ROMAN HISTORICAL COINS

DEDICATION

To my old friend and first teacher,
Thomas Wellington Ward
of San Diego, California

ROMAN HISTORICAL COINS

CLIVE FOSS

LONDON

Typeset by Setrite Typesetters
and printed and bound in Great Britain by
Biddles Ltd., Guildford Survey, England.
for the publishers
B.A. Seaby Ltd.
8 Cavendish Square
London W1M OAJ

Distributed by
B.T. Batsford Ltd.
P.O. Box 4, Braintree, Essex CM7 7QY

Foss, Clive
    Roman historical coins.
    1. Coins, Roman — Collectors and collecting
    I. Title
    737.4937   CJ837
    ISBN 0−900652−97−7

Contents

Ambition sigh'd; She found it vain to trust
The faithless Column and the crumbling Bust;
Huge moles, whose shadow stretch'd from shore to shore,
Their ruins ruin'd and their place no more!
Convinc'd, she now contracts her vast design,
And all her Triumphs shrink into a Coin:
A narrow orb each crouded conquest keeps,
Beneath her Palm here sad Judaea weeps,
Here scantier limits the proud Arch confine,
And scarce are seen the prostrate Nile or Rhine,
A small Euphrates thro' the piece is roll'd,
And little Eagles wave their wings in gold.
The medal, faithful to its charge of fame,
Thro' climes and ages bears each form and name:
In one short view subjected to your eye
Gods, Emp'rors, Heroes, Sages, Beauties lie.

Alexander Pope, to Mr Addison

Preface

I undertook this work to provide something I had long hoped to find, a convenient reference for determining the meaning of Roman coin types, and for associating the coins with Roman history. This is not, of course, a novel desire, nor is the subject one never attempted before. In fact, there is a long tradition of books about Roman historical coins, beginning with Joseph Eckhel's *Doctrina Nummorum Veterum* (Vienna 1792–8). He treated the whole of Roman coinage, analysing most major types with eminent good sense, in a clear and elegant Latin. His work, though, is extremely difficult to find, even if it can be read. In more modern times, G. F. Hill offered a general treatment, *Historical Roman Coins* (London 1909) which described and analysed 109 types from the Republic through Augustus, with long and well considered discussions. His book was followed by the more ambitious work of Edward Sydenham, *Historical References on Coins of the Roman Empire*, which listed about 300 types from Augustus to Gallienus, systematically arranged and explained; but this was a selection from the whole, with no attempt to be comprehensive. Most recently Michael Grant, in *Roman History and Coins*, provided a general introduction and appreciation of the subject, without attempting to discuss many coins.

It seemed, therefore, that there was room for a book which would examine the whole corpus of Roman coins, and extract from it those which could be associated with specific historical data. No one since Joseph Eckhel (whose work is by far the best on the subject) had done anything like this, and his volumes have necessarily been left behind by the advance of research, though not as far as one might expect. At first, it appeared that this would be merely a work of compilation, derived from the obvious catalogues. I soon found, however, that the catalogues often did not explain the coins (or did so in vague terms), so that real research proved necessary, and a short project became a long one. Fortunately, it has been a labour of love, for I have long been a collector of Roman coins (I bought my first when I was nine years old), and have never lost my interest in them, thanks to friends and associates, many now long deceased; this book is dedicated to one of them. Although it would be optimistic to hope that a nine-year old could make much of the present volume, I hope that it will be of value to collectors, and to historians, who will find in it more than 2,400 types, with reference to over 10,000 individual coins.

This work could never have been accomplished without help of all kinds, most notably from the American Numismatic Society and its untiring librarian, Frank Campbell. Their excellent index of articles in the numismatic periodicals made it possible to locate information rapidly which otherwise might have taken an extraordinary length of time, if it could be found at all. I am greatly indebted to research assistants, who performed the initial work of putting the data from the catalogues onto cards so that it could be more easily managed: Jeffrey Kelley, Lindsay Gee and Jessica Payne all worked with exemplary accuracy and efficiency. This project was begun in the tranquillity of All Souls College, Oxford, to whose Fellows, especially Peter Fraser, I have many obligations. I worked there with the support of the John Simon Guggenheim Memorial Foundation, whose trustees provided important material support. Illustrations have largely been supplied from Seaby archives with additional material generously supplied by Messrs Christies and Sothebys.

The volume was finished expeditiously thanks to the opportune use of a printer belonging to the Sardis Expedition, for which I am much indebted to Jane Scott and Michael Weishan. I am happy to thank Peter Clayton of Seaby who accepted the work for publication and has offered constant advice and encouragement. Simon Bendall, Theodore Buttrey, Wendell Clausen and Mason Hammond read individual sections and provided helpful comments; I am particularly grateful to Ernst Badian for his careful criticism. Finally, I owe a special debt to Eva Chou, whose modesty precludes longer acknowledgement.

SUPPLEMENTARY NOTE

The following works appeared while this book was in production and are of value for the subject and should be consulted:

C.H.V. Sutherland, *Roman History and Coinage, 44 BC−AD 69* (Oxford 1987): Julio-Claudian types and history.

H. Halfmann, *Itinera principum* (Stuttgart 1986): revised chronology of the travels of Hadrian.

R. Burgess, 'Quinquennial vota and the imperial consulship in the fourth and fifth centuries', *Numismatic Chronicle* 148 (1988) 77−96: Fundamental treatment of the *vota* issues.

Introduction

This work is intended to make correlation between Roman history and numismatics easier by identifying and listing coin types which refer to history. It covers the period from the second century BC through to the fifth century AD, and is based on the standard catalogues of Crawford, Cohen, and *Roman Imperial Coinage* (*RIC*). The types included are those which may be associated with a specific contemporary event, policy or activity, for example the assassination of Julius Caesar, the religious megalomania of Commodus, or the travels of Hadrian. It therefore does not include coins of unspecified or abstract reference − types which depict the Bravery of the Emperor or the Loyalty of the Army, without further detail − or those which commemorate the remote past, as most types of the Republic. The past only appears where it had direct relevance to the present, as, for example, the coins of Antoninus Pius struck to celebrate the 900th anniversary of Rome.

The coins thus provide a survey of a kind of late Republican and imperial propaganda, designed to be seen and widely circulated. They should therefore reflect the image which the government of the day wanted to present to its subjects. I have presumed that the coins were meant to be seen and understood, and that the Romans paid some attention to their types. For this, literary sources offer convincing if sparse evidence, and reason suggests that a great variety of types would only be issued for a purpose. Full discussion of this question, though, would lead far from present purposes; the material to a large extent will speak for itself.

This book is addressed to two audiences: historians who are interested in what the coins might contribute as an historical source, and collectors who want to know what their coins mean. It does not have the professional numismatist in mind to the same extent, for his interests have advanced far beyond the description and analysis of types, and turned to the more technical matters of coin production, mint organisation and establishment of a precise chronology. Consequently, the content of the coins is often not stressed in numismatic literature, and difficult to determine from the standard catalogues. This work is based on those catalogues, notably the *RIC* and the *BMC* for the Empire, and Crawford for the Republic. These, however, do not consistently contain the analysis necessary for the present purpose, and therefore a great range of numismatic literature has been consulted, though it does not appear here since this is not intended as a work with full scholarly apparatus, but a convenient handbook. In addition, I have occasionally introduced an interpretation of my own.

A glance through this book will reveal the constant change in the nature of the coin types, beginning in the late Republic, where contemporary references are gradually inserted among those which reflect the past, usually an individual's family, continuing through Augustus whose coins show the transition from Republic to Empire, building slowly through the first century to reach a height of detail and wealth of types in the period from Hadrian through Severus; then becoming more limited and unvarying in the later third century until the Tetrarchy brought a standardisation which had never before existed; until finally, after a brief flurry of activity and variety under Constantine, the content becomes uniformly monotonous, dealing only with the emperor, his offices and anniversaries, in the fourth and fifth centuries. The last types which could be called historical appear under Justinian and Heraclius, just beyond the range of this work. In all this, the coins reflect the development of the empire and its political system.

This work consists of two parts: a brief introduction which explains how to use the book, and gives details of the most common types in the context of Roman ritual and society; and a catalogue which introduces each reign, lists the types and gives reference for varieties and denominations. It deviates little from the subject, and presumes access to a convenient introduction such as David Sear's *Roman Coins and their Values*, for explanation of systems of denominations and dating. After the next section has been read, the work should be self-explanatory. It concludes with an index, of remarkable types and inscriptions – that is, excluding inscriptions which merely give a date or imperial office, and types which figure standard gods or personifications.

HOW TO USE THIS BOOK

This book is essentially a catalogue of the historical types on the Roman coinage, arranged chronologically with reference to the denominations in which they were struck and the standard catalogues which list them. The types are arranged in sections, according to the emperor who issued them (except for the Republic, see below). Each section begins with an historical introduction which is intended not to give a summary history of Rome, but to provide a context for the coins; it contains full reference to the types. Since many types recur constantly, the next section describes them in more detail than the catalogue, and gives background information which will help to interpret them.

Within each section, the types are arranged according to the date of the event which they commemorate; in most cases, this corresponds roughly (within a year or two) with the date when the coins were issued, but some were struck several years after the event. Dates of these are usually indicated in the references. In its arrangement, this catalogue generally follows that of the standard works, but differs in two respects. Coins struck in the name of a junior colleague are listed with his issues as emperor: thus the issues of Marcus Aurelius Caesar appear under his name, although they were actually issued by Antoninus Pius. Likewise, coins issued in the name of members of the imperial family are listed under their names. Conversely, coins of deified emperors appear under the names of the actual issuer, for consecration was an act of policy by the following emperor. In those cases, and in the case of imperial relatives who appear on the reverses of an emperor's coins, cross-references are given under the individual in question. In principle, each individual who appears on a coin has a separate entry.

The chronological arrangement by emperor naturally prevails through most of the catalogue, but its first three sections are arranged on a different principle, for they deal with the Republic which (in theory, at least) had no one ruler. The first of them, 'The Republic', covers the years 121–54 BC, the second the supremacy of Caesar, and the third the Civil Wars from 44–31 BC. These sections are arranged chronologically without regard for the issuer; thus the coins of Pompey will be found in the first section, those of his followers who opposed Caesar in the second, and those of his sons in the third. The section on the civil wars is necessarily complex, since so many actors were involved; consequently, it has a longer introduction than usual, which not only narrates the history as revealed by the coins, but also sketches the biography of each individual who issued them. This section contains all the issues of the triumvirate; cross-references for those of Octavian are given in the section on Augustus.

In a sense, a similar arrangement for the Tetrarchy, and the whole period of imperial colleges through the mid-fifth century, would have equal merit since types were struck collectively by groups of emperors. In these cases, however, the rapid changes of Augusti and Caesars would make the coinage difficult to follow. It has therefore been arranged conventionally by emperor, with references to indicate how co-rulers use the same types as their senior colleagues.

The catalogue lists historical types, which are a small part of the vast volume of Roman coinage. Many types, therefore, do not appear here at all. The catalogue does not include routine personifications or gods unless they can be associated with a specific context, nor are the numerous vague and optimistic victory types of the third century, for example, included unless they refer to a particular victory. The catalogue is based on a conscientious effort to identify all types which have a specific content, usually with reference to an event, but often to an imperial policy, or an identifiable piece of propaganda. There are, naturally, some types difficult to define: all issues of the civil wars of 68–69 might be considered historical, as well as any coin which bears the portrait of Caesar. In those cases, the principle of specificity has been followed, and those with definable contexts included. In such questions, a certain amount of subjective judgement must be employed. I have therefore included all coins whose interpretation seems reasonably sound, and excluded those whose association with history seems remote or implausible; if anything, I have tried to err on the side of inclusion. There are some types whose appearance suggests that they must refer to something, but for which no explanation is forthcoming; they are omitted, but amount to no more than a few dozen.

The catalogue has two main types of user in mind, those whose primary interest is history, and those who are more concerned with the coinage, especially collectors. For the student of history, use of the book should be straightforward, and desired information about the events celebrated by a particular emperor, or the kind of propaganda he produced, will be found in the appropriate sections. For the collector, reference will be slightly more complicated, and it is primarily to him that the following paragraph is directed.

If you want to find a particular coin, look first in the index, which lists noteworthy types and a few inscriptions. The types are given priority, so that a coin inscribed AEGYPTO CAPTA, for example, will be listed under 'Aegyptus', together with all types relating to Egypt. If that does not help, it will be necessary to determine the date of the coin, easily done by reference to a standard work like Sear's *Roman Coins and Their Values*. That year can then be consulted in the catalogue, but note that arrangement here is by event, not date of issue, so be prepared to look a year or two before or after the date which appears on the coin. Correlation between date and event is provided by the historical introductions at the head of each section. Remember, too, that all types are not historical, and that the majority of Roman coins are necessarily not included here.

Because of the great changes which took place in the coinage during the five hundred years covered here, and the consequent different methods of presentation in the standard catalogues, the format of this catalogue varies according to period, with three basic forms of presentation, for the Republic, the Empire, and the late Empire (from the reforms of Diocletian through Theodosius). Examples should explain the presentation.

The Republic

44 BC The Ides of March
  34 M. Junius Brutus, L. Plaetorius Cestus. Mint: moving with Brutus. *Obv.* BRVT IMP L PLAET CEST, Bearded head of Brutus r. *Rev.* EID MAR, Pileus (cap of freedom) between daggers. Den: *Cr* 508/3

The first line, in all parts of the work, identifies the event and gives its date. For the Republic, the issuer and mint are of prime importance; they appear next, with the sequential number of the coin within the section. The description, in this section only, gives both obverse and reverse, with explanations, where necessary, added in brackets. The entry concludes with the denomination (*see* the abbreviations below) and reference to the catalogue of Michael Crawford, *Roman Republican Coinage*. In virtually all cases, his dating and interpretation have been followed.

The Empire

112 AD The Forum of Trajan, with the Ulpian basilica.

56 FORVM TRAIAN/I (SPQR OPTIMO PRINCIPI), Elaborate façade of building, with columns, statues, etc. Aur: 255−7/*C*167−8. Ses: 630/*C*169; 654

As before, the first line gives date and event. The second gives the sequential number, then the reverse inscription and a brief description of the type. Unless otherwise indicated, the obverse may be presumed to bear the image and superscription of the emperor. Unusual obverses are included where appropriate. The inscription is presented with its variants (minor variants sometimes given in the references below). In this case, TRAIAN/I means that some types have TRAIAN, others TRAIANI, and the words in parentheses appear on some types only; details will be found in the *RIC*. In some cases, abbreviated inscriptions have been expanded by way of explanation: in SPQR vota PRO REditu CAESaris, for example, only the letters in capitals appear on the coin; lower case letters always indicate such expansions. The descriptions given here are usually as concise as possible; full details are in *RIC* (and, even more thoroughly, in *BMC*). Since many types recur constantly, reference should be made to the immediately following section, for fuller explanation, and for the context of the type in Roman ritual and society.

The references indicate the denomination, always abbreviated, and the numbers in *RIC* (numbers alone) and Cohen (numbers preceded by *C*). Semicolons separate varieties; standard catalogue numbers are separated by commas. In cases where several types commemorate the same event, they are arranged not according to alphabetical order of inscriptions, but generally with precious metals preceding the base, and more elaborate types before the simple. Occasionally, coins have been included which do not appear in the catalogues. They are identified by special references, with the name of an author and date of publication; these are explained below. Note that this catalogue does not always correspond to *RIC* and Cohen in its arrangement: the former lists coins by the ruler who struck them, and Cohen according to the portrait which appears on them. Thus *RIC* numbers of the early issues of Aurelius will be found there under Antoninus Pius. Coins which have the head of a co-ruler on the reverse will be listed separately by Cohen under the joint names of the rulers, while here they appear according to the obverse.

Late Empire

362 AD Discovery of a bull representing the god Apis in Egypt (or perhaps symbolic representation of pagan sacrifice; in any case, the closest to a pagan type on this coinage).

9 SECVRITAS REIPVB, Bull stg. r. Æl: Aqu 242−3; Are 313−23; Con 161−4; Cyz 125−8; Her 101−4; Lug 236−8; Nic 118−22; Sir 105−7; Sis 411−13, 417−19; Tes 222−6

The first line provides the usual information, here, as often, with an alternative explanation. Inscriptions and description are given as above, but the catalogue references follow a different system. In this period (294−395), the mints were of great importance, and form the natural basis for presenting the coinage. Since Cohen ignores them, his references are omitted, and the *RIC* alone is given. The mints are abbreviated as they are on the coinage (*see below*), and listed in alphabetical rather than geographical order (as in the *RIC* and other works), since the reader can hardly be expected to carry a map of the Roman empire in his head.

The final period, from Arcadius to Anastasius, is poorly catalogued. Since the *RIC* has not reached these years, use is made of Cohen for the West, Tolstoy for the East, *Roman Silver Coins V* for the silver, and specialised studies, notably Hahn for the reign of Theodosius II. A definitive catalogue for this period is being prepared by Professor Philip Grierson.

Abbreviations of denominations

Æl, 2, 3, 4: bronzes of the late empire, according to size.

Ant(oninianus)
Arg(enteus)
Aur(eus)
Avfrae: Gold fraction
Avq: Quinarius aureus
Cis(tophorus)
Den(arius)
Dra(chma); 2Dra: Didrachm; ½Dra: Hemidrachm
Dup(ondius)
Fol(lis)
Mil(iarense)

Quad(rans)
Qui(narius) (silver)
Sem(is)
Ses(tertius); 2Ses: double sestertius
Sex(tans)
Sil(iqua)
Sol(idus)
Tri(ens)
Trip(ondius)

Abbreviations of mints

Ale(xandria); Amb(ianum); Ant(ioch); Aqu(ilea); Are(late); Car(thage); Con(stantinople); Cyz(icus); Her(aclea); Lon(don); Lug(dunum); Med(iolanum); Nic(omedia); Ost(ia); Rav(enna); Rom(e); Ser(dica); Sir(mium); Sis(cia); T(h)es(salonica); Tic(inum); Tre(veri).

Abbreviated references

P. Bastien (1958): 'Les travaux d'Hercule dans le monnayage de Postume', *RevNum* 6.1: 59−69

—— (1960): 'Emissions de l'atelier de Lyon en 293 et 294', *RevNum* 6.2 (1960/61): 75–112

—— (1983): 'The horse's head and imperial bust on Roman coins', *SAN* 14: 4–8

A. A. Boyce (1965): *Festal and Dated Coins of the Roman Empire. (Numismatic Notes and Monographs* 153). New York.

C. L. Clay (1970): 'Nilus and the Four Seasons on a new As of Septimius Severus', *Numismatic Chronicle* 7. 10: 71–87

G. Elmer (1941): 'Die Münzprägung der gallischen Kaiser', *Bonner Jahrbucher* 176: 1–106

A. N. de Fazi (1977): 'Moneda inedita del emperador Hadrianus de la serie 'adlocutiones' a sus trupos'. *Gaceta numismatica* 44: 74–76

W. Hahn (1979): 'Die östliche gold- und Silberprägung unter Theodosius II', *Litterae Numismaticae Vindobonenses Roberto Goebl Dedicatae*. Vienna: 103–131

P. V. Hill (1964): *The Coinage of Septimius Severus and his Family of the Mint of Rome*. London.

C. M. Kraay (1960): 'Two New Sestertii of Domitian', *ANS Museum Notes* 9: 109–116

—— (1976): 'The Bronze Coinage of Vespasian', *Scripta nummaria romana: Essays Presented to Humphrey Sutherland*, ed. R. A. G. Carson and C. M. Kraay. London

LRBC: R. A. G. Carson, J. P. C. Kent, P. V. Hill, *The Late Roman Bronze Coinage*. London 1965

MonMed: O. Ulrich-Bansa, *Moneta Mediolanensis*. Venice 1949

K. Pink (1949): 'Der Aufbau der römischen Münzprägung in der Kaiserzeit: VII: Probus', *Numismatische Zeitschrift* 73: 13–74

RSC V: C. E. King, *The Roman Silver Coinage*, vol V. London 1987

P. Strauss (1985): 'Ein unedierter Aureus des Domitian aus Judäa', *Festschrift Herbert Cahn*. Basel: 135–139

Count J. Tolstoy (1912): *Monnaies byzantines*. St. Petersburg

FREQUENT AND REPEATED TYPES

Although the Roman coinage displays tremendous variety in the scenes which it represents and in their iconography, a number of subjects constantly recur. These representations constitute the vast majority of the historical types and so are discussed in some detail here, as the catalogue descriptions are usually abridged. The list which follows is naturally not complete, but includes the most frequently used types and subjects.

ADLOCVTIO. An address to the army by the emperor, on a variety of serious occasions – to announce accessions, wars or policies, to encourage the troops, to reward bravery, to suppress revolt, and so on. The emperor is usually represented standing on a tribunal, accompanied by a high officer, addressing a group of soldiers identified by their standards. In the extensive series associated with the travels of Hadrian, the emperor addresses the troops from horseback.

ADVENTVS, PROFECTIO, FORTVNA REDVX, FELICITAS. Imperial journeys were the occasion for a solemn ceremonial of greeting and well-wishing, with sacrifices, prayers, and a great crowd of the public. They involved the places visited in such effort and expense that Augustus tried to avoid arriving or leaving in broad daylight (when the rituals took place) to spare the Italian municipalities. *Adventus* (arrival) and *profectio* (departure) become especially frequent in the third century, at first in reference to Rome, but later, when mints strike distinctive types, in connection with provincial cities. The departure of the emperor was attended by vows to Fortuna Redux ('Fortune who brings back') for a safe return. This cult was established in 19 BC when Augustus returned from the East: instead of the extravagant honours proposed by the Senate, he accepted an altar to Fortuna Redux to be built near the Porta Capena, the gate by which the Appian Way left the city. Domitian built a temple to Fortuna Redux on the Capitoline after his victorious return from Germany. Marcus Aurelius uniquely celebrated Fortuna Dux, apparently with the same significance. When a journey was by sea, as frequently in the second century, vows were made to Felicitas, the good luck of the emperor, to survive the dangers.

Severus 43   Decius 1   Hadrian 108*a*

ANNIVERSARIES. The Romans had a strong sense of the importance of their past and celebrated various sorts of anniversaries, of which three especially figure on the coinage − the celebration of five or ten-year intervals of a reign (*see* VOTA); the recurrent *saecula* (*see* SECULAR GAMES), and the centenaries of the city of Rome. Three of the latter are prominently portrayed − the 900th, celebrated in 147 by Antoninus Pius, the 1000th which fell in the reign of Philip, and the 1100th, marked by a vast coinage by the sons of Constantine. In all cases, the new century could be taken as the beginning of a new age, with symbolism especially evident in the last case. Theories which find traces on the coins of innumerable other anniversaries, notably of temple foundations or of events in the reign of Augustus, seem in general to lack foundation and in most cases are less convincing than alternative explanations of a more immediate nature. For a different point of view, see the ingenious work of Michael Grant, *Roman Anniversary Issues*.

ARMY. The great Roman army, which by the reforms of Augustus comprised some 300,000 men stationed along a frontier of more than 8000 miles, was a professional force of legionaries and auxiliaries who served for a whole career, and one of the elements most essential for the very survival of the empire. It naturally appears on the coinage of all periods, becoming more prominent in the troubles of the third century, and overwhelming in the fourth. Most of the references in these periods, however, are abstract appeals or praises like 'fides militum' or 'gloria exercitus' which, being unspecific, do not find a place here. Specific references are notable under Hadrian, who portrayed the army of each province he visited, and in the late third century, when a new mobile cavalry army was established to deal with the changed tactics of the day. Troops of great importance were the praetorians, the bodyguard of the emperors and the only armed force in Italy. They frequently played a major role in determining the succession to the empire, beginning with Claudius, who features them on his coins. The army was naturally predominant during periods of civil war − 44−30 BC, 68−69 AD and 193−197 AD − when the coinage devotes much attention to the forces involved, as well as the propaganda of the conflicting sides. Some later emperors whose power depended on the favour of the troops, notably Gallienus and Carausius, celebrated the individual legions who supported them. (*See also* TRIUMPH, VICTORY.)

Vitellius 2   Claudius 2   Gallienus 28*l*

BUILDINGS. From the beginning, emperors commemorated their public works on the coinage, by advertising imperial benefactions, or as personal propaganda. Buildings of public utility, such as the market of Nero or the forum of Trajan, share attention with structures which celebrate the piety or victories of the emperor, such as the temple of Augustus restored by Antoninus, or the numerous triumphal arches erected from the time of Augustus through the third century. Rebuilding of Rome, or parts of it, after the frequent fires which devastated the city, was also an important imperial benefaction. The last building to be commemorated is the temple of Rome and Venus, restored by Maxentius. In virtually all cases, the buildings portrayed were at Rome rather than in the provinces, an indication consonant with most other types of the coinage which reveal the overwhelming importance of the capital, and the audience which such propaganda was intended to reach. Benefactions to provincial cities, like dedications to foreign gods, first become frequent in the third century.

Nero 22 Nero 11 Trajan 20

CAESARS. Attribution of the name *Caesar* marked the heir to the throne who, if of age, would participate actively in the ritual and political and military life of the state. Caesars, beginning with Nero, were coopted into the high priestly offices; consequently their coins, especially in the third century, feature the implements of the priests. They also became *princeps iuventutis*, or 'leaders of the Youth' and heads of the equestrian order. The title was originally given by acclamation of the knights (*equites*), who formed the second of the ruling classes after the Senate. Gaius and Lucius Caesars were the first to be so named, then Nero; by the second century, the title became routine, and by the third was often retained after a Caesar became Augustus. In some cases, it was used to indicate the subordinate position of a member of an imperial college.

Diadumenian 1

CHARITIES. Beside the regular distributions of grain which the emperors bestowed on the people of Rome (*see* LIBERALITAS), special charities for the support of poor children in Italy were established by Nerva and greatly extended by Trajan. He gave large sums to the cities on the condition that the interest be devoted to such charity. Hadrian maintained the system and Antoninus Pius expanded it by providing for poor girls in memory of his wife Faustina.

CLVPEVS VIRTVTIS. As part of the honours which Octavian received when he became Augustus in 27, the Senate voted him a golden shield with an inscription praising his *virtus, clementia, justitia* and *pietas*. It frequently appears on his coins with a suitable legend. Similar shields were awarded to Tiberius for *clementia* and *moderatio* (virtues he notably lacked), and to later emperors through Trajan. They are usually represented by a figure of Victory carrying the shield. The type last appears under

Vitellius 7

Antoninus Pius, by whose time the shield was used to celebrate a victory. As such, the type continued through the third century, but without the connotations of the *clupeus virtutis*.

COINAGE. The coinage itself is rarely the subject of coin types, and those that appear are often obscure. Claudius, for example, commemorated the restoration of the weight of the coins, and Alexander Severus claimed credit for restoration of the coinage, but in neither case is the nature of the reform clear from the coins themselves. Likewise, the abundant series of the early fourth century, SAC MON VRB AVGG ET CAESS NN, has no evident connection with the coinage reform of Diocletian. Portrayal of (Juno) Moneta, the patroness of the mint, rarely seems to have topical significance.

CONSECRATIO (*see also* FUNERALS). Popular feeling considered Julius Caesar a god after his assassination, and the triumph of the Caesarians established his official cult. That precedent was followed after the death of Augustus, who refused to allow himself to be worshipped as a god in Rome during his lifetime. Consecration was a solemn act of the Senate, voted to emperors whose memory it favoured. It was not automatic: the efforts of Antoninus to secure the consecration of Hadrian earned him the surname Pius. By the third century, however, the practice became routine. A consecrated emperor became a *divus* (a byform of *deus*, a god) and was worshipped like other gods, with his temple and priests. Octavian built a temple to Divus Julius; a temple of the *divi* on the Palatine, attested in the third century, was probably for the collective worship of emperors whose divinity risked being forgotten. The cult of the deified emperors was renewed by Decius in connection with his campaign against the Christians, as reflected in a remarkable series of antoniniani portraying his deified predecessors.

CONSULS. The supreme magistrates of the Roman republic, always elected in pairs, were the civil and military heads of the state. Under the empire, they naturally lost their powers but continued to preside over the Senate, administer justice, and, most important in the late empire, to give games at their own expense. Most emperors held the consulate, some several times. The last non-imperial consul held office under Justinian. Entry into the office was a solemn event which marked the beginning of the year on 1 January. The consuls, dressed in their elaborate official togas, made a procession from their houses to the Capitoline, where they sacri-

Philip 10

ficed white bulls to Jupiter. They were accompanied by lictors who bore the fasces (symbol of the ancient right to chastise or execute citizens), musicians, senators, magistrates and representatives of the armed forces. The day was a public holiday, with great throngs attending the *processus consularis*. From the time of Trajan, consuls could employ the *ornamenta triumphalia*; the procession thus came to resemble a triumph. The coins frequently depict the emperor as consul, in his chariot in the procession, sacrificing, or standing in his consular robes. In Late Antiquity, when the main function of the consul was to hold the games, he is portrayed as about to throw the *mappa*, or napkin, which signalled their start. The practice was supposed to originate with Nero who, reluctant to leave the banqueting table, threw his napkin from the window and ordered the games to begin.

CORONA CIVICA. An oak wreath awarded for saving the life of a Roman citizen from enemy attack. The crown was a lifetime honour which brought considerable privileges. Caesar received it legitimately; the Senate awarded it to Augustus in 27 for saving the lives of citizens in general by bringing peace; for later emperors through Trajan (Tiberius refused it), the crown was part of the honours on their accession or soon after.

Augustus 26

DONATIVES. Called *congiarium* or *liberalitas*, they appear on the coinage under Nero; the former dies out in the second century. The distributions were made to the people of Rome on special occasions: victories, promotion of colleagues, imperial weddings and others. They consisted of money and of tokens which entitled the bearer to draw supplies, usually of food, from the imperial stores. The emperor handed these in person to the beneficiaries, as portrayed in the characteristic distribution scene of the coinage (in most detail on the bronze) which show the emperor seated on his curule chair on a platform, attended by a prefect and officers or soldiers; a statue of Minerva or Liberalitas often stands in the background. In front, a citizen mounts the steps to the platform with his hand or the

Antoninus Pius 47

fold of his toga extended to receive the gifts. In many cases, the scene is represented symbolically by the figure of Liberalitas alone; she holds the cornucopia of wealth and an accounting board pierced with circular openings for the rapid counting and distribution of the money. These civil donatives were distinct from the military *donativum*, a special gift of money to the troops, notably the praetorians, on the accession of an emperor (as a kind of bribe to guarantee him their acceptance) and on other important occasions. In these cases, the recipients are shown as soldiers. In Late Antiquity, a donation of gold formed a regular supplement to army pay: by the mid-fourth century, it consisted of five solidi and a pound of silver, and was given on accessions and at the fifth anniversary of a reign. It is represented by the frequent VOTA which dominate the late coinage.

FAMILIES (*see also* CAESARS). Since the dynastic spirit was always strong among the Romans – Octavian succeeded at first because he was the adopted son of Caesar – relatives and descendants of emperors are frequently portrayed on the coinage. They appear most commonly, beginning with Augustus, in their role as heirs who would continue the dynasty. Wives and children therefore have a special prominence, while other relatives appear for specific reasons, as for example, the relatives of Caligula who had been killed by Tiberius, or his sisters whom he seduced, or the mothers of Nero and Alexander Severus who played a dominant political role.

Caligula 10

FUNERALS and consecrations of emperors and their relatives form an important subject of the coinage of all periods, as a reflection of the state

| Trajan 61 | Caracalla 68 | Caracalla 70 |

religion in which the emperors became gods. An imperial funeral was an elaborate ceremony which in many ways resembled a triumph. It was a day of public mourning whose main features were the funeral procession and the burning of the pyre. In the first century, the body, carefully embalmed, was carried in the procession, but by the second it was buried with normal funeral rites and the main ceremony involved a wax image of the deceased. This lay in state for a week at the entrance of the palace, flanked by seated senators wearing black robes. The image, dressed in triumphal robes, was then carried by leading knights and senators to the Forum where the first part of the procession was held: images of famous Romans were followed by professional mourners, musicians and dancers; images of the subject nations; representatives of the guilds of artisans; cavalry and infantry; and the magistrates and senate. Hymns were sung in the Forum and a funeral oration delivered from the Rostra. The procession then moved on to the Campus Martius where the image, carried by knights and accompanied by dirges, reached the funeral pyre, a wooden structure filled with brushwood and built in the shape of a tower with three levels, crowned by a gilded chariot. The bier containing the image was set on the tower, a procession of cavalry rode around it, and one of the consuls set it on fire. At that point, an eagle, representing the soul of the deceased, was released from the top of the tower. The funeral games followed a week later. They began with a solemn procession from the Capitoline to the Circus, with statues of the gods and a gilded image of the deceased borne in a chariot drawn by elephants. The games featured horse races and gladiatorial contests. Many aspects of the funeral ritual are portrayed on the coins, especially in the second century.

GOLDEN AGE. The notion that a reign or event might mark the beginning of a new golden age of peace and happiness, such as had existed in mythological times, constantly appears on the coinage, especially in the third century when such an eventuality was ever more remote. It is often associated with special anniversaries, such as the centenaries of Rome, or with imperial megalomania, as on the coins of Commodus. Its imagery includes the phoenix, whose miraculous renewal from the flames symbolised rebirth, the elephant whose supposed longevity was apt for indicating eternity, and Janus who presided over beginnings.

PONTIFICES. The state religion was led by the fifteen members of the college of pontifices, the *XVviri sacris faciundis*, under the direction of the Pontifex Maximus. They were not dedicated to the service of any one god, but supervised the whole religious apparatus, with the aim of maintaining good relations between men and gods. They had precedence over

Civil Wars 55   Nero 3   Marcus Aurelius 1

all magistrates, and jurisdiction over all priests and religious matters; they celebrated the games of Apollo and the Secular Games. The Pontifex Maximus appointed the Vestal Virgins and the *flamines* who headed the worship of individual native gods. Separate from the pontifices was the college of augurs who divined the will of the gods by interpreting signs in the sky. Under the Republic, they had great power because they could stop meetings of the assembly or annul decrees if the auspices had not been properly performed. The various priests, originally coopted into the colleges, were elected by the people in the late Republic (Julius Caesar began his career as *pontifex maximus*, an office he held for life), but were appointed by the emperors. Priests could always hold other civil office (Mark Antony, for example, was an augur throughout his political career), as long as they did not interfere with the duties of the priesthood. From the time of Claudius, it became customary to coopt the heir to the throne into the priestly colleges. Consequently, the signs of their office became a normal type for coins of the Caesars, especially in the third century. They were also frequently depicted in the late Republic to advertise the priesthoods which the political leaders held. The implements usually represented were the *aspergillum, simpulum, praeferculum, secespita*, and *lituus*; earlier coins often have the *apex* and the *securis*. The first four were the instruments of the pontifices: the *aspergillum* was a sprinkler with long ends of horsehair used to cast holy water on the altar, victim and audience; the *simpulum* was a ladle with a long handle used to make libations, primarily of wine; the *praeferculum*, a metal jug, held the wine used in libations; and the *secespita*, a long knife with an ivory handle, was employed to cut the throat of the sacrificial animal and to open its entrails. Augurs used the *lituus*, a curved short staff, to divide the heavens into quarters for the purposes of divination. The *securis*, or axe, which also appears as the sign of the Pontifex Maximus, could be used to kill the victims or to cut them into pieces. The *apex* was a conical wooden cap tied under the chin by long fillets, worn by *flamines* and the Salian priests of Mars.

PRIESTLY IMPLEMENTS: *see* PONTIFICES.

PRINCEPS IVVENTVTIS: *see* CAESARS.

PROVINCES of the empire were frequently portrayed on the coinage in a variety of contexts: in association with wars and conquests, usually as a female in a dejected state; on imperial visits, as the ADVENTVS series of Hadrian; or as the sign of an emperor's origin, a type which becomes frequent with Severus. Antoninus Pius produced a remarkable series portraying the provinces presenting gifts on his accession. In all cases, each province has distinctive attributes which enable it to be identified.

Hadrian 41

Hadrian 81

Decius 7*a*

RELIGION. The state religion, a vital part of the life of emperor and empire, finds a larger place in the coinage than will be apparent here, for most religious types feature a god or a personification without any specific connotation. The most frequent historical religious types deal with dedication or restoration of temples (usually showing the temple, but sometimes its cult image), and sacrifices by or for the emperor (*see* VOTA). Three reigns, however, exhibit special religious types. Antoninus Pius advertised many ancient cults and myths of Rome in connection with the 900th anniversary of the city; the megalomania of Commodus led him to display the gods with whom he felt he had close relations or could be identified; and the installation on the throne of a priest of the sun, Antoninus called Elagabalus, brought a new cult into a prominent place on the coinage. The coins well reflect the religious development of the empire, with the early prominence of the Olympian gods, the rise of the cult of the emperors, the growth of eastern and other local cults (especially under the Severi and later) and finally the demise of paganism under Constantine. After his reign, the religious types are uniformly Christian, with the sole exception of an issue of Julian 'the Apostate'.

REPETITIONS of types. Emperors — or those who were more directly concerned with such matters — frequently copied earlier coin types which attracted their fancy. In some cases, the significance is plainly topical: Antoninus Pius, for example, imitated a type of Drusus showing heads of children in a cornucopia because on both occasions twins were born to the imperial family. When Postumus claimed to restore Gaul, he appropriated a type of Hadrian. In most cases, however, the new type seems merely to have been chosen because it appealed, without special significance.

SECULAR GAMES. Solemn rites and sacrifices with games and performances held at the beginning of a new *saeculum*, a period supposedly equal to the longest span of human life and defined variously as 100 or 110 years. The celebration is first attested in 348 BC, and was revived by Augustus in 17 BC. *Saeculares* were subsequently celebrated by Domitian in 88 and Severus in 204. In each case, the ritual was the same, with three nights and days of solemn sacrifices and stage performances, followed by a week

Philip 1 21

Domitian 32*b*

of games and entertainments. The rites were announced by heralds as games which no one had ever seen or would see again; and by a decree of the Senate ordering an inscription to be carved on a cippus recording that they had been held. Before the games, the emperor distributed *suffimenta*, the incense for ritual purification, to the people, and received from them the offering of the first fruits of the season. The solemn ritual began on the night before 1 June, with the sacrifice of sheep and goats to the Moerae, or Fates, by the banks of the Tiber, and with *sellisternia* held on the Capitol in honour of Juno and Diana. During the day, bulls were sacrificed to Jupiter Optimus Maximus on the Capitoline, then the next night, sacrificial cakes were offered to the goddesses of childbirth by the Tiber, followed by stage performances in a temporary wooden theatre, and more *sellisternia*. The daytime ritual of 2 June consisted of sacrifices of cows to Juno on the Capitol, a banquet for the emperors and the *XVviri sacris faciundis* (*see* PONTIFICES), and the *supplicatio matronarum*, a prayer to Juno by 110 selected married women. That night, a pregnant black sow was sacrificed to Terra Mater by the Tiber, with performances and *sellisternia* following. On the third day, sacrificial cakes were offered to Apollo and Diana on the Palatine, then the *carmen saeculare*, the secular hymn (written by the poet Horace for Augustus' celebration) was performed at the temple of Apollo on the Palatine by twenty-seven boys and twenty-seven girls whose parents were alive. It was repeated at the Capitol after a procession had led there from the Palatine. The actual secular games ended that day with races and games in a circus in the campus Martius, but a week of games, the *ludi honorarii*, followed. Many aspects of the ritual appear on the coins of Augustus, Domitian and Severus. Other secular games were held by Claudius, who used a different reckoning, in 47; the herald who announced them was jeered when he claimed that no one living had ever seen such games or would again. These celebrated the 800th anniversary of Rome, as did the games of Philip two centuries later. His coins reveal that he imported a great range of animals to be exhibited in the entertainments. Maximian held games called secular, apparently at Lugdunum, in 295; nothing is known of their nature, nor of those held by Carausius five years earlier. They may have been real secular games held according to a different calculation, or simply games to mark a new age. The normal celebration should have recurred in 314, but by then the empire was dominated by the Christians, and the practice was abandoned. The celebrations for the 1100th anniversary of Rome, held by the sons of Constantine, apparently retained no trace of the old *saeculares*.

SELLISTERNIUM. A ritual banquet served to images of the gods placed on chairs or couches (in the latter case, called *lectisternium*) in order to gain their favour. *Sellisternia* were held to avert a disaster, such as the plague, or in association with special prayers, as at the secular games. Since deified emperors became gods, *sellisternia* to them, often portrayed on the coinage, formed part of the ritual of their new divine status.

Antoninus Pius 32*b*

TENSA. A rectangular two-wheeled carriage of ivory and silver drawn by four horses, with its front decorated to resemble the façade of a temple. It was used to bear the images of the Capitoline gods – Jupiter, Juno and Minerva – in sacred processions in the Circus. Images of lesser gods were

Titus 26

carried on hand-barrows. Caesar scandalised Rome by having his own image carried into the Circus on a *tensa*, as one of his divine honours. As part of the celebration of Augustus' victories in the East in 19 BC, the Senate had his triumphal insignia displayed in a *tensa* at the Circus games before they were deposited in the temple of Jupiter. Subsequently, deified emperors were honoured by *tensae* dedicated to them and displayed in their funeral processions in the Circus.

TRIUMPH. A solemn ritual celebrated in Rome to honour a general who had won a significant victory over a foreign enemy (not in a civil war). Less important victories, over slaves or pirates, for example, earned a lesser triumph, an *ovatio*, such as Octavian celebrated after Naulochus. A triumph was voted by the Senate to the commanding general. On the agreed day, the *triumphator*, who had to wait outside the city until the triumph was decreed, entered Rome from the Campus Martius through the Porta Triumphalis and paraded past the Circus and through the Forum to the temple of Jupiter on the Capitoline. The procession was long and elaborate; led by senators and magistrates, who were followed by bearers of the spoils of war and of images of conquered regions, and of placards which named defeated nations, captured cities or special accomplishments of the general; then the sacrificial animals; the most important

Republic 15

captives in chains (they were led off to execution before reaching the Capitol); lictors of the general; and finally the *triumphator* himself, dressed in a toga decorated with gold stars (*toga picta*) and an embroidered purple tunic (*tunica palmata*), and standing in a chariot drawn by four horses. He wore a crown of laurel and carried a sceptre decorated with an eagle, and a laurel branch; behind him stood a slave holding a golden crown above his head. In all this, the victorious general took on the attributes of Jupiter. Behind him came his sons on horseback, his officers and the army, singing songs which praised or satirised their general. The procession ended on the Capitoline where the *triumphator* dedicated his laurels to Jupiter and the beasts were sacrificed. A triumph normally lasted one day, but Augustus celebrated for three days for his victories in Dalmatia, Actium and Egypt. Triumphs were common in the Empire; the last was held by Diocletian in 302. Generals who fought in the name of an emperor were not entitled to triumphs themselves, but could receive the *ornamenta triumphalia*, the decorations without the procession. Coins most commonly figure the *triumphator* in his chariot.

VICTORIES. One of the richest series of coins of all periods portrays the wars and victories of the emperor. Most victories are represented symbolically by the figure of a winged Victory walking with a palm branch or trophy, often with a captive at her feet, or inscribing a shield attached to a palm tree. The symbolism began in the republic and assumed a special form under Augustus who set up a statue of Victory (from Tarentum) in his new Senate House in 29 BC. Senators regularly offered sacrifice on the altar before it. The statue was considered to represent the fortune of the empire and was thus the subject of great controversy when the Christian Theodosius removed it. Imperial victories are also frequently represented by the figure of the emperor fighting, or by a captive seated in dejection. Many types figure an anticipated or imaginary victory, as part of a propaganda which becomes universal and banal in the third century: they are generally omitted here, since they cannot be associated with a specific event. Less commonly, the coinage presents scenes from the wars, such as a river crossing, a miraculous success, the conquest of a particular region, or the installation of a foreign king. Such types are most common in the second century. Acclamation as *imperator*, a great honour which a victorious general received from his troops and normally led to triumph, was common in all periods. It was a natural accompaniment of war, as were addresses to the army (*see* ADLOCVTIO).

VOTA. In the practical-minded Roman religion, prayers called *vota* were offered in two stages: they were *suscepta* when formulated as a prayer; then, after the god had granted the requested favour, they were paid, *soluta*, with a sacrifice. There were innumerable vows, public and private. The former often accompanied imperial voyages, wars, marriages and such occasions. The most important for the coinage, however, were the vows undertaken at the beginning of each ten-year period of a reign for its successsful completion. These appear under Trajan and continue into the fifth century. At first, they were held at the end of a *decennium*; they were then paid for the first ten years and offered for the second. In the third century, however, when few emperors lasted ten years, they were held at the beginning of a reign as *vota* (*suscepta*) for a ten-year period.

Under the Tetrarchy and later, the situation becomes much more complicated. During the joint reign of Diocletian and his colleagues, vows were undertaken for the whole imperial college and renewed as appropriate. Matters were often simplified by celebrating vows for Augusti and Caesars together, even though they might not have assumed power in the same years. It also became customary for each emperor to celebrate the vows of his colleagues; his *vota* coins of a given issue, there-fore, might bear a variety of numbers. This can cause much confusion for the collector, especially in the coinage of the fourth century. By that time, the vows were primarily quinquennial, held at the end of each five-year period. They also provided the occasion for a major donative of gold and silver to the troops. Consequently, they were often celebrated early, as for example at the beginning of a major campaign. Determining the exact occasion for vows is thus sometimes difficult, especially since the celebrations were sometimes held at irregular intervals.

The coins of this period normally bear such inscriptions as VOT X MVLT XX, indicating vows paid for the completion of ten years, and undertaken for another decade. A simple VOT V usually indicates the vows undertaken at the beginning of a reign. In the fifth century, the *vota* coinage often appears in two types. The rarer, which usually portrays the emperor wearing consular robes and holding the *mappa* on the obverse, was struck for the actual anniversary festivities, which were normally celebrated by the emperor holding the consulate. The more common series, with a normal obverse bust, was issued for general circulation during the period following the anniversary, so that the *vota* figure is merely equivalent to a date. Although, strictly speaking, these are not historical types, they have been included here for convenience.

True *vota* types end with the reigns of Theodosius II and Valentinian III. Thereafter, the image of Victory inscribing numbers on a shield continues as a frozen type, with no special meaning, while the numbers become increasingly garbled. Such types have not been included.

The Republic

In general, the coinage of the Republic does not deal with contemporary events, but presents symbols or commemorates the families of the individual moneyers who were responsible for each issue. The symbols – most notably the asses with Janus and a prow and the denarii bearing the head of Roma and the Dioscuri – predominate through to the middle of the second century, with the personal types becoming the most frequent in the late second and first centuries. Although these personal types are of great interest in themselves, and reflect much of early Roman history, they usually commemorate the family of the moneyer who struck them. These moneyers were young men of the leading families at the beginning of their careers. The types thus served as personal advertisement, but did not present events or policies of importance at the time. In this, they differ from the coinage of the emperors or even of the warlords who dominated the Republic in the last generations of its existence, for in those cases, the origins of an individual often had a direct bearing on the policies which he followed, or served as rallying points for a party. The coinage of Caesar provides notable examples.

Most of the Republican coinage, therefore, will not be discussed here – it would be worth a book in itself. Instead, the following pages will concentrate on types which may reasonably be taken to refer to contemporary events, as illustrations of the history of the late Republic. These begin in the late second century, with commemoration of the establishment of Roman control over southern Gaul, and become increasingly important in the late first. In each case, the essential historical background will be sketched, but naturally, no attempt will be made to provide a complete and coherent history of the late Republic. Types of all moneyers will be considered together in chronological order, until the rise of Caesar. An outline of his career will be followed by the coins which contain all the historical references of the period. Next, the historical background to the Civil Wars and sketches of its main players will be followed by their coins. The section on Augustus, which contains the coins struck after Actium, will make full reference to this discussion.

The conquest of southern Gaul

The expansion of Roman power into southern Gaul was the result of attacks of the local tribes on the free Greek city of Massilia (Marseilles), a Roman ally. In 125 and 124 BC, the Romans sent forces to restore order in the neighbouring region, which was of great strategic value for controlling the land route from Italy to Spain, where they had two provinces. These successes stirred the main confederation of tribes of the interior, the Arverni, and their allies, the Allobroges, into action. The Allobroges were defeated in 121 by L. Domitius Ahenobarbus (cos. 122);

later the same year, the Arverni were crushed by Q. Fabius Maximus (cos. 121). As a result, the whole of southern Gaul was brought under Roman control, and both victors triumphed in 120. To secure control of the region, the Romans founded the colony of Narbo Martius (Narbonne) under the leadership of Domitius Ahenobarbus and L. Licinius Crassus, who now made his entry into public life.

121 – 119 BC Establishment of Roman control of southern Gaul through victories over the Arverni and Allobroges, and the foundation of the colony of Narbo.

1 L. Furius Philus: Rome 119. *Obv.* M FOVRI L F, Head of Janus. *Rev.* ROMA PHILI, Roma crowning trophy of Gaulish arms. Den: *Cr* 281

2*a* L. Licinius Crassus and Cn. Domitius Ahenobarbus (Duoviri for establishing the colony), with M. Aurelius Scaurus, L. Cosconius, C. Malleolus, L. Pomponius and L. Porcius Licinius: Narbo 118. *Obv.* M AVRELI ROMA, Head of Roma r. *Rev.* L LIC CN DOM SCAVRI, Gaulish warrior (perhaps their king Bituitus) in biga r., hurling spear. Den: *Cr* 282/1

2*b* — — but *obv.* M COSCO M F, and *rev.* without SCAVRI. Den: *Cr* 282/2

2*c* — — *obv.* C MALLE C F. Den: *Cr* 282/3

2*d* — — *obv.* P POMPONI CN F. Den: *Cr* 282/4

2d

2*e* — — *obv.* L PORCI LICI. Den: *Cr* 282/5

The career and triumph of Marius

C. Marius, a native of Arpinum in the hills south-east of Rome, rose from humble origins because of his skill in the military, and in 119 was elected tribune, an office he used to carry out electoral reforms (*3*) whose details are now obscure. He gained real distinction during the war against Jugurtha in Africa, taking command as consul in 107 and bringing the war to a successful conclusion in 105. At this moment, Rome was faced with its greatest threat since Hannibal, when the German tribes of the Cimbri and Teutones descended into southern Gaul and there humiliatingly crushed the Roman army. Marius was elected consul in 104 to deal with the emergency, and re-elected five times in succession, an unprecedented event. He used his power to reform the army and to defeat first the Teutones at Aquae Sextiae in 102, then the Cimbri in Cisalpine Gaul the next year. These victories (*4*) gained Marius a triumph (*5–8*) and unprecedented influence. They had been foretold by the priest of the great mother goddess Cybele; he arrived from her temple at Pessinus in Asia Minor just at this time. While he was in power, Marius, who was more of a soldier than a politician, relied on a radical tribune, Saturninus, to pass measures in his interest. Saturninus, who was instrumental in securing Marius' elections as consul in 102–100, embarked on a major programme of reform which included the sale of grain to the public at a low subsidised price. His proposals attracted the bitter opposition of the senatorial aristocracy, and his excesses led to his murder in 100, but the grain bill was passed and a special coinage (*9*) issued to pay for it. After the fall of Saturninus, Marius was temporarily eclipsed and went into retirement in 99. Nevertheless, a party favourable to his policies continued to exist, and colonies for his veterans were established in Southern Gaul; a vast quantity of coinage (*6–7*) was issued for them.

119 BC   The electoral reforms of Marius as tribune.

    3   P. Licinius Nerva: Rome 113 or 112. *Obv*. ROMA, Bust r. *Rev*. P NERVA, Voter on *pons* (passage to voting area) receiving ballot on l., while another casts his on r. Den: Cr 292/1

          3   5

102 BC   First victories of Marius against the Germans, foretold by the priest of Cybele.

    4   C. Fabius Hadrianus: Rome 102. *Obv*. Bust of Cybele r., sometimes with EX ARGENTO PVBLICO behind. *Rev*. C FABI C F, Victory in biga r., Den: Cr 322/1

101 BC   The triumph of Marius for his German victories. Types 6 and 7 were struck by the Marian party for the colonies in Gaul; type 8 may represent the deliverance of Rome by the victories of Marius.

    5   C. Fundanius: Rome 101. *Obv*. Head of Roma r. *Rev*. C FVNDAN Q, Marius in quadriga r., his young son riding near horse. Den: Cr 326/1

   6*a*   — — *Obv*. Head of Jupiter r. *Rev*. C FVNDA Q, Victory crowning trophy before which captive kneels. Qui: Cr 326/2

   6*b*   T. Cloulius: Rome 98. Types as before but *rev*. T CLOVLI Q. Qui: Cr 332/1

7 C. Egnatuleius: Rome 97. *Obv.* C EGATVLEI C F Q, Head of Apollo r. *Rev.* ROMA Q, Victory inscribing shield attached to trophy. Qui: *Cr* 333/1

8 P. Cornelius Lentulus Marcellinus: Rome 100. *Obv.* ROMA (PECUNIA EROGATA senatus consulto), Bust of Hercules seen from behind. *Rev.* LENT MAR F, Genius of the Roman people crowning Roma. Den: *Cr* 329/1

100 BC The grain bill of Saturninus.

9 L. Calpurnius Piso, Q. Servilius Caepio: Rome 100. *Obv.* PISO CAEPIO Q, Head of Saturn r. *Rev.* AD FRVmentum EMVndum ['for buying grain'] EX S C, *quaestor urbanus* and *quaestor ostiensis* std. on bench; ear of wheat on r. Den: *Cr* 330/1

The Victories of Sulla

L. Cornelius Sulla Felix, born in 138 of a wealthy aristocratic family, entered public life as quaestor in 107, with the task of assisting Marius in Africa. During the Social War (*see* below), Sulla's victories over the Samnites, the most implacable of the Roman foes, gained him the consulate for 88. After a short time in Rome, where he had to establish his control by military force against Marius and his partisans, Sulla left for the East to deal with king Mithradates of Pontus, who had overrun the Roman province of Asia and sent a force to occupy large parts of Greece. In 86, Sulla took Athens after a devastating siege and won a decisive victory at Chaeronea (*15*). He was obliged to settle quickly with Mithradates, however, because his enemies had taken power in Rome. Led by Cinna and Marius, they attacked the city in 87. It was defended for the Senate by the consul Octavius and the general Pompeius Strabo, but plague broke out in their armies and apparently spread to the city. Losses were tremendous, in spite of appeals to the gods (*10–13*), and the troops deserted to Cinna who entered Rome with Marius. They slaughtered their opponents, and Marius was elected to a seventh consulate. He died a few days after assuming office.

Cinna, now in firm control, embarked on a programme to gain popularity by reducing debts, improving the coinage, and restoring the distribution of grain (*14*), which had been curtailed during the Social War. The main efforts of the government, however, were necessarily directed to defence against Sulla, which Carbo led after Cinna was murdered in 84. During the civil war which followed his return, Sulla occupied Rome which barely escaped capture by the Samnites whom he defeated in a bloody battle at the Colline Gate (*16*) of the city. By the end of 82, Sulla was in full control of Rome and the government: he had his enemies proscribed and executed, and assumed the office of dictator. The followers of Marius, however, still held out in Spain, where they were led by Q. Sertorius. Sulla therefore sent an expedition (*17–18*), which soon caused them to flee to Africa. In 81, he held a magnificent triumph to celebrate his victories in the East, and received the honour of a gilded equestrian statue (*20*) from the grateful Senate, whom he re-established in power in a series of major reforms. Sulla also began the rebuilding of the temple of the Capitoline Jupiter (*21*), which had been destroyed by fire in 83, and established a network of military colonies (*19*) in Central Italy. He abdicated his power in 79 and retired to his estates in Campania where he died the following year.

87 BC The siege of Rome by Sulla's enemies: outbreak of the plague with a procession in honour of the gods of the Capitoline (Jupiter, Juno and Minerva) and prayers to Aesculapius.

10*a* L. Rubrius Dossenus: Rome 87. *Obv.* DOSSEN, Head of Jupiter r. *Rev.* L RVBRI, *Tensa* of Jupiter. Den: *Cr* 348/1

10*b* *Obv.* DOS, Head of Juno r. *Rev.* As previous. Den: *Cr* 348/2

10*c* — — *Obv.* DOS, Bust of Minerva r. *Rev.* As previous. Den: *Cr* 348/3

11 — — *Obv.* DOSSEN, Head of Neptune r. *Rev.* L RVBRI, Victory stg. r. before garlanded altar of Aesculapius with snake coiled round top. Qui: *Cr* 348/4

12 — — *Obv.* Head of Janus, altar in centre. *Rev.* L RVBRI DOSSE/N/I, Prow r. As: *Cr* 348/5

13 — — *Obv.* Janiform head of Hercules and Mercury. *Rev.* Prow protruding behind shrine which contains altar of Aesculapius. As: *Cr* 348/6

86 BC Social policy of Cinna, with restoration of grain distribution to the people.

14 M. Fannius, L. Critonius: Rome 86. *Obv.* AED PL, Bust of Ceres r. *Rev.* M FAN L CRI (or CRT) PVBLICO ARGENTO, Two aediles std. on bench, ear of wheat on r. Den: *Cr* 351/1

86–82 BC The victories of Sulla, honoured with two acclamations as imperator (the first example of such iteration in Roman history). The first apparently refers to his victory in Greece; the second to his defeat of the Samnites at the Colline Gate.

15 L. Sulla, L. Manlius Torquatus: Rome, *c.* 82. *Obv.* L MANLI PROQ, Head of Roma r. *Rev.* L SVLLA IM/P/E, Sulla in quadriga r., crowned by Victory. Aur: *Cr* 367/2, 4. Den: *Cr* 367/1, 3, 5

16 L Sulla: Rome (?), *c.* 81. *Obv.* L SVLLA, Bust of Venus; Cupid stg. on r. *Rev.* IMPER ITERV/M, Jug and lituus between two trophies. Aur: *Cr* 359/1. Den: *Cr* 359/2

16 21

82–81 BC The campaign of Sulla against Sertorius.

17 C. Valerius Flaccus (proconsul in Gaul): Massilia 82. *Obv.* Bust of Victory r. *Rev.* C VAL FLA IMPERAT EX S C, Aquila between legionary standards. Den: *Cr* 365/1

18*a* C. Annius, with his quaestors L. Fabius Hispaniensis and C. Tarquitius: N. Italy and Spain: 82–81. *Obv.* C ANNI/VS T F T N PRO COS EX S C, Diademed female bust or head r. *Rev.* L FABI L F HISP Q, Victory in quadriga r. Den: *Cr* 366/1–3

18*b* — — — — *Rev.* C TARQVITI P F Q, Victory in biga r. Den: *Cr* 366/4

81 BC Establishment of military colonies in Italy.

19*a* C. Marius Capito: Rome 81. *Obv.* C MARI C F CAPITO, Bush of Ceres r. *Rev.* Ploughman with yoke of oxen l. Den: *Cr* 378/1a, b

19*b* — — — — but CAPIT on *obv.* and C MARI C F S C on *rev.* Den: *Cr* 378/1c

— — Dedication of equestrian statue by the Senate.

20 A. Manlius: Rome 80. *Obv.* A MANLI A F Q, Bust of Roma r. *Rev.* L SVLL/A FELI/X DIC, Equestrian statue l. Aur: *Cr* 381/1

— — Beginning of the reconstruction of the temple of Capitoline Jupiter (a work not completed until 69).

21 M. Volteius: Rome 78. *Obv.* Head of Jupiter r. *Rev.* M VOLTEI M F, Capitoline temple. Den: *Cr* 385/1

The Social War

The Italian states, long under Roman rule and increasingly Romanised, frequently agitated for the political equality with Rome (most directly expressed by a demand for citizenship) which had become increasingly difficult to acquire by the second century. Their cause was taken up by the tribune Livius Drusus in 91, but his murder put an end to their hopes and they broke into open revolt in the same year. The Italians organised a confederacy called Italia (*22–23*), with its capital at Corfinium in the Apennines, and raised a huge army which initially inflicted severe defeats (*24–27*) on the Roman forces. In 90, however, Rome relented to the extent of granting the citizenship to communities which had not revolted or which would immediately return to allegiance. The consuls Pompeius Strabo and Porcius Cato defeated the Marsi in the north while Sulla, their legate in the south, moved against the bitter resistance of the Samnites.

In 89, a law was passed to grant Roman citizenship to all Italians who applied. This action deprived most of the allies of a reason for fighting, and the war effectively came to end, though the Samnites (*30*) held out in a guerilla war until they were finally defeated by Sulla in 82. In the last stage of the war, in 88, the Samnites sent an embassy to Mithradates of Pontus, the most redoubtable enemy of Rome, asking him to send an army in their support. The king sent only encouragement and gold, which was struck into coins of a Pontic type (*28–29*). Although the Italians gained their immediate objective of political equality, it look a long time for the laws to be put into full effect, and it was only with the census of 70, carried out by Pompey (*34*), that large numbers of Italians were finally enrolled in the citizen body.

The Italian confederacy struck its own coins, with distinctive types and legends in both Latin and the native Oscan of the south. The coinage of the republic, on the other hand, refers to no specific event of the war beside the emergency measure of 91, the *Lex Papiria de aeris pondere* (*31–32*) which allowed for the coinage of silver sestertii and for bronze at half the old weight.

91 BC Organisation of the Italian confederacy.

> 22*a* *Obv.* ITALIA, Head of Italy l. *Rev.* Youth kneeling at foot of standard holding a pig at which eight (sometimes six) soldiers point their swords (the oath of allegiance of the confederate tribes). Den: *Syd* 619–21; 629 (no *obv.* legend)

22a   27

> 22*b* — — but *obv.* VITELIU (in Oscan letters). Den: *Syd* 626
> 22*c* — — but *rev.* Q SILO. Den: *Syd* 634
> 22*d* — — but *obv.* Helmeted head. C PAAPIUS MVTILVS (in Oscan) on *obv.* or *rev.* Den: *Syd* 637
> 23   *Obv.* MVTIL EMBRATVR (=imperator; in Oscan), Helmeted head of Italia. *Rev.* C PAAAPI (in Oscan), Bearded man holding pig at which two soldiers point their swords. Den: *Syd* 640

— — Initial victories over Rome.

> 24*a* *Obv.* VITELIU (in Oscan letters), Head of Italia l. *Rev.* Soldier with foot on Roman standard; bull (symbol of Italy) reclining at r., sometimes with NMI LVVKI M R (name of general, in Oscan). Den: *Syd* 627; 642
> 24*b* — — *Obv.* C PAAPIVS MVTILVS (in Oscan); *rev.* VITELIV (Oscan). Den: *Syd* 638
> 25   *Obv.* Bust of Italia, crowned by Victory. *Rev.* Soldier stg. with foot on Roman standard; bull on r.; tree with four shields attached on l. Den: *Syd* 630
> 26   *Obv.* Head of Bacchus r. *Rev.* VITELIV (Oscan), Italian bull trampling Roman wolf. Den: *Syd* 628
> 27   — — *Obv.* MVTIL EMBRATVR (Oscan); *Rev.* C PAAPI (Oscan) Den: *Syd* 641

88 BC Material help from Mithradates of Pontus.
  28 *Obv.* Bust of Italia crowned by Victory. *Rev.* Soldier greeting ambassador (?) who has debarked from ship in background. Den: *Syd* 632
  29 *Obv.* Head of Bacchus. *Rev.* MI IEIVS MI (Oscan), Thyrsus tied with fillet resting on cista mystica on which is fawn's skin. (Copied from types of Amisus in Pontus, Mithradates' main port.) Aur: *Syd* 643
— — Last resistance of the Samnites.
  30 *Obv.* as 22*d*; *Rev.* as 24, but legend SAFINIM (Oscan: 'of the Samnites'). Den: *Syd* 639
91 BC Roman issues according to the Lex Papiria.
  31 D. Silanus: Rome 91. *Obv.* E LEGE PAPIRIA, Bust of Roma r. *Rev.* D SILANVS L F, Victory in biga r. Ses: 337/4
  32*a* Lege Papiria de aeris pondere: Rome 91. *Obv.* I, Head of Janus. *Rev.* L P D A P, Prow. As: *Cr* 338/1
  32*b* — — *Obv.* S, Head of Saturn r. *Rev.* As previous. Sem: *Cr* 338/2
  32*c* — — *Obv.* Head of Minerva r., four raised dots behind. *Rev.* As previous, with four raised dots. Tri: *Cr* 338/3
  32*d* *Obv.* Head of Hercules r., three raised dots. *Rev.* As previous, with three raised dots. Quad: *Cr* 338/4

The victories of Pompey and his rule in Rome

Cn. Pompeius Magnus, born in 106, gained his first military experience under his father, Pompeius Strabo, in the Social War in 89. His military skills were recognised by Sulla, who sent him to Africa, where he destroyed the Marian forces led by Domitius Ahenobarbus and King Iarbas of Numidia in 81; for this he received a triumph, though he was only 25 and had held no high public office. He then conducted the campaign against the rebel Sertorius in Spain, and returned to Rome after his victory in 71. He received a second triumph (*33*) and the consulate for 70, in spite of the opposition of the Senate. During his period in office, he made many reforms, restoring the tribunes to power, giving greater participation in the government to the businessmen (*equites*) and reviving the office of censor, which he used to enrol an unprecedentedly large number of Italians (*34*) in the citizen body, thus effecting the final reconciliation between them and Rome.

In 67, Pompey was granted extensive powers to deal with the pirates in the eastern Mediterranean. He extirpated them with rapid efficiency, then moved against their ally, the old adversary of Rome, King Mithradates, whom he drove to refuge and finally suicide in 63. In 64, he deposed the last Seleucid king and made Syria a Roman province and in the next year moved to Judaea (*35*), then torn by civil strife. He captured Jerusalem and restored order to the country while his lieutenant Scaurus received the surrender of Arethas (*36*), the king of the neighbouring Nabataeans. By his victories and settlements, Pompey reorganised the whole East and made greater and richer conquests than any Roman before. He returned to Rome in 62 and celebrated his third triumph *(37—39)*; he had in the previous year received the signal honour of the *corona civica (38—39)*, an oak-wreath, for his services in saving the lives of Roman citizens.

By now, Pompey was faced with open opposition from the Senate. He therefore organised a coalition of the most powerful men in Rome and together with Crassus and Julius Caesar took over the state. The senatorial government was powerless against the combination of force which is improperly called the 'first triumvirate'. In 58, Caesar as consul carried out reforms suitable to the three leaders, then assumed the governorship of Gaul where he made extensive conquests of his own. Pompey stayed in Rome, while Crassus set out for eastern conquests, only to meet disaster and death in 53. Meanwhile, C. Memmius had expanded Roman control of Asia Minor by gaining victories in Bithynia *(40)*.

After the death of Crassus, and with his assumption of a sole consulate in 52, Pompey became supreme in Rome; he would have gained absolute power in the city in 53, a time of increasing anarchy, had he not been opposed by the consul Valerius Messala *(41)*. His increasingly autocratic tendencies also stirred much opposition among the aristocracy, and the hopes of liberty *(42)* were never far away. Pompey gradually broke with Caesar and attempted to gain full control of the empire. In the civil war which began in 49, Pompey fled Italy before Caesar's rapid advance, and withdrew to Illyricum, then Greece, where he was defeated at Pharsalus in 48. He hoped to take refuge in Egypt, but was murdered as he attempted to land there.

71 BC Pompey's second triumph, for his victories in Spain, with reference to his earlier successes in Africa.

    33 Pompey: Rome 71. *Obv.* MAGNVS, Head of Africa r.; lituus behind. *Rev.* PROCOS, Pompey in triumphal quadriga r., Victory flying above; his elder son rides the fore horse. Aur: Cr 402/1

70 BC Pompey's censorship, with Rome and Italy reconciled by the enrolment of new citizens.

    34 Q. Fufius Calenus, P. Mucius Scaevola (Cordus): Rome 70 *Obv.* HO VIRT KALENI, Jugate heads of Honos and Virtus. *Rev.* ITAL RO CORDI, Italia and Roma clasping hands. Den: Cr 403/1

        34   37

63 BC   Pompey's eastern campaigns: surrender of a ruler in Judaea, variously identified as Dionysius of Tripolis or Aristobulus the High Priest.

     35   A. Plautius: Rome 55. *Obv.* A PLAVTIVS AED CVR S C, Head of Cybele r. *Rev.* BACCHIVS IVDAEVS, Figure kneeling before camel (the enigmatic legend has given rise to a variety of explanations). Den: *Cr* 431/1

— —   Surrender of king Arethas of Nabataea to Scaurus.

     36   M. Aemilius Scaurus, P. Hypsaeus: Rome 58. *Obv.* M SCAVR AED CVR EX S C (REX ARETAS), Camel with kneeling figure before. *Rev.* P HVPSAEVS AED CVR C HVPSAE COS PREIVER CAPTVM (many variations in legend), Jupiter in quadriga l. Den: *Cr* 422/1

62 BC   The triumph of Pompey, and award of the *corona civica*.

     37   Faustus Cornelius Sulla: Rome 56. *Obv.* S C, Bust of Venus r. *Rev.* FAVSTVS (in monogram), Three trophies (for Pompey's three triumphs); jug l., lituus r. Den: *Cr* 426/3

     38   — — *Obv.* S C FAVSTVS (in monogram), Head of Hercules r. *Rev.* Globe surrounded by three small wreaths and one large one; below, *aplustre* and ear of wheat. (Small wreaths = Pompey's three triumphs; large wreath = *corona civica*). Den: *Cr* 426/4

     39   L. Vinicius: Rome 52 *Obv.* CONCORDIAE (or −AI), Head of Concord r. *Rev.* L VINICI, Victory walking r., carrying palm branch decorated with four wreaths (symbolism as previous type; the obverse probably reflects the hope of good relations between Pompey and Caesar). Den: *Cr* 436/1

58 BC   Victories of Memmius in Bithynia, exact nature unknown, though they did earn him the title imperator. (Memmius is best known in literary history; the poet Catullus accompanied him to Bithynia and the poem of Lucretius, *De rerum natura*, was dedicated to him.)

     40   C. Memmius: Rome 56. *Obv.* C MEMMI C F, Head of Ceres. *Rev.* C MEMMIVS IMPERATOR, Kneeling captive before trophy. Den: *Cr* 427/1

40

54 BC   Opposition in Rome to Pompey's growing autocracy.

     41   M. Valerius Messalla: Rome 53. *Obv.* MESSAL F, Bust of Roma. *Rev.* Sceptre with wreath below curule chair (the subjection of royalty to the rule of the Republic, symbolic of

the temporary defeat of Pompey's attempt at one man rule
by the moneyer's father, cos. 53). Den: *Cr* 435/1

42   M. Junius Brutus: Rome 54. *Obv.* LIBERTAS, Head r. *Rev.*
BRVTVS, Brutus the elder (Rome's first consul, 509 BC, responsible for deposing the kings, and reputed ancestor of the
moneyer, later Caesar's assassin), walking between lictors.
Den: *Cr* 433/1

JULIUS CAESAR

C. Julius Caesar was born in 100 BC, the descendant of an ancient
patrician family which traced its ancestry back to Aeneas and Venus, and
the nephew of Marius. He received an education which enabled him to
become one of the greatest speakers and writers of the day, and in 81 was
sent to the court of Bythinia and received the *corona civica* for saving the
life of Roman citizens. He rose through public offices, becoming Pontifex
Maximus in 63 and propraetor in Spain in 62−61, an office he filled with
great success. On his return to Rome in 60, he refused a triumph, but
reached an agreement with Pompey and Crassus to form a coalition of the
three most powerful men in Rome and take over the government. As
consul in 59, he carried out the policies of this alliance, gaining for
himself the proconsular power in Cisalpine and later Transalpine Gaul, a
position renewed in 55. He used these years to effect extensive conquests
(1−6), adding a large and rich province to the empire and gaining a reputation for military skill and the devotion of his legions. During these
wars, he was acclaimed imperator by his troops *(7)*.

Although Caesar had many supporters to look after his interests in
Rome while he was in Gaul, opposition to him grew and attracted
Pompey, who desired to establish his sole rule. By agreement with
Pompey, Caesar had arranged to stand for the consulate for 48 in ab-
sentia, but in January 49, his enemies triumphed, Pompey was given
dictatorial powers, and Caesar was ordered to disband his legions. After
reflecting, Caesar crossed the Rubicon, the boundary of his province, and
a new civil war began. Despite the resistance of the consuls, loyal to
Pompey *(8)*, Caesar rapidly occupied Italy *(9)*, and hastened to Spain
where he defeated the Pompeian forces *(10−11)*. The consuls, meanwhile,
had fled to Sicily and then to Asia *(12−14)*, where they led the Republican
opposition.

During this campaign, Caesar was made dictator on the motion
of Lepidus. He held that office a short time, returned to Rome, where he
was elected consul for 48, then set out against Pompey whose fate was
decided at the battle of Pharsalus *(15)* in August 48. On the night before
the battle, Caesar, after seeing an omen, vowed to build a temple to his
ancestress, Venus Genetrix, should he be victorious. This temple *(33)*
eventually became the centre of his new forum in Rome. Caesar now
received the office of dictator *(16)* for a year. Defeated, Pompey fled to

Egypt where he was killed. Caesar followed, spent the winter in Egypt where he met Cleopatra and had to fight the Ptolemaic forces, then moved north to Asia Minor. His rapid victory at Zela in Pontus over Pharnaces, the son of Mithradates, and his Pompeian adherents, justified the message 'veni, vidi, vici'. He returned to Rome in October 47.

After arranging to be consul for the year 46, Caesar crossed to Africa, where the Pompeian forces had gathered (*17−19*), and crushed them at Thapsus in April (*20−24*). He now accepted a dictatorship (*25−26*) to last for ten years (it was renewed annually, so that he became dictator for the fourth time in April 45), returned to Rome and celebrated an elaborate triumph (*29−30*) for his victories in Gaul, Egypt, Pontus and Africa. His honours included a chariot with four white horses, equivalent to that of the sun-god, and a radiate golden crown, also symbolic of the sun (Civil Wars *38−39*), which would be carried into the theatres to represent him. In addition, he was awarded a curule (*27−28*) chair with the right to sit between the consuls in the Senate, and a temple of Liberty (*31*) was decreed to honour his liberation of Rome. He now embarked on his numerous building projects (*32−33*) and reforms, of which the introduction of the Julian calendar has proved the most permanent.

War was not yet over, however, for the sons of Pompey had assembled a force in Spain to carry on the resistance to Caesar (*34−35*). These were Cn. Pompeius Magnus, who had commanded the Pompeian fleet and moved to Africa after Pharsalus, and Sextus Pompeius (*see* Civil Wars). Caesar crossed over and defeated them at Munda in March 45. Cnaeus was killed, but Sextus survived (*39*) to maintain the hopes of his party. Caesar was now supreme in the Roman world. When the news of Munda reached Rome, the senate voted Caesar the title of imperator (*37*) for life, with the right to wear a laurel wreath, and proposed to build a temple in honour of his clemency (*38*), for Caesar, unlike Marius and Sulla, did not massacre his opponents.

In April, Caesar had entered his fourth term as dictator (*36*) and received the right to wear the golden crown of the triumphator whenever he attended the circus games (in 44, he began to wear it on other public occasions: cf. *37, 42*). After his return to Rome in October 45, Caesar received honours more characteristic of a monarch than a magistrate. They culminated in the title *pater patriae* (*40*), the unprecedented office of dictator *in perpetuo* (*43−44*) and extravagant adulation, which included a golden throne to be exhibited in the Circus with his golden crown on it as a sign of his power even when he was absent (Civil Wars *37*). Caesar was to be worshipped as a god (*42*), with temples, altars and a priest. In February 44, as part of his preparation for a great campaign against the Parthians, Caesar was offered a royal diadem which he refused. His tendency toward monarchy, however, was too manifest and extreme for many leaders of the Roman aristocracy, who organised a plot and assassinated the unarmed dictator as he entered the theatre of Pompey, where the Senate was temporarily meeting, on the Ides of March (*45*).

58–49 BC   Victories of Caesar in Gaul, with acclamation as imperator. Type *3* refers to his capture of Massilia, whose patron goddess was Artemis, in 49 BC.

1   L. Hostilius Saserna: Rome 48. *Obv.* Head of Gaulish female r. *Rev.* L HOSTILIVS SASERNA, Victory walking r., carrying Gallic trophy. Den: *Cr* 448/1

2   —— *Obv.* Head of bearded Gaulish male r. *Rev.* (Legend as 1), Charioteer and (perhaps British) warrior in biga r. Den: *Cr* 448/2

2   15

3   —— *Obv.* Head of Gaulish female r. *Rev.* (Legend as *1*), Artemis stg. facing, with stag. Den: *Cr* 448/3

4   D. Junius Brutus Albinus: Rome 48. *Obv.* Head of Mars r. *Rev.* ALBINV/S BRVTI F, Two Gallic horns crossed; oval shield above, round shield below. Den: *Cr* 450/1

5   Caesar: mint moving 48–47. *Obv.* LII (perhaps a reference to Caesar's age), Diademed female head r. *Rev.* CAESAR, Gallic trophy. Aur: *Cr* 452/1. Den: *Cr* 452/2; 452/4–5 (captive below trophy). Qui: *Cr* 452/3 (*obv.* head veiled)

6   Caesar: Spain 46–45. *Obv.* Head of Venus r. or l.; Cupid behind. *Rev.* CAESAR, Male and female Gaul below trophy. Den: *Cr* 468/1, 2

7   C. Caesar: Gaul 47 (? Date and interpretation uncertain). *Obv.* Head of Venus r. *Rev.* (C) CAESAR IMP, Trophy; at foot, on l. chariot (perhaps the British *essedum*); on r., shield with two spears and Gallic horn. Den: *Cr* 482/1

49 BC   Resistance of Pompeians in Rome.

8   Cn. Nerius: Rome 49 *Obv.* NERI Q VRB, Head of Saturn r. *Rev.* L LENT C MARC COS, Legionary eagle between standards of *hastati* and *principes*. Den: *Cr* 441/1

——   Liberation of Rome from autocracy (of Pompey).

9   C. Vibius Pansa: Rome 48. *Obv.* LIBERTATIS, Head of Libertas r. *Rev.* C PANSA C F C N, Roma, std., crowned by Victory. Den: *Cr* 449/4

——   Resistance of the Pompeian forces in Spain.

10   Cn. Calpurnius Piso, Terentius Varro: Spain 49. *Obv.* CN PISO PROQ NVMA, Head of Numa r. *Rev.* MAGN PROCOS, Prow r. (reference to Pompey's victories at sea). Den: *Cr* 446/1

11   —— *Obv.* VARRO PROQ, Terminal bust of Jupiter r. *Rev.* MAGN

PROCOS, Sceptre between eagle and dolphin (symbolic of Pompey's domination of land and sea). Den: *Cr* 447/1

— — Pompeian resistance continues in Sicily, then Asia.

12 L. Cornelius Lentulus, C. Claudius Marcellus: Sicily, Asia 49. *Obv.* Triskeles with head of Medusa (symbol of Sicily). *Rev.* LENT MAR COS, Jupiter holding thunderbolt and eagle (statue of Jupiter by Myron, erected in Syracuse in 460 BC). Den: *Cr* 445/1

13 — — *Obv.* L LENT C MARC COS, Head of Apollo r. *Rev.* Q, type as previous. Den: *Cr* 445/2

14 — — *Obv* Head of Jupiter r. *Rev.* L LENTVLVS C MARC COS, Statue of Diana of the Ephesians. Den: *Cr* 445/3

48 BC Preparations for the campaign against Pompey: Caesar adopts a standard with a bull because of an omen. When he was sacrificing at a festival on the Alban Mount in December 49, the bull escaped and swam across a lake; Caesar took this as an omen for his successful crossing to Greece. The bull was also the symbol of Bovillae, ancestral home of the Julii, because of a similar incident.

15 L. Livinius Regulus: Rome 42 (posthumous issue for Caesar). *Obv.* Laureate head of Caesar r. *Rev.* L LIVINEIVS REGVLVS, Bull charging r. Den: *Cr* 494/24

— — Second dictatorship of Caesar combined with celebration of his offices of Pontifex Maximus and augur.

16 Caesar: struck in the East 47. *Obv.* CAESAR DICT, Axe and sacrificial vessel. *Rev.* ITER, Jug and augur's wand. Aur: *Cr* 456/1

47—46 BC The Pompeian resistance, advertising its base in Africa.

17 Q. Metellus Pius Scipio, P. Crassus Jun.: Africa 47—46. *Obv* Q METELLVS SCIPIO IMP G T A, Lion-headed Genius Terrae Africae stg. facing. *Rev.* P CRASSVS IVN LEG PRO PR, Victory stg. facing. Den: *Cr* 460/4

18 — — *Obv.* CRASS IVN LEG PRO PR, Head of Utica wearing mural crown r., between ear of wheat and caduceus; prow below. *Rev.* METEL PIVS SCIP IMP, Trophy between lituus and jug. Den: *Cr* 460/3

19 Q. Metellus Scipio, Eppius: Africa 47—46. *Obv.* Q METELL SCIPIO IMP, Head of Africa r. *Rev.* EPPIVS LEG F C, Hercules stg. facing. Den: *Cr* 461/1

46 BC Victory of Caesar in Africa.

20 T. Carisius: Rome 46. *Obv.* (S C), Bust of Victory r. *Rev.* T CARISI, Victory in biga or quadriga r. Den: *Cr* 464/4, 5

21 — — *Rev.* Roma std. l. on pile of weapons. Qui: *Cr* 464/6

22 C. Considius Paetus: Rome 46. *Obv.* PAETI, Head of Venus r. or l. *Rev.* C CONSIDI, Victory in quadriga l. Den: *Cr* 465/3, 4

23 — — *Obv.* Bust of Minerva r. *Rev.* C CONSIDI, Victory in quadriga r. Den: *Cr* 465/5

24 — — *Obv.* PAETI, Head of Venus r. *Rev.* C CONSIDI/VS, Victory walking r. or l., holding trophy. Qui: *Cr* 465/6, 7

—— Third dictatorship of Caesar.

25 L. Munatius Plancus: Rome 45. *Obv*. C CAES DIC TER, Bust of Victory r. *Rev*. L PLANC PR/AEF VRB, Jug. Aur: *Cr* 475/1. 1/2 Aur: *Cr* 475/2

26 C. Clovius: uncertain mint 45. *Obv*. CAESAR DIC TER, Bust of Victory r. *Rev*. C CLOVI PRAEF, Minerva stg. l., holding trophy. Æ: *Cr* 476/1

—— Award to Caesar of a curule chair after Thapsus.

27 C. Considius Paetus: Rome 46. *Obv*. Head of Apollo r. *Rev*. C CONSIDI/VS PAETVS (OR PAETI), Curule chair on which lies wreath. Den: *Cr* 465/1.2

28 Lollius Palicanus: Rome 45. *Obv*. HONORIS, Head of Honos r. *Rev*. PALIKANVS, Curule chair, sometimes with wreath. Den: *Cr* 473/2

—— Triumph of Caesar, with special gifts of money to the troops and people, and advertisement of Caesar's titles.

29 L. Papius Celsus. Rome 46. *Obv*. TRIVMPVS, Head of Triumphus r. *Rev*. L PAPIVS CELSUS III VIR, Eagle placing stick on fire while eagle fans flames (a reference to the moneyer's family). Den: *Cr* 472/2

30 C. Caesar: Rome (?) 46. *Obv*. COS TERT DICT ITER, Head of Caesar r. *Rev*. AVGVR PONT MAX, Priestly implements; on r., D or M (for Donativum or Munus). Den: *Cr* 467/1

46–45 BC Construction of temples. A temple of Libertas was vowed as part of the honours to Caesar at his triumph. At that time, the temple of Felicitas was under construction; it was dedicated by Lepidus in 45 or 44. Caesar himself began a temple to his patron, Venus Genetrix; it was the centrepoint of his new forum. The following interpretations are hypothetical: 31 could simply reflect Caesar's claim to be the liberator of Rome, while 32 may represent Caesar's battle-cry 'Felicitas' at Thapsus. The figure on 33 has been identified as the cult image for the temple of Venus.

31 Lollius Palicanus: Rome 45. *Obv*. LIBERTATIS, Head of Liberty. *Rev*. PALIKANVS, Rostra on which stands tribune's bench (a family reference). Den: *Cr* 473/1

32 —— *Obv*. FELICITATIS, Head of Felicitas r. *Rev*. PALIKANVS, Victory in biga r. Den: *Cr* 473/2

33 Mn Cordius Rufus: Rome 46. *Obv*. RVFVS IIIVIR, Jugate heads of Dioscuri r. *Rev*. MN CORDI/VS, Venus stg. l., with Cupid perched on her shoulder. Den: *Cr* 463/1

—— Organisation of the Pompeian resistance in Spain.

34 Cn. Pompeius Magnus, M. Poblicius: Spain 46–5 *Obv*. M POPLICI LEG PRO PR, Head of Roma r. *Rev*. CN MAGNVS IMP, Hispania welcoming Pompey Jr., about to disembark from ship. Den: *Cr* 469/1

35a Cn. Pompeius Magnus, M. Minatius Sabinus: Spain 46–5. *Obv*. CN MAGNVS IMP F (several variations), head of Pompey the Great. *Rev.* M MINAT SABIN PR Q, Baetica welcoming disembarking Pompey. Den: *Cr* 470/1a

35*b*   — — Baetica greeting Pompey while Tarraco, kneeling, presents shield. Den: *Cr* 470/1b

35*c*   — — Baetica greeting Pompey while Tarraco crowns him. Den: *Cr* 470/1c, d

35   38

45 BC   April. Caesar dictator for the fourth time, with right to wear the golden crown of the triumphator.

36   M. Mettius et al.: Rome 44 *Obv.* CAESAR DICT QVART, Head of Caesar r., wearing golden crown. *Rev.* M METTIVS, Juno Sospita in biga r. Den: *Cr* 480/2

45 BC   Award of special, permanent title imperator after battle of Munda. (The types with IMPER were perhaps struck immediately after the Ides of March.)

37*a*   L. Aemilius Buca, M. Mettius, P. Sepullius Macer: Rome 44. *Obv.* CAESAR IMP/ER, Head of Caesar r., wearing golden crown; priestly implements behind. *Rev.* M METTIVS, Venus stg. l., holding Victory. (Den: *Cr* 480/3; 480/17 (no implements on *obv.*).

37*b*   — — but *rev.* L AEMILIVS BVCA. Den: *Cr* 480/4; 480/18 (no implements on *obv.*).

— —   Award of a temple to the Clemency of Caesar by the Senate (never finished), with celebration of Caesar's games, perhaps those of the Parilia, the birthday of Rome (see also type 40*b*).

38   P. Sepullius Macer: Rome 44. *Obv.* CLEMENTIAE CAESARIS, Tetrastyle temple. *Rev.* P SEPVLLIVS MACER, Acrobat (*desultor*) riding two horses r. Den: *Cr* 480/20

45−44 BC   Continuing resistance of the Pompeians in Spain under Sextus Pompey.

39   Sextus Pompeius: Spain 45−44. *Obv.* SEX MAGN/VS (PIVS) IMP, Head of Pompey the Great. *Rev.* PIETAS Pietas stg. l. (Pietas was the Pompeian battlecry at Munda). Den: *Cr* 477/ 1−3

45 or 44 BC   Award of title pater patriae.

40*a*   C. Cossutius Maridianus, P. Sepullius Macer: Rome 44. *Obv.* CAESAR PARENS PATRIAE, Wreathed head of Caesar r., wearing veil of Pontifex Maximus; lituus before, apex behind. *Rev.* C COSSVTIVS and MARIDIANVS arranged in form of a cross; A A A F F in angles. Den: *Cr* 480/19

  40*b* — — *Rev.* as 38. Den: *Cr* 480/20

44 BC Fifth consulate of Caesar.

  41   C. Caesar: Rome 44. *Obv.* CAESAR DIC QVAR, Bust of Venus r. *Rev.* COS QVINC in laurel wreath. Aur: *Cr* 481/1

— — Divine honours for Caesar, represented by the star of divinity, which he shared with his ancestress Venus.

  42   P. Sepullius Macer: Rome 44. *Obv.* CAESAR IMP, Head of Caesar r., wearing golden crown; star behind. *Rev.* P SEPVLLIVS MACER, Venus stg. l., holding Victory and sceptre, sometimes with star at base of sceptre. Den: *Cr* 480/5

44 BC February (?). Award of the dictatorship for life.

  43   L. Aemilius Buca: Rome 44. *Obv.* CAESAR DICT PERPETVO, Wreathed head r. *Rev.* L BVCA, Fasces and caduceus crossed; axe, globe and crossed hands in angles. Den: *Cr* 480/6

  44*a*   L. Aemilius Buca, M. Mettius, C. Cossutius Maridianus: Rome 44. *Obv.* CAESAR DICT (IN) PERPETVO, Head of Caesar r., wearing golden crown and sometimes veil. *Rev.* Venus std. r. or l., holding Victory, L BVCA: Den: *Cr* 480/7−8

  44*b* — — — — P SEPVLLIVS MACER: Den: *Cr* 480/9−14

  44*c* — — — — C MARIDIANVS: Den: *Cr* 480/15−16

        44   45

——— The Ides of March.

  45   M. Junius Brutus, L. Plaetorius Cestus: Mint: moving with Brutus 43−2. *Obv.* BRVT IMP L PLAET CEST, Bearded head of Brutus r. *Rev.* EID MAR, Pileus (cap of freedom) between daggers. Den: *Cr* 508/3

THE CIVIL WARS

The following section treats the coinage from the assassination of Caesar in 44 to the battle of Actium in 31. Names of individuals who form the subject of biographical sketches after the introduction are in bold type.

After the Ides of March, the situation in Rome was confused, for the tyrannicides had no clear plan for taking power. **Brutus** and **Cassius** occupied the Capitoline, while **Antony**, who was consul with Caesar, convened a meeting of the Senate at which a general amnesty was declared.

He restrained **Lepidus**, whose troops had occupied the Forum, and delivered a eulogy at Caesar's funeral on 20 March which inflamed the populace against the liberators. Popular loyalty to the dictator's memory was also manifested at the games of the Parilia (*1*) held in April to celebrate the victory of Munda. Antony, now dominant with the support of Caesar's veterans, had himself assigned the provinces of Gaul, which would offer a firm base for power.

In May, however, Antony was faced with the unwelcome arrival of C. Octavius (**Augustus**, in the next section), the great nephew of Caesar who had been adopted in the latter's will and had come to Rome to claim his rights. His name roused the support of the troops and people, and he showed his devotion to his adoptive father's memory by attempting to display his golden throne and crown (*37*) at the games in May and July. Both times he was thwarted by Antony, but during the games of Caesar's victory in July, a comet appeared and was promptly identified as the manifestation of Caesar's soul; Octavius consequently had a star placed on the head of Caesar's statues (*31*; Augustus 69). He now became the heir of Caesar's popularity and the chief rival of Antony. Needing more substantial support, however, Octavius, who held no public office, illegally raised an army from his father's veterans and occupied Rome in November. Antony, unable for the moment to fight him, patched up an agreement and set out for Gaul.

The province which Antony had appropriated was already occupied by a defender of the Republic, Decimus Brutus, who held it from Caesar. His strategic location and powerful army were a threat to the Caesarians, whose enemies now began to scatter and organise: Brutus and Cassius, in danger in Rome, had left for parts unknown. Antony, therefore, marched against Decimus and besieged him when he withdrew to Mutina in Cisalpine Gaul. Meanwhile, in Rome, the elder statesman Cicero had emerged from retirement to lead the resistance against Antony. He persuaded the senate to make an ally of Octavius, who was given the title propraetor and command of an army together with the consuls Hirtius and Pansa. In their enthusiasm, the Senate awarded him an equestrian statue (*2*). Although both consuls were killed in the fighting, the campaign was a success, and Antony withdrew to Gaul (*3–4*). For his part in the victory, Octavius received the title imperator (*2*).

The Senate, however, decreed greater honours to the liberators: Decimus Brutus held a triumph, and Brutus and Cassius were not only confirmed in the provinces which they had occupied but given superior power over all other governors in the East. Brutus became proconsul of Macedonia, Illyricum and Achaea, where he defeated **C. Antonius** (*19*), Antony's brother, to whom Macedonia had originally been assigned, as well as the Thracian tribes (*20–23*). Cassius, meanwhile, had taken Syria, and most of the Roman east. The Republican leaders engaged also in a war of propaganda, in which they portrayed themselves as champions of Liberty (*24–30, 41–43*). In the West, Lepidus, governor of Hither Spain and southern Gaul, had reconciled **Sextus Pompey**, who had been conducting a guerrilla war in Spain to the Republic. In return for his support, Pompey received an extraordinary command over the coasts and fleets.

The favour of the government toward the assassins and its neglect of his interests alienated Octavius, while Lepidus, instead of fighting Antony, joined him (*5*). In May 43, Octavius demanded the consulate (made vacant by the death of both incumbents at Mutina) and when the Senate hesitated, brought up his army. The Senate, fortified by new legions which arrived from Africa (*6*), prepared to resist, but its troops deserted and Octavius entered the city. In August, he was duly elected consul (*7*) and had his adoption by Caesar ratified. He now officially became C. Julius Caesar Octavianus, known to modern convenience as Octavian, a name he never used; for contemporaries, he was simply Caesar.

After a brief stay in Rome, Octavian marched against Antony but instead of fighting a war reached an arrangement with him and Lepidus at Brundisium in November. The three agreed to take over the state under the title *IIIviri reipublicae constituendae* 'Triumvirs for reorganising the Republic' (*8–11*), which gave them superiority over all other officials. Octavian resigned his now superfluous consulate. Each took control of a province, with Italy to be held in common: Antony received Gaul, Lepidus Spain and Octavian Africa and the islands. Possession of those territories, however, was dubious, for **Cornificius** controlled Africa for the Senate (*50*) and Sextus Pompey took advantage of his naval command to seize power in the islands. The triumvirs marched on Rome, where the helpless Senate confirmed them in power for five years, through the end of 38. By this act, the Republic finally came to an end.

The triumvirs began their career by an act of bloody vengeance on their enemies, the infamous proscriptions, whose most famous victim was Cicero. Many were chosen, however, for their wealth; and the profits from confiscations enabled the three to strike an abundant series of gold coins (*12–18*). The year 42 opened with the official deification of Caesar (*31–39*). Octavian, who could now style himself '*divi filius*' (a title he only began to use in 40), had a star, representing the comet of 44, placed on the head of the statues of Caesar (*31*), to whom a temple (*83*: begun in 36 BC) was authorised and equestrian statues (*36*) were erected in all the cities of Italy. Antony became the high priest of the cult (*38–39*).

The triumvirs now prepared to move against the defenders of the Republic. Lepidus was left to manage Italy, while Antony and Octavian moved toward Greece. Octavian stopped to deal with Sextus Pompey who had seized Sicily and was threatening to blockade the Italian coast. Although Italy was successfully defended by **Salvidienus**, the Caesarian fleet was defeated off Rhegium while Octavian watched. Pompey celebrated a triumph and was acclaimed imperator for the second time (*44–47*). Octavian and Antony nevertheless managed to cross to Illyricum, but they had hardly landed when the Republican fleet under **Staius Murcus** and **Ahenobarbus** (*48*) took control of the sea and cut off their retreat. In gratitude for his successes at sea, Ahenobarbus vowed a temple to Neptune (*49*).

By this time, the Republicans had gained considerable success. With the formation of the triumvirate, Brutus and Cassius knew that war was inevitable. They therefore met in Smyrna to plan action against Rhodes and the Lycians, whose fleets might pose a danger in their rear as they moved westward. In the spring of 42, Cassius attacked, defeated and plundered Rhodes (*40−41*), while the fleet of Brutus, commanded by **Casca**, conquered the Lycian cities (*42−43*). The successful liberators met at Sardis in the summer, and were there proclaimed *imperatores*; they then crossed into Macedonia with a huge army. The war and the fate of the Republic were decided in two battles at Philippi in October and November. Brutus and Cassius committed suicide in defeat. Before the battle, Octavian, in hope of victory, vowed to build a temple in Rome to Mars the Avenger (Augustus 55). The triumvirate was victorious, but far from controlling the whole empire. Cornificius held out in Africa until the end of the year (*50*), and Sextus Pompey, firmly in control of Sicily, was reinforced by the fleet of Murcus (*51*), while Ahenobarbus maintained control of the Ionian Sea.

The triumvirs, nevertheless, proceeded to reorganise the government. Many legions were demobilised, and the provinces were divided, with Antony, the real victor at Philippi, receiving the lion's share, and Lepidus being virtually excluded. Octavian was assigned the difficult task of finding land for the discharged troops in Italy, to be confiscated from sixteen cities (*54*). The unpopularity which this aroused was exploited by Antony's wife Fulvia and his brother **Lucius**, consul (*52−53*) for 41. The war they started was settled by Octavian's capture of Perusia, where Lucius had taken refuge, in February 40. Octavian owed his victory to his friend Salvidienus, whom he rewarded with the governorship of Gaul and the promise of the consulate (*65*).

Antony, meanwhile, had gone to Asia Minor to settle affairs and raise money. Late in 41, his activities took him to Tarsus where he met **Cleopatra**, who made such an impression that he followed her to Egypt and stayed there through most of the next year. During his absence in 40, the Parthians, led by Pacorus and the renegade **Labienus** (*56*), invaded Roman territory. Pacorus conquered Syria and Judaea, where he installed a favourable king, Antigonus, while Labienus proceeded to Asia Minor, gaining the adherence of partisans of the Republican cause. Antony's governor **Plancus** put up enough resistance to earn the title imperator (*55*), but soon was obliged to withdraw to the islands.

Because of the situation in Italy, it appeared that war between the triumvirs was inevitable, and would be much to Octavian's disadvantage, since Antony had not only the prestige of his victory at Philippi, but controlled the sea, thanks to his recent alliance with Ahenobarbus (*57*) and Pompey, and had loyal legions in Gaul. Instead, however, Antony and Octavian met at Brundisium (*58−61*) in October 40 and made an agreement which essentially gave Octavian control of the West, while Antony took the East, where he planned a great campaign against the Parthians. Antony married Octavian's sister **Octavia** (*62−64*), and set out eastwards, after both triumvirs had visited Rome and arranged a settlement with Sextus Pompey, who was recognised as governor of Sicily and Sardinia in the spring of 39; he in turn agreed to supply the grain he had threatened to cut off from Rome. In the same year, Octavian secured his position in the West by the victory of his lieutenant **Calvinus** (*67*) who pacified Spain after a major revolt.

In spite of the treaty, Octavian had no intention of resigning control of Sicily and the seas to Sextus, and attacked him in 38. His fleet, however, was defeated (*69*) in the straits of Messina between Sicily and Italy. Octavian, needing new ships, met with Antony at Tarentum (*71−78*), where their mutual suspicions were allayed. Octavian promised Antony legions for his eastern expedition and received 120 ships to use against Sextus Pompey. The triumvirate was renewed for another five years. Octavian entrusted the fleet to his friend Agrippa, who had already won impressive victories in Gaul (*70*); Lepidus, now ruling Africa, promised reinforcements. The war was decided by the battle of Naulochus (*80−82*) in September 36; the fleet of the last defender of the Republic was defeated, and Sextus fled to the east. Lepidus was the second casualty of the war: when he tried to claim excessive credit for the success and to reassert his position in the triumvirate, he was humiliated and deposed by Octavian who left him only the title *pontifex maximus*, which he exercised in exile. Octavian was now supreme in the West. He used his position to stress the memory of Caesar, and his descent from the Julian family by beginning construction of the temple of Divus Julius (*83*) in 36, and by celebrating the festival of his ancestress, Venus Genetrix (*87−88*), in 34.

After the meeting at Brundisium, Antony had returned to the East, where his immediate task was the war against Parthia. In 39, his general **Ventidius** drove the Parthians from the Roman east (*66*), defeated and killed Labienus, and was rewarded with a triumph in Rome. Antony followed up his success the next year by receiving the surrender of King Antiochus of Commagene, for which he gained a third imperatorial salutation (*84*). The new governor of Syria, **Sosius**, drove back another Parthian attack, and captured Jerusalem (*79*) in 37, where he installed Herod as king. Meanwhile Antony had had to postpone his planned great expedition, to sail west and meet Octavian at Tarentum, whence he returned with little but promises. He was now free for his major aim. In preparation, he reduced the Roman provinces to three and assigned large areas to the responsibility of the local client rulers, of whom the most important was **Cleopatra** of Egypt. For the moment, these dispositions, and even Antony's open affair with the queen, by whom he had two children, were accepted at Rome.

In the spring of 36, Antony left Syria with a large army, planning to strike through Media into the Persian heartland. The treachery of his ally, Artavasdes of Armenia, however, brought failure and considerable losses. In the next year, therefore, Antony achieved a measure of compensation by invading Armenia and making a treaty with the king of Media, to whom large parts of Armenia were assigned. By this arrangement, Antony consolidated his eastern frontiers. The major campaign, however, came in 34, when Antony conquered Armenia and led its king in triumph to Alexandria; the kingdom was made into a Roman province. As part of the celebrations, Caesarion, the son of Caesar and Cleopatra, was proclaimed co-ruler of Egypt and the queen received the grandiose title 'Queen of Kings' (*85*). Kingdoms, not all of them in Antony's control, were bestowed upon his children by Cleopatra, while Antony's other son, **Marcus Antonius Junior**, was also honoured (*86*). After a further campaign, Antony had secured the Roman position in the East by establishing a network of client kingdoms, which now included Media. He appeared to be the dominant figure in the Roman world.

The two leaders, inevitably headed for conflict, entered into a war of words in 33, in which Octavian stirred public opinion in Italy against Antony by portraying him as dominated by an oriental queen determined to establish her dominion over Rome. The triumvirate expired at the end of 33, and the two consuls, Ahenobarbus and Sosius, both favourable to Antony, took office. When their attempts to censure Octavian failed, and he appeared in the Senate with an armed guard, they fled east, together with 300 senators. They met Antony at Ephesus, where he had gathered an army of thirty legions (*90*) and a great fleet. Octavian, now in control, but without a legitimate position, secured Italy by a sort of plebiscite in which the entire population swore an oath of personal allegiance to him. He deposed Antony from all offices and prepared to move against him (*89*). Antony, meanwhile, was subject to divided counsel, as some of his advisers wanted him to dispense with Cleopatra who, thanks to the propaganda of Octavian, had become a political liability. However, he persisted in his loyalty to the queen, and prepared for battle. The fleet of Octavian, commanded by Agrippa, met the forces of Antony, now reduced by desertion – Ahenobarbus and Plancus were among the most notable to take the side of Octavian before the final showdown – at Actium in September 31. The victory was complete and decisive. Cleopatra sailed off to Egypt, followed by Antony, who stopped at Cyrenaica in a vain effort to secure the legions of Scarpus (*91–94*). After a delay in Egypt, he and Cleopatra committed suicide in 30. Octavian had triumphed and Rome was an autocracy, well on its way to becoming an empire.

AGRIPPA

M. Vipsanius Agrippa, born in Dalmatia in 63 BC of an equestrian family, was a schoolmate and close friend of Octavian whom he accompanied to Rome in 44. Under the triumvirate, he rose to high rank, played a major role in the Perusine war in 40, and won victories in Gaul against local rebellions and German attacks. These brought him a consulate (*70*; cf. *31–33*). He commanded the fleets at Naulochus and Actium and gained the right to wear both mural and rostral crowns (Augustus *87, 89*). His success made him the natural heir for Augustus, who had no sons. He married Augustus' daughter Julia in 21 and received the tribunician power in 18; it was renewed five years later. Agrippa, however, died in 11 BC on his return from campaigning on the Danube. For his coins, *see also* Augustus *85−89*; Caligula *11*.

AHENOBARBUS

C. Domitius Ahenobarbus, descendant of one of the most ancient republican aristocratic families, though son of a bitter enemy of Caesar, was pardoned by the dictator. He nevertheless joined the conspirators and came to command their fleet, with which he inflicted a severe defeat on the Caesarian fleet of Domitius Calvinus who was attempting to convey troops to Greece for the battle of Philippi. Ahenobarbus thereby gained the title imperator (*48*). After Philippi he still controlled a fleet in the Ionian Sea, but in 40 joined Antony (*57*) who made him governor of Bithynia. There, he took part in the campaigns against the Parthians and Sextus Pompey who attempted to carve out a territory in Asia Minor. Consul in 32, he fled Rome to join Antony at Ephesus, and became a commander of his fleet. A few days before the battle of Actium, he deserted to Octavian, but died shortly after. He was the great-grandfather of the emperor Nero.

ANTONY

Marcus Antonius was the son of a general of the same name and of Julia, the sister of Caesar. His grandfather was a famous orator who perished in the proscriptions of Marius. Born in 83, he first attained high public office in 57. He attached himself to Caesar and rose to power through him. He fought with Caesar in Gaul, became quaestor in 52, and augur in 50. He commanded part of the army at Pharsalus and became *magister equitum*, the chief assistant of the dictator, in 48. After a temporary eclipse caused by his own corruption and extravagance, he was consul with Caesar in 44, and proposed royal power for him. His career subsequent to the Ides of March is included in the outline above, where reference to his coins will be found.

GAIUS ANTONIUS

Gaius, the brother of Mark Antony, was legate of Caesar in 49 and urban praetor in 44. In 43, the Senate, dominated by Antony, appointed him governor of Macedonia (*19*) which was then occupied by Brutus. When he attempted to take the province, he was blockaded in Apollonia and captured by Brutus, who executed him with some reluctance in 42.

LUCIUS ANTONIUS

Lucius, the youngest brother of Mark Antony, became quaestor in Asia in 50 and tribune in 44. In that office, he actively supported his brother's interests after the assassination of Caesar, earning the surname Pietas (*53*) as a sign of his devotion. As consul (*52*) in 41, with the encouragement of Antony's wife Fulvia, he led an uprising against Octavian, who was then unpopular because of his land redistribution. Lucius briefly gained control of Rome, but withdrew to Mutina, where he was besieged by Octavian. He surrendered in February 40, was pardoned, and disappeared from history.

MARCUS ANTONIUS JUNIOR

The elder son of Antony and Fulvia, Marcus was born *c.* 43 and betrothed as a child to Julia, daughter of Octavian; he apparently took part in his father's Armenian wars, and was honoured in the triumph which followed (*86*). After Actium, Antony conferred the *toga virilis* on him in the hope that he and Caesarion would assume power in Egypt, and sent him on a fruitless peace mission to Octavian. He was executed in 30 after the death of Antony.

BRUTUS

M. Junius Brutus, who became Q. Caepio Brutus when he was adopted by his uncle after the early death of his father, began his career as a moneyer in 60. At that time, he was an opponent of the autocracy of Pompey (Republic *42*) and an advocate of the Republican liberty he always supported. After serving in Cyprus and Cilicia, he returned to Rome in 52 and became a noted lawyer, often in conflict with Pompey. Their difficulties were resolved, however, and Brutus joined Pompey and fought on his side at Pharsalus. After Pompey's fall, Caesar forgave Brutus and made him his friend and governor of Cisalpine Gaul, an office he filled with distinction in 46–45. Caesar designated him as urban praetor in 44 and planned to have him made consul for 41, but when he took the perpetual dictatorship in February 44, Brutus joined the opposition, and was a leader of the plot which culminated in the Ides of March (Caesar *45*). The assassination made him violently unpopular with the populace of Rome and he withdrew to Greece. After being declared a public enemy in November 44, he raised an army, and took control of Macedonia and Illyricum. The Senate now changed sides and confirmed his position early in 43. Brutus defeated C. Antonius, to whom Macedonia had been assigned, and won victories over the Thracians which gained him the title imperator. Together with Cassius, whom he met at Sardis, Brutus fought the Caesarians at Philippi, where he committed suicide after defeat in November 42. For his coins, see the narrative above.

CALVINUS

Cn. Domitius Calvinus entered public life in 62, and became consul in 54 through bribery and the influence of Pompey. In 49, however, he commanded part of the Caesarian forces at Pharsalus and thereafter became governor of Asia, where his defeat by Pharnaces, son of Mithradates, was avenged by Caesar at Zela. Had the dictator survived 44, Calvinus would have been his master of horse. During the campaign of Philippi, Calvinus, in command of the Caesarian fleet, was defeated by Ahenobarbus and Staius Murcius and barely escaped to Brundisium. His consulate in 49 was followed by a proconsulate in Spain, where he won major victories (67) against tribes in revolt, and earned a triumph. He is last mentioned, as holding a priestly office, in 20.

CASCA

P. Servilius Casca Longus, the assassin of Caesar who struck the first blow, was tribune in 43 but left Rome to take up the Republican cause. He commanded the fleet of Brutus in the successful campaign against Lycia (42−43), and perished at Philippi.

CASSIUS

C. Cassius Longinus achieved distinction in 53 when, after commanding under Crassus at the disaster of Carrhae, he escaped and successfully defended Syria against Parthian attack. He fought on the side of Pompey in the civil war, but was pardoned by Caesar and became his legate. Opposition to Caesar's autocracy, however, led him to organise the conspiracy of the Ides of March. Assigned the province of Cyprus after the assassination, he went instead to Syria, which he seized from the legitimate governor. This gave him a base and an army for resisting the triumvirs, so he then moved north to take over Asia Minor after winning a decisive victory at Rhodes. He joined forces with Brutus at Sardis and together they met defeat and death at Philippi. For his coins, see above.

CLEOPATRA

Cleopatra VII, the last Ptolemaic queen of Egypt, has a place in the Roman coinage because of her association with the leaders of the Republic. She became queen in 52 at the age of seventeen, but was soon driven out by her brother and co-regent Ptolemy XIV. It was at this point that Caesar appeared in Syria, following Pompey. He took up the cause of the queen, restored her to power, and made her his mistress. She bore him a son and lived with him in Rome until the Ides of March, when discretion and unpopularity brought her back to Egypt. In 40, she met Mark Antony at Tarsus and soon brought him under her dominion. She had three children by him, and she and they received provinces and kingdoms from Antony when he ruled the East. At his triumph over the Armenians in 34, he awarded her the grand title Queen of Kings (*85*). Their liaison became the subject of hostile propaganda at Rome, and was used to stir the people against Antony. War followed, and at Actium Cleopatra sailed away from the battle with her fleet. Antony followed her to Egypt, and there they both committed suicide in 30. The last major kingdom of the East was now Roman.

CORNIFICIUS

Q. Cornificius, who took control of Illyricum for Caesar during the civil war, was appointed by him to govern Syria, then Africa. After the Ides of March, he held Africa for the Senate and remained loyal to them when the triumvirate was formed. He sent troops to Sextus Pompey and gave refuge to survivors of the proscriptions. When Sextius, governor of the adjacent province of Africa Nova, attacked him in the name of the triumvirs, Cornificius was at first successful and acclaimed imperator (*50*), but was defeated and killed by the end of 42.

LABIENUS

Q. Labienus, whose father Titus fell fighting Caesar at Munda in 45, was sent by Brutus and Cassius as ambassador to the Parthian king, Orodes. After Philippi, he cooperated with the Parthians in overrunning Asia Minor, much of which he occupied with the help of the Parthian cavalry and the local republican resistance. The victories he gained earned him the title imperator (*56*), but when Antony organised the counterattack in 39, Labienus was defeated by Ventidius and killed.

LEPIDUS

M. Aemilius Lepidus, descendant of an ancient and rich noble family, was born in 89 and rose through public office until he became urban praetor in 49. He was a partisan of Caesar, and moved to make him dictator in his absence at the siege of Massilia. As a reward, he became governor of Hither Spain, where his successes earned him the title imperator and a triumph. He was consul with Caesar in 46, and his Master of Horse in 45; he ran affairs in Rome while the dictator was absent. Lepidus warned Caesar of a plot against him on 14 March 44, and after the assassination rallied the populace against the murderers. Antony had him made *pontifex maximus*, then governor of Hither Spain and southern Gaul, where he brought Sextus Pompey over to the side of the government. Declared a public enemy like Antony (*5*), he joined him and Octavian to form the triumvirate (*9, 11, 17−18*) in 43. He was consul the next year and governor of Africa after Philippi. In 36, however, after participating in the defeat of Sextus Pompey, he was deposed from office by Octavian, but remained Pontifex Maximus until his death in exile in 12 BC.

OCTAVIA

Octavia, the sister of Octavius, was first married to C. Marcellus, by whom she had three children (one of them being Marcellus, later designated as Augustus' successor). After the death of her husband, she was married to Antony in 40 (*62−64*), as part of the entente between the triumvirs. It was through her efforts that Antony and Octavian were reconciled at Tarentum (*73−76*) in 37, but Antony left her for Cleopatra the next year and divorced her in 32. She nevertheless took care of his children, and through their two daughters became the grandmother of the emperor Claudius and great-grandmother of his wife Messalina. She died in 11 BC.

PLANCUS

L. Munatius Plancus, who fought with Caesar in Gaul and Africa, became governor of Transalpine Gaul in 44, and attempted to relieve the siege of Decimus Brutus at Mutina in 43. He then joined Antony, celebrated a triumph for his victories in Gaul, and became consul with Lepidus in 42. Antony made him proconsul of Asia (*55a*) after the Perusine war and there he confronted the invasion of Labienus. Although he gained some successes which justified a second acclamation as imperator (*55b*), he was forced to take refuge in the islands. As governor of Syria in 35, he was responsible for the murder of Sextus Pompey. He deserted to Octavian in 32, and remained in favour. It was he who proposed that Octavian be given the title Augustus in 27. The date of his death is unknown. Early in his career, he assumed the priestly office of *VIIvir epulonum*, whose characteristic jug appears on his coins (*55*; Caesar *25*).

SALVIDIENUS

Q. Salvidienus Rufus Salvius was a boyhood friend of Octavian who in 42 entrusted him with the defence of Italy against Sextus Pompey. He won a victory at Rhegium which earned him the title imperator, but his fleet was in turn badly defeated by Pompey soon afterwards (*44−47*). Salvidienus played a major role in the Perusine war against L. Antonius in 41; his efforts there on behalf of Octavian were rewarded by the governorship of

Gaul and the consulate (*65*) for 39. Nevertheless, he entered into treasonous correspondence with Antony, who betrayed him to Octavian. He committed suicide after being condemned in 40.

SEXTUS POMPEY

Sextus Pompeius Magnus, the younger son of Pompey the Great, born in 67, withdrew to Africa after Pharsalus and then to Spain after Thapsus. He there joined his brother in resisting Caesar, and after the brother's death at Munda, carried on a guerrilla war. In 44, he reached an accord with Antony through the mediation of Lepidus and became *praefectus classis et orae maritimae*, with authority over the coasts and fleets of the republic. Later the same year, however, he was proscribed. He thereupon took the fleet he commanded, conquered Sicily, and won a significant victory over the fleet of Octavian in 42. In celebration, he assumed the title 'son of Neptune' (*44—47*). After Philippi, he received many refugees including Staius Murcus and his fleet. In 40, during the hostilities between Antony and Octavian, he took Sardinia and finally, when he threatened to blockade the coast, his position was recognised by Octavian in 39. When Octavian nevertheless attacked him the next year, Sextus defeated his fleet (*69*) in the straits of Messina. His position was greatly weakened, however, when Octavian received reinforcements from Antony, and in 36, his domain collapsed at the battle of Naulochus (*80—82*). Sextus fled to the east, hoping to establish a base in Asia Minor, but came into conflict with Antony and his generals and was captured and executed in 35.

SCARPUS

L. Pinarius Scarpus, the grandson of Caesar's sister, fought with his relative Octavian at Philippi, then joined Antony, who eventually put him in charge of Cyrenaica with four legions to defend Egypt against attack from the west. After Actium, Antony sought the support of Scarpus' army, but he turned it over to Cornelius Gallus, the governor of Africa, and remained in office in Cyrenaica until 27. He thus struck coins with both Antony and Octavian (*91—94*).

STAIUS MURCUS

Although he had been a legate of Caesar, Murcus joined the assassins and was named as commander of the fleet by Cassius. He took Rhodes and gained command of the sea; together with Ahenobarbus, he defeated the Caesarian fleet commanded by Calvinus. After Philippi, he joined Sextus Pompey (*51*), but was murdered at Syracuse in 39.

VENTIDIUS

P. Ventidius Bassus became a friend of Caesar, who raised him to the Senate, and in 44, joined Antony whose cause he served in the Perusine war. In 39, his victorious campaigns drove the Parthians from Asia Minor and Syria and earned him the title imperator (*66*). When the Parthians again attacked in 36, Ventidius crushed them decisively. His successes roused the jealousy of Antony, who dismissed him from service, but he celebrated a triumph in Rome in 36, after which he disappears from history.

Coinage of the Civil Wars

44 BC April. Festival of the Parilia, with games and demonstrations in favour of Caesar.

    1 P. Sepullius Macer: Rome 44. *Obv*. Veiled head of Antony r., with short beard (of mourning); lituus before, jug behind. *Rev*. P SEPVLLIVS MACER, Acrobat with two horses. Den: *Cr* 480/22

43 BC (ITALY), April. Siege of Mutina: award of title imperator and equestrian statue to Octavius.

    2 C. Caesar (Octavius): Italy 43. *Obv*. C CAESAR IMP, Bearded head of Octavius r. *Rev*. S C, Equestrian statue l. Den: *Cr* 490/1; 490/3, 497/1 (*obv*. III VIR R P C; struck as triumvir)

—— April-November: Antony, in Gaul, as enemy of the Senate, advertising his connection with Caesar.

    3 M. Antonius: Gaul 43. *Obv*. M ANTON IMP (R P C), Bearded head of Antony r. *Rev*. CAESAR DIC, Laureate head of Caesar r. Den: *Cr* 488/1, 2

—— April-November: Antony in Gaul: advertisement of his base Lugdunum. The figure XL apparently represents Antony's age.

       2   9

    4 M. Antonius: Gaul 43. *Obv*. Bust of Victory (sometimes identified as Fulvia) r. *Rev*. LVGVDVNI A XL, Lion walking r. Qui: *Cr* 489/5

—— May-November. Alliance of Antony and Lepidus.

    5 M. Antonius: Gaul 43. *Obv*. M ANTON (COS) IMP, Lituus, jug and raven. *Rev*. M LEPID (COS) IMP, Priestly implements. Den: *Cr* 489/1, 2. Qui: 489/3 (legends abbreviated)

— — July. Resistance of the Senate to Octavius with legions from Africa.
6   L. Cestius, C. Norbanus: Rome 43. *Obv.* Bust of Africa r.
Rev. L CESTIVS C NORBA PR (EX) S C, Helmet (or two snakes) on
curule chair. Aur: *Cr* 491/1
— — August. Octavius marches on Rome and becomes consul; advertisement of relation with Caesar.
7   C. Caesar: Rome 43. *Obv.* C CAESAR COS PONT AVGUR, Bearded
head of Octavian. *Rev.* C CAESAR DICT PERP PONT MAX, Head of
Caesar r. Aur: *Cr* 490/2
— — November. Creation of the triumvirate, celebrated with an extensive series of gold coins struck from the profits of the proscriptions, advertising the real or mythical ancestry of the triumvirs, and their harmony.
8   M. Antonius: Cisalpine Gaul 43. *Obv.* M ANTONIVS III VIR R P
C, Bearded head r. *Rev.* C CAESAR III VIR R P C, Bearded head
r. Aur: *Cr* 492/1
9   — — *Rev.* M LEPIDVS III VIR R P C, Bearded head r. Aur:
Cr 492/2
10   C. Caesar: Cisalpine Gaul: 43. *Obv.* C CAESAR III VIR R P C PONT
AVG, Bearded head r. *Rev.* M ANTONIVS IM III VIR R P C AVG,
Bearded head r. Aur: *Cr* 493/1
11   M. Lepidus: Italy 42. *Obv.* LEPIDUS PONT MAX III VIR R P C,
Bearded head r. *Rev.* CAESAR (IMP) III VIR R P C, Head of
Octavian r. Aur: *Cr* 495/1. Den: *Cr* 495/2
12   L. Livinius Regulus, P. Clodius, L. Mussidius Longus, C.
Vibius Varus: Rome 42. *Obv.* M ANTONIVS III VIR R P C, Head r.
Rev. L REGVLVS IIII VIR A P F, Hercules (ancestor of the Antonii)
std. on rock Aur: *Cr* 494/2
13   — — — — *Rev.* C VEIBIVS VAARUS, Clasped hands. Aur:
Cr 494/11
14   — — — — *Obv.* C CAESAR III VIR R P C, Head of Octavian r.
Rev. L REGVLVS IIII VIR A P F, Aeneas carrying Anchises. Aur:
Cr 494/3
15   — — — — *Rev.* P CLODIVS M F IIII VIR A P F, Venus std. facing,
embracing Cupid with her left hand. Aur: *Cr* 494/6
16   — — — — *Rev.* As 14. Aur: *Cr* 494/12
17   — — *Obv.* M LEPIDVS III VIR R P C, Head r. *Rev.* L REGVLVS IIII
VIR A P F, Vestal Aemilia stg. 1. Aur: *Cr* 494/1
18   — — — — *Rev.* As 14. Aur: *Cr* 494/10
43 BC (The East). Gaius Antonius assigned to govern Macedonia.
19   C. Antonius: moving mint 43. *Obv.* C ANTONIVS M F PROCOS,
Female bust r. *Rev.* PONTIFEX, Priestly implements. Den:
Cr 484
— — Victories of Brutus over the Thracians.
20   Q. Caepio Brutus, C. Flavius Hemii: moving mint 43–2.
Obv. Head of Apollo r. *Rev.* Q CAEPIO BRVTVS IMP, Two captives
below trophy. Den: *Cr* 503/1

19

25

21 —— *Obv.* C FLAV HEMIC LEG PRO PR, Bust of Apollo r. *Rev.* Q
CAEP BRVT IMP, Victory crowning trophy. Den: *Cr* 504/1

22 Q. Caepio Brutus, M. Servilius: moving mint 43–42. *Obv.* M
SERVILIVS LEG, Head of Libertas r. *Rev.* Q CAEPIO BRVTVS IMP,
Trophy. Aur: *Cr* 505/4. Den: 505/5

23 M. Brutus, Pedanius Costa: moving 43–2. *Obv.* COSTA LEG,
Head of Apollo r. *Rev.* BRVTVS IMP, Trophy. Den: *Cr* 506/2

43–42 BC Republican propaganda, with emphasis on Liberty.

24 C. Cassius, M. Aquinus: moving 43–2. *Obv.* LIBERTAS M
AQVINVS LEG, Head of Libertas r. *Rev.* C CASSI PR COS (or IMP),
Tripod with cauldron. Aur: *Cr* 498/1; 499/1

25 C. Cassius, Cornelius Lentulus Spinther: moving 43–2. *Obv.*
LEIBERTAS C CASSI IMP, Head of Libertas r. *Rev.* LENTVLVS
SPINT, Jug and lituus. Aur: *Cr* 500/2,4. Den: 500/3,5

26 Brutus: moving 43–2. *Obv.* LEIBERTAS. Head of Libertas r.
Rev. CAEPIO BRVTVS PRO COS, Plectrum, lyre and laurel branch.
Den: *Cr* 501/1

27 Brutus, L. Sestius: moving 43–2. *Obv.* L SESTI PRO Q,
Head of Libertas r. *Rev.* Q CAEPIO BRVTVS PRO COS, Tripod.
Aur: *Cr* 502/1. Den: 502/2

28 —— —— *Rev.* —— Victory walking r. Qui: *Cr* 502/3

29 Brutus, Pedanius Costa: moving 43–2. *Obv.* LEIBERTAS, Head
of Libertas r. *Rev.* Crossed prow-stem and anchor. Qui: *Cr*
506/3

30 —— *Obv.* L BRVTVS PRIM COS (Brutus the Liberator of Rome
from the kings), Head of L. Junius Brutus r. *Rev.* M BRVTVS
IMP COSTA LEG, Head of Brutus r. Aur: *Cr* 506/1

42 BC January. Deification of Caesar, with a temple (*83*), a star placed
on his statues, and erection of equestrian statues. Display of Caesar's
golden throne and crown are probably to be associated, as perhaps
are the more symbolic types of Antony, the high priest of the cult,
who by showing the sun-god commemorated Caesar's triumph of
46, where he was decreed a chariot with four white horses, and his
subsequent honour of a radiate crown. Both of these were attributes of the Sun and thus quasi-divine honours for Caesar. Some
of the types of Octavian (who could now call himself '*divi filius*')
were struck in later years.

31 Octavian, Agrippa: moving 38. *Obv.* IMP DIVI IVLI F TER III VIR

R P C, Laureate head of Caesar r. with star on forehead. *Rev.*
M AGRIPPA COS DESIG in field. Den: *Cr* 534/1

32   — — *Obv.* DIVOS IVLIVS DIVI F, Heads of Caesar and Octavian
vis-a-vis. *Rev.* as previous. Den: *Cr* 534/2

33   — — *Obv.* IMP CAESAR DIVI IVLI F, Bearded head r. *Rev.* As
previous. Den: *Cr* 534/3

34   C. Caesar: Italy *c.* 38. *Obv.* CAESAR DIVI F, Bearded head of
Octavian r. *Rev.* DIVOS IVLIVS, Wreathed head of Caesar r.
Æ: *Cr* 535/1

35   — — *Obv.* as previous, but star before head. *Rev.* DIVOS
IVLIVS in wreath. Æ: *Cr* 535/2

36   C. Caesar, L. Cornelius Balbus: moving 41. *Obv.* C CAESAR III
VIR R P C, Head r. *Rev.* POPVL IVSSV, Galloping equestrian
statue l. Den: *Cr* 518/2

37   C. Caesar: moving 42. *Obv.* CAESAR III VIR R P C, Hear r. *Rev.*
Wreath (golden crown) resting on curule chair inscribed CAESAR
DIC PER (or PR or PE). Den: *Cr* 497/2

37   38

38   M. Antonius: moving 42. *Obv.* M ANTONI IMP, Bearded head r.
Rev. III VIR R P C, Bust of Sol in distyle temple. Den: *Cr* 496/1

39   — — *Obv.* Bearded head of Antony r. *Rev.* M ANTONIVS III VIR
R P C, Radiate head of Sol r. Den: *Cr* 496/2; 496/3 (IMP on
obv.)

— —   Spring: Campaigns of Cassius and Brutus in Asia Minor, with
victories over Rhodes and the Lycians, the latter gained under the
command of Casca Longus. Type 43 also symbolically reflects the
Ides of March by portraying the emblems of royalty being broken
by Victory, as does 41 with its untied diadem (the crown of a
Hellenistic king).

40   C. Cassius, M. Servilius: moving 42. *Obv.* C CASSI IMP, Head
of Libertas r. *Rev.* M SERVILIVS LEG. *Aplustre* (stern ornament
of ship). Aur: *Cr* 505/1. Den: 505/2

41   — — — — *Rev.* Crab holding *aplustre*; rose (of Rhodes) and
untied diadem on l. Den: *Cr* 505/3

42   Brutus, Casca Longus: moving 42. *Obv.* BRVTVS IMP, Bearded
head of Brutus r. *Rev.* CASCA LONGVS, Trophy resting on prow.
Aur: *Cr* 507/1

43   — — *Obv.* CASCA LONGVS, Head of Neptune r. *Rev.* BRVTVS
IMP, Victory walking r., breaking diadem; broken sceptre below.
Den: *Cr* 507/2

—— Summer. Meeting of Brutus and Cassius at Sardis, with acclamation of both as imperator by the assembled army. (Included above, as types 20–23, 40–43.)

—— Summer. Victory of Sextus Pompey over the Caesarian fleet at Rhegium, with advertisement of his family and honours to Neptune, whose son he claimed to be. The victory provided Sextus with his second acclamation as imperator. The reverse of type 47 is an illustration of piety, such as Sextus bore to his father's memory.

44*a* Q. Nasidius: Sicily 42 (?). *Obv.* NEPTVNI, Head of Pompey the Great r. *Rev.* Q NASIDIVS, Sea-battle with two ships each side. Den: *Cr* 483/1

44*b* —— —— but *rev.* ship sailing r. Den: *Cr* 483/2

45 Sex. Pompey: Sicily 42–40. *Obv.* MAG PIVS IMP ITER, Head of Sex. Pompey r. *Rev.* PRAEF CLAS ET ORAE MARIT EX S C, Heads of Pompey the Great and Pompey Jr. vis-à-vis. Aur: *Cr* 511/1

46 —— *Obv.* —— Head of Neptune r. *Rev.* —— Naval trophy. Den: *Cr* 511/2

46   48

47 *Obv.* —— Head of Pompey the Great r. *Rev.* —— Neptune stg. l. between the Catanaean brothers, each of whom carries his father in his shoulders. Den: *Cr* 511/3

—— Summer. Victory of Ahenobarbus over the Caesarian fleet, with vows to build (or restore) the temple of Neptune in the Campus Martius, an action apparently completed when Ahenobarbus was consul in 32.

48 Ahenobarbus: moving 41. *Obv.* AHENOBAR, Bearded head (probably of one of the moneyer's ancestors) r. *Rev.* CN DOMITIVS IMP, Trophy on prow. Den: *Cr* 519/2

49 —— *Obv.* AHENOBAR, Male head r. *Rev.* CN DOMITIVS L F IMP NEPT, Tetrastyle temple. Den: *Cr* 519/1

—— Resistance of the Republicans in Africa, led by Cornificius.

50*a* Q. Cornificius: Africa 42. *Obv.* Head of Jupiter Ammon l. *Rev.* Q CORNVFICI AVGVR IMP, Juno Sospita crowning Cornificius. Aur: *Cr* 509/1. Den: 509/2

50*b* *Obv.* Head of Africa r. *Rev.* As previous. Aur: *Cr* 509/3. Den: 509/4

50*c* *Obv.* Head of Tanit l. *Rev.* As previous. Den: *Cr* 509/5

42 BC November–41 BC. Independent command of the sea by Staius Murcus. This is earliest of the 'restitutor' types.

51 Murcus: moving 42–41. *Obv.* Head of Neptune r. *Rev.* MVRCVS IMP, Male figure raising female; trophy behind. Den: *Cr* 510/1

51   52b

41 BC   Consulate of L. Antonius. Type 53 features his cognomen 'Pietas'.

52*a*   M. Antonius, M. Barbatius, M. Cocceius Nerva: moving 41. *Obv.* M ANT IMP AVG (III) VIR R P C M NERVA PROQ P, Head of Antony r. *Rev.* L ANTONIVS COS, Head of Lucius Antonius r. Aur: *Cr* 517/4. Den: 517/5

52*b*   As previous, but *obv.* legend ends M BARBAT Q P. Aur: *Cr* 517/1 Den: *Cr* 517/3

53*a*   Antony: moving 41. *Obv.* ANT AVG IMP III VIR RPC, Head of Antony r. *Rev.* PIETAS COS, Fortuna stg. l. Aur: *Cr* 516/1. Den: *Cr* 516/2−3

53*b*   − − As previous, but *rev.* Pietas stg. l. Aur: *Cr* 516/4. Den: *Cr* 516/5

41−40 BC   Redistribution of land and settlement of veterans by Octavian. According to Professor Badian, this type may have secondary or even prime reference to the reforms of the moneyer's famous homonymous ancestor, the tribune of 133.

54*a*   Ti. Sempronius Gracchus: Rome 40. *Obv.* DIVI IVLI F, Bearded head of Octavian r. *Rev.* T SEMPRON GRACCVS IIII VIR Q DESIG, Standard, eagle, plough and measuring rod. Den: *Cr* 525/2

54*b*   *Obv.* (SC), Laureate head of Caesar r. *Rev.* As previous, sometimes with SC. Den: *Cr* 525/3−4

54a   56

40 BC   Parthian invasion of Asia Minor: initial successes of Antony's proconsul Plancus, giving him an imperatorial acclamation, followed by the victories of Labienus, made possible by his Parthian cavalry. Labienus' coins were struck for the Republican contingents who followed him.

55*a*   M. Antonius, L. Munatius Plancus: moving 40. *Obv.* M ANTON IMP AVG III VIR R P C, Lituus and jug. *Rev.* L PLANCVS PRO COS, Thunderbolt, jug and caduceus. Aur: *Cr* 522/1. Den: 522/2

55*b* — — As previous, but *rev.* inscription L PLANCVS IMP ITER. Aur: *Cr* 522/3. Den: 522/4

56 Labienus: moving 40. *Obv.* Q LABIENVS PARTHICVS IMP, Head r. *Rev.* Parthian horse r., with bridle and saddle to which bowcase and quiver are attached. Aur: *Cr* 524/1. Den: 524/2

— — Summer. Adherence of Ahenobarbus to Antony.

57 M. Antonius, Cn. Domitius Ahenobarbus: moving 40. *Obv.* ANT IMP III VIR RPC, Head r. *Rev.* CN DOMIT AHENOBARBVS IMP, Prow r. Aur: *Cr* 521/1. Den: 521/2

— — October. Reconciliation of Antony and Octavian at Brundisium, and marriage of Antony and Octavia. The ivy wreath of 63 and 64 and the reverse of 64 refer to Antony's triumphal reception in Ephesus as an incarnation of the god Dionysus (Bacchus).

58 M. Antonius: moving 39. *Obv.* M ANTON IMP III VIR R P C, Head r. *Rev.* CAESAR IMP (PONT) III VIR R P C, Head r. Aur: *Cr* 528/1. Den: 528/2,3

59 C. Caesar, M. Antonius: moving 39. *Obv.* CAESAR IMP, Bearded head r. *Rev.* ANTON(IVS) IMP, Head r. Aur: *Cr* 529/1. Den: 529/2

60 — — *Obv.* ANTONIVS IMP, Head r. *Rev.* CAESAR IMP, Caduceus. Den: *Cr* 529/3

61 — — *Obv.* III VIR R P C, Head of Concordia r. *Rev.* M ANTON C CAESAR (IMP), clasped hands holding caduceus. Qui: *Cr* 529/4

62 M. Antonius: moving 39. *Obv.* M ANTONIVS IMP III VIR R P C, Head r. *Rev.* Head of Octavia r. Aur: *Cr* 527/1

63 M. Antonius: Ephesus 39. *Obv.* M ANTONIVS IMP COS DESIG ITER ET TERT, Head r., wearing ivy wreath. *Rev.* III VIR R P C, Bust of Octavia on cista mystica. Cis: *Syd* 1197

64 — — *Obv.* — — Jugate heads of Antony and Octavia. *Rev.* — — Statue of Bacchus on cista mystica. Cis: *Syd* 1198

64   69

40 BC Successes of Salvidienus in the Perusine war, rewarded with the promise of the consulate.

65 C. Caesar, Q. Salvidienus Salvius. *Obv.* C CAESAR III VIR RPC, Bearded head r. *Rev.* Q SALVIVS IMP COS DESIG, Thunderbolt. Den: *Cr* 523/1

39 BC Spring. Victories of Ventidius in Asia Minor, with acclamation as imperator.

66   M. Antonius, P. Ventidius: East 39. *Obv.* M ANT IMP III V R P C, Bearded head r. *Rev.* P VENTIDI PONT IMP, Jupiter Victor stg. facing. Den: *Cr* 531/1

— —   Victories of Calvinus in Spain for Octavian.

67   Cn. Domitius Calvinus: Osca 39. *Obv.* OSCA, Head of Hercules r. *Rev.* DOM COS ITER IMP, Priestly implements. Den: *Cr* 532/1

38 BC Further victories over the Parthians, won by Ventidius and culminating in the surrender of Antiochus of Commagene to Antony.

68   M. Antonius: moving 37. *Obv.* (M) ANT AVGV/R III VIR R P C, Head r. *Rev.* IMP TER, Trophy. Den: *Cr* 536/1−4

— —   Victory of Sextus Pompey over the fleet of Octavian at Messina, in the strait which contained Scylla and Charybdis.

69   Sextus Pompey: Sicily 38. *Obv.* MAG PIVS IMP ITER, Ship with aquila on prow before lighthouse of Messina surmounted by statue of Neptune. *Rev.* PRAEF CLAS ET ORAE MARIT EX S C, (with variations), Scylla, wielding rudder. Den: *Cr* 511/4

— —   Victories of Agrippa in Gaul, rewarded with the consulate (*See also 31−33*).

70   C. Caesar, M. Agrippa: moving 38. *Obv.* IMP CAESAR DIVI IVLI F, Bearded head r. *Rev.* M AGRIPPA COS DESIG in field. Den: *Cr* 534/3

37 BC Spring. Meeting of Antony and Octavian at Tarentum, with renewal of the triumvirate, each thus becoming *triumvir iter*. Contribution of ships by Antony for Octavian's war against Sextus Pompey.

71   C. Caesar: moving 37. *Obv.* IMP CAESAR DIVI F III VIR ITER R P C, Bearded head r. *Rev.* COS ITER ET TER DESIG, Priestly implements. Den: *Cr* 538/1

72   — — *Obv.*— — Tripod, inscribed R P C, with cauldron. *Rev.* — — within laurel wreath. Den: *Cr* 538/2

73a   L. Calpurnius Bibulus, L. Sempronius Atratinus, M. Oppius: Tarentum (?) 37. *Obv.* M ANT IMP TER COS DES ITER ET TER III VIR R P C, Heads of Antony and Octavia vis-à-vis. *Rev.* L BIBVLVS M F PR DESIG, Antony and Octavia in quadriga drawn by hippocamps; below, HS on l. Ses: *Syd* 1255.

73b   — — As previous, but *rev. leg.* L ATRATINVS AVGVR COS DESIG. Ses: *Syd* 1261

73c   — — but *rev.* M OPPIVS CAPITO PRO PR PRAEF CLASS F C. Ses: *Syd* 1265

74a   — — *Obv.* — — Jugate heads of Antony and Octavian facing head of Octavia. *Rev.* Three galleys sailing r., I below; legend as 73a. Trip: *Syd* 1256

74b   — — — — *rev.* legend as 73b. Trip: *Syd* 1262

74c   — — — — *rev.* legend as 73c. Trip: *Syd* 1266

75a   — — *Obv.* As 73. *Rev.* Two galleys sailing r., B below. Legend as 73a. Dup: *Syd* 1257

75b   — — — — *Rev.* legend as 73b. Dup: *Syd* 1263

75c — — — — *Rev.* legend as 73c. Dup: *Syd* 1267
76a — — *Obv.* As 74. *Rev.* Galley sailing r., A below. Legend as 73a. As: *Syd* 1258
76b — — — — *Rev.* legend as 73b. As: *Syd* 1264
76c — — — — *Rev.* legend as 73c. As: *Syd* 1268
77a — — *Obv.* Head of Antony, legend as 73. *Rev.* Galley without sail r. Legend as 73a. Sem: *Syd* 1259
77b — — *Rev.* legend as 73c. Sem: *Syd* 1269
78a — — *Obv.* Janiform head. Legend as 73. *Rev.* Stem of prow, ●● beside. Legend as 68a. Sex: *Syd* 1260
78b — — — — *Rev.* legend as 68c. Sex: *Syd* 1270
— — July. Defeat of Parthians and capture of Jerusalem by C. Sosius, acclaimed imperator for his victories.
79 C. Sosius, Zacynthus 37. *Obv.* ZA, Head of Antony r. *Rev.* Judaea and Antigonus std. below military trophy. Æ: *Syd* 1272

36 BC September. Defeat of Sextus Pompey by Octavian and Agrippa at Naulochus; coins struck several years after the event.
80 Octavian: Italy 29−27. *Obv.* Bust of Diana r. *Rev.* Temple enclosing military trophy on naval base; triskelis in pediment, IMP CAESAR on architrave. Aur: 273/*C*121
81 — — *Obv.* Head of Octavian r. *Rev* IMP CAESAR, Military trophy (detail of previous). Den: 265/*C*119−120
82a Augustus: Lugdunum 15−13. *Obv.* AVGVSTVS DIVI F, Head r. *Rev.* IMP X/I/I SICIL, Diana stg. half l. Aur: 172/*C*145; 181; 194/*C*169. Den: 173/*C*146; 175; 182−3/*C*168; 195/*C*170
82b — — — — *Rev.* IMP XII SICIL, Diana adv. r. Aur: 196/*C*176. Den: 197/*C*172

82a   83

— — Beginning of construction of the temple of Divus Julius in Rome; it was completed in 29.
83 C. Caesar: moving 36. *Obv.* IMP CAESAR DIVI F III VIR ITER R P C, Bearded head l. *Rev.* COS ITER ET TER DESIG, Tetrastyle temple with veiled figure within and DIVO IVL on architrave. Aur: *Cr* 540/1. Den: 540/2

35 BC Celebration of Antony's victories in Armenia and accord with the king of Media.
84 M. Antonius: moving 36. *Obv.* ANTONIVS AVGVR COS DES ITER ET TERT, Head r. *Rev.* IMP TERTIO III VIR R P C, Armenian tiara; crossed bow and arrow behind. Den: *Cr* 539/1

34 BC Triumph for Antony's victories in Armenia, with titles granted to Cleopatra and her family, and celebration of Antony's heir.

    85   M. Antonius: moving 34—32. *Obv.* ANTONI ARMENIA DEVICTA, Head r., Armenian tiara behind. *Rev.* CLEOPATRAE REGINAE REGVM FILIORVM REGVM, Bust r. Den: *Cr* 543/1

    85   90t

    86*a*   — — *Obv.* M ANTON M F M N AVG IMP TERT, Head r. *Rev.* COS ITER DESIGN TERT III VIR R P C, Head of M. Antonius junior r. Aur: *Cr* 541/1

    86*b*   — — *Obv.* ANTON AVG IMP III COS DES III III V R P C, Head r. *Rev.* M ANTONIVS M F F, Head of M. Antonius jr. r. Aur: *Cr* 541/2

— — Festival of Venus Genetrix celebrated by Octavian in Rome, with advertisement of the descent of the Julian family from the goddess.

    87   Octavian: Italy *c.* 32. *Obv.* Head of Octavian l. or r. *Rev.* Venus, seen from behind, stg. r., leaning on column. Den: 250/*C*62

    88   — — *Obv.* Head of Venus r. *Rev.* Octavian stg. l. with spear, r. hand outstretched. Den: 251/*C*70

32 BC Preparations by Octavian for war against Antony, with address to the troops.

    89   Octavian: Italy 32. *Obv.* Bust of Pax r. *Rev.* CAESAR DIVI F, Octavian stg. r., holding spear and raising hand in *adlocutio*. Den: 253/*C*72

— — Preparations of Antony for war against Octavian: the army of Antony, for whose pay this vast series was struck.

    90   M. Antonius: moving 32—31. All have *obv.*: ANT AVG III VIR R P C, Ship r. and *rev.*: Aquila between standards (unless specified).

        a CHORTIVM PRAETORIARVM; Aur: *Cr* 544/1

        b CHORTIS SPECVLATORVM, Three standards decorated with wreaths and prow. Den: *Cr* 544/112

        c LEG PRI. Den: *Cr* 544/13

        d LEG II. Den: *Cr* 544/14

        e LEG III. Den: *Cr* 544/15

        f LEG IIII (or IV). Aur; *Cr* 544/2. Den: *Cr* 544/16,17

        g LEG V. Den: *Cr* 544/18

        h LEG VI. Aur: *Cr* 544/3. Den: 544/19

        i LEG VII. Den: *Cr* 544/20

j   LEG VIII. Den: *Cr* 544/21

k   LEG VIIII (or IX). Den: *Cr* 544/22,23

l   LEG X. Den: *Cr* 544/24

m LEG XI. Den: *Cr* 544/25.

n   LEG XII (ANTIQVAE). Aur: *Cr* 544/4. Den: 544/9,26

o   LEG XIII. Aur: *Cr* 544/5. Den: 544/27

p   LEG XIIII (or XIV). Aur: *Cr* 544/6. Den: 544/28,29

q   LEG XV. Den: *Cr* 544/30

r   LEG XVI. Den: *Cr* 544/31

s   LEG XVII (CLASSICAE). Den: *Cr* 544/10,32

t   LEG XVIII (LYBICAE). Den: *Cr* 544/11,23

u   LEG XVIIII (or XIX). Aur: *Cr* 544/7. Den: 544/34,35

v   LEG XX. Den: *Cr* 544/36

w LEG XXI. Den: *Cr* 544/37

x   LEG XXII. Den: *Cr 544/38*

y   LEG XXIII. Den: *Cr* 544/39

31–27 BC   Command of Scarpus in Africa, with the title imperator for victories over the Libyan tribes soon after his arrival. Types 92 and 93, issued after Scarpus' surrender to Octavian, commemorate the victory at Actium.

91   M. Antonius, Pinarius Scarpus: Cyrenaica 31. *Obv.* M ANTO COS III IMP IIII, Head of Jupiter Ammon r. *Rev.* SCARPVS IMP LEG VIII, Aquila between standards. Den: *Cr* 546/1

92   — — — — *Rev.* ANTONIO AVG SCARPVS IMP, Victory stg. r. Den: *Cr* 546/2,3

93   C. Caesar, Pinarius Scarpus: Cyrenaica 30–27. *Obv.* AVGVR PONTIF, Head of Jupiter Ammon r. *Rev.* IMP CAESAR DIVI F, Victory on globe r. (the Victory of Tarentum; see Augustus 17). Den: *Cr* 546/4

94*a*   — — *Obv.* IMP CAESARI SCARPVS IMP, Open r. hand. *Rev.* DIVI F AVG PON, Type as previous. Aur: *Cr* 546/5. Den: *Cr* 546/6

94a

94*b*   — — but *obv.* SCARPVS IMP; *Rev.* CAESARI DIVI F. Den: *Cr* 546/7. Qui: 546/8 (no globe under Victory)

The Empire

AUGUSTUS

Triumvir 43 BC/Augustus 27 BC−14 AD

C. Octavius, the great-nephew of Julius Caesar, was born in Rome in 63 BC, and rose to power after the Ides of March and the announcement of his adoption by Caesar. His career as imperator, triumvir and consul, from 44 to 31 BC, is included in the narrative of 'the Civil Wars'.

Octavian spent the winter after the battle of Actium in Samos, then crossed to Asia, which he reincorporated into the Roman realm (*1*) then proceeded to the peaceful conquest of Egypt (*2*) which became his when Antony and Cleopatra committed suicide. Octavian finally returned to Rome in 29, to receive tremendous honours: he celebrated a triple triumph (*3−9*) for his victories in Illyricum, at Actium and in Egypt, while triumphal arches (*10*) and a rostral column (*11*) in the Forum were dedicated by a grateful Senate. These victories, which restored the Roman realm to its rightful extent, brought honours to Terminus, the god of boundaries (*12−13*); and by including Egypt, which had not been Roman, they justified an extension of the *pomoerium* (*14*), the sacred limit of the city which was expanded when territory was added to Rome.

In recognition of these successes, the people of Asia proposed to set up an official cult in his honour; he allowed it on condition that the worship be directed to himself together with the goddess Rome (*56*). At this time, the temple of Divus Julius (already featured on the coins (Civil Wars *83*) before its completion) was dedicated, as was the new Senate house, or Curia, adorned with images to celebrate the victories (*15−17*). The battle of Actium had taken place below a headland which contained a shrine of Apollo; consequently, the god was honoured at Rome with a new temple (*18−20*) on the Palatine, near the house of Octavian, decorated with outstanding works of Greek art. It was dedicated in 28.

Since 32, when the triumvirate expired, Octavian had ruled by his own authority as consul, reinforced by an oath of loyalty from the whole population of Italy. In 27, the Senate granted him supreme power, expressed in the honorary title Augustus, which became part of his name. With it went the right to decorate the doorposts of his house with two laurel branches and the oak wreath, or *corona civica*, awarded to those who had saved the life of Roman citizens. In addition, a golden shield, the *clupeus virtutis*, was dedicated in the curia and inscribed with the emperor's four cardinal virtues: *virtus, clementia, iustitia* and *pietas*. Reflections of these honours figure on the coinage (*21−30*) throughout the reign.

The next two years saw Augustus absent in Spain, where a series of hard campaigns was fought to subjugate the tribes of the interior. Since the emperor fell ill, the wars were led by his legate, Carisius. Their success was crowned by the foundation in 25 of Emerita (*31—34*), a colony for discharged troops designed to ensure permanent Roman domination of the area. Augustus again became critically ill in 23, and arranged for Agrippa to succeed him if he should succumb. Upon his recovery, he effected a major reorganisation by which he gave up the consulate and its numerous routine duties and assumed instead the power of a tribune (*35*), annually renewed for the rest of his life; this became the basis for his rule. The following year saw major internal reforms, and much construction, including the dedication of a temple to Jupiter Tonans (*36*), the god of storms, to celebrate Augustus' miraculous escape when lightning barely missed him during the Spanish campaign.

In 21, Augustus set out for the East to reorganise the administration and deal with frontier problems. He passed through Greece, where the temple of Zeus at Olympia (*37*) was apparently restored, then crossed to Asia where he carried out major reforms. His visit may have provided the occasion for dedicating the temple of Rome and Augustus (*56*) authorised at Pergamum in 29.

Meanwhile, Tiberius, Augustus' stepson and most successful general, advanced to Armenia, where he installed a new king and re-established Roman influence (*38—43*). These operations seemed to provide such a menace that king Phraates of Parthia voluntarily returned the standards which the Romans had lost at Carrhae in 53, in Syria in 40, and in the retreat of Antony in 36, together with the surviving captives (*44—50*). This cancellation of past humiliation was a great occasion which the Senate considered deserving of a triumph. Augustus, with his usual restraint, refused to mount the triumphal car, accepting only the symbolic *ornamenta triumphalia*. He did, however, allow his triumphal insignia to be displayed in the *tensa* or sacred car of the god Mars (*52—54*). In addition, a triumphal arch (*49—51*) was erected, as was a temple on the Palatine to Mars Ultor (*55*), where the standards were stored and displayed. The temple, to the 'Avenger' had been vowed by Octavian at Philippi to celebrate the vengeance of the god of war on the assassins of Caesar. When Augustus returned to Rome in 19, the Senate and people proposed further honours, but he accepted only an altar to Fortuna Redux (*63—64*), to be set up near the gate through which he entered the city.

Not long after, Augustus relieved the Senate of the burden of providing free grain (*66*) to the populace of Rome by paying for it himself, and the Via Flaminia, the great military highway between Rome and the northern Adriatic, was completed. In 27, Augustus had entrusted repair of the roads to the Senate, with this major exception, though in fact he personally financed a great deal of road construction. Completion of these projects was commemorated by statues on triumphal arches (*57—62*), some apparently in Rome, others in Spain, where much of the road construction was carried out.

In the year 17, a comet (*67—68*) appeared in the heavens, and was taken to be a reappearance of the soul of Julius Caesar (which had first manifested itself as a comet in 44), and the auspicious occasion for inaugurating a new age. Augustus then, together with Agrippa, assumed the leadership of the college of priests in charge of festivals, the *XVviri sacris faciundis* (*70*), and conducted the secular games with great magnificence. A herald (*71–72*) announced them, and the Emperor with the other members of the college distributed *suffimenta* (*73*), perfumes and inflammable substances, to the people to be used in purificatory rites. The ceremonies featured a hymn, written by the poet Horace and still preserved.

In the following year, Augustus left Rome again, this time for a long stay in Gaul and on the frontier. The Senate undertook vows for his health and safety (*75–76*) when he left, and further vows for his health (*77*) when he fell ill during the campaigns. Most of the fighting was done by Tiberius, who defeated the German tribes and conquered the province of Rhaetia (*78, 80*), thus ensuring the security of the passes into Italy. On Augustus' return, in 13, the Senate made offerings of thanks (*81*) which included the dedication of a shield with his image (*82–83*), and held games in honour of Jupiter in celebration. Because of the addition of a new province, Augustus was able to extend the *pomoerium* (*79*) of Rome.

While Augustus was busy in Gaul, Agrippa had been making impressive gains in the East, where he put down a revolt in the client kingdom of Bosporus. He refused the offered triumph (*84*), but did accept renewal of his tribunician power (*85–86*), which in effect made him heir apparent. Since Agrippa was married to Augustus' daughter Julia, a dynasty (*87–88*) was now established, and the succession apparently ensured. Unfortunately for these plans, Agrippa died in 12, leaving his sons Gaius and Lucius, who were still too young to assume public office. In the same year, on the death of Lepidus the triumvir, who had long held the office, Augustus assumed the role of *pontifex maximus*, the head of the state religion. Since the high priest was obliged to live in a public residence, Augustus gave part of his own house (*90–91*) to the state. At the same time, he presented an official residence to the Vestal virgins and undertook construction of a new temple of Vesta (Tiberius 7) on the Palatine, adjacent to his own house.

Once again, in 10 and 8, Augustus was in Gaul, to settle affairs of the province. During his stay, the great altar (*92*) and monumental complex at Lugdumum was dedicated as the centre for the imperial cult in the provinces of Gaul. These campaigns, which saw the defeat of German tribes (*93*) and further conquests in the Danube regions, were the first in which Gaius Caesar (*94*), now of age, participated. His introduction to public life was the occasion for much celebration. Gaius assumed the title of *princeps iuventutis* or head of the equestrian order in 5, to be joined by his brother Lucius in 2 BC. This honorary title, which first appears on Roman coins (*95*) at this time, was used to designate the heir to the throne. Unfortunately for the plans of Augustus, both the brothers died young: Lucius in 2 AD under mysterious circumstances, and Gaius in 4 AD of wounds received while fighting in Armenia.

After the vast issues in honour of Gaius and Lucius, the coinage of Augustus abandons reference to contemporary events until the end of the reign, even though the period was marked by great expansion of the empire in the Balkans (as well as the disastrous defeat of Varus in Germany in 9 AD). Only one final issue, in 13 AD, celebrated the victories of Tiberius (96–97) in Germany and recognised him as the successor to the aged emperor. Augustus conducted the census at Rome in 13 and 14, then departed on a journey to Naples. On his return to Rome, he fell ill and he died at Nola in August 14, in the same room in the country villa where his father had died, and on the fifty-seventh anniversary of his own first consulate. His body was brought to Rome, to the great mausoleum he had constructed, and he was consecrated a month later.

The coinage of Augustus well reflects the great transformation of Rome from a republic to an empire: the earliest, 'imperatorial' types are typical issues of the army leaders of the time. Coins up to 12 BC are still struck by moneyers and bear their names, but the last twenty-five years of the reign produced a coinage which is sparse and uninformative, its types dominated by the emperor and his family.

Coinage as imperator, triumvir and consul: 44–31 BC

43 BC   The battle of Mutina: award of title imperator to Octavian and dedication of an equestrian statue to him. March on Rome and assumption of the consulate. *See* Civil Wars *2, 7.*

——   Formation of the triumvirate. *See* Civil Wars *8, 10, 11, 14–16.*

42 BC   Deification of Julius Caesar. *See* Civil Wars *31–37.*

41–40 BC   Settlement of veterans in Italy. *See* Civil Wars *54.*

40 BC   Reconciliation with Antony at Brundisium. *See* Civil Wars *58–61.*

38 BC   Victories of Agrippa in Gaul. *See* Civil Wars *70.*

37 BC   Renewal of the triumvirate at Tarentum. *See* Civil Wars *71–72.*

36 BC   Victory over Sextus Pompey at Naulochus. *See* Civil Wars *80–82.*

——   Beginning of construction of the temple of Divus Julius. *See* Civil Wars *83.*

34 BC   Celebration of the festival of Venus Genetrix. *See* Civil Wars *87–88.*

Consul January 31–January 27

30 BC   Asia and the East regained from Antony and Cleopatra.

    1   ASIA RECEPTA, Victory on cista mystica between snakes. Qui: 276/C14

——   Conquest of Egypt.

    2   AEGVPT/O CAPTA, Crocodile r. Aur: 544/C1. Den: 275/C2,3; 545) C4

29 BC   Triple triumph for victories of Illyricum, Actium and Egypt, with honours to Neptune and Apollo, and erection of a triumphal arch and a rostral column in the Forum. As a special privilege, the

1   8

triumphal insignia were displayed in the sacred *tensa* of Jupiter Capitolinus in the procession to the Circus.

3   CAESAR DIVI F, Victory holding palm in biga r. Aur: 260–1/C67

4   *Obv.* Victory stg. on prow. *Rev.* CAESAR DIVI F (or IMP CAESAR), Augustus in triumphal quadriga r. Den: 263/C75; 264/C115

5   CAESAR DIVI F, *Tensa* 1. or r., surmounted by four miniature horses. Aur: 258–9/C76–7

6   (No legend), Laurel wreath intertwined with prows (*corona rostrata*). Den: 473/C335

7   (No legend), Victory stg. on prow. Qui: 474/C328

8   *Obv.* (No legend), Bust of Victory. *Rev.* CAESAR DIVI F, Octavian as Neptune stg 1., r. foot on globe. Den: 256/C60

9   CAESAR DIVI F, Apollo Actius std. r. on rock. Den: 256/C61

10   IMP CAESAR on architrave of arch bearing figure of Octavian in quadriga. Den: 267/C123

11   *Obv.* Head of Apollo r. *Rev.* IMP CAESAR, Rostral column surmounted by statue. Den: 271/C124

— —   Honours to the god of boundaries, Terminus, for the victories which restored the Roman realm to its full extent.

12   IMP CAESAR, Figure of Terminus (herm) on thunderbolt. Den: 269/C114

13   *Obv.* Head of Terminus r., thunderbolt behind. *Rev.* Octavian std. on curule chair holding small figure of Victory. Den: 270/C116

— —   Extension of the *pomoerium* of Rome, the result of the conquest of Egypt. (This type has also been taken to refer to the foundation of colonies in general.)

14   *Obv.* (No legend), Head of Apollo r. *Rev.* IMP CAESAR, Octavian ploughing with yoke of oxen. Den: 272/C117

— —   Dedication of the new Curia, or Senate House, with two images of Victory: one on its pediment, and the other within, a famous statue brought from Tarentum.

15   Curia with colonnaded base; IMP CAESAR on architrave, and Victory on globe on apex of pediment. Den: 266/C122

16   IMP CAESAR, Victory on globe, wings spread: detail of previous type. Aur: 268/C113

17   CAESAR DIVI F, Victory on globe, holding wreath and palm (the victory of Tarentum). Den: 254–5/C64–6

15   19

28 BC   Dedication of the temple of Actian Apollo. It contained a statue of Apollo playing the lyre and various works of art, notable among them four statues of cows by the Greek sculptor Myron; these frequently figure on the coinage as symbols of the victory of Actium.

18   IMP X/II ACT, Apollo holding plectrum and lyre. Aur: 170/ C143; 179/C164; 190/C166−7; 192/C162. Den: 171/C144; 180/ C165; 191; 193/C163

19   C ANTIST VETVS IIIVIR APOLLINI ACTIO, Apollo on platform holding lyre and sacrificing over altar. Den: 365−6/C343

20   AVGVSTVS, Cow r. or l., head lowered. Aur: 536−8/C26−7

Augustus January 27 BC−August 14 AD

27 BC   Award of the title Augustus, with the right of the emperor to decorate his doorposts with laurel branches and an oak wreath, and grant of the *clupeus virtutis*. These events were long celebrated on the coinage, and the oak wreath became the standard obverse type of the sestertius.

21   AVGVSTVS S C, Eagle on oak wreath; laurel branches behind. Aur: 277/C30

22a   *Obv.* G TVRPILIANVS III VIR FERO, Bust of Feronia r. *Rev.* CAESAR AVGVSTVS, Two laurel branches flanking oak wreath enclosing O C S. Aur: 286/C478

22b   *Obv.* L AQVILLIVS FLORVS III VIR, Triskelis. *Rev.* As previous. Aur: 302/C356

The following all have *Obv.* OB CIVIS SERVATOS, Oak wreath flanked by laurel branches, and *Rev.* Name of moneyer (as below) III VIR A A A F F around S C. All are sestertii.

23a   Q AELIVS L F LAMIA: 323/C341
23b   C MARCI L F CENSORIN AVG: 325/C454
23c   T QVINCTIVS CRISPINVS (SVLPIC): 327−30/C508, 510
23d   M SANQVINIVS Q F: 341/C520
23e   P LICINIVS STOLO: 345/C441
23f   TI SEMPRONIVS GRACCVS: 348/C524
23g   C ASINIVS C F GALLVS: 370/C367
23h   C CASSIVS C F CELER: 374/C407

23*i*   C GALLIVS C F LVPERCVS: 377/*C*434
23*j*   CN PISO CN F: 380/*C*377
23*k*   L NAEVIVS SVRDINVS: 383/*C*471
23*l*   C PLOTIVS RVFVS: 387/*C*501

23*h*   27

24   CAESAR AVGVSTVS, two laurel branches. Aur: 26/*C*45; 50/*C*46.
     Den: 33/*C*48; 51/*C*47
25*a*   *Obv.* TVRPILIANVS III VIR, Head of Liber r. *Rev.* AVGVSTO OB
     C S in oak wreath. Aur: 278
25*b*   *Obv.* TVRPILIANVS III VIR FERON, Bust of Feronia r. *Rev.* As
     previous. Aur: 279/*C*476
25*c*   *Obv.* M DVRMIVS III VIR HONORI, Head of Honos r. *Rev.* As
     previous. Aur: 312/*C*426
26   OB CIVIS SERVATOS, oak wreath. Aur: 29; 76. Den: 40/*C*210−1;
     75/*C*210; 77/*C*208
27   CAESAR AVGVSTVS, Two laurel branches flanking S P Q R
     arranged around shield inscribed CL V. Aur: 52/*C*50, 52. Den:
     36/*C*51, 53
28   OB CIVIS SERVATOS, Shield inscribed S P Q R CL V in oak wreath
     Aur: 30/*C*216; 78/*C*214. Den: 79/*C*213, 215
29*a*   S P Q R, Victory flying r., holding wreath above shield
     inscribed (SPQR) CL V which rests against a column. Aur: 31,
     61/*C*290; 88/*C*288; 90. Den: 45/*C*289; 46; 48/*C*291; 89; 94−5
29*b*   S P Q R, Victory flying r., about to attach shield inscribed CL V
     to column. Aur: 32
29*c*   S P Q R, Victory flying r., holding branch and wreath above
     shield inscribed CL V (or holding shield). Aur: 91. Den: 47
29*d*   S P Q R CL V, Victory flying r., holding plain shield. Den: 92
29*e*   S P Q R, Victory stg. facing, holding shield inscribed (SPQR)
     CL V. Aur: 62/*C*286. Den: 49; 93/*C*287
30*a*   CAESAR AVGVSTVS, Shield inscribed CL V. Den: 34−5
30*b*   S P Q R, Same type. Den: 43−4/*C*292
30*c*   Shield inscribed SPQR CL V. Den: 42/*C*293
25 BC   Victories in the Spanish wars, and foundation of Emerita.
31   P CARISIVS LEG PRO PR, Trophy on heap of weapons. Den: 4−
     5/*C*402−3

32 — — Trophy on head of kneeling captive. Den: 6/*C*404

33 P CARISI LEG, Victory crowning trophy; dagger and curved sword at base. Qui: 1/*C*386−7

34 P CARISIVS LEG PRO PR, City wall with EMERITA inscribed above gate. Den: 9−10/*C*397−8

34   35

23 BC Award of the tribunician power; this title becomes the standard type for dupondii. All have *Obv.* AVGVSTVS TRIBVNIC POT in oak wreath, and *Rev.* Name of moneyer (as below) III VIR A A A F F around S C. All are dupondii.

35*a* Q AELIVS LAMIA: 324/*C*342

35*b* C CENSORINVS L F AVG: 326/*C*452

35*c* (T) CRISPINV/S SVLPICIAN/VS: 331−4/*C*505, 507

35*d* T QVINCTIV/S CRISPINVS: 335−6/*C*509

35*e* M SANQVINIVS Q F: 342/*C*521

35*f* P (LICINIVS) STOLO: 346; 347/*C*440, 442

35*g* TI SEMPRONIVS GRACCVS: 349/*C*525

35*h* CASINIVS (C F) GALLVS: 371−2/*C*368

35*i* C CASSIVS CELER: 375/*C*408

35*j* C GALLIVS LVPERCVS: 378/*C*435

35*k* CN PISO C F: 381/*C*378

35*l* L SVRDINVS: 384/*C*472

35*m* C PLOTIVS RVFVS: 388/*C*502

22 BC Dedication of the temple of Jupiter Tonans.

36 IOV/IS TON/ANT/IS, Image of Jupiter holding thunderbolt in hexastyle temple. Aur: 27 59; 63/*C*178; 66/*C*184. Den: 64−5; 67/*C*185, 179−80

21 BC Restoration of temple of Zeus at Olympia by Agrippa.

37 IOVI OLV/M, Hexastyle temple with round shield in pediment and palmettes on top. Den: 472/*C*182

20 BC Successful campaigns of Tiberius in Armenia.

38 ARMENIA CAPTA, Victory slaughtering bull. Aur: 514/*C*8

39 — — Sphinx std. r. Aur: 513/*C*10

40 CAESAR DIVI F ARMEN CAPTA (or RECE) IMP VIIII, Armenian stg. facing, holding spear and bow. Den: 518−20/*C*58−9

41 ARMENIA CAPTA (or RECEPTA), Tiara, quiver and bow case. Den: 515−7/*C*11−13

41   49

42*a*   *Obv*. (P PETRON) TVRPILIAN/VS IIIVIR, Head of Liber r. *Rev*.
CAESAR DIVI F ARME CAPT, Armenian kneeling r. Den: 290/
C488; 292/C489

42*b*   *Obv*. TVRPILIANVS IIIVIR FERO, Head of Feronia r. *Rev*. As
previous. Den: 291/C487

42*c*   *Obv*. L AQVILLIVS FLORVS IIIVIR, Bust of Virtus r. *Rev*. As
previous. Den: 306/C360

43   *Obv*. As previous. *Rev*. CAESAR DIVI F ARMINIA CAPTA,
Armenian stg. facing. Den: 307/C361

— —   Recovery of captives and standards from the Parthians (*44–58*);
ornamenta triumphalia decreed for Augustus who refused a full
triumph, but accepted the signal honour of having his triumphal
insignia – the eagle-tipped sceptre, the laurel crown, and the *toga
picta* worn over the *tunica palmata* – displayed in the *tensa* or
sacred car of Mars, before being deposited in his temple (*52–54*);
construction of the temple of Mars Ultor (*55*), where the standards
would be stored (it was dedicated in 2 BC); and erection of a
triumphal arch to celebrate the peaceful victory (*49–51*).

44*a*   *Obv*. TVRPILIANVS IIIVIR, Head of Liber r. *Rev*. CAESAR AVGVSTVS
SIGN RECE, Parthian kneeling r., Den: 287/C485

44*b*   *Obv*. (P PETRON) TVRPILIAN/VS IIIVIR FERON, Head of Feronia r.
Rev. As previous. Den: 288–9/C484, 486

44*c*   *Obv*. L AQVILLIVS FLORVS IIIVIR, Head of Sol r. *Rev*. As previous.
Den: 304/C358

44*d*   *Obv*. (Same legend), Bust of Virtus r. *Rev*. As previous.
Den: 305/C359–60

44*e*   *Obv*. M DVRMIVS IIIVIR. Bust of Hercules r. *Rev*. As previous.
Den: 314/C428

45   SIGNIS RECEPTIS, Aquila and standard flanking SPQR Aur:
85/C264, 266. Den: 86–7/C265, 267

46   SIGNIS PARTHIC/IS RECEPT/IS in three lines. Den: 523–6/C255,
257

47   SIGNIS RECEPTIS, Mars, standard over shoulder, holding aquila.
Aur: 60; 80/C258, 261. Den: 41; 58; 81–4/C259–60, 262

48   SIGNIS (PARTHICIS) RECEPTIS, Capricorn r. Aur: 521–2/C256,
263

49   CIVIBVS ET SIGN MILIT A PART RECVP/ER, Triple triumphal arch
surmounted by quadriga flanked by figures holding standard
and aquila. Aur: 131, 133; 135/C82. Den: 132/C85; 134/C84;
136–7/C83

50 SPR SIGNIS RECEPTIS, Single arch inscribed IMP (I) X TR PO/T (I)V supporting quadriga. Cis: 508−10/*C*298

51 L VINICIVS,Triumphal arch inscribed SPQR IMP CAE and surmounted by quadriga bearing Augustus; two smaller arches by sides supporting archer and slinger. Den: 359/*C*544

52 *Obv.* SPQR PARE/NTI CONS SVO, *Toga picta* over *tunica palmata* between eagle sceptre and laurel crown. *Rev.* CAESARI AVGVSTO, Decorated *tensa* r. Den: 96−101/*C*78, 80

52   55*c*

53 SPQR, *Tensa* of Mars containing eagle-tipped sceptre. Aur: 107/*C*273; 109; 111−12/*C*276. Den: 108/*C*274; 110/*C*275; 113/*C*279

54 SPQR, *Tensa* with eagle sceptre within tetrastyle temple. Aur: 114; 116; 118/*C*278. Den: 115/*C*280; 117/*C*281; 119−20/*C*279; 120A (hexastyle temple)

55*a* MARTIS VLTORIS (variously abbreviated), Image of Mars holding aquila and standard in round (or hexastyle) temple. Aur: 28/*C*204; 68/*C*193; 73/*C*197. Den: 39; 69−72/*C*194−5, 200−1; 74/*C*196, 198

55*b* MAR VLT, Round temple containing aquila and standards. Aur: 104/*C*189. Den: 103: 105−6/*C*190−1

55*c* MART VLTO, Round temple containing vexillum. Cis: 507/*C*202

−− Completion (?) of the temple of the imperial cult at Pergamum, the seat of the Commune of Asia; the temple had been authorised by Augustus in 29.

56 COM ASIAE, Hexastyle temple inscribed ROM ET AVGVST. Cis: 505−6/*C*86

−− Reform of the system of building and financing roads, commemorated by four different arches, perhaps erected in Spain where many roads were built.

57 QVOD VIAE MVNitae SVNT, Augustus, crowned by Victory in biga of elephants on single arch which stands between roofed porticoes. Aur: 141/*C*230; 143

58 −− but double arch on viaduct. Aur: 140/*C*229

59*a* *Obv.* As 44*b* (Turpilianus). *Rev.* AVGVSTVS CAESAR, Augustus stg. in biga of elephants l. (detail of one of previous). Den: 280−4/*C*480−1

59*b*   *Obv*. s 44*d* (Aquillius Florus/Virtus). *Rev*. As previous. Den: 301/*C*354

59*c*   *Obv*. M DVRMIVS III VIR, Head of Honos r. *Rev*. As previous. Den: 311/*C*427

60   (Legend as 57−8), Augustus, crowned by Victory, in horse-drawn quadriga on double arch on viaduct. Den: 144−5/*C*231, 233−4

61   − − Two arches, each bearing an equestrian statue and trophy, on viaduct. Den: 142/*C*235

61   64

62*a*   Cippus inscribed SPQR IMPeratori CAESari QVOD viae Munitae sunt EX EA Pecunia Quae Iussu senatus AD Aerarium Delata EST. Den: 360−1/*C*541−2

62*b*   *Obv*. SPQR IMP CAES on pedestal of equestrian statue before city walls and gate. *Rev*. As previous. Den: 362/*C*543

19 BC   Return of Augustus to Rome, with dedication of altar to Fortuna Redux, and vows for his continued health.

63   FORT/VN RED/V CAES AVG SPQR inscribed on altar. Aur: 53/*C*103, 105; 55/*C*107. Den: 54/*C*104, 106; 56/*C*108

64   *Obv*. Q RVSTIVS FORTVNAE ANTIAT, Busts of Fortuna Victrix and Fortuna Felix on portable shrine. *Rev*. CAESARI AVGVSTO EX S C Ornamented altar inscribed FOR RE. Den: 322/*C*513

65   IOVI VOT SVSC PRO SAL CAES AVG SPQR in oak wreath. Den: 57/*C*183

18 BC   Procession in honour of Augustus taking charge of the distribution of free grain to the populace.

66*a*   *Obv*. L AQVILLIVS FLORVS IIIVIR, Head of Sol. *Rev*. CAESAR AVGVSTVS S C, Quadriga with modius-shaped car containing ears of wheat. Den: 303/*C*357

66*b*   *Obv*. M DVRMIVS IIIVIR HONORI, Head of Honos r. *Rev*. As previous. Den: 313/*C*429

67   78

17 BC Appearance of a comet, supposedly the soul of Caesar, taken as inaugurating a new age.

67   DIVVS IVLIVS, Comet with vertical tail. Den: 37−8/*C*97−9; 102

68   M SANOVINIVS IIIVIR, Head of young Caesar (?) r., comet above. Aur: 337. Den: 338/*C*1.

The following type, whose date and interpretation are disputed, may be associated with the same event.

69   L LENTVLVS FLAMEN MARTIALIS, Augustus, l. hand resting on shield inscribed CL V, crowning image of Caesar who holds Victoriola and has star above head. Den: 415/*C*419

—— Celebration of the Secular Games: assumption of the priesthood, announcement by the herald, and distribution of the *suffimenta*.

70   L MESCINIVS RVFVS IIIVIR, Cippus inscribed IMP CAES AVG LVD SAEC; XV sacris FACIUNDIS at sides. Den: 354−5/*C*461

71   *Obv.* AVGVST DIVI F LVDOS SAE, Herald holding caduceus and shield decorated with star. *Rev.* As 68. Aur: 339/*C*5. Den: 340/*C*6

72   IMP, Altar inscribed LVDI SAECVLI flanked by priest and herald. Aur: 138/*C*112. Den: 139/*C*188

73   L MESCINIVS, AVG SVFfimenta POPVLO, Augustus std. on platform inscribed LVD S giving *suffimenta* to two citizens. Aur: 350/*C*466

—— (Date uncertain). Rebuilding of the Regia, destroyed by fire in 36 and reconstruction of the sacred shields, *ancilia*, which had fallen from heaven in the reign of Numa. The type may also reflect participation of the Salian priests, who carried the *ancilia*, in the Secular Games.

74a   P STOLO IIIVIR, *Apex* between *ancilia*. Den: 343/*C*438

74b   *Obv.* AVGVSTVS TR POT, Equestrian statue of Augustus. *Rev.* As previous. Den: 344/*C*439

16 BC Campaigns of Augustus in Gaul: vows for a safe return; vows and sacrifices for his recovery from illness.

75   VOTA PVBLICA SVSCEPTA PRO SALute ET REDitu IOVI OPTIMO MAXIMO SACRum, Mars stg. Aur: 147/*C*320; 149; 151. Den: 146/*C*327; 148/*C*321; 150/*C*324−6; 152; 153/*C*322

76a   L MESCINIVS RVFVS, Mars stg. r. on pedestal inscribed SPQR VOTA PRO REDitu CAEsaris. Den: 351−2/*C*463

76b   As previous, but base inscribed SPQR VOTA PVBLICA SVSCEPTA PRO salute ET REDitu AVGusti. Den: 353/*C*464

77   *Obv.* C ANTISTI VETVS IIIVIR, Bust of Victory r. *Rev.* PRO VALETVDINE CAESARIS SPQR, Priest making libation over altar to which victimarius leads bull. Aur: 369

15 BC Conquest of Rhaetia, the occasion (at an uncertain date) for extending the *pomoerium* of Rome.

78   IMP X, Tiberius and Drusus (or one of them) presenting branch to Augustus std. on platform. Aur: 163−4/*C*130, 132, 134. Den: 162/*C*131; 165/*C*133, 135

79   C MARIVS TRO IIIVIR, Augustus ploughing with ox-team before city walls. Aur: 402

14 BC Defeat of the German tribes.

80   L CANINIVS GALLVS IIIVIR, long-haired barbarian kneeling r., offering vexillum. Den: 416

13 BC Offerings of thanks to Jupiter on return of Augustus from Germany, with dedication of a shield bearing his image by the Senate.

81   *Obv.* IOVI optimo MAXIMO SPQR VOTA suscepta PRO salute IMPeratoris CAESaris QVOD PER EVm RES PVblica IN AMPliore ATque TRANquilliore statu EST in oak wreath. *Rev.* L MESCINIVS RVFVS IIIVIR, Cippus inscribed IMP CAES AVGV COMMuni CONSensu. Den: 358/*C*462

82   *Obv.* S C OB REM PVblicam CVM SALVTE IMP CAESAR AVGVS CONSERVATAM, Image of Augustus on shield. *Rev.* As 94*b* Den: 356/*C*465

82   92

83   *Obv.* As previous. *Rev.* L MESCINIVS RVFVS IIIVIR, Cippus inscribed IMP CAES AVGV COMMuni CONSensu. *Rev.* As 81. Den: 357

— — Victories of Agrippa in the East, for which he refused a triumph; hence his absence from the triumphal quadriga.

84   C MARIVS C F TRO IIIVIR, Palm branch in quadriga r. Den: 399/*C*456

— — Renewal of Agrippa's tribunician power, and designation as successor, with consequent establishment of a dynasty; further honours consisting of an equestrian statue.

85   (Legend as previous), Augustus and Agrippa stg., with attributes of tribunes. Den: 397/*C*457; 400/*C*458

86   C SVLPICIVS PLATORIN, Augustus and Agrippa std. on platform decorated with rostra. Den: 406−7/*C*529

87*a*   M AGRIPPA PLATORINVS IIIVIR, Head of Agrippa, wearing combined mural and rostral crown. Aur: 409/*C*2

87*b*   M AGRIPPA COS TER COSSVS LENTVLVS. Same type. Den: 414/*C*3.

87*c*   (Legend as 87*a*), Bare head of Agrippa r. Den: 408/*C*3

88   C MARIVS TRO IIIVIR, Head of Julia between those of Gaius and Lucius Caesars. Den: 404−5/*C*1, 2

89   COSSVS CN F LENTVLVS, Equestrian statue of Agrippa on pedestal decorated with prows. Den: 412/*C*418

12 BC Election of Augustus as Pontifex Maximus, and transformation of part of Augustus' house into public property.

    90   L CANINIVS GALLVS IIIVIR, Cippus inscribed comitia caesaris AVGVSTI (interpretation hypothetical). Den: 418/*C*384

    91   L CANINIVS GALLVS OB C S, Laurel wreath above door flanked by laurel branches. Aur: 419/*C*385

10 BC Dedication of the altar of Lugdunum and creation of the Community of the Gauls.

    92   ROM ET AVG, Elaborately decorated altar. Ses: 229/*C*239; 231/*C*236. Dup: 232. As: 230/*C*240; 233/*C*237. Sem: 234/*C*238

8 BC Defeat and submission of German tribes.

    93   IMP XIIII, Cloaked figure presenting infant to Augustus std. on platform. Aur: 200. Den: 281/*C*175 1/*C*174

— — First campaigns of Gaius Caesar, in Gaul.

    94   C CAES AVGVS F, Gaius galloping r.; eagle between standards behind. Aur: 198/*C*38. Den: 199/*C*40

2 BC Advertisement of Gaius and Lucius Caesars as heirs to the imperial power: Gaius became *princeps iuventutis* in 5, Lucius in 2 BC.

    95   C L CAESARES AVGVSTI F COS DESIG PRINC IVVENT, Gaius and Lucius stg. facing. Aur: 206, 209/*C*42. Den: 207–8, 210–12/*C*43

95

13 AD Triumph of Tiberius for victories in Germany, and renewal of tribunician power, marking him as successor.

    96   TI CAESAR AVG F TR POT XV, Tiberius in quadriga r. Aur: 221/*C*299; 223. Den: 222/*C*300; 224/*C*301

    97   (Same legend), head r. Aur: 225/*C*1. Den: 226/*C*2

LIVIA

Livia Drusilla, also called Julia Augusta, was born in 58 BC, and married Tiberius Claudius Nero in 43. Augustus, who met her in 39, took her from her husband in 38, though she was pregnant with Drusus. They had a long and successful marriage, but no children. She accompanied Augustus on his travels and campaigns and accumulated great wealth; her status rose after his adoption of her son, Tiberius. On the death of Augustus, she was adopted into the Julian family by his will and gained the title Augusta. She died in 29, after surviving a serious illness in 22 (Tiberius *17*). Tiberius, who came to hate her, refused consecration; it was only granted by her grandson Claudius in 42 (Claudius *8*).

AGRIPPA

See Civil Wars.

JULIA

The only child of Augustus, and his first wife Scribonia, Julia was born in 39 BC and married C. Marcellus in 25. When he died, she married Agrippa, whom she accompanied to the East in 17−13. On his death, Augustus forced her to marry Tiberius, an arrangement which pleased neither. When he went to Rhodes in exile, she stayed in Rome, where she carried on affairs with many members of the aristocracy, and may have been involved in a plot to replace Tiberius as heir to the throne. For reasons now mysterious, Augustus exiled her to the prison island of Pandataria in 2 BC. She remained there until starved to death by order of Tiberius in 14. She appears on Augustus *88*; other representations are questionable.

GAIUS AND LUCIUS CAESARS

Gaius, born in 20 BC to Julia and Agrippa, was the oldest grandson of Augustus. At the age of three, he was adopted by the emperor, who educated him personally and in 8 BC presented him to the troops in Gaul. At the age of fourteen, he entered into the priestly offices and accepted a consulate, which he was to fill five years later. He became *princeps iuventutis*, was awarded a silver shield and spear by the equestrian order, and was plainly intended to be Augustus' successor. In the spring of 1 BC, he set out for the East, where the Parhinas had seized control of Armenia, and entered his consulate in Syria in 1 AD. The war in Armenia, was successful and a supporter of Rome was installed on the throne, but he soon died, and the war continued. During the operations, Gaius was severely wounded, and died at Limyra in Asia Minor in 4 AD.

Lucius, the younger brother of Gaius, was born in 17 BC and immediately adopted by Augustus. He became *princeps iuventutis* in 3 BC, an occasion for which Augustus assumed the consulate and gave a donative (not recorded on the coinage). After assisting at the dedication of the temple of Mars Ultor in 2 AD, he was sent to Spain to gain experience of the West, as Gaius was to the East. However, he fell ill on the journey and died at Massilia in the same year.

For the coins of Gaius and Lucius, *see* Augustus *88, 94, 95*.

TIBERIUS

August 14−March 37

Tiberius Claudius Nero, born in November 42 BC, was the son of an homonymous father of the ancient family of the Claudii and of Livia.

When he was four, his mother married Octavian, by whom she had no further children; consequently, the stepsons of the future emperor soon rose to prominence. Tiberius participated in the triumph for the victory of Actium, received a thorough education in Greek, and rose through the usual offices. He accompanied Augustus on the Spanish campaign and himself led the successful war in Armenia (Augustus *38−43*) in 20 BC. During the reign of his stepfather, his main accomplishments were military. In 15, he led the campaigns which culminated in the conquest of Rhaetia (Augustus *78*) and in 13, as consul for the first time, conducted the honours to the emperor on his return.

When Agrippa died in 12, Tiberius was forced, with great reluctance, to marry Julia, daughter of Augustus. During the succeeding years, he was active on campaign in Illyricum and Dalmatia, receiving the *ornamenta triumphalia* and the title imperator. Together with Augustus, he dedicated the great altar of Lugdunum (*1*; cf. Augustus *92*) in 10, and in the following two years participated in the ultimately unsuccessful conquest of Germany, earning a triumph and a second consulate. He gave the spoils of the war to the restoration of the temple of Concord (*2*), which he dedicated in 10 AD. In 6 BC, he gained the tribunician power, and thus close association in the rule of the empire, yet the following years, until 2 AD, saw him in eclipse, as he withdrew to Rhodes to study and to make way for the rising Caius and Lucius Caesars. After the death of the latter in 4 AD, however, Tiberius was adopted by Augustus, and assumed the name Tiberius Julius Caesar as well as the tribunician power for ten years. For most of the remaining years of Augustus, he was occupied with wars in Germany and the Danube region, earning a triumph (*14*; Augustus *96*) for his success in Pannonia. Finally, in 13, he received the power of proconsul and was thus recognised as successor to the throne.

When Augustus died in August 14, Tiberius succeeded without serious opposition, and in the next month conducted the funeral and consecration (*3−13*) of his stepfather. He became priest of the imperial cult, and in 15 assumed the office of Pontifex Maximus. In 17, he showed great generosity toward the cities of Asia which had been struck by a devastating earthquake (*15*), but himself only left Rome once during the first twelve years of his reign. On that occasion, he spent a year in Campania to deal with serious local problems, but returned in 22 when Livia was extremely ill. Her recovery was marked by public prayers and honours, including the use of a special carriage, or carpentum (*18*). At about this time, Tiberius was honoured by the Senate with shields (*16−17*) which celebrated his moderation and clemency, on the model of the *clupeus virtutis* of Augustus. In 27, Tiberius withdrew to the Isle of Capri, and never returned to Rome. The reign was generally peaceful, with minor disturbances and problems on the eastern frontier easily put down. Tiberius lived longer than any other Roman emperor; he died at the age of 78 in November 37 on his way back to Rome. His coinage resembles that of the last years of Augustus by maintaining an abstract monotony which rarely reflects historical events.

Imperator, under Augustus

10 BC Dedication of the great altar of Lugdunum, presided over by Tiberius together with Augustus.

1 ROM ET AVG, Altar of Lugdunum (Augustus *92*) Ses: 240−1/
*C*28−30; 247−8/*C*36−7. Dup: 235−6/*C*31, 33; 244/*C*37. As: 237−8/*C*31, 33; 242/*C*34; 245/*C*37. Sem: 239/*C*32; 243; 246/*C*38

10 AD Dedication of the temple of Concord, rebuilt by Tiberius; celebrated by coins struck twenty-five years later.

2 *Obv.* (No legend), Hexastyle temple of Concord, decorated with statues. *Rev.* TI CAESAR DIVI AVG F AVGVST P M TR P XXXVI/I (or XXXIIX) around S C. Ses: 55; 61/*C*116; 67/*C*133

Sole ruler, 14−37 AD

14 Funeral and consecration of Augustus. Most of the types have direct reference to Augustus and to his cult on the Palatine hill, site of the temple of *7* and the altar of *10*, which Tiberius dedicated to his stepfather's providence in arranging for the succession.

3 DIVOS AVGVST DIVI F, Bare head r., star above. Aur: 23−4/*C*28−9

4 *Obv.* DIVO AVGVSTO SPQR, Statue of Augustus in car drawn by quadriga of elephants. *Rev.* TI CAESAR DIVI AVG F AVGVST P M TR POT XXXVI/I (or XXXIIX) around S C. Ses: 56/*C*102; 62/*C*108; 68/*C*125

5 *Obv.* DIVVS AVGVSTVS PATER, Augustus, radiate std. 1.; altar before. *Rev.* As previous, but TR POT XXIIII. Ses: 49/*C*74

6 *Obv.* DIVO AVGVSTO SPQR, Shield inscribed OB CIVES SER in oak wreath supported by capricorns. *Rev.* As type 4. Ses: 57; 63/*C*109; 69/*C*129

7 *Obv.* DIVVS AVGVSTVS PATER, Radiate head 1. *Rev.* S C, Round temple (of Vesta on the Palatine, built by Augustus) flanked by statues of calf and lamb on high bases. Dup: 74−6/*C*142

8 *Obv.* As previous *Rev.* S C, Victory alighting 1., resting shield inscribed SPQR (*clupeus virtutis*) on cippus. Dup: 77−8/*C*141

9 *Obv.* As previous. *Rev.* S C in oak wreath (*corona civica*), Dup: 79/*C*143

10 *Obv.* As previous, but head r. or 1. *Rev.* PROVIDENT, altar enclosure with double door. As: 80−81/*C*146

11 *Obv.* As type 7, with star above, thunderbolt before. *Rev.* S C, Seated female figure, perhaps Livia. As: 71−3/*C*151

12 *Obv.* As type 7. *Rev.* S C, Eagle stg. on globe. As: 82/*C*155

13 *Obv.* As type 7. *Rev.* S C, Winged thunderbolt. As: 83/*C*158

14−15 Celebration of triumphs under Augustus.

14 TR POT XVI/I IMP VII, Tiberius in triumphal quadriga. Aur: 1, 3/*C*1−2. Den: 2, 4/*C*8

17 Restoration of cities of Asia destroyed by earthquake.

15   *Obv.* CIVITATIBVS ASIAE RESTITVTIS, Tiberius std. 1. *Rev.* TI CAESAR
DIVI AVG F AVGVST P M TR POT XXIIII around S C. Ses: 48/*C*70

15

17

22 (?)   Award of honorific shields by the Senate.
   16   CLEMENTIAE, Facing bust on shield. Den: 38/*C*4
   17   MODERATIONI/S, Same type. Dup: 39/40/*C*5−6
23   Public prayers and honours to Livia on her recovery from illness.
   18   SPQR IVLIAE AVGVST, Ornamented carpentum drawn 1. by mules.
   Rev. As 15. Ses: 50/*C*74

DRUSUS

Drusus Julius Caesar, son of Tiberius, born about 13 BC, was favoured by
Augustus, who made him *princeps iuventutis* in 2 AD and by his father,
under whom he campaigned successfully in Illyricum. His victories earned
him a triumph and a commemorative arch in the Forum. He received the
consulate the following year and the tribunician power (*2*) in 22, a sign
that he was considered as an eventual successor to the throne. Since his
wife Livilla had produced twins (*1*), Tiberius Gemellus and Germanicus,
in 19, continuation of the dynasty seemed secure. The jealousy of Tiberius'
adviser Sejanus, however, led him to seduce Livilla, who poisoned Drusus
in 23.

19   Birth of twins to Drusus and Livilla.

1 *Obv*. (No legend), Heads of two small boys in crossed cornucopiae; caduceus between. *Rev*. DRVSVS CAESAR TI AVG F DIVI AVG N PONT TR POT II around S C. Ses: 42/*C*1

22 Award of the tribunician power.
2 PONTIF TRIBVN POTEST ITER around S C. As: 45/*C*2

NERO CLAUDIUS DRUSUS

Drusus, the son of Livia and younger brother of Tiberius, was born in 38 BC and raised in the household of Augustus. He rose early to high office, and in 15 BC led campaigns in Rhaetia which earned him the *ornamenta triumphalia*. In 13, he governed Gaul and from 12 to 9 won great victories in Germany (*1*), where he died in 9 BC as the result of a fall from his horse. He was buried in the mausoleum of Augustus, and received a triumphal arch on the Appian way (*2*). He was the father of Germanicus, and of Claudius, who struck all his coins (*see also* Claudius 9).

9 Victories in Germany, and award of triumphal arch.
1 DE GERMANIS, Two oblong shields crossed before standard. Aur: 73/*C*5. Den: 74/*C*6
2 DE GERM/ANIS on architrave of triumphal arch surmounted by equestrian statue and trophies. Aur: 69/*C*1; 71/*C*3. 2Dr: 125 (no legend); 126. Den: 70/*C*2; 72/*C*4

ANTONIA

Antonia, the daughter of Mark Antony and Octavia, born in 36 BC, married Nero Claudius Drusus, and gave birth to Germanicus, Livilla who married Drusus, son of Tiberius, and Claudius. She revealed the intrigues of Sejanus to Tiberius, and protected her grandson Caius from him. When Caius became emperor, he made Antonia Augusta, but poisoned her soon after. Coins were struck in her honour by Claudius (*10–11*).

GERMANICUS

Germanicus Julius Caesar, son of Nero Claudius Drusus and Antonia, and thus grandson of Livia and Mark Antony and nephew of Tiberius, was born about 15 BC. Augustus obliged Tiberius to adopt him in 5 AD, and the next year he married Agrippina; he was evidently intended as the eventual successor to the throne. He led campaigns under Tiberius in the Danube region in 7–9 AD, received a major command in Germany in 13, and fought there until 16, when he recaptured the standards which had been lost in the disastrous defeat of Varus in 9. For this, he received a triumph in 17 (*1*). The next year, he was sent east with special powers which enabled him to establish Artaxias on the Armenian throne (2), but he died at Antioch in 19, perhaps poisoned. Coins were struck in his honour by his son Caligula (*see* Caligula 5−7).

17 Victories in Germany, with recovery of standards.
    1 *Obv.* GERMANICVS CAESAR, Germanicus in triumphal quadriga r. *Rev.* SIGNIS RECEPT DEVICTIS GERM, Germanicus stg. l., holding standard. Dup: 57/C7
18 Victories in Armenia and establishment of Artaxias as king.
    2 ARTAXIAS GERMANICVS, Germanicus stg. facing, crowning stg. Artaxias. 2Dr: 59

AGRIPPINA

Vipsania Agrippina, daughter of Agrippa and Julia, was born in 14 BC, and married Germanicus in 9 AD. She accompanied her husband, by whom she had nine children, on his campaigns, and returned to Rome after his death. Tiberius, who hated her, exiled her to the isle of Pandateria, where she committed suicide in 33. Caligula brought her ashes to Rome, and honoured her with circus games, annual sacrifices and a series of coins (Caligula 8−9).

NERO AND DRUSUS CAESARS

Nero, the eldest son of Germanicus and Agrippina, was born in 7 AD, and honoured, together with his brother Drusus, by Tiberius after the death of the emperor's own son Drusus. Tiberius, however, urged by Sejanus to eliminate the entire family of Germanicus as a possible threats to his rule, sent Nero into exile in 30 and had him starved the following year. Drusus, born in 8, similarly enjoyed high honours under Tiberius. Led by hopes of the succession, he intrigued with Sejanus against his own brother, but was nevertheless denounced for conspiracy and imprisoned in the cellar of the imperial palace where he was starved to death in 33. Nero and Drusus were refused burial by Tiberius; they received posthumous honours from their younger brother Caius (Caligula *10*).

CALIGULA
March 37−January 41

Gaius Julius Caesar Germanicus, the son of Germanicus and Agrippina, was born at Antium in 12 AD. The soldiers of the Rhine, where he spent much of his childhood, gave him his nickname, 'little boot'; he was always officially known as Gaius Caesar. He survived the plots of Sejanus and after 31 was favoured by Tiberius, whom he succeeded with the support of the praetorian prefect Macro in 37. One of his first acts, therefore, was to hold a special parade of the praetorians (*1*) to pay the thousand sesterces a head bequeathed to them by Tiberius.

In August 37, Gaius dedicated the temple of Divus Augustus (*2−5*) and brought the ashes of his mother Agrippina and his brothers Nero and Drusus to the capital; he celebrated the memory of the members of his family (*5−10*) who had been destroyed by Tiberius and Sejanus, and set up circus games and annual sacrifices in honour of Agrippina. He also remembered his grandfather Agrippa (*11*), for whom a massive series of coins was struck now and in succeeding years. He gave special honours to his three sisters (*12*), having them mentioned in the oath of allegiance sworn by all subjects, and making them honorary vestals. The latter seemed especially inappropriate, since Caligula is reputed to have slept with all three. Early in 38, the Senate awarded him the title *Pater Patriae* (*13*), and in 39, he repealed the sales tax of ½% (*14*). This had originally been instituted by Augustus at the rate of 1% after the financial crisis of the Civil Wars; Tiberius had reduced it by half.

The coinage of Caligula refers infrequently to events of the day; it ignores the campaigns in Germany, and the monomania of the emperor, who eventually had himself worshipped in a special temple. His extravagances and cruelties finally led to his murder by the troops in January 41.

37 Payment to the praetorian guard of the bequest of Tiberius.

  1 ADLOCVTIO COH, Gaius on platform addressing troops. Ses: 32/
     *C*1; 40/*C*2; 48/*C*3

— — Dedication of the temple of Divus Augustus.

  2a *Obv.* C CAESAR AVG GERMANICVS P M TR POT, PIETAS in exergue,
      Pietas std. 1. *Rev.* DIVO AVG, Gaius, with attendants, sacrificing
      before hexastyle temple. Ses: 36/*C*9

  2b — — *Obv.* C CAESAR DIVI AVG PRON AVG P M TR P III/I P P. Ses:
      51/*C*11

  3a (No legend), Radiate head of Augustus r., between stars.
      Aur: 1/*C*10. Den: 2/*C*11

  3b DIVVS AVG PATER PATRIAE, Radiate head r. Aur: 3/*C*4; 9/*C*4;
      15/*C*1; 23/*C*6. Den: 4/*C*5; 6/*C*9; 10/*C*5; 16/*C*2; 24/*C*7; 31/*C*8

  4 *Obv.* DIVVS AVGVSTVS S C, Radiate head 1. *Rev.* CONSENSV
     SENAT ET EQ ORDIN P R, Augustus std. 1. on curule chair. Dup:
     56/*C*87

— — Return of ashes of family members and celebration of their memory,
     combined with previous. Type *9* shows the carpentum in which the
     image of Agrippina was borne to the Circus.

  5 *Obv.* GERMANICVS CAES TI AVG/V (F) COS II γ M, Bare head r.
     Rev. DIVVS AVGVSTVS, Radiate head 1. Dra: 60−62/*C*2

  6 GERMANICVS CAES P C CAES AVG GERM, Bare head r. Aur:
     11/*C*3; 17/*C*1; 25/*C*6. Den: 12/*C*4; 18/*C*2; 26/*C*5

  7a *Obv.* GERMANICVS CAESAR TI AVGVST F DIVI AVG N, Bare head 1.

Rev. C CAESAR AVG GERMANICVS PON M TR POT around S C. As: 35/*C*1

7*b*   — — C CAESAR DIVI AVG PRON AVG P M TR POT III P P around S C. As: 43; 50/*C*4

8   AGRIPPINA MAT C CAES AVG GERM, Bust r. Aur: 7/*C*3; 13/*C*1; 21/*C*5. Den: 8/*C*4; 14/*C*2; 22/*C*6; 30/*C*7

9   *Obv.* AGRIPPINA M F MAT C CAESARIS AVGVSTI, Bust r. *Rev.* SPQR MEMORIAE AGRIPPINAE, Carpentum drawn by mules. Ses: 55/*C*1

9

12

10*a*   *Obv.* NERO ET DRVSVS CAESARES, Nero and Drusus riding r. *Rev.* C CAESAR AVG GERMANICVS PON M TR POT around S C. Dup: 34/*C*1

10*b*   — — C CAESAR DIVI AVG PRON AVG P M TR POT III/I P P around S C. Dup: 42/*C*2; 49/*C*3

11   *Obv.* M AGRIPPA L F COS III, head l., with rostral crown. *Rev.* S C, Neptune stg. l. As: 58/*C*3

— —Special honours to Caligula's three sisters.

12   AGRIPPINA DRVSILLA IVLIA, Three sisters, as Securitas, Concordia, and Fortuna, stg. facing. Ses: 33/*C*4; 41

38   Award of the title *pater patriae*

13   SPQR P P OB C/IVES S/ERVATOS in oak wreath. Aur; 27/*C*20. Den: 19/*C*19; 28/*C*21. Ses: 37/*C*24; 46/*C*25; 53/*C*26

39   Remission of the ½% sales tax.

14*a*   *Obv.* C CAESAR DIVI AVG PRON AVG, Pileus between S C. *Rev.* PON M TR P III P P COS DES III around REMISSA CC. Quad: 39/*C*5

14*b*   — — PON M TR P III/I COS TERT around R CC. Quad: 45/*C*6; 52/*C*7

14

CLAUDIUS

January 41–October 54

Tiberius Claudius Nero Germanicus was born at Lugdunum on 1 August 10 BC, the day the great altar was dedicated (*5*). He was the son of Nero Claudius Drusus and Antonia, grandson of Livia and Mark Antony, brother of Germanicus and uncle of Caligula. Because of frequent illnesses and a speech defect, he was generally left out of public life, but in 14 AD became priest of Divus Augustus (*10–11*). He gave a speech in the Senate on the fall of Sejanus, and another to congratulate Caligula on his accession in 37. He married Messalina in 39, and became the father of Britannicus in 41. When Caligula was murdered in January 41, the praetorians proclaimed the surprised and reluctant Claudius emperor in their camp in Rome (*1–2*); they favoured him as the son of Germanicus, and because of the generous bribe he offered. After brief resistance, he was recognised by the Senate which had hoped to restore the republic. They bestowed on him the now habitual *corona civica* (*3*), and the *clupeus virtutis* (*4*), no doubt with special significance, since Claudius had saved the lives of Roman citizens by ending the reign of Caligula.

Claudius proclaimed his intention to follow the policies of Augustus, and restored stability after the follies of Caligula. He received the title *pater patriae* (*7*) in January 42, and celebrated the long-delayed consecration of Livia (*8*), which Tiberius had refused. He also honoured Augustus and his own parents Drusus and Antonia (*9–11*). The same year saw victories in Germany (*12*), and the beginning of construction of the new port of Ostia, ultimately finished by Nero (*see* Nero *24*). In 43, the Roman legions began the conquest of Britain, which justified a triumph (*13–14*) in 44.

By this time, Messalina had given birth to three children (Messalina *1*), and a dynasty seemed firmly established, but the empress's debaucheries and open infidelity led to her execution in 48. Claudius then married his niece Agrippina; to cement the relationship, her son Nero was engaged to Claudius' daughter Octavia. In 50, Claudius made Agrippina Augusta (*15–16*) and adopted Nero (*17*; *see also* Nero *1–2*). To ensure the succession of Nero rather than Britannicus, Agrippina fed Claudius a dish of poisoned mushrooms, with fatal effect, in October 54.

41 Accession, with the support of the praetorians.
    1 IMPER RECEPT inscribed on battlements of praetorian camp, within

1   3

which soldier holding standard stands in gabled enclosure. Aur:
7/*C*40; 19/*C*42; 25/*C*43; 36/*C*45. Den: 8/*C*41; 20; 26/*C*44; 37/*C*46

2   PRAETOR RECEPT, Claudius clasping hands with praetorian. Aur:
11/*C*77; 23; 29/*C*80. Den: 12/*C*78; 24/*C*79

— —Recognition by Senate, with award of *corona civica* and *clupeus
virtutis*.

3   EX S C OB CIVES SEVATOS in oak wreath. Aur: 5/*C*33; 15/*C*34.
Den: 6; 16/*C*35. Ses: 96/*C*39; 112

4   (No legend), Flying Victory holding shield inscribed OB C S.
Avq: CNR XIV. 193

— —Celebration of the great altar of Lugdunum, perhaps on the occasion
of Claudius' fiftieth birthday.

5   ROM ET AVG, Altar of Lugdunum. Quad: 1/*C*81

41–43   (date uncertain). Reform of the coinage; details uncertain. The
letters on the scale apparently stand for Pondus Nummorum
Restitutum, 'Weight of the coins restored'.

6   *Obv.* TI CLAVDIVS CAESAR AVG around hand holding scales above
P N R. *Rev.* PON M TR P IMP (P P) COS DES IT (or COS II) around S C.
Quad: 85/*C*71; 89, 91/*C*73

42   Award of the title *pater patriae*.

7   SPQR P P OB S C in oak wreath. Aur: 40/*C*86; 48/*C*88; 50/*C*91;
53/*C*92; 59; 63/*C*95. 2Dr: 123/*C*76 (no SPQR). Den: 41; 49/*C*89;
54/*C*93; 60/*C*94; 64/*C*96

— —Consecration of Livia, with honours to Augustus and Claudius'
parents Nero Claudius Drusus and Antonia. The reverses of *10*
and *11* refer to Claudius' role as priest of Divus Augustus.

8   *Obv.* DIVVS AVGVSTVS, Radiate head r. *Rev.* DIVA AVGVSTA,
Livia std. 1. Dup: 101/*C*93

9   NERO CLAVDIVS DRVSVS GERMAN IMP, Triumphal arch. Ses: 98,
114/*C*48

10   *Obv.* ANTONIA AVGVSTA, Bust r. *Rev.* SACERDOS DIVI AVGVSTI,
Two torches. Aur: 67/*C*4. Den: 68/*C*5

11   — — TI CLAVDIVS CAESAR AVG P M TR P, Claudius, veiled stg. 1.,
holding simpulum. Dup: 92/*C*6

— —Victories in Germany.

12.   DE GERMANIS inscribed on triumphal arch surmounted by equestrian statue between trophies. Aur: 3; 35/*C*28. Den: 4/*C*27

44   Triumph for victories in Britain.
13   DE BRITANN on triumphal arch surmounted by equestrian statue between trophies. Aur: 30/*C*16; 33/*C*17; 44. Den: 34/*C*18; 45/*C*19
14   − − Claudius in triumphal quadriga l. 2Dr: 122/*C*15
50   Award of the title Augusta to Agrippina and adoption of Nero.
15*a*   AGRIPPINAE AVGVSTAE, Bust r. Aur: 80/*C*3. Den: 81/*C*4
15*b*   AGRIPPINA AVGVSTA CAESARIS AVG, Bust r. Cis: 117/*C*2
16   *Obv.* TI CLAVD CAESAR AGRIPP AVGVSTA, Jugate busts l. *Rev.* DIANA EPHESIA, Cult image of Diana. Cis: 119/*C*1
17   NERO CLAVD CAES DRVSVS GERM PRINC IVVENT, Bust r. Aur: 82/*C*4. Den: 83/*C*5

MESSALINA

Valeria Messalina, born about 25, was married to Claudius at an early age, and became the mother of Octavia, Britannicus and Antonia. Although made the head vestal, she became notorious for her debauchery and viciousness, and was responsible for the deaths of many members of the imperial family and aristocracy. She was finally executed in 48 for open adultery.

48 (?)   Celebration of the dynasty of Claudius.
1   OCTAVIA BRITANNICVS ANTONIA, Britannicus standing between Octavia and Antonia. 2Dr: 124

BRITANNICUS

Claudius Tiberius Britannicus, the son of Claudius and Messalina, was born about 41 and was originally named Germanicus. The Senate awarded him the new name to honour Claudius' conquest of Britain at the time of his birth. He was regarded as the heir to the imperial power until Claudius married Agrippina, by whom he was displaced in favour of her son Nero. Soon after his accession, Nero poisoned Britannicus at a banquet. For his coins, *see* Messalina *1* above.

AGRIPPINA the Younger

Julia Agrippina, born in 15, was the daughter of Germanicus and Agrippina the elder. In 28, she married Domitius Ahenobarbus; their son was Nero. Exiled by Caligula in 39, she was recalled by her uncle Claudius, who married her in 49 and made her Augusta (Claudius *15*) the following year. After poisoning Claudius in 54, she enjoyed a brief period of supremacy while her son was still a minor (Nero *4−5*), but fell from favour and was killed on his orders in 59.

NERO

Caesar 50/Augustus October 54−June 68

L. Domitius Ahenobarbus Nero Claudius Caesar was born in Antium in 37, the son of Domitius Ahenobarbus and Agrippina the Younger. He entered public life at an early age and rose rapidly after the marriage of his mother to Claudius. To secure his place in the succession, he was engaged to Claudius' daughter Octavia in 49 and finally adopted by Claudius in 50. When he donned the *toga virilis* in 51, Nero received great honour: he was consul designate, with tribunician power, *princeps iuventutis* (*1−2*), and was coopted by the Senate into the high priesthoods (*3*). He married Octavia in 53 and assumed supreme power when his mother had Claudius murdered in 54.

Nero was swiftly recognised by the Senate, who awarded him the now habitual *corona civica* (*4*), but remained firmly under the domination of his mother, whose image ostentatiously adorns the initial coinage (*4−5*). One of Nero's first acts was the funeral and consecration of his adopted father (*6−8*). He soon had to turn his attention to the East where the Parthians occupied Armenia. When Nero appointed Domitius Corbulo to defend Roman interests in the region, the Parthians withdrew and the grateful Senate awarded Nero the *clupeus virtutis* of Augustus (*9*). At that time or soon after he assumed the title of *pater patriae* (*10*).

Three activities dominated the reign of Nero and are clearly reflected in his coinage (which naturally neglects his notorious extravagances and cruelties): his great building projects; his wars, especially in the East; and his love of the arts. First of the buildings to be erected was a vast wooden amphitheatre in the Campus Martius, whose opening in 57 was apparently the occasion for a donative to the people (*11*). It was followed two years later by the great *macellum*, the market on the Caelian hill (*12*). Troubles continued in Armenia when the king of Parthia claimed the country for his brother in 58. The Romans responded in strength; Corbulo's victory near the Armenian capital in 58 was rewarded by celebration (*13*) and erection of a triumphal arch (*14*) in honour of the emperor. The arts were featured in the Neronia (*15*), a festival established in 60 on the model of the Olympic games, to be held every five years, with athletic and artistic competitions. This was presumably the occasion for a second donative (*16*) to the people, and honours to Apollo (*17*). Because of Nero's later extravagant artistic performances, the coinage which features Apollo playing the lyre was taken by contemporaries to represent the emperor himself in his favourite role.

In 61, when the great British revolt of Boadicea was suppressed by Paulinus, the Senate erected commemorative statues (*18−19*) showing the head of the vanquished enemy beneath the foot of Rome. By this time, Nero had freed himself of all restraint by murdering his mother, his tutors, and finally his wife Octavia. He married Poppaea Sabina (*20*) in 62 and began to indulge his artistic and other passions. In the middle of 64, his activities were interrupted by a devastating fire which destroyed a large part of Rome. The government had to undertake a massive and expensive programme of rebuilding (*21*), which included restoration of the sacred temple of Vesta (*22*) in the Forum. The following year, however, brought celebration, as peace was established on all the frontiers, and the temple of Janus, kept open when there was war anywhere in the empire, could ostentatiously be closed (*23*), for the first time since the reign of Augustus. The victory celebrations culminated when Tigranes of Armenia arrived in Rome in 66 to receive his crown from the hands of Nero.

Peace did not last, however, for in the next year a major revolt broke out in Judaea. Nero went to Greece where, far from making preparations for war, he indulged all his love of the arts in an extravagant tour which brought the finances of the empire near to ruin and reflected the emperor's lack of interest in practical affairs. When the pay of the troops fell behind, Julius Vindex, governor of Gaul, revolted. Although he was suppressed, his place was taken by Galba, governor of Spain. Loyalty to Nero rapidly collapsed, and when he was condemned by the Senate to a horrible death, he very reluctantly committed suicide.

As Caesar, under Claudius, 50−54

50 Adoption by Claudius and appointment as consul designate and *princeps iuventutis*; grant by the Senate of all the high priesthoods.
  1   COS DES PRINCI IVVENT on shield within laurel wreath. Cis: 121/*C*82
  2   EQVESTER ORDO PRINCIPI IVVENT on shield; spear behind. Aur: 78/*C*96. Den: 79/*C*97. Ses: 108/*C*99

2   14

  3   SACERD COOPT IN OMN CONL SVPRA NVM EX S C, *Simpulum* and *lituus* above tripod and patera. Aur: 76/*C*311. Den: 77/*C*312. Dup: 107

As Augustus, 54−68

54−55 Supremacy of Agrippina and award of *corona civica*.

4   *Obv.* AGRIPP AVG DIVI CLAVD NERONIS CAES MATER, Busts of Nero and Agrippina vis-à-vis. *Rev.* NERONI CLAVD DIVI F CAES AVG GERM IMP TR P around oak wreath enclosing S C. Aur: 1/*C*6; 3. Den: 2/*C*7

5   AGRIPPINA AVGVSTA MATER AVGVSTI, bust r., sometimes veiled 2Dr: 607–8/*C*1–2. Dra: 610–1.

54 Funeral and consecration of Claudius.

6   AGRIPPINA AVG DIVI CLAVD NERONIS CAES MATER, Images of Divus Claudius and Fides Praetorianum in quadriga drawn by elephants. Aur: 6/*C*3. Den: 7/*C*4

7   *Obv.* DIVVS CLAVDIVS AVGVSTVS, Head l. *Rev.* *Tensa*, or sacred chariot, of the god Claudius r., surmounted by four miniature horses flanked by Victories. Aur: 4/*C*31. Den: 5/*C*32

8   DIVOS CLAVD AVGVST GERMANIC PATER AVG, Head r. 2Dr: 613/*C*1; 619–20. Dra: 621/*C*3; 622

55 Award of *clupeus virtutis* for successes in Armenia.

9*a*   VICT AVG, Victory alighting l., holding round shield. Avq: 10/*C*336

9*b*   S C, Victory flying l., holding shield inscribed SPQR (struck 65–67). As: 312–16/*C*28–9, 297; 351–2, 368/*C*298–9; 473–8/*C*290–3; 540–8, 605–6/*C*302–3

——Award of the title *pater patriae*. This became the standard type for the following five years, with the date changing annually.

10   PONTIF MAX TR P II P P around oak wreath enclosing EX S C. Aur: 8/*C*204. Den: 9/*C*205

57 First donative, probably on completion of the amphitheatre in the Circus Maximus.

11   CONG I DAT POP, Donation scene with Nero, official, citizen and child; Minerva and Liberalitas in background. Ses: 151–5; 394, 434–5, 501–4/*C*68–70

59 Completion of the new market, *Macellum Augusti*, on the Caelian hill.

12*a*   MAC AVG, Domed building surrounded by porticoes. Dup: 109–111/*C*357; 373–4/*C*127; 399–402/*C*128–9

12*b*   —— with mark of value, II, in exergue. Dup: 184–9/*C*130

58 Victories of Corbulo in Armenia.

13   ARMENIAC, Victory advancing r. 2Dr: 615. ½Dr: 616/*C*32

14   S C, Elaborately decorated triumphal arch. Ses: 143–150, 392–3, 432–3, 498–500/*C*306–310

60 Establishment of the quinquennial festival, the Neronia, with a donative and honours to Apollo, patron of the arts.

15*a*   CER/TAM/EN QVINQuennale ROM/AE constitutum, Decorated table bearing urn and wreath. Sem: 91–2, 228–30, 486–8, 559–63/*C*49–57, 60, 65

15*b*   —— with mark of value S above table. Legend variously abbreviated. Sem: 231–248, 427–8/*C*47–8, 58–9, 61–4

16*a*   CONG II DAT POP R, Type as *11*. Ses: 100–1, 156–7, 576/*C*72–7

17*b*   23

16*b* CONG II DAT POP, Donation scene with Nero, prefect, attendant and citizen; Minerva and tetrastyle building in background. Ses: 102, 158−62, 505−6/*C*78−81

17*a* PONTIF MAX TR P IMP P P, Apollo r., in flowing robes, playing lyre. As: 77−82, 414−17, 451−5/*C*196−202

17*b* — — with mark of value, I, in exergue. As: 205−12, 384−5/ *C*203

17*c* As 17*a*, but no legend. As: 73−6/*C*354

61 Victories of Paulinus in Britain, suppressing the revolt of Boadicea, celebrated with commemorative statues erected by the Senate. The second type, 17, may refer to the victories of Corbulo in Armenia.

18 PONTIF MAXIM TR P VII (VIII, VIIII, IX) COS III P P EX S C, Virtus (or Roma) stg. l. with foot on head of enemy wearing crown with points; pile of weapons beside. Aur: 25/*C*129; 31/*C*225; 36/ *C*229; 40/*C*232. Den: 26/*C*220; 32/*C*226; 37; 41/*C*233

19 — — Roma stg. r., holding round shield, foot on head of enemy; pile of weapons beside. Aur: 27/*C*221; 33/*C*227; 38/ *C*230; 42/*C*234. Den: 28/*C*222; 34; 39/*C*231; 43/*C*235

62 Marriage with Poppaea.

20 AVGVSTVS AVGVSTA, Nero stg. beside Poppaea. Aur: 44, 56/*C*42. Den: 45, 57/*C*43

64−8 Rebuilding of Rome after the great fire.

21*a* ROMA, Rome std. l. (several varieties). Aur: 54/*C*257. Den: 55, 65/*C*258; 70/*C*259. Ses: 272−82, 329−36, 356−7, 360−1, 398, 442−3, 515−17, 590−4/*C*260−2, 264−71, 273−8, 284−5. Dup: 292−8, 343−5, 363, 365/*C*263, 279−83, 286

21*b* — — Rome std. r. Ses: 358−9, 369/*C*287. Dup: 364

21*c* PON/TIF MA/X TR P/OT IMP P P, Same type. Sem: 88, 90, 222−3, 424−6, 479−85, 549−58/*C*189, 193−5

21*d* — — with mark of value, S, before head. Sem: 221/*C*178; 224−5/*C*331; 226−7/*C*332

21*e* — — No legend or mark of value. Sem: 89

— — Rebuilding of temple of Vesta commenced; it was finished by Vespasian (*see* Vespasian 52−4).

22 VESTA, Round hexastyle temple. Aur: 61/*C*334. Den: 62/*C*335

65 Closing of the temple of Janus, symbol of universal peace.

    23a PACE P R TERRA MARIQ PARTA IANVM CLVSIT, Temple of Janus, with door variously to r. or l. Aur: 50, 58/*C*114. Den: 51. Ses: 263−71, 323−8, 353−5, 438−9, 510−12, 583−5/*C*133−4, 136−40, 143−5, 152, 154−5, 158−62. Dup: 283−8, 337−8/ *C*135, 150−1. As: 300−5, 421, 468−72, 537−9/*C*132, 141−2, 147−9, 153, 156−7

    23b PACE P R VBIQ PARTA IANVM CLVSIT, Same type. Dup: 289−91, 339−42, 362/*C*165−6, 169−70. As: 306−11, 347−50, 366−7/ *C*163−4, 167−8, 171−6

65 (Date uncertain). Completion of the new harbour at Ostia, begun by Claudius.

    24a AVGVSTI POR OST, View of the port of Ostia with surrounding buildings and ships within, and reclining god Tiber; several varieties. Ses: 178−83/*C*33−41

    24b − − PORT AVG SC. Ses: 440−1, 513−4, 586−9/*C*250−4

THE CIVIL WARS

March 68−January 69

The incompetence and misgovernment of Nero eventually provoked a revolt led in March 68 by the propraetor C. Julius Vindex, who had his base in Lugdunum. Since he was descendant of a Gaulish royal family which had only received Roman citizenship in the previous generation, he could not hope for supreme power himself, and therefore called on Galba, the governor of Spain, to free the human race from the tyrant Nero. Meanwhile, Vindex had rapid success in Gaul, raising an army reputed to number 100,000, and throwing Rome and Nero into a panic. The inhabitants and legions of the Rhine, however, refused to take his side, and loyal troops commanded by Verginius Rufus defeated and killed Vindex in May.

The coinage of this revolt (*1−11*), which shows that it was neither a native Gaulish uprising nor undertaken to restore the republic, indicates a desire for constitutional imperial government, and features the slogans of the rebels. Although in a sense all the coins of the wars could be considered historical, only those which reflect the propaganda or base of the revolt are included here. A related series of coins with similar slogans (*12−19*) is associated with mints in Spain, and was evidently issued in that province before Galba, who supported Vindex, assumed the title of imperator in April 68.

During the revolt of Vindex, another province fell away from Nero, when the governor of Africa, Clodius Macer, threw off his allegiance to Nero in April 68 (*see* below).

A third series of anonymous coins (*20−27*) may be associated with a later stage of the civil wars, the revolt of Vitellius which began on

1 January 69 when the legions of Upper Germany refused to renew their oath of allegiance to Galba. The soldiers revolted in the name of the Senate and People of Rome, but soon proclaimed their general, Vitellius, as emperor. At first he refused the imperial title, until it could be conferred on him by the Senate. One series of these coins features legions involved in the revolt — the 15th of Castra Vetera in Lower Germany, and the First Italica, based at Lugdunum — which played a major role in Vitellius' success. The latter, though not named, is indicated by its distinctive boar's-head standard (*RIC* 201*f*. offers a different interpretation of this coinage). Another major series features the loyalty of the armies and the praetorians, as well as their concord, and was evidently intended as propaganda to suborn the praetorians loyal successively to Galba and Otho. All these coins may be dated to the early months of 69.

68 The revolt of Vindex, March—May 68. Coins struck in Gaul, bearing the slogans of the rebels.

1   *Obv.* PAX ET LIBERTAS, Clasped hands holding caduceus. *Rev.* SIGNA P R, Aquila between standards. Den: 57

2   — — *Rev.* SPQR in oak wreath. Den: 58/*C*424

3   *Obv.* ROMA RESTITVTA, Helmeted bust r. *Rev.* IVPPITER CONSERVATOR, Jupiter std. l. Den: 60—1/*C*370

4   — — *Rev.* IVPPITER LIBERATOR, Same type. Den: 62/*C*374

5   — —*Rev.* SIGNA P R, Type as 1. Den: 63

6   *Obv.* SALVS GENE/R/IS HVMANI, Victory stg. on globe. *Rev.* SPQR (OB C S) in oak wreath. Aur: 71/*C*419. Den: 68; 69/*C*428; 72—3/*C*420—1; 74/*C*423; 77

6a — — *Rev.* SIGNA P R, Types as 1. Den: 70

7   — — *Rev.* MARS VLTOR, Mars advancing r. Den: 67/*C*409

8   *Obv.* SALVS GENERIS HVMANI, Victory stg. r., inscribing V on shield. *Rev.* SPQR (OB C S) in oak wreath. Den: 75/*C*422; 76

9   *Obv.* SALVS GENERIS HVMANI, Winged Nemesis adv. r. *Rev.* SPQR in oak wreath. Den: 74/*C*423

10 *Obv.* SALVS ET LIBERTAS, Helmeted female figure stg. l. *Rev.* SPQR in oak wreath. Aur: 65/*C*417. Den: 66/*C*418

11 — — *Rev.* SIGNA P R, Type as 1. Den: 64/*C*411

— —Support for Vindex in Spain, coins struck March—April 68, with reference to the provinces in revolt, and further slogans. Type 9 refers to the mineral wealth and mints of Spain, the sources of money to finance the revolt.

12 *Obv.* CONCORDIA HISPANIARVM ET GALLIARVM, Busts of Hispania and Gallia vis-à-vis. *Rev.* VICTORIA P R, Victory in biga r. Den: 15

13 *Obv.* HISPANIA S C, Bust r. *Rev.* SPQR in angles of spears crossed over shield. Den : 135/*C*429

14 *Obv.* HISPANIA, Bust r. *Rev.* MARTI VLTORI, Mars stg. facing. Den: 23/*C*375

15 *Obv.* MONETA, Bust of Juno Moneta r. *Rev.* SALVTARIS, Cap of Vulcan above anvil with hammer and tongs (equipment for striking coins). Den: 30/*C*402

16   *Obv.* LIBERTAS RESTITVTA, Bust r. *Rev.* SPQR on round shield in oak wreath. Aur: 26/*C*430

17   *Obv.* LIBERTAS, Bust r. *Rev.* RESTITVTA, Pileus between two daggers (reminiscence of the EID MAR coin of Brutus). Den: 24−5/*C*394−5

18   *Obv.* ROM/A RENASC/ES, Roma stg. r., holding Victory. *Rev.* BON/I EVENT, Bust r. Aur: 8/*C*397. Den 11/*C*400

19   *Obv.* ROMA VICTRIX, Roma stg. l. *Rev.* SALVS PVBLIC, Bust r. Den: 36/*C*401

69   The revolt of Vitellius: the legions, with slogans and appeal to the praetorians of Rome.

20   *Obv.* GALLIA, Bust r. *Rev.* FIDES: Clasped hands holding standard decorated with boar's head [standard of Legio I Italica]. Den: 131/*C*361

21   *Obv.* LIBERTAS RESTITVTA, Bust r. *Rev.* CONCORDIA, Concord stg. l., holding standard with boar's head. Den: 132/*C*358

22   − − *Rev.* MARS ADSERTOR, Mars stg. facing holding boar's head standard. Den: 133/*C*376

23   *Obv.* ADSERTOR LIBERTATIS, Head of Mars r. *Rev.* LEGION XV PRIM, Victory stg. r. Den: 130

24   *Obv.* FIDES EXERCITVVM, Clasped hands. *Rev.* CONCORDIA PRAETORIANORVM, Concord stg. l. Den: 118/*C*359

25   *Rev.* CONCORDIA PROVINCIARVM, Same type. Den: 119/*C*360

26   − − *Rev.* FIDES PRAETORIANVM, Clasped hands. Den: 121/*C*363

27   − − *Rev.* VESTA P R QVIRITIVM, Bust r. Den: 126/*C*364

24   Macer 1

CLODIUS MACER

April−September/October 68

L. Clodius Macer, the propraetor of Africa and commander of the Legion III Augusta based in Numidia, revolted against Nero in April 68, relying on the strength of his position and fleet, and his ability to cut off the grain supply of Rome. He rebelled in the name of the Senate, raising a new legion, I Macriana, and attempting to extend his control over Sicily, but was murdered on the orders of Galba after he assumed power in Rome.

68   Honours to Africa and to its Third Legion, Macer's main support. 'Liberatrix' in these types refers to Africa as the hoped source of liberation for Rome, and appears on the reverse as the by-name of both Legions III and I.

1*a*   *Obv.* L CLODI MACR/I LIBERA/TRIX S C, Bust of Africa r. *Rev.* LEG III AVG LIB, Aquila between two standards. Den: 1−4/C7, 3

1*b*   — — *Rev.* LEG I LIB MACRIANA. Den: 5−6/C8

2*a*   *Obv.* L C/LODI MACRI S C, Lion's head r. *Rev.* As previous. Den: 7−11/C5

2*b*   — — *Rev.* LEG I LIB MACRIANA. Den: 12

3   *Obv.* L CLODI MACRI S C, Bust of Victory r. *Rev.* as 1*a*. Den: 13−18/C4

4   *Obv.* L CLODI MACRI S C, Libertas stg. r. (probably the badge of the new legion). *Rev.* As 1*b* and 2*b*. Den: 19−21/C1−2

— —Advertisement of Macer's position as governor.

5   PROPRAE AFRICAE, Warship r. (details vary). Den: 34−42/C12−13

— —Honours to Macer's capital and advertisement of his claims to Sicily.

6   *Obv.* L C/LODI MACRI CARTHAGO S C, Bust of Carthage r. *Rev.* SICILIA, Head of Medusa over triskeles. Den: 22−29/C10−11

GALBA

Imperator April 68/Augustus June 68−January 69

Servius Sulpicius Galba, scion of an ancient Republican family which claimed to trace its ancestry to Jupiter (*2*), was born at Terracina in 3 BC. He was a favourite of the empress Livia (*14*) under whose influence he rose early to high office and who left him a considerable sum in her will. Consul in 33, he successfully governed Germany and Africa, receiving the *ornamenta triumphalia* and the friendship of Caligula and Claudius. Nero named him governor of Hispania Tarraconensis, where he received news of the revolt of Gaul while he was holding court in New Carthage (*1*). Upon receiving letters from Vindex which called on him to be liberator of the human race, he accepted leadership of the revolt. He was much encouraged by the priest of Jupiter at Clunia, who discovered an ancient oracle which announced that the ruler of the world should come from Spain. It was there that he assumed the title imperator and moved actively against Nero (*2−3*). At first, he refused the title Augustus in deference to the Senate who alone could confirm it (*16*), but assumed full imperial rank when news arrived of the death of Nero. He was swiftly recognised by the Senate (*15*).

The coinage of Galba's revolt features the propaganda slogans of the civil war (*10−13*; cf. *17−18*), his devotion to Livia (*14*) which gave him a connection with the house of Augustus, and the provinces of Spain and Gaul (*4−9*), the bases of the revolt. In reward for their help, he cancelled the 2½% customs duty which had prevailed at the provincial borders (*19−23*). As Augustus, Galba continued to strike these types, adding advertisement of his piety toward the Senate (*16*) and toward the Julian *gens* into which he got himself adopted (*24*). There is naturally no mention of the parsimony and cruelty which rapidly destroyed his popularity and led to his murder by the troops after only four months in the capital.

Imperator, April–June 68

68 Revolt of Galba. Several of these types (indicated by *) continued to be struck after Galba became emperor, and bear the title Augustus rather than imperator.

– – Commemoration of his speech in Cathago Nova accepting leadership against Nero.

    1   ADLOCVTIO, Galba on platform with officers addressing troops. *Ses: 462–8/C1–6

– – Receipt of favourable prophecy in Clunia and acceptance of the title *imperator*. In this type, Galba is seated in the presence of the city goddess because he is figured in the guise of his ancestor Jupiter.

    2   HISPANIA CLVNIA SVLpicia, Stg. female figure (Clunia) presenting Palladium to seated Galba. *Ses: 469–73/C86–8

    3   IMP, Galba riding r. Aur: 227/C96. Den: 145; *156/C94; 228/C97

– – Support of the provinces, especially Spain and Gaul.

    4   CONCORDIA PROVINCIARVM, Concord stg. l. Aur: 104, *117, *119, *181–2/C37, 41–2. Den : 35, 49, 54, *118, *120, 125 (PROVINCIA), 126, *149, *180, *183/C31–6, 38–40

    5   GALLIA HISPANIA, Gaul and Spain clasping hands. Aur: 17. Den: 15/C73; 16; 18; 109; *154

        5   9

    6*a*   HISPANIA, Spain stg. l. Aur: 20; *192; *225. Den: 19–21/C80; 50; *144; *155/C82; *190–1/C83; *193; *226/C85

    6*b*   – – Bust r. Den: 1–3/C75–7; 86, 515/C78

    7*a*   *Obv.* SER GALBAE HISPANIA, Bust of Spain r. *Rev.* S P Q R in angle of two spears crossed under round shield. Den: 516

    7*b*   – – but *obv.* legend SER SVLPICI GALBAE IMP A. Den: 517/C283

    7*c*   – – SER SVLPICIVS GALBA. Den: 518

    8   GALLIA, Bust of Gaul r. Den: 85/C72

    9   TRES GALLIAE, Three busts r. Den: 89–92

– – Propaganda slogans of the Civil War.

    10*a*   LIBERTAS RESTITVTA, Libertas stg. l. Aur: 8/C134. Den: 9/C135

    10*b*   – – Head l. Den: 7/C132

11   ROMA RENASC/ENS, Roma stg. l. or r. When struck by Galba
       as Augustus, this type probably also commemorated the con-
       tinuing rebuilding of Rome after the great fire. Aur: 24; 40/
       C196; *58; 87; *194; *198; *201–3. Den: 25–9/C209–10;
       41–3/C196; *57/C197; 88/C215; 95/C213; *160–2/C201;
       *195–7; *199–200/C100; *204; *229–30/C208
12   ROMA VICTRIX, Roma stg. l. Aur: 44, *59/C222, 224. Den: 45,
       53, *60/C221, 223
13   SALVS GENE/RIS HVMANI, Salus sacrificing over altar. Aur:
       *146–7, *206, *208, *212, *213, *231/C232–3, 235, 237,
       239. Den: 96–7, *171–2, *205, *207, *209–11, *214, *232/
       C234, 236, 238, 240
– –   Honours to Livia, and advertisement of Galba's connection with
       the family of Augustus. 14b was the major type of Galba's silver as
       emperor, when he felt a continuing need to proclaim this association.
14a   AVGVSTA, Livia std. l. *Ses: 331–8/C11–12; 432
14b   DIVA AVGVSTA, Livia stg. l. *Aur: 55; 142/C46; 184/C54; 188;
       223/C57. Den: 13–14/C43–4; 36/C45; *52/C48; *143/C47;
       *150–3/C52–3; *185–7/C55–6; *189; *224/C58. *As: 65–7/
       C49–50

Augustus June 68–January 69

– –   June: Recognition of Galba by the Senate.
15a   SPQR OB C/IV/ES S/ER/VATOS in oak wreath. Aur: 61, 163–5,
       169/C286. Den: 62, 166–8, 170/C285, 287–8. Ses: 259–72,
       317, 404–10, 454–5/C289, 295, 297, 300–3, 305. Dup: 286–
       90, 416–19/C296, 298–9, 304

15a

15b   (EX S C) OB CIVES SER/VATOS in oak wreath. Ses: 385–6, 434–
       5/C59–62
– –   Celebration of the respect for the Senate which kept Galba from
       assuming the imperial title without its consent.
16   SENATVS PIETATI AVGVSTI, Genius of the Senate crowning stg.
       Galba who holds Victory. Ses: 489/C280

— — Realisation of war propaganda by restoration of freedom and of Rome. Type *17* may also have reference to restoration of a famous statue of Libertas in the city and *18* to the rebuilding of Rome, and perhaps to the establishment of a charity for children.

17 LIBERTAS RESTITVTA, Galba raising kneeling Libertas; Roma stg. in background. Ses: 479−80/*C*135−7

18 ROMA RESTI, Galba raising kneeling Roma, who holds child. Ses: 485/*C*219−20

— — Winter. Abolition of the 2½% customs duty, a reward to Gaul and Spain for their support. The captives on type *20* probably represent financial officials of Nero who plundered the province and denounced Galba. Types *21−23* are those of the regular coinage struck for use in the western provinces.

19 XXXX REMISSA, Galba crowned by victory stg. in triumphal arch surmounted by quadriga. Ses: 134/*C*348

20 QVADRAGENS/VMA/E REMISSA/E, Three captives followed by officer advancing toward triumphal arch. As: 77−84/*C*165−7

21 AVGVSTA R XL, Livia std. l. Ses: 433

22 LIBERT/AS AVG/VST R XL, Livia stg. l. Ses: 438−41/*C*102, 104. As: 293, 296, 327, 422/*C*98−9, 103

23 ROMA R XL, Rome stg. l. Ses: 450/*C*194

— — Adoption of Galba into the Julian family.

24 PIETAS AVGVSTI, Pietas sacrificing at altar decorated with image of Aeneas, Anchises and Iulus (the altar of the Julian *gens*). Ses: 483/*C*160

— — Rebuilding of the temple of Honos and Virtus, completed by Vespasian (Vespasian *51*).

25 HONOS ET VIRTVS, Honos and Virtus stg. facing each other. Ses: 474−8/*C*89−92

OTHO

January−April 69

No historical types.

VITELLIUS

Imperator January 69/Augustus April−December 69

Aulus Vitellius, born in 12 AD, was the son of L. Vitellius, one of the leading statesmen of the early empire (*see* following section). He grew up on Capri and rose to high office through the influence of his father and his close connections with the imperial court. He was consul in 48, held the high priesthoods (*9*) and was made governor of Lower Germany by Galba in 68. When the troops renounced their allegiance to Galba on 1 January 69, they turned to Vitellius, who assumed leadership of the revolt (*1−5*;

cf. Civil Wars *21−28*), though refusing the imperial title; he was content to call himself Germanicus and imperator. He soon gained the allegiance of Gaul, Spain and Britain. Meanwhile, Galba was murdered and Otho proclaimed in his place; consequently the army of Vitellius marched against him rather than its original adversary, crossed into Italy and won a decisive victory between Cremona and Verona in April 69.

The Senate then recognised Vitellius, with all the customary honours. He entered Rome in July, but almost immediately had to face the revolt of Vespasian, to which he reacted with remarkable passivity. Forces loyal to Vespasian soon entered northern Italy, and won a major victory at Cremona in October. Vitellius held out in Rome until December when he made an agreement with Fl. Sabinus, brother of Vespasian, to abdicate. The people and praetorians, however, refused to accept the proposal. Sabinus was forced to withdraw to the Capitoline, where he was besieged and killed, with great damage to the buildings, and Vitellius was obliged to remain emperor until the forces of Vespasian arrived and put him to death on 20 December. His coinage celebrates his far more distinguished father (*10−11*), as well as the son (*12*) whom he hoped would eventually succeed him.

Imperator, January−April 69

69 Revolt of Vitellius: propaganda stressing the loyalty of the rebel troops and appeal to the praetorians, with celebration of Spain. Much of the coinage of this period was anonymous: *see* Civil Wars *20−27*.

1 CONSENSVS EXERCITVVM, Mars advancing l. Aur: 4−5; 22/*C*23; 26; 49/*C*27; 64 (struck as Augustus). Den: 6; 20−1; 23/*C*24; 24−5; 48; 50−1. As: 40/*C*25

1 9

2*a* FIDES EXERCITVVM, Clasped hands; sc in exergue. Aur: 52/*C*30. Den: 47 (no sc); 53/*C*31; 54; 67/*C*36. As: 42/*C*34
2*b* FIDES EXERCITVVM in two lines. Den: 27−30/*C*32−3
,3 CONCORDIA PRAETORIANVM, Concordia stg. l. Den: 19/*C*22
4 FIDES PRAETORIANVM, Clasped hands. Den: 55/*C*37
5 CONSENSVS HISPANIARVM, Hispania stg. l. As: 41/*C*29

Augustus April—December 69

69　Recognition by the Senate: award of *corona civica* and *clupeus virtutis*.

6　SPQR OB C/IV S/ER in oak wreath. Aur: 82/*C*85. Den: 69A; 83/*C*86. Ses: 122, 159/*C*87

7　VICTORIA AVGVSTI, Victory adv. 1., holding shield inscribed SPQR. Aur: 61. Den: 62—3. As: 46

8　— — Victory inscribing OB CIVES SER on shield affixed to palm tree. Ses: 123/*C*94

— —Celebration of Vitellius' past: his priesthoods and his distinguished father.

9　XV VIR SACR FAC, Dolphin above and raven below tripod with lebes. Aur: 85, 108/*C*113. Den: 70, 86, 109/*C*111—12, 114—16

10　L VITELLI/VS COS III CENSOR, Bust of L. Vitellius r., in consular robes. Aur: 7/*C*1 (III COS); 76—7/*C*3; 98. Den: 99/*C*2

11*a*　— — L. Vitellius std. l. in consular robes. Aur: 94, 96/*C*54. Den: 95, 97/*C*55.

11*b*　L. VITELL CENSOR II, Same type. Ses: 114, 134—5/*C*53

— —The future of Vitellius: his children, by whom he hoped to found a dynasty.

12　LIBERI/S IMP GERMAN/ICI, Busts of Vitellius' son and daughter vis-à-vis. Aur: 8/*C*8; 78, 100, 102/*C* 1, 3, 6. Den: 57, 79, 101, 103/*C* 2, 4—5, 7

LUCIUS VITELLIUS

L. Vitellius, father of the emperor Vitellius, was closely connected with the family of Augustus. He married Antonia Minor, daughter of Octavia, and rapidly rose to high office. In 18, he led Roman forces in Armenia, and in 34 held his first consulate. He settled problems in Judaea by deposing the procurator Pontius Pilate in 37, and in the next year became governor of Syria. His greatest successes came under Claudius, whom he flattered obsequiously. He shared the consulate with the emperor in 43 and was left in charge of Rome during Claudius' campaigns in Britain. He was censor with Claudius in 49, and maintained his high position at court until his death in 51. His influence was responsible for the rise and success of his less able son whose coins celebrate the father (Vitellius *9—11*).

VESPASIAN

July 69—June 79

Titus Flavius Vespasianus was born in the Sabine country of Italy in November, 9 AD. Through the influence of his brother who was a senator, he entered on a public career, rising to a successful command in Britain under Claudius. During the reign of Nero, he fell from favour until the outbreak of the great Jewish revolt, in which the whole country rose against the Romans and inflicted severe defeats on them, caused the emperor to entrust the war to him. With the assistance of his son Titus, he assembled a large army and moved on the offensive in 67. In two campaigning seasons, he recovered the whole country except Jerusalem, winning in the process a naval victory (*40*) on the Sea of Galilee. News of the civil war and proclamation of Galba, however, caused operations to be suspended.

Vespasian was reserved toward Galba, recognised Otho, but became an enemy of Vitellius, whose success, achieved by the German legions, was resented by the troops of the East. The officers in Judaea and the governor of Egypt proclaimed Vespasian emperor (*1–2*) on July 69 and he soon attracted the allegiance of the entire Roman East, as well as Spain (*3–5*). He swiftly named his sons Titus and Domitian as Caesars (*6–10*), clearly stating a dynastic policy which might bring stability. He made Antioch his headquarters, and there struck his first coins. Vespasian's forces soon reached Italy, and by the end of the year Rome was in his hands and Vitellius was dead. The Senate recognised Vespasian as emperor in December, awarding the full imperial honours and granting high rank to his sons (*11–15*). During the fighting, however, Vespasian's brother, who had led resistance from the Capitoline, was killed and the buildings there were destroyed by fire.

The first year of the reign was marked by serious problems: a native chief, Civilis, led a revolt in Gaul which threatened Roman rule. His forces defeated the legions on the Rhine and captured their standards, but after a long campaign led by Domitian, the standards were recaptured (*41*). The Sarmatians invaded Moesia, and the Jewish war continued. During this time, Vespasian stayed in Alexandria, while Titus pursued the siege of Jerusalem. Finally, in the autumn, Vespasian arrived in Rome (*16–18*) where his victories were celebrated (*20–21*) and he received the civic crown (*19–20*) and the titles *pater patriae* and 'restorer of liberty (*19, 22–23*). The grateful Senate also commemorated the goodwill which he showed towards them (*24*). He designated his sons as consuls (*25*) for the next year, and embarked on a programme of reform of the government.

Vespasian was especially active in rebuilding Rome, still largely ruined after the great fire of 64 (*26–27*). He devoted particular attention to the Capitol, where the site of the temple of Jupiter Optimus Maximus was reconsecrated in July 70; the temple itself was rebuilt by about 75 (*28*). Other reconstructions included the temple of Vesta in the Forum (*52–54*) and that of Honos and Virtus by the walls (*51*). The greatest of Vespasian's constructions was a new forum, adjacent to the Forum of Augustus. Beside the temple of Peace (*57*), dedicated in 75, it contained colonnades and numerous outstanding works of ancient art (*58–59*), some brought from Greece, others taken from Nero's demolished palace.

Titus captured Jerusalem in October 70, a victory which brought the Jewish war to a close, and re-established Roman rule (*29–40*). Peace was now universal, the temple of Janus was closed, and the mood of the time was reflected in a large series of coins which figure the goddess Pax (*42–43*). In 71 Titus returned to Rome (*46–47*) to celebrate a splendid triumph with his father (*48–50*) for the victory which was long commem-orated in the coinage, and by the triumphal arch still standing in the Roman Forum. In the same year, he was designated as *imperator* (*45*), effectively being named co-ruler, while Domitian was given a second consulate. Vespasian now devoted himself to reforming the army and establishing colonies. Trouble soon broke out in Britain, however, and Roman forces were occupied there for some years. In the East, on the other hand, an easy victory was gained when the king of Commagene was deposed and his kingdom annexed to the empire in 72. Internal reforms were also important, among them the reorganisation of the Senate and introduction of many new members from the provinces which Vespasian carried out as censor in 73 (no special types, but mentioned in the obverse legends).

The rest of the reign saw many events of universal interest: wars on the eastern frontier and in Britain, the end of Jewish resistance in Judaea and suppression of outbreaks in Egypt and Cyprus, extension of the empire and expansion of the citizenship, internal reforms and suppression of conspiracies. The coinage, however, reflects none of these, but continues to celebrate earlier events or to portray stock types, mentioning only the successive consulates of the emperor (*55–56, 60, 62*) and the award of the *clupeus virtutis* (*61*) by the Senate in 77.

Some of the early issues of Vespasian imitate types of Galba, whose memory he honoured. Types *23* and *51* are taken directly from Galba's coinage, while *22* and *26* reflect the slogans of the civil wars whose aims were now realised, and *24* uses a Galban image with a different legend to show the continuing reverence of the emperor for the Senate.

69 June Proclamation of Vespasian as emperor.
1   TR POT COS, Vespasian and his sons in quadriga r. Aur: 273
2   IMPER, Vespasian galloping l. Den: 271/*C221*
— — Revolt and success of Vespasian, based on the support of the armies, and of Spain, which was rewarded by a grant of citizenship.
3   CONSEN/SVS EXERCIT/VS, Two soldiers clasping hands. Den: 259/*C78*; 284/*C79*; 305–6/*C78*
4   CONSENSVS EXERCITVVM, Mars advancing l. Den: 225
5   HISPANIA, Hispania stg. l. Aur: 256/*C201*
— — Foundation of a dynasty: proclamation of Titus and Domitian as Caesars. Some of these types were struck until 73.
6   IMP T CAESAR inscribed on shield resting on crossed spears. Aur: 369
7a   IMP T FLAVIVS CAESAR AVG F, Head of Titus r. Aur: 351/*C6*; 351*a*

7*b*   T FLAVIVS VESPASIANVS CAESAR, Head r. Aur: 352

7*c*   IMP CAES VESP AVG P TRI P COS II, Head of Titus r. Aur: 357/ C2−5; 357*a*

8*a*   LIBERI IMP AVG VESPAS, Facing heads of Titus and Domitian. Den: 313−14/C10−11; 321/C1; 330/C2

8*b*   − − Titus and Domitian stg. facing. Den: 315/C248; 322/C249; 331/C250

      8*b*   28

9   CAESARES VESP AVG FILI, same type. Aur: 3/C52; 270/C570.

10*a*   CAE DVM ET T CAES IMP VESPAS, Head of Titus r. Aur: 359/C1

10*b*   − − Facing heads of Titus and Domitian Aur: 358/C8, 9

− −December. Recognition of Vespasian by the Senate, with grant of full honours, including the priesthoods, and of Titus and Domitian respectively as consul and praetor.

11*a*   AVGVR PON MAX, Priestly implements. Den: 1/C41; 29/C42

11*b*   AVGVR TRI POT, Same type. Den: 30/C43; 42/C45; 80 (struck in 74).

12   T ET DOM C EX S C, Titus and Domitian std. facing each other on platform; two togate figures between. Ses: 404/C533; 404*a*

13*a*   TITVS ET DOMITIANVS PRINC IVVEN, Titus and Domitian riding r. Aur: 27

13*b*   T/ITVS ET DOMIT/IAN CAESARES PRINC IV/(V)EN, Titus and Domitian riding r. (preceded by foot-soldier on Ses). Aur: 292, 292*a*/C538. Ses: 390/C534. As: 391/C535

14   − − Titus and Domitian std. l. Aur: 24/C540; 293/C543−4. *Den: 25−26a*/C542, 545

15   CAESAR AVG F COS CAESAR AVG F PR, Facing heads of Titus and Domitian. Aur: 2/C4. Den: 2/C5; 283/C6. As: 386/C12

70   Arrival of Vespasian in Rome, with sacrifice to Fortuna Redux. Type *18* was repeated for the arrival of Titus in 70 (*see 46 below*) and frequently later in the reign, apparently without topical significance.

16   IMP V P P COS II DESIG III, Rome greeting Vespasian. Aur: 265/C209

17   ROMA ET AVGVSTVS COS ITERVM TRIBVN POT, Rome presenting Victory to Vespasian. As: 385/C422

18*a*   COS ITER FORT RED, Fortune stg. l. Aur: 4/C83; 276/C81. Den: 4/C84; 31; 276/C82; As: 387/C85

18*b*   FORTVNAE REDVCI, Same type. Ses: 402/*C*185; 409/*C*186
—— Celebration of Vespasian's victories, with award of the *corona civica* and of the title *pater patriae*; restoration of liberty, and establishment of good relations with the Senate.
19*a*   SPQR in oak wreath. Aur: 66/*C*515. Den: 57/*C*517; 66/*C*516
19*b*   OB CIVES SERVATOS around oak wreath. Den: 17/*C*275
19*c*   SPQR (P P) OB C/IV/ES S/ER/VATOS in oak wreath. Aur: 298. Den: 291/*C*525. Ses: 457–9, 592/*C*528–31; 737. Dup: 651/*C*265. As: 547/*C*527
19*d*   EX S C OB CIV SER in oak wreath. As: *Kraay (1976)* 49.
20   VICTORIA AVG/VSTI, Victory inscribing OB CIV SER on shield attached to palm tree (*cf* Type *39b*). Ses: 464/*C*591–2; 466/*C*621–3
21   VICTORIA IMP VESPASIANI, Victory stg. l. on globe. Den: 268/*C*630–1
22   SPQR ADSERTORI LIBERTATIS PVBLIC/AE in oak wreath Ses: 411/*C*518; 455–6/*C*519–22
23*a*   LIBERTAS RESTITVTA, Vespasian raising kneeling female; Roma stg. behind. Ses: 430/*C*262
23*b*   —— Libertas stg. l. Den: 290/*C*261
24   CONCORDIA SENATVI, Vespasian crowned by Genius of the Senate. Ses: 418/*C*76
—— Titus and Domitian designated as consuls.
25   IMP AVG F COS DESIGN II CAESAR AVG F COS DESIG, Facing heads of Titus and Domitian. As: 412/13 (*see Kraay 1976*, 50)
—— Rebuilding of Rome.
26   ROMA RESVRGE(N)S, Vespasian raising Rome. Aur: 310/*C*427. Den: 310. Ses: 407/*C*424; 445/*C*424; 520/*C*426; 735/*C*425
27   ROMA, Rome std. reclining on the seven hills; wolf and twins below, Tiber in front. Ses: 442/*C*404–5
—— Reconsecration of the site of the temple of Jupiter on the Capitoline. The type was repeated 74–77, probably to celebrate completion of the reconstruction.
28   S C, Hexastyle temple. Ses: 452/*C*490; 553/*C*491; 577/*C*488; 591/*C*493 750/*C*491. As: 496/*C*486; 765/*C*489
—— Fall of Jerusalem and defeat of the Jewish revolt, commemorated in a long series of coins struck until the end of the reign.
29*a*   IVDAEA, Judaea std. mourning at foot of trophy. Aur: 15/*C*225. Den: 15/*C*226; 34/*C*228; 45; 254; 266/*C*226; 288/*C*227
29*b*   —— As previous, but hands tied behind back. Aur: 16; Den: 16/*C*229
29*c*   —— As previous, but palm tree in background. Aur: 287/*C*230; Den: 287/*C*231
30   IVDAEA CAPTA, Judaea std. mourning under palm tree, behind which stands Vespasian. Ses: 427/*C*239; 733
31   —— Judaea mourning under palm behind which stands Jewish captive with hands tied. Ses: 424–6/*C*232–8

30

40

32 IVD/AEA CAP/TA, Judaea std. at foot of palm tree, mourning; weapons around As: 393/*C*224; 489/*C*244; 490/*C*246−7 (IVDEA); 491/*C*245 (IVDEA); 595/*C*240; 596 (IVDEA); 762/*C*240

33 IVDAEA DEVICTA, Judaea stg. with hands tied before palm tree. Den: 289/*C*243

34 DEVICTA IVDAEA, Victory inscribing SPQR on shield attached to palm tree below which Judaea sits mourning. Ses: 419/*C*142

35 DE IVDAEIS, trophy. Aur: 301/*C*139. Den: 301/*C*140

36 (No legend), Judaea seated mourning before palm tree; Vespasian stg. on r. Den: 41a; 363/*C*645

37 S C, Vespasian stg. with foot on prow; suppliant Jew and Jewess at his feet; palm tree behind. Ses: 525/*C*479

38 VICTORIA AVGVSTI, type as 17. Aur: 53/*C*644

39a − − Victory inscribing shield attached to palm tree; Judaea std. mourning below. Ses: 397/*C*627; 468/*C*625−6, 628

39b − − Victory inscribing OB CIV SER on shield. Ses: 467/*C*624

40 VICTORIA NAVALIS, Victory stg. on prow. Dup: 481/*C*633; 745/*C*636. As: 503/*C*632−4; 551/*C*637; 562/*C*638; 601/ *C*639; 767/ *C*639

− − Defeat of revolt of Civilis and recapture of the legionary standards.

41 SIGNIS RECEPTIS, Victory flying r., offering an aquila to Vespasian who stands l. on platform. Ses: 461/*C*510−12

− − Universal peace established.

42 PAX AVGVSTI, Vespasian raising woman who wears a mural crown. Aur: 356/*C*322

43 PACI ORB TERR AVG, Bust r., with mural crown. Aur: 334/ *C*293. Den: 317−18/*C*291−2; 324/*C*289; 327; 334/*C*294; 338

71 Third consulate of Vespasian.
    44*a* cos III, Vespasian in quadriga r. Ses: 524/*C*476; 536/*C*477
    44*b* s c, Same type. Ses: 451/*C*475
——Designation of Titus as *imperator* and Domitian as consul for the second time.
    45 CAES AVG F DES/IG IMP AVG F COS DES/IG IT/ER s c, Titus and Domitian stg. facing each other. Ses: 413−15/*C*46, 50
——June. Return of Titus to Rome.
    46 COS III FORT RED, Fortuna stg. l. Aur: 11/*C*98; 280/*C*96. Den: 11/*C*99; 281/*C*97; 299.
    47 NEP RED: Neptune stg. l., foot on globe. Aur: 35/*C*272. Den: 361/*C*274
——Triumph of Vespasian and Titus for the victory in Judaea, and celebration of the temple of Isis in which they spent the night before the triumph.
    48 TRIVMP AVG, Triumphal procession: Vespasian in quadriga, trumpeter, captive etc. Aur: 294/*C*567
    49*a* VICTORIA AVGVSTI, Vespasian in quadriga r. Aur: 54/*C*642. Den: 54/*C*643
    49*b* IMP, Same type. Aur: 44
    49*c* (No legend), same type. Den: 364/*C*643
    50 s c, Tetrastyle temple of Isis with semicircular pediment. Ses: 453/*C*484; 537/*C*485
——Restoration of the temple of Honos and Virtus, destroyed by fire.
    51 HONOS ET VIRTVS, Honos and Virtus stg., facing each other. Ses: 423/C202−3
73 Dedication of the temple of Vesta, rebuilt after the great fire under Nero.
    52*a* VESTA, Round temple with statues. Aur: 59/*C*582; 69/*C*578; 580; 304/*C*581. As: 547/*C*578; 659/*C*351; 705/*C*615
    52*b* s c, Round temple with four columns. Ses: 736/*C*485
    53 VESTA, Vesta stg. l. Den: 40/*C*572; 50/*C*574; 60/*C*575
    54 —— Vesta std. l. Dup: 567n.

    52   57

74 Fifth consulate.
    55 PON MAX TR P COS V, Vespasian std. r. Den: 76−7/*C*363−4
75 Sixth consulate.
    56 PON MAX TR P COS VI, Vespasian std. r. Den: 94/*C*365
——Dedication of the temple and Forum of Peace, with its collection

of works of art, including bronze statues of cows by Myron and Phidias.

57 PON MAX TR P COS VI/I, Peace, naked to waist, std. l., holding branch (the cult image in the temple). Den: 90/*C*366; 101, 101A/*C*373−4

58 COS V/II, Heifer advancing r. with head outstretched (the heifer of Myron). Aur: 71/*C*105; 96/*C*117. Den: 71/*C*106

59 COS VII, Cow stg. r. (the cow of Phidias). Aur: 97/*C*116. Den: 96/*C*118

77 Eighth consulate.

60 COS VIII, Vespasian crowned by Victory. Aur: 105/*C*130

— —Award of the *clupeus virtutis* by the Senate.

61 S C, Victory advancing l., holding shield inscribed S P Q R. Dup: 743/*C*465; 757/*C*466−8. As: 599, 599A/*C*466−7

79 Ninth consulate.

62 COS VIIII, type as 60. Aur: 112/*C*138

DOMITILLA the Elder

Flavia Domitilla, descendant of an Etruscan family with Roman citizenship, married Vespasian and became the mother of Titus, Domitian and Domitilla. She died before Vespasian became emperor, and neither gained the title Augusta nor was consecrated, but coins were struck in her memory (Titus *29*).

DOMITILLA the Younger

Flavia Domitilla, daughter of Vespasian and Domitilla, also died before Vespasian became emperor. She was consecrated and coins were struck in her memory (Titus *30*).

TITUS

Caesar 69/Imperator July 71/Augustus June 79−September 81

Titus Flavius Vespasianus, who bore the same name as his father but was known unusually by his *praenomen*, was born in 39, and raised and educated at the imperial court. After his first military distinction in Germany at the age of twenty, he rose through the normal civic offices. Great fame came after Vespasian put him in charge of a legion for prosecuting the Jewish war. When Nero was killed, Titus was sent to Rome as an emissary to Galba, but he, too, was killed before Titus could arrive. Titus then returned to the East, where he played an active role in his father's proclamation as emperor, and in the continuing war in Judaea.

Titus was consul for the first time in 70 with Vespasian, and, when his father left for Rome, assumed control of the operations in Judaea, which he brought to a successful conclusion by the capture of Jerusalem in September (*1–8*), an event which was celebrated as the beginning of an era of peace (*9*). He returned to Rome (*11–12*) in June 71 to celebrate a great triumph (*13*) with Vespasian, who in the following month gave him the title imperator and the tribunician power, thus making him co-ruler (*10*). He held this power constantly from 71, was consul most years (*17, 20*), and assumed the office of censor in 73. In 72, he gave his first donative (*14*) to the people; the occasion is unknown. His coinage as Caesar, like that of his father, also celebrates the rebuilding of Rome (*15–16, 18–19*).

In 79, Titus was awarded the *clupeus virtutis* (*21*), and in the same year celebrated the consecration of Vespasian (*24–29*) and of Domitilla the younger (*30*), as well as the memory of his mother Domitilla (*31*), who was apparently not consecrated. The year 79 saw notable victories in Britain and the disastrous eruption of Mount Vesuvius, which caused the emperor to stay a considerable time in Campania to help restore the region. While Titus was away, a devastating fire destroyed much of the monumental centre of Rome, and the city was struck by the plague. As a result, the senate decreed a special supplication to the gods in the form of a *sellisternium*, (*33–36*) where a banquet was served in the company of images of the gods set out on thrones. Late in the year the new Colosseum, begun by Vespasian, was dedicated (*37–38*), the occasion for celebrations and games (*39*). In the summer of 81, Titus set out for the Sabine country where he fell ill and died of a fever in September. He was rumoured to have been poisoned by his brother Domitian.

Caesar, 69–71

(*See also* Vespasian *6–10, 12–15, 25, 45.*)

70 Victory in Judaea.
1   IVDAEA DEVICTA, Victory writing IMP T CAES on shield attached to palm. Aur: 373/*C*119
2   IVDAEA CAPTA, Judaea std. mourning under palm, behind which stands Titus (Vespasian *30*). Ses: 608/*C*113
3   IVD/AEA CAP/TA, Judaea std. mourning under palm behind which stands Jewish captive (Vespasian *31*). Ses: 91–3/*C*108–9, 111, 114. As: 128/*C*115
4   – – Judaea std. mourning under palm; some variation (Vespasian *32*). As: 620/*C*116; 653; 784/*C*117–18. Sem: 141/*C*112
5   (No legend), Judaea std. mourning before palm tree; Emperor stg. on r. (Vespasian *36*). Aur: 160/*C*391. Den: 367/*C*392
6   S C, Titus stg. with foot on prow; two Jews kneel at his feet; palm tree on l. Ses: 638/*C*234

7 — — Judaea std. mourning below palm; weapons around. Sem: 812/*C*225

8 VICTORIA NAVALIS S C, Victory stg. on prow (Vespasian *40*). As: 627/*C*387; 662/*C*386; 789—90/*C*388—9

— —Universal peace established.

9 PACI ORB TERR AVG, Bust r. (Vespasian *43*) Den: 343/*C*127

Co-ruler with Vespasian, 71—79

71 Designation of Titus as imperator and Domitian as consul for the second time.

10 CAESAR DOMITIAN COS DES II, Domitian riding r. Ses: 605/*C*27; 628/*C*28; 635/*C*29

— —June. Return of Titus to Rome.

11 FORTVNAE REDVCI, Fortuna stg. l (Vespasian *18b*). Ses: 607/*C*43; 643

12 NEP RED, Neptune stg. l., foot on globe (Vespasian *47*). Aur: 155/*C*120. Den: 155/*C*121; 366/*C*122

— —Triumph for victory in Judaea.

13 (No legend), Titus in quadriga r. or l. Aur: 159/*C*393—4. Den: 163; 368/*C*395. Ses: 612/*C*228; 629/*C*229, 231; 637/*C*230, 645/*C*226, 232. As: 658/*C*227

72 First donative; occasion unknown.

14 CONGIAR PRIMVM P R DAT, Donation scene with Titus, attendant, citizen and Minerva. Ses: 606/*C*46

73 Rebuilding of temple of Jupiter on the Capitoline.

15 S C, Hexastyle temple of Jupiter. Ses: 681/*C*243; 102/*C*244 (struck 80); As: 656a/*C*242

— —Rebuilding of temple of Vesta in the Forum.

16 VESTA, Round temple with statues (Vespasian *52*). Aur: 157/*C*350; 162/*C*349; 171/*C*347—8; 180

74 Third consulate.

17 PONTIF TR P COS III, Titus stg. l. Den: 174/*C*161

75 Dedication of the Forum of Vespasian, with the temple of Peace and ancient works of art.

18*a* PONTIF TR P COS IIII, Peace std. l. (Vespasian *57*). Den: 185/*C*162

18*b* PON MAX TR P COS VI, Same type. Den: 200/*C*154

19 COS V, Cow of Myron (Vespasian *58*) Aur: 187—9/*C*51, 53—4. Den: 187/*C*52

79 Seventh consulate.

20 TR POT VIII COS VII, Titus in quadriga l. Den 207/*C*333

— —Award of *clupeus virtutis* by the Senate.

21 S C, Victory stg. l., holding shield inscribed SPQR. Aur: 81/*C*206

Sole ruler, 79–81

79   Succession to the throne, through the foresight of Vespasian.
    22   PROVIDENT AVGVST, Vespasian presenting globe to Titus. Ses: 97–8/*C*178–180
    23   s c, Titus on horseback, receiving Palladium from Rome. Ses: 104/*C*223–4
——Funeral and Consecration of Vespasian
    24   DIVVS (AVGVSTVS) VESPASIAN/VS, Vespasian std. l., wearing radiate crown. Aur: 32/*C*72. Ses: 144–6/*C*206–8
    25   DIVO AVG VESP SPQR, Statue of Vespasian in quadriga of elephants. Ses: 143/*C*205
         (The following all have obverse DIVVS AVGVSTVS VESPASIANVS, head r.)
    26   EX s c, *Tensa* or chariot of the god Vespasian. Aur: 60/*C*145. Den: 60–61/*C*146–7
    27   EX s c, Victory placing shield on trophy; captive std. at foot. Aur: 59/*C*143. Den: 59*a*, *b*/*C*144

27   33

    28   EX sc, Shield resting against cippus on which stands urn; laurels on either side. Aur: 62/*C*148. Den: 62/*C*149
    29   s c on shield supported by two capricorns; globe below. Aur: 63/*C*496. Den: 63/*C*497
——Consecration of Domitilla the younger, sister of Titus, with honours to the memory of Domitilla the elder, his mother.
    30   *Obv.* DIVVS VESPASIANVS AVGVSTVS, Head r. *Rev.* DIVA DOMITILLA AVGVSTA, Bust r. Aur: 69/*C*1. Den: 69/*C*2
    31*a*   *Obv.* IMP T CAES DIVI VESP F AVG P M TR P P P COS VIII around s c. *Rev.* MEMORIAE DOMITILLAE SPQR, Carpentum drawn by two mules. Ses: 153/*C*1
    31*b*   —— Same type, *Rev.* legend DOMITILLAE IMP CAES VESP AVG SPQR. Ses: 154/*C*3
80   Eighth consulate.
    32   s c, Titus in quadriga r. Ses: 101/*C*233
——*Sellisternium* to supplicate the gods to remove the plague.
    33   TR P IX IMP XV COS VIII P P, Winged thunderbolt (of Jupiter) on draped table. Aur: 23/*C*315. Den: 23/*C*316
    34   —— Ears of wheat (of Ceres) on throne. Aur: 24/*C*312. Den: 24a, b/*C*311, 313
    35*a*   —— Dolphin (of Neptune) below curule chair. Den: 27A

35*b*   — — Dolphin on tripod. Aur: 27/*C*320, 322. Den: 27/*C*321, 323

36   — — Wreath on two curule chairs. Aur: 25/*C*317. Den: 25/*C*318−19

— —   Dedication of the Colosseum and accompanying games.

37   s c, The Colosseum, with the Meta Sudans on r. Ses: 110/*C*400

37

38   — —, The Meta Sudans. Dup: 115−*C*246

39   TR P IX IMP XV COS VIII P P, Elephant. Aur: 22/*C*300−2. Den: 22−3/*C*303−4

DOMITIAN

Caesar 69/Augustus September 81−September 96

T. Flavius Domitianus, the younger son of Vespasian, was born in Rome in October 51. When his father was proclaimed emperor, Domitian became Caesar and *princeps iuventutis* (*1*), and was designated praetor (Vespasian *15*) for 70 and consul (Vespasian *25*) for 71. After escaping from the fire on the Capitoline, he administered Rome until Vespasian arrived in the summer of 70. He shared the command of the war against Civilis in Gaul, rode in the triumph of Vespasian and Titus (*5*) in 71, and was consul in 72 (Vespasian *45*; Titus *10*), but generally had little power or responsibility under Vespasian. Titus, similarly, failed to give him the tribunician power, but shared the consulate with him in 80, and clearly indicated him as successor to the throne. His types as Caesar thus generally repeat those of his father and brother.

As Titus lay dying, Domitian hastened to the praetorian camp in Rome, and was proclaimed emperor. He proceeded to consecrate Titus, an event celebrated in an unusually small and rare series of coins (*10*) and to dedicate the arch in the Roman Forum, which honoured the Jewish victories, to his memory. He carried out much other construction in Rome, including the rebuilding of the temple of Jupiter on the Capitoline (*11, 42*), recently destroyed by fire. The same fire had consumed the temple of Juno Moneta, home of the Roman mint. Coin production was therefore moved to a new site near the Colosseum, whose opening in about 84 was celebrated by an extensive series of coins (*25*) featuring the first appearance of Moneta Augusti, who was to become a stock type. Domitian also completed construction of his father's Forum of Peace (*27*) early in his reign.

In 82, he married Domitia, and made her Augusta; they soon had a son, but he died in infancy and was consecrated (Domitia *1−2*). The early years of the reign were marked by the victories of Agricola in Britain, which led Roman troops into the highlands of Scotland and gave Domitian an additional proclamation as imperator (*23*). Far greater, though, were the Roman victories in Germany, led by the emperor himself. The Chatti were severely defeated and the Roman frontier extended beyond the Rhine. The victories were marked by the award of the title Germanicus, a triumph celebrated with great festivities, the erection of a triumphal arch (*22*) and an abundant series of coins (*12−20*), which were struck for several years. After the war, Domitian raised the pay of the troops by a third, to 300 denarii (*24*). Like his father and brother, Domitian held the office of censor, but in December 85, assumed it in perpetuity (*26*), an unprecedented action which foreshadowed the extravagant autocracy which was to mark the reign.

The greatest celebration of the reign was that the Secular Games in 88 (*28−36*), when circus races and sacrifices marked the return of the *saeculum*, calculated from the celebration by Augustus in 17 BC. Further troubles in Germany followed with the revolt of Saturninus and his legions. Domitian set out for the frontier, only to find that the revolt had been suppressed before he arrived. He proceeded from there to a large-scale campaign against the Marcomanni, Quadi and Dacians which resulted in major victories, establishment of firm control over the northern frontier, and a triumph (*37−38*) in 89.

Domitian had great military success, defeating the Germans and Sarmatians by 92, and annexing parts of Germany and Transjordan; but none of these events found a place in the coinage. Meanwhile, relations between emperor and Senate were deteriorating; conspiracies were frequent and executions and confiscations widespread, recalling the worst days of Tiberius or Nero. Domitian also scandalised Rome by carrying on an open affair with his niece Julia, whom he consecrated after her death from an abortion in 91 (*39−40*). Finally, the hated emperor succumbed in 96 to a conspiracy organised at court with the help of his wife Domitia.

Domitian was an enthusiastic builder whose projects transformed the face of Rome. A series of coins struck toward the end of the reign, perhaps in commemoration of its fifteenth anniversary, feature some of his monuments: the temple of Minerva (*43*), the triumphal arch for the German wars (*22*), an equestrian statue erected in the Forum in 91 (*47*), and a shrine within the magnificent Domus Flavia (*41*), part of the palace on the Palatine which was greatly enlarged. He also restored the temple of Serapis (*44*), the temple of the deified emperors (*45*) and the shrine of the Great Mother, Cybele (*46*). With the exception of the temples, the commemorative buildings of Domitian perished in the general *damnatio memoriae* which the Senate in vengeance inflicted upon his name.

Caesar, 69–81

69 Proclamation as Caesar and *princeps iuventutis*, a title celebrated on the coinage for several years.
   1   PRINC/EPS IVVENT/VTIS, Domitian on horseback, galloping l. or r. Cis: 76/*C*373 (struck by Titus). As: 697/*C*400; 711/*C*401 (PRINCIP); 716/*C*402; 728/*C*388 (*See also* Vespasian *8–10*, *12–15*.)
70 Designation as consul. (*See* Vespasian *25*.)
——Victory in Judaea.
   2   VICTORIA NAVALIS S C, Victory stg. r. (Vespasian *40*). As: 692/*C*636; 707/*C*637
——Birthday of Domitian, celebrated by Titus in the East with games.
   3   IMP T CAES AVG on shield. Aur: *Strauss* (1985)
——Universal peace established.
   4   PACI ORB TERR AVG, Bust r. (Vespasian *43*) Den: 350/*C*337
71 Designation as consul for the second time. (*See* Vespasian *45* and Titus *10*.)
——Triumph for victories in Judaea.
   5   S C, Domitian in quadriga r. As: 688/*C*476; 700/*C*477
72 Rebuilding of temple of Jupiter Capitolinus (Vespasian *28*).
   6   S C, Hexastyle temple. As: 689/*C*533; 703/*C*534; 793 (struck 77)
73 Rebuilding of the temple of Vesta.
   7   VESTA, Round temple with statues (Vespasian *52*). Aur: 230/*C*614. As: 690/*C*616; 705/*C*615
79 Consecration of Vespasian.
   8   DIVO VESP, Lighted altar with panel in front. Cis: 75/*C*95
80 *Sellisternium* to supplicate gods against the plague.
   9   PRINCEPS IVVENTVTIS, Helmet (of Minerva) on throne. Aur: 47/*C*398. Den: 47/*C*399

Sole emperor, 81–96

81 Consecration of Titus.
   10   DIVO AVG T DIVI VESP F VESPASIANO, Titus, radiate, std. l.; altar in front. Ses: 437–8/*C*98–9
82 Rebuilding of temple of Capitoline Jupiter after second fire.
   11   CAPIT RESTIT, Tetrastyle temple with statues and decoration. Cis: 222/*C*23
83 Victories and conquests in Germany.
   12   S C, Domitian riding, spearing fallen German. Ses: 257/*C*483; 284/*C*484; 317/*C*485; 344/*C*486–7; 361

13   s c, Domitian stg. with German kneeling at his feet holding shield. Ses: 258/*C*488; 285/*C*489; 318/*C*490

14   s c, Domitian stg., with Rhine reclining below. Ses: 259/*C*503; 286/*C*504; 319/*C*505; 345/*C*506; 362/*C*507; 389/*C*508

14   29

15   s c, Domitian and general clasping hands over altar, escorted by two or three soldiers. Ses: 260/*C*496; 288/*C*497; 320−1/*C*498, 502; 346/*C*499; 402/*C*500

16*a*   s c, Domitian stg., crowned by Victory. Ses: 322/*C*510; 347/*C*511; 363/*C*512; 390/*C*513; 403/*C*514; 415/*C*515

16*b*   — — As previous, with Minerva stg. by Domitian. Ses: 404/*C*516

17   s c, Victory inscribing DE GER on shield set on trophy; captive at feet. Ses: 255/*C*469; 282/*C*470; 315/*C*471; 359/*C*475

18   s c, Trophy between std. captives. Dup: 266/*C*539

19   GERMANIA CAPTA, Trophy between seated Germania and standing German captive; weapons on ground. Ses: 252/*C*135; 278/*C*136; 312; 341/*C*137

20*a*   IMP VIIII (or XI or XII or XIII or XIIII) COS XI (or XII or XIIII) CENS POT P P, Germania std. on a shield in an attitude of mourning; broken spear below. Aur: 72/*C*188 (VIIII . . .XI); 77/*C*199 (XI. . . XII); 83/*C*206 (XII. . .XII); 90/*C*211, 103/*C*224 (XIII. . .XII); 111/*C*291 (XIIII. . .XIIII) Den: 69/*C*177 (VIIII . . .XI); 103/*C*226 (XIII. . . XII)

20*b*   GERMANICVS COS XIIII, Same type. Aur: 127/*C*148

— —Sacrifice of thanks to Domitian's patron goddess Minerva, in her shrine in the Palace.

21   s c, Domitian sacrificing in front of shrine. Ses: 256/*C*491; 283/*C*492; 316/*C*493; 343/*C*495; 360/*C*494

— —Erection of a triumphal arch to celebrate the victories.

22   s c, Triumphal arch with two arches crowned by quadrigae of elephants. Ses: 261/*C*530; 391/*C*672 (struck 90); 416/*C*531 (struck 96)

84 Triumphs in Britain, with award of the title *imperator* for the seventh time.

23   P M TRIB P IMP VII P P, Horseman attacking enemy; decapitated corpse below. Ses: *Kraay (1960)* 109

— — Increase in military pay by giving a new 'imperial' *stipendium*, in addition to the three already existing.

24   STIP AVG DOMITIAN S C, Domitian addressing troops. Ses: *Kraay (1960)* 114

— — Establishment of a new mint to replace that in the temple of Juno Moneta; first appearance of Moneta Augusti. This type was struck until the end of the reign.

25   MONETA AVGVST/I, Moneta stg. l., holding scales and cornucopiae. Dup: 327/C328; 350/C330. As: 242A/C323; 248/C324; 301/C326; 337; 354/C329; 372/C331; 387A; 395/C332; 408/C333; 423/C334

85   Assumption of a perpetual censorship.

26   IMP XIIII COS XIII CENSOR PERPETVVS P P around S C. Dup: 357/C231

86   Completion of the Forum of Peace (alternatively, restoration of the Augustan Ara Pacis).

27   PACIS, Altar on steps flanked by priests. As: 336/C338

88   Secular Games: types portray the announcement; the distribution of purifying incense (*suffimenta*) to the people; reception of grain (*fruges*) from them; sacrifice of an ox to Jupiter (first day) and a black sheep and goat to the Moerae (first night); prayer of matrons to Juno, dictated by the Emperor; procession of children in honour of Apollo and Diana (third day); and sacrifice of a black sow to Terra Mater (third night).

Unless noted, all have the legend COS XIIII LVD SAEC (FEC).

28   Cippus in wreath. Aur: 115/C69. Den 115/C70−1

29   Herald stg. or advancing; legend inscribed on cippus on l. Aur: 119/C75. Den 116−17/C73−4, 76−7. Qui: 118/C78. Dup: 380/C72

30   Legend adds SVF P D, Domitian std. on platform gives fumigants to citizen accompanied by child; temple in background. Ses: 376/C81

30

31a

31a   Legend adds A POP FRVG AC, Two citizens offering fruges to Domitian std. on platform Ses: 375/C82

31b   — — Domitian and citizens hold paterae over vessels on platform. Ses: 375a/C83

32a   Domitian sacrificing over altar; on l., victimarius with goat and lamb (or ox); musicians on r.; temple of Jupiter Stator in background. Dup: 365/C88; 381−2/C87, 89. As: 386/C90

32b   Similar, but no victimarius. As: 385/C85−6

33   Domitian dictating prayer to three kneeling matrons; temple in background. Ses: 377/C80

34   Three children in procession before Domitian and togate companion. Ses: 379/C79

35   Domitian sacrificing over altar; Tellus reclining on l.; victimarius with sow on r.; musicians in background. Ses: 378/C84

36   Domitian sacrificing over altar; Tellus (or Tiber) reclining and musicians stg. on r.; wooden theatre in Campus Martius in background. Dup: 383/C91. As: 387/C92

89   Victories over German and Dacian tribes, and triumph.

37   GERMANICVS COS XIIII (or XV or XVI), Domitian in quadriga l. Aur:
128/C146 (XIIII); 165 (XV); 185/C161 (XVI). Den: 165/C155 (XV)

38   GERMANICVS COS XV (XVI or XVII), Germania std. in attitude of mourning. Aur: 164/C156 (XV); 184/C163 (XVI); 202/C169 (XVII)

91   Consecration of Julia, niece and mistress of Domitian.

39   *Obv.* DIVA IVLIA (AVGVSTA), Diademed bust r. *Rev.* (AVGVSTA), Image of Julia in biga of elephants. Aur: 219−20/C1, 19

40   DIVAE IVLIAE AVG DIVI TITI F SPQR, Carpentum drawn by two mules. Ses: 400/C9; 411/C10

95   The buildings of Domitian, celebrated on the fifteenth anniversary of his reign. (*See also 11, 22, 25, 27.*)

41   (No legend), Distyle temple containing throned image; Victories or warriors before temple l. and r. (Probably a shrine within the temple of the Gens Flavia in the palace.) Aur: 203/C671. Ses: 413/C522

42   IMP CAESAR, Temple of Jupiter Capitolinus, rebuilt. Den: 207/C174

43 IMP CAES, Round Temple of Minerva, built by Domitian. Den: 206/*C*171
44 — — Temple of Serapis in the Campus Martius, rebuilt by Domitian. Den: 204/*C*172
45 IMP CAESAR, Temple of the Deified Emperors on the Palatine, rebuilt. Den: 208/*C*175
46 IMP CAES, Shrine of the Magna Mater (Cybele) in the Circus Maximus, rebuilt. Den: 205/*C*170
47 S C, Equestrian statue of Domitian r. Ses: 414/*C*482

47

JULIA, daughter of Titus

Julia, the daugther of Titus and Marcia Furnilla, born in 64, was given the title Augusta by her father, and seduced by her uncle Domitian while Titus was still alive. She was married to her cousin Fl. Sabinus, who was consul in 82 and killed by Domitian a few years later. Thereafter, Domitian lived openly with Julia until she died from an abortion in 90. She was consecrated in the following year (Domitian *39–40*).

DOMITIA

Domitia Longina, daughter of Nero's most famous general Domitius Corbulo, born between 50 and 55, was taken from her first husband by Domitian, first as his mistress, then his wife after 70. Their son, who was perhaps called Vespasian, was born in 73 and died in infancy. He was consecrated after Domitian became emperor (*1–2*). Domitia's infidelities, which reputedly included a liaison with Titus, caused her repudiation and exile, but she was taken back by Domitian after the death of Julia. She helped to organise the plot which killed Domitian in 96, and long survived him, living in great wealth until *c.* 140.

73 (Coins struck 81–3). Death and consecration of the infant son of Domitian and Domitia.
  1 DIVVS CAESAR IMP DOMITIANI F, Baby boy std. on globe. Aur: 213/*C*10. Den: 213/*C*11

2   DIVI CAESAR/IS MATRI (or MATER), Domitia std. l., extending r. hand to child who stands facing her. Ses: 440−1/C6−8

NERVA

September 96−January 98

M. Cocceius Nerva, born in 30, had a distinguished career, receiving the *ornamenta triumphalia* under Nero and serving as consul in 71 and 94. When Domitian was murdered, the conspirators raised the elderly jurist to the throne (*1*). He gave a donative, addressed the troops (*2−3*), took measures against informers and recalled the victims of Domitian, whose memory was condemned to oblivion. From the beginning, the reign was troubled by plots and the hostility of the praetorians, whose fondness for Domitian eventually forced Nerva to surrender his murderers. He sought the favour of the troops (*4*; significantly, the commonest of his types), and finally gained security in October 97 by adopting the governor of Upper Germany, Ulpius Traianus, whose legions provided a firm military base for the regime. Trajan succeeded to the throne without opposition when Nerva died four months later.

In domestic policy, Nerva was concerned to correct the excesses of Domitian and to reduce the burdens of the citizens, especially of the poor, as far as possible. To this end, he established a distribution of free grain in Rome (*5*), lent money to farmers at low rates of interest, instituted endowments for the support of poor children (*6*), and took over the cost of maintaining the imperial post (*7*), which had formerly fallen on the municipalities. His generosity extended to other than Italians when he abolished the system of false accusation which had been abused by Domitian in collecting the special tax imposed on the Jews (*8*) to support the temple of Jupiter Capitolinus.

96 Accession, by choice of the Senate, with donative and address to the troops.

    1   PROVIDENTIA SENATVS, Nerva, holding globe, facing Genius of the Senate. Ses: 90/*C*129

    2   CONGIAR P R, Distribution scene with Nerva, officer and citizen; statues of Minerva and Liberalitas in background. Ses: 56/*C*37; 57/*C*39

    3   ADLOCVT AVG, Nerva on platform addressing troops; temple in background. Ses: 50/*C*1

−−Efforts to secure the good will of the praetorians (who nevertheless remained hostile).

    4   CONCORDIA EXERCITVVM, Clasped hands. Aur: 2/*C*15; 14/*C*19. Den: 2/*C*16; 14/*C*20; 26/*C*22. Ses: 54. As: 53/*C*17; 69/*C*18; 79/*C*21; 95/*C*23.

    4*b*   −− Clasped hands holding aquila on prow. Aur: 3/*C*24; 15/

C28; 27/C33. Den: 3/C25; 15/C29; 27/C34. Ses: 54; 70/C27; 80/C30; 96/C35. Dup: 55/C26; 81/C32; 97/C36. As: 80/C31

97 Free distribution of grain established in Rome.

    5   PLEBEI VRBANAE FRVMENTO CONSTITVTO, Modius containing wheat ears and poppy. Ses: 89/C127; 103

—— Charity for poor children.

    6   TVTELA ITALIAE, Nerva std. l., extending r. hand to Italia; boy and girl between them. Ses: 92/C142

—— Assumption of costs of imperial post by the government.

    7   VEHICVLATIONE ITALIAE REMISSA, Two mules grazing, shafts and harness behind. Ses: 93/C143; 104/C144

—— Abolition of system of collecting the Jewish tax.

    8   FISCI IVDAICI CALVMNIA SVBLATA, Palm tree. Ses: 58−9/C54−5; 72/C56; 82/C57

8

TRAJAN

Caesar October 97/Augustus January 98−September 117

Marcus Ulpius Traianus was born in the Roman colony of Italica in Spain in 53 AD, the son of a successful general and statesman (*see* below). From the age of nineteen, he spent many years in the military, gaining both considerable experience and the respect and loyalty of the troops. He then rose in public life to become consul in 91 under Domitian, a reward for his valuable role in the German campaigns. During the reign of Nerva he was governor of Germania Superior, and was engaged in improving the frontier defences when he was chosen as Nerva's adopted son and successor (*1*) in October 97.

Trajan remained on the frontier, where the situation demanded his presence, even after he became sole emperor (the first not of Italian birth) in January 98. Assured of the loyalty of his troops (*2−3*) and of the Senate, which awarded him the *corona civica* and the *clupeus virtutis* (*4−5*), he ordered the consecration of Nerva (no coins at the time; *64*), and continued his work of pacification of the German frontier (*6*). From there he proceeded to the Danube, taking measures to ensure the security of the Roman provinces against possible aggression from the Dacians, and paving the way for future advances. Trajan finally entered Rome in 99 where, as one of his first acts, he gave a generous donative to the troops and the people, with magnificent games (*7*). In the following year (or possibly in 103), he was awarded the title *optimus princeps* (*9–10*), which appears on the majority of his coins.

Trajan's first years in Rome were occupied with building projects in the city – a triumphal arch (*8*) in honour of the German campaigns was completed and a major rebuilding of the Circus Maximus begun – and in the provinces, where military works and roads attracted as much attention as civic buildings. Work was especially active in the Danube region in preparation for the invasion of Dacia which began in 101. The emperor led the army in person and in the course of two campaigns crushed the Dacian power, establishing Roman garrisons beyond the Danube, and reducing the rest of Dacia to a vassal state. He returned to Rome where his victories (*12–16*) earned him the title *Dacicus* (*11–12*), and celebrated a triumph (*11*), marked by another donative (*17*) to the people, gladiatorial contests and other entertainment, as well as a triumphal arch on the Capitoline dedicated to Jupiter the Greatest and Best (*18*).

In 103, during Trajan's fifth consulate (*19*), the rebuilding of the Circus Maximus (*20*) was completed and other projects continued, but the government's main efforts were directed to the north where the Dacian king Decebalus failed to maintain the terms of the treaty; his massacre of the Roman garrisons in 105 provoked a new and more decisive war. This time, a bridge (*21*) was built across the Danube (*22–23*), and the army marched deep into the Dacian heartland. The capital Sarmizegethusa was taken with its accumulated treasures and Decabalus was driven to suicide in despair. His head was cut off and brought to Rome to be displayed (*39–41*). A new province was added to the empire, Roman control of the north coast of the Black Sea was assured, and the whole frontier given greater security. This great victory was the occasion for another triumph (*24*) and for a vast coinage (*25–38*), which continued for several years, some of it struck to celebrate the tenth anniversary of the reign.

While the Dacian war was being brought to a successful conclusion, a more peaceful expansion was taking place in the East, where the Roman forces annexed the kingdom of Nabatea after the death of its last king. The region became the province of Arabia (*46*) in 106. Trajan stayed in Dacia after the war to arrange the organisation of the new province (*42*), whose creation, by expanding the boundaries of the empire, justified an extension of the *pomoerium* of Rome (*45*). He returned to Rome in 107, and celebrated a magnificent triumph and games. As part of the ceremonial opening of the circus games, he addressed the people (*47*), to whom he gave a third and exceptionally abundant donative (*48*).

The next few years were marked by the great building projects which changed the face of Rome. Trajan had already restored the temples of Honos and Venus Genetrix (*43–44*) prior to his decennalia. He now opened the great baths which replaced the Golden House of Nero in 109. They were fed with waters from southern Etruria by a new aqueduct, the

Aqua Traiana (*53*). The Via Traiana (*54*), which ran from Beneventum to Brindisi, was completed at about the same time. The greatest project was the Forum of Trajan (*55*) which comprised a temple, twin libraries of Greek and Latin works, a basilica (*56*), a market, and the column (*57–58*) which bears the sculptured record of the Dacian wars. The buildings were dedicated at the end of 112 and the column somewhat later. The major rebuilding of the harbour of Portus (*59*) at the mouth of the Tiber was also completed in these years.

The government was concerned with the welfare of its subjects in other ways. Before 100, Trajan had expanded the endowments which Nerva had established for poor children in Italy. He maintained this charity, celebrating it and the consequent 'Restoration of Italy' (*49–52*). In 112, Trajan's sister Marciana died and was consecrated (*60–62*). The consecration of his father, also called Marcus Ulpius Traianus (*63–64*) soon followed, although he had been dead since 100 or earlier; action at this time referred to the prospective war against Parthia, for the elder Trajan had won a triumph in the earlier Parthian campaign of 75/76.

The period of peace was an interlude before the beginning of the war designed to destroy the power of Parthia and annex it to the Roman empire. Parthian activities in Armenia provided the pretext: their king had appointed his nephew, Parthamasiris, to rule that kingdom in violation of a long-standing agreement with Rome, and Parthian connections with Decebalus during the Dacian wars added to Roman hostility. Trajan left the capital (*65–66*) in October 113 for Athens, where he received a Parthian embassy proposing a compromise which he rejected. After spending the winter at Antioch, he arrived on the frontier, where he was met by the client princes of the East. The emperor confirmed or replaced them (*67*) and advanced into Armenia, where Parthamasiris met him (*68*). The Parthian prince prostrated himself, throwing his diadem at Trajan's feet, expecting to be crowned again with it, according to custom. Trajan, however, kept the crown, had Parthamasiris executed, and annexed Armenia to the Roman empire. This event led to his proclamation as imperator for the seventh time (*69*).

Trajan returned to his winter quarters in Antioch, where he miraculously escaped death by earthquake when a figure of superhuman size, evidently Jupiter, led him from a collapsing building (*70*). In the spring of 115, he again set out for the East, and rapidly conquered northern Mesopotamia and part of Adiabene beyond the Tigris. Mesopotamia, like Armenia, was incorporated into the empire (*71*), and Trajan received his eighth acclamation as imperator (*72*). The following year brought the most spectacular success, as Trajan completed the conquest of Adiabene, then advanced down the Tigris to Babylon to capture the Parthian capital, Ctesiphon, by mid-summer; Parthia seemed completely defeated (*74*), and Trajan assumed the title Parthicus (*76*); these events coincided with the twentieth anniversary of his reign (*77*).

From Ctesiphon, Trajan made an excursion to the Persian Gulf, then returned to Babylon where he received news of rebellions in Armenia and Mesopotamia. Although these were soon suppressed, he decided that the Romans could not hope to maintain direct control of Parthia. He appointed Parthamaspates, the son of the Parthian king, to rule there in the Roman interest (75), and returned to Antioch. Revolts and civil disturbances were now widespread: fighting between Jews and gentiles was causing considerable slaughter in Cyprus, Cyrene and Egypt; Moors and Berbers were restive; and there were rumours of threats on the northern frontier. Trajan decided to return to Rome, but only managed to reach Selinus in Cilicia, on the southern coast of Asia Minor, where he died suddenly in August 117. Trajan supposedly adopted Hadrian on his deathbed, but the coin which purports to celebrate this (78) and to have been struck before news of his death reached Rome, may in fact have been issued by the party favourable to Hadrian as evidence for the adoption.

97 Adoption by Nerva.

 1   PROVID TR P COS II P P, Trajan receiving globe from Nerva. Aur: 28/*C*318. Den: 28/*C*319

98 Death of Nerva: address to the troops in the field, and their swearing of the oath of loyalty to Trajan.

 2   S C, Trajan and officer on platform addressing soldiers. Ses: *Strack* 308−9

 3   FIDES EXERCIT, Trajan in priestly robes clasping hand of soldier over altar; two others stand behind. Ses: 439/*C*147

— —Accession to imperial power, with award of the *corona civica* and *clupeus virtutis*.

 4   SPQR OB CIV SER in oak wreath. Ses: 421/*C*362

 5   TR POT COS II/I (DES IIII) (P P), Victory walking l., holding shield inscribed SPQR. As: 395/*C*614; 417/*C*628; 425

98−99 Subjugation of tribes along the Rhine.

 6*a* P/ONT M/AX T R P COS II/I P P, Germania std., holding olive branch. Aur: 5/*C*207; 15/*C*290; 35/*C*220. Den: 5/*C*208

 6*b* (Same legend: COS III), Germania std., resting head on hand. Aur: 36/*C*221

99 Return to Rome, with donative and erection of triumphal arch.

 7   COS II CONG P R, Donation scene with Trajan, officer, Liberalitas and citizen. Ses: 380−1/*C*55

 8   TR POT COS III P P, Triumphal arch. Ses: 419−20/*C*632−3

100 Award of title *optimus princeps* by the Senate.

 9   (COS V P P) SPQR OPTIMO PRINC/IPI in oak wreath. Aur: 148/*C*101−2; 149/*C*363; 150/*C*581. Ses: 476/*C*582. Dup: 477/*C*584. As: 476/*C*583

 10 TR POT COS IIII P P, Genius of the Senate presenting globe to Trajan (this type, struck in 101, could also be a belated reference to Trajan's accession). Ses: 437/*C*642

101−2 First Dacian war: triumph of Trajan and award of the title *Dacicus*, donative to the people, and dedication of a triumphal arch to Jupiter Optimus Maximus.

11 DACICVS COS IIII P P, Trajan in triumphal quadriga. Aur: 48
12*a* — — Victory stg. on prow. Den: 46/*C*128
12*b* — — Victory walking l. Den: 47
13 P M TR P COS IIII P P, Trajan erecting trophy over Dacian. Aur: 70−1/*C*254
14 — — Trajan crowned by Victory. Aur: 69/*C*251. Den: 69/*C*253
15 TR P VII IMP IIII COS V P P, Roma receiving Victory from Trajan; captive at feet. Ses: 453/*C*601
16 TR P VII IMP IIII COS IIII DES V P P, Trajan stg. before std. Roma who extends her hands to a kneeling Dacian. Ses: 448/*C*598; 449 (no Dacian)
17 COS V CONGIAR SECVND, Donation scene, as 7. Ses: 450/*C*61
18 SPQR OPTIMO PRINCIPI, Triumphal arch inscribed I O M, shown in considerable detail. Ses: 572−4/*C*547−8 (details vary)

103 Fifth consulate.
19*a* P M TR P COS V P P, Trajan in quadriga l. Aur: 86/*C*262; 90/*C*547
19*b* (COS V P P) SPQR OPTIMO PRINCIPI, Same type (r. or l.) Aur: 137/*C*92. Den: 137−141/*C*93−4. Ses: 532/*C*495. Dup: 553/*C*494
— — Rebuilding of the Circus Maximus.
20 SPQR OPTIMO PRINCIPI, the Circus Maximus. Ses: 571/*C*545−6

106 Preparations for the second Dacian war: crossing into Dacia by a bridge and with the aid of the god of the Danube who helped to overcome Dacia.
21 SPQR OPTIMO PRINCIPI, Bridge with tower at each end, boat below. Ses: 569/*C*542. Dup: 570/*C*544. As: 569/*C*543

21   22

22 COS V P P SPQR OPTIMO PRINC DANVVIVS, The Danube reclining. Den: 100−1/*C*136−7
23 SPQR OPTIMO PRINCIPI, The Danube forcing kneeling Dacia to the ground. Ses: 556−9/*C*525−6
— — Triumph over the Dacians, and celebration of the victory in an abundant series of coins struck for several years. All have legend SPQR OPTIMO PRINCIPI unless otherwise specified. Several of these types were struck in honour of the tenth anniversary of the reign (*see below*).

24   DACICVS COS V P P, Trajan in triumphal quadriga. Aur: 77/ *C*134

25   Trajan on horseback thrusting spear at fallen Dacian. Aur: 208−9/*C*501. Den: 208/*C*502. Ses: 534−7/*C*503−4; 543/*C*508. Dup: 538−9/*C*506; 541; 544−5/*C*510. As: 536/*C*505; 540; 542/*C*507; 543/*C*509

26   Trajan presenting a Dacian to the Senate. Aur: 215/*C*527−8

27   Trajan crowned by Victory. Den: 212−13/*C*514−15

28*a*   DACICVS COS V P P, Dacia std. r. or l., mourning. Aur: 78/*C*135

28*b*   DAC CAP COS V P P SPQR OPTIMO PRINCIPI, Same type. Den: 97−8/*C*119−20

28*c*   Dacia std. mourning on shield. Den: 216−19/*C*529−30

28*d*   Dacia std. at foot of trophy. Den: 220−3/*C*537−8

28*e*   Dacia std. on pile of arms before trophy. Ses: 560/*C*531; 564−6/*C*534−6. Dup: 563/*C*533. As: 561−2/*C*532

29*a*   DAC CAP COS V SPQR OPTIMO PRINCIPI, Dacian, hands bound, std. on pile of arms. Den: 96/*C*118

29*b*   − − Dacian stg., hands bound; weapons on ground. Den: 99/*C*121

30*a*   Kneeling Dacian presenting shield to Trajan. Den: 214/*C*522

30*b*   IMP IIII COS IIII DES V P P, Same type. As: 447/*C*174

31*a*   Victory inscribing DACI. CA on shield affixed to palm. Den: 234/*C*450; 286/*C*451

31*b*   Same type, but shield inscribed VIC DAC. Ses: 527−8/*C*452, 454; 530/*C*453. Dup: 531/*C*456. As: 529/*C*455

31*c*   COS V P P SPQR OPTIMO PRINC, Type as 31*a*, but shield attached to trophy. Den: 130/*C*80

32   − − Trophy with shields, swords and javelins. Den: 147/*C* 98−100

33   P M TR P COS V P P, Trophy and captive. Den: 88/*C*264

34*a*   DACICVS COS V P P, Victory flying r. Qui: 73/*C*130

34*b*   − − Victory walking r. Qui: 74−5/*C*131−2

34*c*   − − Victory std. l. Qui: 76/*C*133

35   Trajan, crowned by Victory, stg. l. on platform decorated with festoons and eagles; captives below. Ses: 551−2/ *C*519−21

36   Dacian kneeling at feet of stg. Roma. Ses: 485−6/*C*386; 488/ *C*390. Dup: 487/*C*389. As: 486/*C*387

37   Dacian kneeling at feet of std. Pax. Ses: 510−1/*C*419, 421. Dup: 512/*C*422. As: 510/*C*420

38   Shield inscribed DACIA CAPTA, with curved sword. As: 585/ *C*570

− − Suicide and decapitation of Decebalus, whose head was brought to Rome and exhibited.

39   SPQR OPTIMO PRINCIPI, Trajan stg. l. with foot on head of Decebalus. Aur: 210/*C*511. Ses: 547/*C*512

40   − − Pax stg. l. with foot on head of Decebalus. Den: 190/

> C400. Ses: 503−4/C406, 506. Dup: 505/C410 As: 503/C408; 506/C409

41 — — Roma std. l. with foot on head of Decebalus. Ses: 489/C391. Dup: 490/C393. As: 489/C392

— — Pacification of Dacia, a symbolic type issued in 112/4.

42 DACIA AVGVST PROVINCIA, Dacia std. on rock, with children holding wheat and grapes around her. Ses: 621−2/C125. Dup: 623/C126−7

— — Tenth anniversary of the reign, with celebration of temples which Trajan had restored.

43 (COS V P P) SPQR OPTIMO PRINCIPI, Octastyle temple of Honos adorned with statues; cult image within. Aur: 145−6/C97. Ses: 575/C552. Dup: 576/C554. As: 575/C553

42   46b

44 SPQR OPTIMO PRINCIPI, Octastyle temple of Venus Genetrix flanked by porticoes of the Forum of Julius Caesar; fountain of Appiades before. Ses: 577/C549. Dup: 578/C551. As: 577/C550

— — (Date uncertain): Extension of the *pomoerium* of Rome, the result of the recent conquests.

45 SPQR OPTIMO PRINCIPI, Trajan as priest, ploughing with team of oxen. Ses: 567−8/C539

— — Annexation of Arabia.

46a COS V P P SPQR OPTIMO PRINCIPI, Arabia stg. l., camel at feet. Aur: 142−3/C88, 90. Den: 142/C89

46b (COS V P P) SPQR OPTIMO PRINCIPI ARAB ADQ/IS/IT. Aur: 94−5/C88, 90. Den: 94/C89; 244−5/C26. Ses: 465−6/C32; 610/C27; 612/C29; 614/C34. Dup: 467−8/C36, 38; 613/C31; 615. As: 466/C33; 611/C30; 614/C35

107 Return of Trajan to Rome, with speech to the people and third donative.

47 SPQR OPTIMO PRINCIPI, Trajan on platform in Circus, addressing people. Ses: 553−4/C523−4

48 CONGIARIVM TERTIVM, Donation scene, as on type 7. Ses: 469/C45

108−110 (Date uncertain): Expansion of Nerva's charity to poor children, considered as a 'restoration' of Italy.

49 ALIM ITAL COS V P P SPQR OPTIMO PRINC, Trajan stg. l., extending hand to two children. Aur: 93/*C*15; 230/*C*16

50 ALIM ITAL SPQR OPTIMO PRINCIPI, Abundantia stg. l., child at feet. Den: 243/*C*9. Ses: 459/*C*7; 604/*C*10; 606/*C*14. Dup: 460; 605/*C*12, 13. As: 459/*C*8; 604/*C*11

51 — — Woman holding child, with another at feet, stg. before Trajan std. on curule chair. Ses: 461/*C*17. Dup: 462/19. As: 461/*C*18

52 REST ITAL (COS V P P) SPQR OPTIMO PRINC, Trajan raising kneeling Italy; two children between them. Aur: 105/*C*326. Den: 106. Ses: 472–3/*C*327. Dup: 470/*C*179 (ITALIA REST)

51   54

109–113 Building programme of Trajan in Rome and Italy.
109 Aqueduct of Trajan, which fed his new baths.

53 AQVA TRAIANA SPQR OPTIMO PRINCIPI, River god reclining in grotto. Ses: 463/*C*20; 607–8/*C*23. Dup: 464/*C*22; 609/*C*25. As: 463/*C*21; 607–8/*C*24

— — The highway of Trajan, from Beneventum to Brundisium.

54 VIA TRAIANA SPQR OPTIMO PRINCIPI, Woman reclining l., holding wheel and branch. Aur: 266/*C*647. Den: 266–7/*C*648. Ses: 636–40/*C*649–50. Dup: 641/*C*652. As: 639/*C*651

112 The Forum of Trajan, with the Ulpian basilica.

55 FORVM TRAIAN/I (SPQR OPTIMO PRINCIPI), Elaborate façade of building with columns, statues, etc. Aur: 255–7/*C*167–8. Ses: 630/*C*169; 654

56 BASILICA VLPIA, Façade of Trajan's basilica. Aur: 246–8/*C*42–3. Ses: 616–18/*C*44

55   57*b*

113 Trajan's Column, set up in his Forum.

57*a* SPQR OPTIMO PRINCIPI, Column surmounted by statue of Trajan;

two eagles at base. Aur: 235/*C*556; 292/*C*557; 379. Den: 239/ *C*559; 292−3/*C*558; 313/*C*560. Ses: 579−80/*C*555; 600−2/*C*564, 561; 678/*C*359; 680/*C*361; 683. Dup: 603/*C*563; 679/*C*360. As: 600

57*b*   COS VI P P SPQR OPTIMO PRINC, Same type. Den: 238/*C*116

57*c*   P M TR P COS VI P P SPQR, Same type. Den: 356/*C*284

— — Column bearing the owl of Minerva, probably a symbolic representation of the previous as a sign of the wisdom of Trajan, who built his column between his two libraries; but possibly an actual, otherwise unknown, column dedicated to Minerva.

58*a*   SPQR OPTIMO PRINCIPI, Column surmounted by owl on base decorated with eagles. Ses: *BMC* p181n

58*b*   SENATVS POPVLVSQVE ROMANVS, Owl column without base. Ses: *BMC* 1025/*C*357

— — New harbour, the Portus Traiani, near Ostia.

59   PORTVM TRAIANI, Trajan's harbour, ships within, surrounded with warehouses. Ses: 471/*C*305; 631−2/*C*306

112 Funeral and consecration of Marciana.

All have *obv.* DIVA AVGVSTA MARCIANA, Bust r.

60   CONSECRATIO, Carpentum drawn by two mules. Aur: 746/*C*9. Den: 746/*C*10. Ses: 749/*C*11

61   EX SENATVS CONSVLTO, Image of Marciana on car drawn by two elephants. Den: 747/*C*12. Ses: 750/*C*13

62   Eagle walking l. on sceptre. Aur: 743/*C*3; 745/*C*7. Avq: 744/ *C*5. Den: 743/*C*4; 745/*C*8. Ses: 748/*C*6

112 or 113 Consecration of Trajan's father, in connection with the Parthian war; this was also the occasion to celebrate the memory of Trajan's adoptive father, Nerva.

63*a*   DIVVS PATER TRAIAN, Bust of Trajan Sr. r. Aur: 762−4/*C*2−3. Den: 251−2/*C*140

63*b*   — — Trajan Sr. std. l. Den: 251−2/*C*140

64   DIVI NERVA ET TRAIANVS PAT, Busts of Nerva and Trajan Pater vis-à-vis. Aur: 726−7

113 Departure for the Parthian war, with prayers for a successful return.

65   AVGVSTI PROFECTIO (or PROFECTION AVG), Trajan on horseback preceded and followed by soldiers. Aur: 263/*C*309; 297/*C*40; 314/*C*40. Ses: 633/*C*310; 662/*C*311

66*a*   FORT RED SPQR OPTIMO PRINCIPI, Fortuna std. l. Aur: 253/*C*155. Den: 253/*C*156; 254

66*b*   FORT RED (PARTHICO) (P M TR P) COS VI P P SPQR, Same type. Aur: 308/*C*148; 318/*C*153; 319; 321/*C*151. Den: 308/*C*149; 316−7 (struck 116); 318/*C*154; 320/*C*152

66*c*   FORT RED SENATVS POPVLVSOVE ROMANVS, Same type. Ses: 651− 2/*C*157−8. Dup: 653/*C*160. As: 652/*C*159

114 First actions: kingdoms assigned to client princes of the East.

67   REGNA ADSIGNATA, Three kings stg. before Trajan std. on platform. Aur: 366−7/*C*324. Ses: 666/*C*325

— — Submission of Parthamasiris and annexation of Armenia, with acclamation of Trajan as imperator for the seventh time.

    68 REX PARTHVS, Trajan std. on platform receiving Parthamasiris; five soldiers behind. Aur: 263a; 310−12/*C*369. Ses: 669/*C*330

67   70

    69 IMPERATOR VII, Trajan std. on platform, addressing soldiers. Aur: 309/*C*175

115 Trajan's miraculous escape from the earthquake at Antioch.

    70 CONSERVATORI PATRIS PATRIAE, Large figure of Jupiter holding thunderbolt, protecting Trajan. Aur: 249−50/*C*46. Den 249/*C*47. Ses: 619, 643/*C*48−9

— — Conquest of Mesopotamia and capture of Ctesiphon, the occasion for two more proclamations as imperator.

    71 ARMENIA ET MESOPOTAMIA IN POTESTATEM P R REDACTAE, Trajan stg. between reclining figures of Armenia, Tigris and Euphrates. Ses: 642/*C*39

71

    72 IMPERATOR VIII, Trajan on platform addressing troops. Aur: 322/*C*177. Den: 323. Ses: 655−6/*C*176

    73 IMPERATOR VIIII, Same type. Ses: 657−8/*C*178

116 Conquest of Parthia and appointment of a new king.

    74 PARTHIA CAPTA P M TR P COS VI P P SPQR, Trophy between std. Parthian captives. Aur: 324−5/*C*184, 186. Den: 324/*C*185

    75 REX PARTHIS DATVS, Trajan std. on platform presenting Parthamaspates to kneeling Parthia. Ses: 667−8/*C*328.

75

— — Award of the title *Parthicus* by the Senate.

    76*a*   DAC PARTHICO P M TR POT XX COS XI P P S C in oak wreath. As: 644/*C*122; 646/*C*124; 647−8. Sem: 645/*C*123; 649−50

    76*b*   (P M) TR POT XX COS VI P P around oak wreath containing S C (PARTHICO in *obv.* legend). As: 659/*C*286; 684. Sem: 660/*C*287

— — Vows on the 20th anniversary of the reign (counted from the adoption of Trajan).

    77   VOTA SVSCEPTA P M TR P COS VI P P SPQR, Genius of the Senate and Genius of the Roman People sacrificing over altar. Aur: 371−4/*C*654−5, 657. Den: 372/*C*656

117   Adoption of Hadrian (*see* introduction).

    78   HADRIANO TRAIANO CAESARI, Bust r. Aur: 724*a*

PLOTINA

Pompeia Plotina, born at Nemausus in Gaul about 70, married Trajan before he became emperor. The title Augusta, at first refused, was awarded her by 105. She accompanied Trajan on his eastern campaigns in 113, and brought his body back to Rome four years later. She greatly favoured Hadrian, helping his rise to power and, according to rumour, being instrumental in having him adopted − or in falsifying documents to prove that he had been. Plotina died in 121 and was consecrated by Hadrian, although she only appears on his coins in connection with the consecration of Trajan (*9−12*). She evidently dedicated or restored the altar of Pudicitia Plebeia on the Quirinal, shrine of an ancient plebian cult.

112   Dedication(?) of the altar of Pudicitia.

    1   ARA PVDIC, Altar of Pudicitia. Aur: 733/*C*4. Den: 733/*C*5

1

TRAJAN PATER

M. Ulpius Traianus, a native of Spain, came to Rome in the time of Nero and soon rose to high office. He commanded in the Jewish war under Vespasian, and became the first of his family to gain the consulate. During his governorship of Syria in 75, he earned the *ornamenta triumphalia* by defeating a Parthian invasion, and subsequently governed Asia and held high priesthoods. He died before 100, and was consecrated by his son (Trajan *63−64*).

MARCIANA

Ulpia Marciana, sister of Trajan, was offered the title Augusta together with Plotina when Trajan became emperor. She, too, refused it, though it was conferred before 105. Little is known of her life. She died in 112 and was immediately consecrated (Trajan *60−62*). Since her daughter had two daughters − one of whom married Hadrian − she could reasonably hope to be the ancestress of a dynasty (*1*).

112 The grandchildren of Marciana, hopes of the dynasty.
    1 CAES AVG GERM DAC COS VI P P, MATIDIA AVG F, in ex., Matidia std l., between two children, Sabina and Matidia. Aur: 742/C1. Den: 742/*C2*

MATIDIA

Matidia, daughter of Marciana and niece of Trajan, was born about 68 and assumed the title of Augusta when her mother died in 112. This was the first time that both a sister and niece of an emperor had received the title. The honour no doubt reflected the affection of her uncle, who treated her like a daughter. She married a certain L. Vibius, by whom she had two daughters (*1* and Marciana *1*), Matidia the younger and Sabina who married Hadrian. When Matidia died in 119, Hadrian consecrated her (Hadrian *24−25*; cf. *12*) and built her a temple in the forum of Trajan.

112 Celebration of Matidia's family.
    1*a* PIETAS AVGVST, Matidia stg., with hands on heads of Sabina and Matidia. Aur: 759/*C9*. Den: 759/*C10*
    1*b* − − Matidia holding daughters in her arms. Den: 760/*C12*

HADRIAN
August 117−July 138

Publius Aelius Hadrianus was born in January 76 in Italica in southern Spain, the home of his cousin Trajan. When his father died in 86, Hadrian became the ward of Trajan, who provided for his education in

Rome, where he began his lifelong admiration for Greek culture. He entered a career in public life, rising to command a legion and govern provinces, and in 100 married Vibia Sabina, Trajan's great-niece. Hadrian was chief of staff for the Parthian expedition of 113, and when the emperor returned from the East, he was left as governor of Syria with orders to carry on the war.

In August 117, Trajan died suddenly in southern Asia Minor; when the news reached Antioch, the troops proclaimed Hadrian emperor and the Senate swiftly recognised him. Trajan had supposedly adopted Hadrian on his deathbed, but persistent rumours maintained that the story and the letters of adoption had been forged with the support of Plotina. In any case, the adoption and relationship with Trajan were important in imperial propaganda and find a prominent place in the coinage (*1–5*).

Hadrian spent his first winter as emperor in Asia Minor, visited and pacified the Danube frontier in the spring, and arrived at Rome in July 118 (*13–14*). He gave a donative to celebrate his accession (*15*) and vows for his health and safety (*16*) were undertaken. One of his first acts was the deification of Trajan (*6–8*), which he had requested from the Senate before he reached Rome. At the same time, he honoured his supporters in Trajan's family, Plotina and Matidia (*9–12*), thus stressing his member-ship in the dynasty. Hadrian refused a triumph for himself, but celebrated it in honour of the victorious deceased emperor (*17*), and held Parthian games in his memory.

Once established in power, Hadrian followed a policy of peace and consolidation after the wars of Trajan's reign. He swiftly suppressed revolts in Mauretania, Palestine and elsewhere, then settled the eastern frontier by abandoning the conquests of Trajan, leaving the neighbouring states to their own kings, who would rule them as clients of Rome. He did, however, keep Arabia for its strategic value, and Dacia, where many Roman colonists had settled. In Rome, he faced considerable unpopularity for executing four high-ranking senators accused of conspiracy. To gain the favour of the people, he provided gladiatorial and wild beast shows, and he embarked on a series of reforms of which the most spectacular involved remitting 900 million sesterces of back taxes and burning the records in the Forum of Trajan (*18*). Hadrian also extended the benefits which Trajan had granted to orphans in Italy, an act celebrated as a restoration of liberty (*19*). His generosity was reflected in the lavish titles which appear on the coins (*20–21*).

In 119, Hadrian assumed his third and last consulate, which is often used as the sole indication of a date between that year and the end of the reign. Consequently, the chronology and interpretation of the coins are sometimes difficult to establish. He gave sumptuous games to the people on his birthday in 119, apparently the occasion for another donative (*22*). It was about this time that the revolt of the Brigantes in Britain, which had begun under Trajan, was brought to an end (*23*). Matidia, the emperor's mother-in-law, died in the autumn of 119, and her funeral and consecration (*24–25*) were celebrated.

The year 121 saw the beginning of the extensive travels of Hadrian, which were to dominate the rest of the reign. In April, he reorganised the festival of the birthday of Rome by instituting new circus games (*29*), an occasion for great celebration, with a donative (*30*), which was considered as marking the beginning of a new golden age (*31−33*). At the same time he began the construction of the great temple of Rome and Venus, dedicated to the eternity of the city and the ancestress of the imperial family. He then left on his travels, accompanied by vows (*34−37*) for his safe return.

Hadrian's travels were almost continuous from 121 to 133; during that time he spent no more than two or three years in Rome. The record of the travels, therefore, which figures prominently on the coins, is central to the history of the reign. It suffers, however, from problems in coordinating the coins with other sources, themselves often unclear. The sequence presented here is generally accepted, but many details remain uncertain. Although Hadrian was a great seeker of knowledge, he did not travel primarily for pleasure, but to gain a direct view of the condition of the empire. In each province he investigated local conditions, instituted needed reforms, and reviewed the local troops. The coins thus form three specific series, celebrating his arrival (ADVENTVS), his work of restoration (RESTITVTOR), and his attention to the army (EXERCITVS). The coins which celebrate the travels (and sometimes provide the only evidence for a visit) were struck as one great series toward the end of the reign, perhaps to celebrate its twenty-fifth anniversary. For present purposes, however, it seemed most useful to arrange them according to the date of travel, so that they may be associated with the events they commemorate. In addition, the general series, which names and portrays provinces without specific reference to imperial activities, has been included in the sequence, as another reflection of the travels.

In 121, Hadrian left Rome for Gaul and the northern frontier (*38−44*), where he visited and strengthened the defences of the Rhine and upper Danube. He crossed to Britain (*45−47*) in the following spring; construction of his wall across the island, one of the most striking survivals of his reign, may have begun on this occasion. He then returned to Gaul, passed on to Spain (*48−51*) and spent the winter in Tarraco. During 123, he crossed to Mauretania (*52−54*) where he suppressed a revolt of the Moors before returning to Spain and departing for Asia (*55−57*) in the autumn. After a winter spent at Ephesus, Hadrian progressed northward to Bithynia, and restored its capital, Nicomedia (*58−60*), which had been destroyed by an earthquake. He then sailed to Trebizond, returning by an inland route which brought him to Claudiopolis, the home of his future favourite Antinous, whom he probably met at this time. In 125, he visited Phrygia (*61−62*), where he restored the tomb of the great Athenian general Alcibiades, then sailed from Ephesus to Rhodes and Athens, where he spent the winter. Much of 126 was occupied with a tour of the ancient Greek sites in the province of Achaea (*63−64*); in the autumn he sailed to Sicily (*65−66*).

Finally, late in 126, Hadrian returned to Rome and celebrated his arrival by a donative to the people (*67–73*). His stay in the capital coincided with the tenth anniversary of his accession (*74–77*) and in April 128, he received the title Pater Patriae (*74, 82*). He made an excursion to Africa (*78–81*), where he reviewed the troops and passed laws to stimulate agriculture before setting out on his second great journey, which took him to most of the provinces of the East.

During the winter of 128/9, Hadrian stayed in Athens, receiving many local honours and granting benefits to the city in the form of buildings and games. In the spring, he returned to Ephesus, where he reorganised the precious metal coinage of Asia (*83*), then moved east to Cappadocia (*84–85*) where he met the client kings of the East. He travelled through Cilicia (*86*) to Syria (*87*) and Arabia (*88–89*), and made his base in Antioch. The year 130 saw Hadrian proceed through Judaea (*90–91*), where he made a momentous decision to restore Jerusalem as a Roman colony and to build a temple to Jupiter on the sacred site of the temple of Solomon. He continued to Egypt (*92–96*), where Antinous drowned under rather mysterious circumstances during a cruise up the Nile. The distressed emperor established a cult in his honour; it appears on the local but not the imperial coinage, though representation of Hadrian as the Egyptian god Horus (*113*) probably reflects the decoration of the cenotaph which he built in Rome to honour Antinous. Hadrian stayed at Alexandria and visited Libya (*97*) before returning to Antioch in 131. In the following year, he made a voyage to the Balkans, visiting Thrace, Moesia, Dacia and Macedonia (*98–104*) before returning once again to Athens for the winter. By this time, the great Jewish revolt had broken out, and Hadrian went to supervise field operations in person before returning to Rome late in 133.

Hadrian's final (and definitive) return (*105–8*) to Rome was celebrated by a donative (*109*) and vows for the welfare of the emperor (*110*) and was apparently the occasion for an address to the praetorian guard (*111–12*). He remained in or near the capital for the rest of his reign, overseeing his various grand building projects. The greatest of these, the temple of Rome and Venus (*114–16*), was completed in 135; the others — the Pantheon, the villa at Tibur, and the mausoleum by the Tiber — do not figure on the coinage. Hadrian was now ageing and in such poor health that it was obviously necessary to make provision for the succession. His choice fell on L. Ceionius Commodus, who thereupon changed his name to L. Aelius Caesar. The adoption, in 136, was the occasion for another imperial donative (*117–19*)

Late in 136, Sabina died and was consecrated (*120–2*). Although Hadrian now stayed in Rome, his concern for the provinces was still strong: in 136 or 137, he sent a legate to restore the organisation and finances of the province of Bithynia (*124*), which produced a new local silver coinage. The year 137 brought the twentieth anniversary of the reign and new vows (*125–6*), but the following New Year's Day was attended by disaster when Aelius suddenly died. His place was filled by

T. Aurelius Antoninus, who in his turn adopted Marcus Aurelius and Lucius Verus, the son of Aelius. Hadrian's illness then grew worse, and he died on 10 July 138.

117 Adoption of Hadrian by Trajan
  1 PARTHIC DIVI TRAIAN AVG F P M TR P COS P P, Trajan presenting globe to Hadrian. Aur: 2a/*C*1008; Den: 2/*C*1009
  2 Same legend, with ADOPTIO, Trajan and Hadrian stg., clasping hands. Aur: 3/*C*34; Den: 3/*C*4, 22/*C*5−6

2

  3 ADOPTIO TRIBVNIC POTEST, Same type., Den: 22C/*C*7
  4 DAC PARTHICO P M TR P COS P P, Type as *l.* Ses: 534a, b/*C*523
− − The following is a symbolic representation of the same event, portrayed as the intervention of heaven.
  5 PROVIDENTIA DEORVM, Hadrian holding roll in l. hand and raising r. to receive sceptre from flying eagle. Ses: 589a/*C*1207; Dup: 602/*C*1208
− − Consecration of Trajan.
  6 *Obv.* DIVI TRAIANO PARTH AVG PATRI, Bust r.; *Rev.* (No legend), Radiate phoenix stg. r. Aur: 27/*C*658, 28/*C*659
  7 DIVO TRAIANO (PART AVG) PATRI, Bust r. Aur: 23/*C*3; (no AVG) 24−5/*C*1−2, 4
  8 DIVVS TRAIAN AVG PARTH PATER, Trajan std l. Ses: 627a/*C*552
− − Dynastic continuity, associated with the consecration of Trajan and honours to Hadrian's supporters Plotina and Matidia.
  9 *Obv.* As no. 6 *Rev.* PLOTINAE AVG, bust r. Aur: 29/*C*1, 30/*C*2
  10 *Obv.* of Hadrian; reverse as no 9. Aur: 32/*C*1; Qui: 32A, 33/*C*2
  11 *Obv.* PLOTINA AVG DIVI, head r. *Rev.* TRAIANI PARTHICI, Vesta std. r. Avq: 31/*C*10
  12 *Obv.* PLOTINAE AVG, Bust r. *Rev.* MATIDIAE AVG, Bust r. Aur: 34/*C*1
118 Arrival in Rome, with vows of thanks to Fortune.
  13 PONT MAX TR POT COS II ADVENTVS AVG, Seated Roma clasping hands with stg. Hadrian. Ses: 547/*C*91; Dup: 554/*C*92
  14*a* PARTHIC DIVI TRAIAN AVG F P M TR P COS P P FORT RED, Fortuna std. l. Den: 5/*C*750

14*b* (PARTH F) DIVI NERV NEP P M TR P COS FORT RED, Same type. Aur: 10; 15/*C*741. Den: 10/*C*749; 15/*C*742

14*c* DAC PARTHICO P M TR P COS P P FORT RED, Same type. Ses: 536/ *C*740

14*d* PONT MAX TR POT COS (DES II) FORT RED. Same type. Ses: 541/ *C*751; 543/*C*755; 551/*C*756 (COS II). Dup: 541/*C*752; 545

14*e* P M TR P COS (DES) II FORT RED, Same type. Aur: 18/*C*743; 41/ *C*745. Den: 18/*C*744; 41/*C*746

—— Donative to the people, on arrival.

15 PONT MAX TR POT COS II LIBERALITAS AVG, Donation scene with Hadrian, an attendant, Liberalitas and a citizen. Ses: 552/ *C*914

—— Vows for the health and safety of the Emperor.

16 P M TR P COS II VOT PVB, Pietas stg. r. Den: 47/*C*1475, 52/*C*1476 (COS DES III), 141/*C*1479 (COS III)

—— Triumph in honour of Trajan.

17 *Obv.* DIVI TRAIANO PARTH AVG PATRI, bust r. *Rev.* TRIVMPHVS PARTHICVS, Trajan in quadriga r. Aur: 26/*C*585

—— Cancellation of debts and burning of promissory notes.

18 RELIQVA VETERA HS NOVIES MILL ABOLITA, Lictor holding fasces setting fire to a heap of papers, sometimes with two or three citizens. Ses: 590–3/*C*1210–13

—— Grants to the poor children of Italy whom Trajan had assisted.

18

19

19 P M TR POT COS III S C LIBERTAS RESTITVTA, Hadrian std. on platform extending r. hand; facing him, woman holding child and placing hand on head of second child. Ses: 568/*C*949

— — Celebration of the generosity of the emperor.

20 LOCVPLETATORI ORBIS TERRARVM, Donation scene, with Hadrian, Liberalitas and two citizens. Ses: 585/*C*950

21 RESTITVTORI ORBIS TERRARVM, Hadrian raising woman with turreted crown who holds globe. Ses: 594a/*C*1285, 594*b*; Dup: 603

119 Second donative, on Hadrian's birthday.

22 P M TR P COS III LIBERALITAS AVG, Donation scene, as *15*. Ses: 567/*C*915

— — Suppression of revolt in Britain.

23 PONT MAX TR POT COS III BRITANNIA, Britannia std., resting head on hand. As: 577/*C*197

23   27

— — Consecration of Matidia.

24 *Obv.* DIVA MATIDIA AVGVSTA, bust r. *Rev.* CONSECRATIO, Eagle on sceptre (several varieties). Aur: 424/*C*3; Den: 423/*C*1−2; 425−6/*C*4−6

25 — — *Rev.* PIETAS AVG, Pietas sacrificing at altar. Den: 427/*C*7

120 Honours to Hercules of Gades, the patron of Trajan's and Hadrian's native country, perhaps associated with dedication of a temple to him by the banks of the Tiber

26 P M TR P COS III, Hercules stg. in flat-roofed distyle shrine; below Tiber (or Oceanus), or facing head and prow; or facing head and head of Jupiter. Aur: 56−8/*C*1083, 1087−8

27 — — Hercules and two females stg. in same shrine; below, Tiber and prow, or prow and head, or fish and Tiber. Aur: 59−61/*C*1084−6

28 P M TR P COS III HERC GADIT, Hercules stg. r.; prow and Tiber beside him. Aur: 125/*C*814

121 Reorganisation of festival of birthday of the city, with new circus games, and a donative. The occasion was taken to mark the beginning of a new golden age symbolised by the phoenix of renewal and Janus, the god of beginnings, and presided over by Jupiter, whose bestowal of power on Hadrian is celebrated here.

29 ANN DCCCLXXIIII NATali VRBis primum CIRCenses CONstituti, Genius of the Circus reclining r., holding wheel; three obelisks in background. Aur: 144/*C*161; Ses: 609/*C*164

29

38

30*a* P M TR P COS III LIBERAL AVG, Donation scene with Hadrian and one or more citizens, sometimes accompanied by Liberalitas and officer. Den: 129−32/*C*908−13

30*b* LIBERALITAS AVG III S C, Donation scene with Hadrian, officer, soldier and citizen. Ses: 582/*C*930

31 P M TR P SAEC AVR, Hadrian stg. r. in oval frame, holding phoenix on globe. Aur: 136/*C*1321; Den: 136

32 P M TR P COS III, Janus stg. front. Aur: 162/*C*1070

33 P M TR P COS III, Jupiter presenting globe to Hadrian. Aur: 109/*C*1164

— — Departure of Hadrian on his travels, here seen in the military aspect of setting out for the field; and the symbolic, with the ship indicating a long voyage.

34 P M TR P COS III EXPED AVG, Hadrian on horseback r., raising hand. Ses: 613/*C*592

35 P M TR P COS III, Galley l. or r. Den: 112−13/*C*1173−4

— — Vows for Hadrian's safe return.

36 P M TR P COS III (V S PRO RED), Hadrian and Genius of the Roman people sacrificing over altar. Aur: 140/*C*1485; 109A

37*a* P/ONT M/AX TR P/OT COS III FORT RED, Fortuna std. l. Den: 122/*C*747. Dup: 571/*C*759. As: 578/*C*760; 617

37*b* FORTVNAE REDVCI, Same type. Dup: 599/*C*784–5

—— Travels in Gaul, Germany, the Rhine and Danube (Rhaetia and Noricum), and Britain.

38 ADVENTVI AVG GALLIAE, Hadrian and Gaul sacrificing over altar. Ses: 884/*C*31, 32, 34; Dup/As: 885/*C*33, 35

39 RESTITVTORI GALLIAE, Hadrian raising Gaul. Den: 324/*C*1247–8, 325/*C*1257; Ses: 950/*C*1249, 1251, 1255. Dup/As: 951/*C*1252–4, 1249

40 EXERCITVS GERMANICVS, Hadrian addressing troops. Ses: 920/*C*573, 921/*C*562 (EXERC GERMAN)

41 GERMANIA, Germania stg. facing. Den: 302–4/*C*802–7

42 EXERCITVS RAETICVS, Hadrian addressing troops. Ses: 928–30/*C*578–82

43 ADVENTVI AVG NORICI, Hadrian and Noricum. Ses: 904/*C*73

44 EXERCITVS NORICVS, Hadrian addressing troops. Ses: 927/*C*565

45 ADVENTVI AVG BRITANNIAE, Hadrian and Britain. Ses: 882/*C*28

46 EXERC BRITAN/NICVS, Hadrian addressing troops. Ses: 913/*C*555, 912/*C*556

47 BRITANNIA, Britain std. on pile of stones, resting head on arm. Ses: 845/*C*194. Dup/As: 846/*C*195–6

122 Travels in Spain.

48 ADVENTVI AVG HISPANIAE, Hadrian and Spain. Aur: 319. Den: 319/*C*36. Ses: 886/*C*37, 39, 40. Dup: 887/*C*38, 41

49 RESTITVTORI HISPANIAE, Hadrian raising Spain Aur: 327/*C*1258–9. Den: 326–7/*C*1260–2, 1270. Ses: 952/*C*1271–2, 954/*C*1263, 1265, 1268. Dup/As: 953/*C*1273, 955/*C*1264, 1266–7, 1269

50 EXERC HISPAN/ICVS, Hadrian addressing troops. Ses: 922–3/*C*563–4

51 HISPANIA, Hispania reclining l., rabbit in front. Aur: 305/*C*821, 824, 828. Den: 306/*C*822, 825, 830; 305/*C*834–7, 839. Ses: 851/*C*826, 829, 832, 840. Dup/As: 852/*C*823; 827; 831, 833, 838, 841–2

123 Voyage to Mauretania.

52 ADVENTVI AVG MAVRETANIAE, Hadrian and Mauretania. Ses: 897/ *C*63, 899/*C*66–7, 901/*C*70. Dup/As: 898/*C*65, 900/*C*68–9, 902/*C*71

53 EXERCITVS MAVRETANICVS, Hadrian addressing troops. Ses: 924–5/*C*575–6

54 MAVRETANIA, Mauretania leading or standing in front of horse. Ses: 854–6/*C*952–5; 858/*C*959, 961; 859/*C*957. Dup/As: 857/ *C*953; 860/*C*958, 960

123–125 Travels in Asia Minor, with specific reference to imperial generosity in rebuilding Nicomedia, the capital of Bithynia, after the devastating earthquake of 123.

55 ADVENTVI AVG ASIAE, Hadrian and Asia. Ses: 880/*C*24–5

56 RESTITVTORI ASIAE, Hadrian raising Asia. Ses: 945–6/*C*1235–7. Dup/As: *BMC* 1799*

56

57   ASIA, Asia stg. l. on prow. Den: 301/*C*188−90
58   ADVENTVI AVG BITHYNIAE, Hadrian and Bithynia. Ses: 881/
     *C*26−7
59   RESTITVTORI BITHYNIAE, Hadrian raising Bithynia. Ses: 947/
     *C*1242−4; 948/*C*1238, 1240. Dup/As: 949/*C*1239, 1241
60   RESTITVTORI NICOMEDIAE, Hadrian raising Nicomedia. Ses: 961/
     *C*1283
61   ADVENTVI AVG PHRYGIAE, Hadrian and Phrygia Ses: 905/*C*74
62   RESTITVTORI PHRYGIAE, Hadrian raising Phrygia. Ses: 962/*C*1286,
     1288, 1290−1; 964. Dup/As: 963/*C*1287, 1289
126 Travels in Greece and Sicily.
63   RESTITVTORI ACHAIAE, Hadrian raising Achaea. Aur: 321/*C*1214.
     Ses: 938/*C*1206, 1218, 1220. Dup/As: 939/*C*1217, 1219
64   ADVENTVI AVG SICILIAE, Hadrian and Sicily. Ses: 906/*C*75−6
65   RESTITVTORI SICILIAE, Hadrian raising Sicily. Ses: 965/*C*1292,
     1294. Dup/As: 966/*C*1293, 1295
66   SICILIA, Triskeles with Medusa-head; Scylla, figures and light-
     house below. Ses: 871/*C*1407
− − Return to Rome, with sacrifice of thanks to Neptune, who had
     safely brought Hadrian back across the sea; an address to the
     people in the Forum, and a donative. (The presence of the children
     on type *69b* may suggest a connection with the charities of Trajan:
     see type *19*.)
67   COS III NEP RED, Neptune stg. r. Ses: 650/*C*981
68   COS III, Galley l. or r. Den: 195−6/*C*447−8
69*a* − − Hadrian stg. in front of temple of Divus Julius, address-
     ing three citizens. Ses: 639−41/*C*416−9
69*b* − − Similar, but Hadrian stg. between two children. Ses:
     695/*C*1388−9
70   COS III LIBERALITAS AVG IIII, Donation scene with Hadrian,
     Liberalitas and citizen. Ses: 648−9/*C*931−3
− − The following types are perhaps to be associated with the return to
     Italy and end of the first period of travel.
71   ADVENTVI AVG ITALIAE, Hadrian and Italy. Aur: 320/*C*42−3,
     45. Ses: 888/*C*46, 48. Dup/As: 889/*C*47, 49−50
72   RESTITVTORI ITALIAE, Hadrian raising Italy. Aur: 328/*C*1274.
     Ses: 956/*C*1275−6. Dup/As: 957/*C*1277

73   ITALIA, Italy stg. l. Den: 307/*C*867−9

127 Tenth anniversary of the reign, with congratulations from the Senate, celebrated as the renewal of the golden age, and probable occasion for a new donative.

    74   SPQR AN F F HADRIANO AVG P P in oak-wreath. Ses: 736/*C*1424

    75   COS III, Janus stg. front. As: 662−3/*C*281−2

    76   − − Amalthean goat suckling Jupiter. As: 670/*C*426

    77   LIBERALITAS AVG COS III (P P), Liberalitas stg. r. Den: 216/ *C*918−21; 217/*C*926−7; 363−4/*C*916−17. Ses: 712/*C*922; 713/ *C*928−9 (P P COS III). Dup/As: 729/*C*923−5

128 Visit to Africa, seen as a new military departure.

    78   COS III EXPED AVG, Hadrian on horseback r. Ses: 644−6/ *C*589−91

    79   ADVENTVI AVG AFRICAE, Hadrian and Africa. Aur: 315−6/*C*8. Den: 316/*C*9. Ses: 872/*C*10−11, 13; 874−5/*C*14−15. Dup/As: 873/*C*12

    80   RESTITVTORI AFRICAE, Hadrian raising Africa. Aur: 322/*C*1221− 2; 323/*C*1231. Den: 322/*C*1223; 323/*C*1229, 1230. Ses: 940/ *C*1232; 941/*C*1224, 1226, 1228. Dup/As: 942/*C*1227, 1229

    81   AFRICA, Africa reclining l. Aur: 299/*C*136. Den: 299/*C*137−41. Ses: 840/*C*142, 144; 842/*C*148. Dup/As: 841/*C*143, 146.

− − Hadrian in Rome: concord with the Senate, celebrated by granting of the title *pater patriae*.

    82   COS III, Roma, stg. between Hadrian and the Senate, drawing their right hands together. Aur: 349/*C*350−1

129 Travels in the East: Asia Minor, where the system of coinage was renewed by restriking the cistophori of Augustus and introducing new local types; travels to Syria and Arabia.

    83   *Obv.* IMP CAESAR AVGVSTVS, Head of Augustus r. *Rev.* HADRIANVS AVG P P RENOvavit, Hadrian stg. l. Cis: 532/*C*576

    84   EXER CAPPADOCICVS, Hadrian addressing troops. Ses: 914/*C*553

    85   CAPPADOCIA, Cappodocia stg. l. Ses: 847/*C*200, 204, 206, 208, 210. Dup/As: 848/*C*201−4, 207, 209, 211

    86   ADVENTVI AVG CILICIAE, Hadrian and Cilicia. Ses: 883/*C*29, 30

    87   EXERC/ITVS SYRIAC/VS, Hadrian addressing troops. Ses: 931−7/ *C*568−70, 583−588

    88   ADVENTVI AVG ARABIAE, Hadrian and Arabia. Ses: 878/*C*20−2. Dup/As: 879/*C*23

    89   RESTITVTORI ARABIAE, Hadrian raising Arabia. Ses: 943/ *C*1233−4. Dup/As: 944

130 Travels in Judaea and Egypt.

    90   ADVENTVI AVG IVDAEAE, Hadrian and Judaea. Ses: 890/*C*54−5; 893/*C*56; 894/*C*52−3. Dup/As: 891−2/*C*56−8.

    91   IVDAEA, Hadrian greeting Judaea, who is sacrificing and is accompanied by three children. Ses: 853/*C*872

    92*a*   ADVENTVI AVG ALEXANDRIAE, Hadrian and Alexandria. (This is the only ADVENTVS type to name a city rather than a province). Aur: 317/*C*16. Ses: 876/*C*17.

92*b* — — Serapis and Isis greeting Hadrian and Sabina. Aur: 318/
C18. Ses: 877/*C*19.

93 EXERCITVS ALEXANDRINVS, Hadrian addressing troops. Ses: *De
Fazi (1977)*

94*a* ALEXANDRIA, Alexandria stg. l. Den: 300/*C*154−6

94*b* — — Alexandria reclining. Ses: 843/*C*157−9. Dup/As: 844/
*C*160−1

95 AEGYPTOS, Egypt reclining; ibis in front. Aur: 296/*C*96−8, 105,
108. Den: 297/*C*99−104, 106, 107. Ses: 838/*C*110, 112, 116,
118. Dup/As: 839/*C*111, 113−14, 117.

96*a* NILVS, Nile reclining, leaning on Sphinx; hippopotamus in
front, crocodile below. (Numerous varieties.) Aur: 308/*C*982,
3. Den: 309−311/*C*987, 989−91. Ses: 861/*C*992−4; 863/*C*997−
8; 865−7/*C* 999−1001; 870/*C*986. Dup/As: 862/*C*995−6; 864/
*C*1002; 868/*C*984−5; 869/*C*988.

96*b* (No legend), Same type Aur: 312−14/*C*1497−9

96*c* S C, Same type with children and Egyptian. Ses: 781/*C*1377−8

96a

131 Voyage to Cyrenaica

97 RESTITVTORI LIBYAE, Hadrian raising Libya. Ses: 958/*C*1278

132 Travels in the Balkans, to Thrace, Moesia, Dacia and Macedonia.

98 ADVENTVI AVG THRACIAE, Hadrian and Thrace. Ses: 907/*C*77−8

99 ADVENTVI AVG MOESIAE, Hadrian and Moesia. Ses: 903/*C*72

100 EXERC MOESIACVS, Hadrian addressing troops. Ses: 926/*C*654

101 EXERC/ITVS DACICVS, Hadrian addressing troops. Ses: 915−
919A/*C* 557−9, 561−2, 571−2

102 DACIA S C, Dacia std. l. on rock. Ses: 849/*C*526, 528, 530. Dup/
As: 850/*C*527, 529−33

103 ADVENTVI AVG MACEDONIAE S C, Hadrian and Macedonia. Ses:
895/*C*59, 61. Dup/As: 896/*C*60, 62

104 RESTITVTORI MACEDONIAE, Hadrian raising Macedonia. Den:
329. Ses: 959/*C*1279, 1281−2. Dup/As: 960/*C*1280

133 Return to Rome, and end of the travels; sixth donative; payment of
vows for the emperor's return, and an address to the Praetorian
guard.

105 ADVENTVS AVG/VSTI, Rome std. or stg. clasping hands with stg.
Hadrian. Aur: 224−6/*C*79, 80, 84. Den: 227/*C*94. Ses:
740−2/*C*81−2, 85, 87, 95. Dup/As: 793−4/*C*83, 86, 88−90

106 FORT/VNAE REDVCI, Hadrian clasping hands with Fortuna. Aur:

243. Den: 243/*C*761; 248/*C*788−9 Ses: 761−2/*C*790, 793, 795.
Dup/As: 813−4/*C*791, 792, 794

106   108*c*

107*a*   FORTVNAE REDVCI, Fortuna std. 1. Den: 242; 247/*C*782−3, 787

107*b*   FORT RED COS III (P P), Same type. Den: 211/*C*734; 360/*C*724,
726. Ses: 707/*C*735−6, 738; 851; 969/*C*725, 728−30. Dup/As:
723/*C*737, 739; 724 (FORTVNAE REDVCI); 973/*C*733

108*a*   FELICITATI AVG/VSTI (COS III P P), Galley r. or l. Den: 209−10/
*C*652, 654−6; 239/*C*651; 240/*C*712−3

108*b*   COS III, Same type. Den: 351−2/*C*445

108*c*   FELICITATI AVG COS III P P, Ship moving r. or l. with steersman
and rowers; standard at stern, Neptune at prow (several
varieties). Ses: 703−6/*C*657−8, 661−6, 668, 670−3, 675, 677,
679−82, 684−90, 694−5, 697−701, 703, 705. Dup/As: 718−
22/*C*659−60, 667, 678, 683, 691, 693, 696, 702, 704, 706−8

108*d*   COS III, Ship with rowers and pilot. As: 673/*C*446; 674/*C*449

109   LIBERALITAS AVG VI, Liberalitas stg. l. Aur: 253/*C*934. Den:
253/*C*935, 938, 939. Ses: 765/*C*936, 941. Dup/As: 817/*C*937,
940

110   Vows: some of these types, struck between 134 and 138
could refer to vows undertaken on the twentieth anniversary
of the reign and on the adoption of Aelius.

110*a*   VOT PVB, Genius of the Senate and Genius of the Roman
people sacrificing. Aur: 288/*C*1472−4

110*b*   VOTA PVBL/ICA, Hadrian sacrificing, with attendant, victimarius
and bull, and fluteplayer. Aur: 289/*C*1480. Ses: 792

110*c*   VOTA PVBLICA, Hadrian sacrificing. Den: 290/*C*1481−4

111   ADLOCVTIO, Hadrian addressing troops. Ses: 739/*C*1

112   COH PRAETOR, Hadrian addressing officers and soldiers; several variants. Ses: 908/*C*236; 911/*C*239. Dup/As: 909−10/
*C*237−8

134 Dedication of a cenotaph to Antinous in Rome, decorated with a
statue of Hadrian as the Egyptian god Horus.

113   S C, Hadrian as Horus stg. r., foot on crocodile. Ses: 782/
*C*1380−2, 1384. Dup/As: 830/*C*1383, 1385

135 Dedication of the great temple in the Forum dedicated to Roma Aeterna and Venus Felix (who here make their first appearance on the Roman coinage).

114*a* SPQR, Decastyle temple. Ses: 783/*C1420*−2

114*b* SPQR EX S C, Decastyle temple with statues, columns and elaborate decoration. Ses: 784/*C1423*

115 ROMA/E AETERNA/E, Roma std. l. (Temple cult image.) Aur: 263/*C1303*; 263A/*C1299*−1300; 265/*C1311*, 1313. Den: 265/*C1312*, 1314. Ses: 774−5/*C1301*−2

116 VENERIS FELICIS, Venus std. l. (Cult image.) Aur: 280/*C1447*−8. Den: 280/*C1449*

136 Adoption of Aelius, celebrated with a donative and by types which recall Hadrian's own adoption by Trajan.

117 AELIVS CAESAR, Bust r. Dup/As: 986−9/*C1*, 2

118 DIVIS PARENTIBVS, Busts of Trajan and Plotina jugate or vis-à-vis; stars over heads. Aur: 232A, B/*C1*, 2

119*a* LIBERALITAS AVG VII, Liberalitas stg. l. Aur: 254/*C942*, 944. Den: 254/*C943*

119*b* −− Donation scene, with Hadrian, Liberalitas and citizen. Ses: 766/*C945*

−− Consecration of Sabina

120 *Obv.* DIVA AVG SABINA, Bust r. *Rev.* CONSECRATIO, Sabina borne aloft by eagle. Aur: 418−19/*C27*−29. Ses: 1051/*C30*

121 *Obv.* As previous. *Rev.* CONSECRATIO, Eagle stg. on sceptre. Den: 420−1/*C31*−2, 34. Ses: 1052/*C33*

122 *Obv.* As previous. *Rev.* PIETATI AVG, Altar. Den: 422/*C56*

122   123

−− Restoration of the *Auguratorium* on the Palatine, where Romulus took the auspices for the foundation of Rome.

123 ROMVLO CONDITORI, Romulus adv. r. Aur: 266/*C1315*; 370. Den: 266/*C1316*−18. Ses: 653; 776/*C1320*

136 or **137** Reorganisation of the administration and finance of Bithynia, with issue of a new coinage by the provincial league.

124 COM BIT, Tetrastyle or octastyle temple with ROM S P AVG in frieze; some types have one or two cult images. Cis: 459−462/*C242*−6

137 Twentieth anniversary of the reign, with an image symbolising the continuity and stability of the golden age.

125 VOTA SVSCEPTA in oak-wreath. Aur: 291/*C*1486−7
126 TELLVS STABIL, Tellus stg. or reclining l. Den: 276−8/
*C*1425−7, 1429−30. Ses: 791/*C*1432. Dup/As: 835/*C*1434

138 Adoption of Antoninus
127 IMP (T AELIVS) CAES(AR) ANTONINVS, bust r. Dup/As: 990−1/
*C*1, 2

SABINA

Vibia Sabina, the daughter of Matidia and great-niece of Trajan, married Hadrian before 101, making Hadrian the obvious heir to the throne. Sabina gained the title of Augusta by about 120, but little is known of her life, though late sources maintained that her relations with Hadrian were extremely poor. She died in 136 or 137 and was consecrated (Hadrian *120−122*).

AELIUS

Caesar August 136−January 138

L. Ceionius Commodus was the descendant of an old Etruscan family; his father and grandfather had been consuls. While he held the consulate in 136, he was adopted by Hadrian and made heir to the empire (Hadrian *117−19*). He then changed his name to L. Aelius Caesar. In 137 he held the governorship and a major military command in Pannonia (*1*), after which he returned to Rome (*2*), where he died suddenly on 1 January 138.

137 Governorship of Pannonia.
1 TR POT COS II PANNONIA, Pannonia stg. l., holding vexillum (several varieties). Ses: 1059−60/*C*24, 26, 29, 31. Dup/As: 1071−3/*C*25, 27−8, 32−3

1

−− Return to Rome.
2 TR POT COS II, Std. Roma greeting stg. Aelius. Dup/As: 1069/*C*48

ANTONINUS PIUS

Caesar February 138/Augustus August 138–March 161

Titus Aurelius Fulvius Boionius Arrius Antoninus was born at Lanuvium in Latium in 86 AD of a respectable family which originated in Nemausus in Gaul: his father and both grandfathers had been consuls. Antoninus grew up in a villa near Rome and eventually entered public life, rising to become consul in 130 and proconsul of Asia about five years later. As a close adviser of Hadrian and a leader of the senate, it was natural for the emperor to look to him as his successor upon the untimely death of Aelius. He was formally adopted in February 138 and changed his name accordingly to Titus Aelius Caesar Antoninus. Since Antoninus's own sons had died prematurely, Hadrian arranged for him to adopt the nephew of his wife Faustina along with the son of Aelius (*1*), so that the succession would be assured for a further generation; they later became the emperors Marcus Aurelius and Lucius Verus.

When Hadrian died in July 138, Antoninus succeeded smoothly to the imperial power. He soon had his adoptive father consecrated (*2*) in spite of opposition from the Senate, among whom Hadrian had lost most of his popularity. These efforts earned him the surname Pius. It was customary on the accession of a new emperor for the provinces to send a special gift, the *aurum coronarium*. Pius remitted this entirely for Italy and reduced it by half for the rest of the empire, an act commemorated in a series of coins which figure the privinces (*5–18*). These were struck in 139, the year when the young Marcus Aurelius was made Caesar (*3*), an event celebrated by the first (*4*) of the many donatives which Antoninus gave. In 140, Aurelius assumed the consulate with his adoptive father, apparently the occasion for a second donative (*19–22*). Faustina, the emperor's wife died in the following year and was consecrated; a temple (*33–34*) was erected in her honour and an exceptionally rich series of coins (*25–32*) celebrated her memory, together with the establishment of an endowment for the support of poor girls (*35–36*), comparable to the charities of Nerva and Trajan. The same year saw the completion of the great temple of Rome and Augustus, begun by Hadrian (*23–24*).

Although the reign was generally peaceful, a serious revolt in Britain erupted and was only suppressed in 143. This victory justified the proclamation of Antoninus as imperator for the second time (*37–40*), and, apparently, the third donative (*41*). The government now attempted to bring security to the province by constructing a new wall north of that of Hadrian. At about the same time a revolt broke out in Mauretania, and was not put down until 150. Similarly, there were troubles in Dacia, Egypt and Judaea, none of them serious enough to demand the personal attention of the emperor who, in striking contrast to his predecessor, is recorded never to have left Italy. During these years, the Romans settled the affairs of client kingdoms by appointing kings for the Armenians (*42*) and Quadi (*43*), a Germanic tribe of the Danube frontier. Little is known of these events.

Antoninus became consul (*44*) for the fourth (and last) time in 145, again with Marcus Aurelius, who in this year married Faustina the daughter of the emperor (*45*). The wedding was celebrated with vows (*46*), a donative (*47–48*), and the award of the *corona civica* to Antoninus (*49*). The central event of the reign was the 900th anniversary of the foundation of Rome (*50*) on 21 April 147, an event long anticipated by a remarkable series of coins which figured the ancient legends of the foundation and early history of the city (*55–69*). The celebrations featured magnificent games (*51–52*), with exotic animals from all parts of the empire, as well as another donative (*53–54*). It was at about this time that Pius restored the lighthouse of Ostia, granting added security to the grain supply of the city (*70*). The following year was the tenth anniversary of Antoninus' accession, the occasion for public vows (*71–72*). In 149, twins (*73*) — a boy and a girl — were born to Marcus Aurelius and the younger Faustina, whose previous sons had died in infancy. In 151, the temple of the deified Hadrian was dedicated, provoking a sixth largess (*74–75*).

The coinage records few events for the last years of the reign, which are extremely obscure. War broke out again in Britain in 155 with a revolt of the Brigantes; coins celebrating its suppression (*79*) figure a mourning Britannia, quite different from earlier representations. Two events of these years are frequently marked by the coinage: the unusual occurrence of a twentieth anniversary of a reign, in 158, with vows completed for its fulfilment and undertaken for its continuation (*80–84*) — the occasion for an eighth donative (*85–86*) and the dedication of a statue to the emperor (*87*). In that year or the next, the temple of Divus Augustus was restored (*88*). During these years, Faustina was producing children (*89–90*; Faustina II, *1–11*) at an impressive rate, guaranteeing the future of the dynasty, if only, as it now appeared with the death of her sons in infancy, through the female line. (Ironically, the son who outlived his father was born in 161, just after the death of Antoninus.) Finally, in the last year of the reign, Aurelius and Verus shared the consulate (*91*), the occasion for yet another donative, the ninth and last (*92–94*). In March of the same year, Pius died peacefully in his suburban villa and was succeeded without a problem by his adopted sons.

Caesar, 138

138 Adoption of Aurelius and Verus.
   1   TRIB POT COS PIETAS, Pietas stg. l., extending hands over two small togate figures. Ses: 1085/*C*606
138 Consecration of Hadrian
   2a   *Obv.* DIVVS HADRIANVS AVGVSTVS, head r. *Rev.* CONSECRATIO, Eagle bearing Hadrian aloft. Aur: 389A/*C*270
   2b   *Obv.* As previous. *Rev.* CONSECRATIO, Eagle on globe. Den: 389B/*C*271
139 Adoption of Marcus Aurelius as Caesar and consul designate, celebrated by the first donative.

3 AVRELIVS CAES AVG PII F COS DES, Head or bust. Aur: 411; 413–14/C1, 5. Den: 411–12/C2–4, 6. Ses: 1206/C7, 11. Dup: 1207. As: 1208, 1210/C8–10, 12

3

8

4a (LIBERALITAS) COS II, Donation scene, with Pius, Liberalitas and citizen. Ses: 534/C168; 537

4b P M TR P COS II S C LIBERALITAS (AVG), Donation scene; some variation. Ses: 540–2/C480–82

— — Provincial types, celebrating remission of the *aurum coronarium*. All show the personification of the province (in one case, a city) with appropriate attributes. Most hold a crown.

5 AFRICA COS II, Africa stg. Ses: 574–6/C21, 24. Dup: 592/C23. As: 596/C25

6 ALEXANDRIA COS II, Alexandria stg. Ses: 577–8/C26, 28. Dup: 593/C27

7 ASIA COS II, Asia stg. Ses: 579/C64–5

8 CAPPADOCIA (COS II), Cappadocia stg. Ses: 580/C120; 1056

9 DACIA COS II, Dacia stg. Ses: 581/C347

10 HISPANIA COS II, Hispania stg. Ses: 582/C413

11 MAVRETANIA COS II, Mauretania stg. Ses: 583–5/C551–3; 748 (COS III, type repeated 140/144)

12 PHOENICE COS II, Phoenicia stg. Ses: 587/C596

13 SCYTHIA COS II, Scythia stg. Ses: 588/C777

14 SICILIA COS II, Sicily stg. Ses: 589/C786–7. Dup: 595/C788

15   SYRIA COS II, Syria stg. Ses: 590/*C*794−6
16   THRACIA COS II, Thrace stg. Ses: 591/*C*816
The final coins of this series represent areas which were not under Roman control, perhaps as a reflection of renewed claims to Trajan's conquests.
17   ARMENIA COS II, Armenia stg. Ses: *BMC* p. 188
18   PARTHIA COS II, Parthia stg. Ses: 586/*C*572

140   Joint consulate with Marcus Aurelius, celebrated with a second donative.
19   TR POT COS III, Pius with small figures of Aurelius and Verus in triumphal quadriga l. Aur: 93/*C*190, 191
20   − − Pius and Aurelius std. on platform, flanked by lictors. Aur: 92/*C*913. Ses: 628/*C*763−4
21   AVRELIVS CAES(AR) AVG PII F COS, Head or bust. Aur: 415−21/*C*13, 16, 18−19, 25−26. Den: 415, 417, 421/*C*14−15, 17, 20−22. Ses: 1211−19a/*C*28, 30, 33−4, 37. Dup: 1220/*C*32, 36, 38. As: 1222−9/*C*29, 31, 35, 39−41
22   LIBERALITAS AVG II, Donation scene, with Pius, Liberalitas and citizen. Aur: 74/*C*483

141   Completion of the temple of Venus and Rome, begun by Hadrian.
23   VENERI FELICI, Decastyle temple, decorated with statues. Ses: 651−2/*C*1074−5. Dup: 673/*C*1076
24*a*   ROMAE AETERNAE, Same type. Ses: 622−3/*C*699, 700, 702−3. Dup: 664/*C*701
24*b*   ROMA/E AETERNA/E, Rome std. l. Ses: 621; 621A/*C*694

− −   Death and deification of Faustina, commemorated in coinage which probably continued until the end of the reign. All have obverse DIVA AVG FAVSTINA or variant, with bust r.
The funeral.
25*a*   AETERNITAS, Image of Faustina in car drawn by two elephants with drivers. Aur: 352/*C*53−4. Ses: 1112−13/*C*57, 59. Dup/As: 1166/*C*58
25*b*   EX S/ENATVS C/ONSVLTO, Same type. Aur: 390/*C*204. Ses: 1139−40/*C*201, 203
25*c*   PIETAS AVG, Same type. Dup/As: 1198/*C*270−1
26   EX S C, Carpentum drawn r. by two mules. Aur: 389/*C*196. Den: 389/*C*197. Ses: 1141/*C*198−200
27   CONSECRATIO Three-storey funeral pyre surmounted by image of Faustina in biga. Ses: 1135−6/*C*186, 188−9. Dup/As: 1189/*C*187
Symbolic types.
28   CONSECRATIO, Faustina and Sol in quadriga. Aur: 383/*C*167−9
29   − − Eagle bearing Faustina skyward. Ses: 1133−4/*C*182−3, 185. Dup/As: 1188/*C*184
30   − − Victory carrying Faustina skyward. Ses: 1132/*C*172
31   AETERNITAS, Star. Den: 355/*C*63

Sellisternium in honour of the goddess Faustina.
32a AETERNITAS, Throne against which rests sceptre; peacock in
   front. Den: 353/*C*61
32b AVGVSTA, Same type with variations. Den: 373–7/*C*131–2
— — Dedication of altar and temple.
33 PIET/AS AVG, Altar with door in front. Dup/As: 1191/*C*256–60
34a AETERNITAS, Decorated hexastyle temple containing statue of
   Faustina. Aur: 354/*C*64. Ses: 1115/*C*65, 67, 69, 71. Dup/As:
   1168/*C*66, 68, 70
34b (No legend), Same type. Aur: 406/*C*316–7. Ses: 1152/*C*274
34c AED DIV FAVSTINAE, Same type. Den: 343/*C*1
34d DEDICATIO AEDIS, Same type. Den: 388/*C*191–2. Ses:
   1137–8/*C*193–4
34e PIETAS AVG, Same type. Den: 396/*C*253. Ses: 1148/*C*254. Dup/
   As: 1195/*C*255
— — Endowment for poor girls in Italy, in memory of Faustina
35 PVELLAE FAVSTINIANAE, Building in two storeys containing
   Pius, women carrying children, and other figures. Aur: 397–
   8/*C*261
36 — — Pius and Faustina std. on platform, welcoming men
   with children. Den: 399/*C*262. Ses: 1149/*C*263

36   37

143 Victories in Britain, marked by the award of the title imperator for
the second time, and by a third largesse, with celebration of the
training of the troops.
37a BRITANNIA, Britannia std. on rock or globe. Ses: 742/*C*116
37b IMPERATOR II BRITAN/NIA, Same type. Ses: 743–5/*C*115, 119
38 IMPERATOR II BRITAN, Victory stg. on globe. Aur: 113/*C*113.
   Ses: 719/*C*114
39 IMPERATOR II, Victory advancing l., holding shield inscribed
   BRITAN or SPQR. Dup: 725/*C*443. As: 732/*C*442
40 DISCIPLIN AVG, Antoninus advancing r., followed by officer
   and three soldiers.
41 LIBERALITAS AVG III, Donation scene with Pius, Liberalitas
   and citizen. Aur: 75/*C*484–5, 487–8. Den: 75/*C*486. Ses:
   608A/*C*489
— — Kings appointed for the Armenians and Quadi.
42 REX ARMENIIS DATVS, Pius crowning king of Armenia. Ses:
   619/*C*686

42

43   REX QVADIS DATVS, Pius crowning king of the Quadi.
       Ses: 620/C687−8; 1059/C689
145   Antoninus consul for the fourth time.
44   COS IIII, Pius in slow quadriga l. or r. Aur: 161/C1178 (no
       legend). Ses: 766−7/C319, 320
— —   Marriage of Marcus Aurelius and Faustina, the occasion for public
       vows, a fourth donative, and award of the *corona civica*.
45*a*   CONCORDIAE, Small figures of Aurelius and Faustina clasping
       hands over altar and before larger figures (probably statues)
       of Pius and the elder Faustina. Ses: 601/C146−7
45*b*   *Obv.* DIVA AVG FAVSTINA, Bust r. *Rev.* As previous.
       Ses: 1129/C161.
       This type is associated with Diva Faustina because newly-
       wed couples made a sacrifice at the altar of Concord in her
       temple.
46   VOTA PVBLICA, Concord stg. behind Aurelius and Faustina
       who clasp hands. Aur: 402/C294

47

47   LIB/ERALITAS AVG IIII (COS IIII), Donation scene with Pius,
       Liberalitas and citizen. Aur: 140−1/C494−6. Den: 141/C497.
       Ses: 774/C 498. As: 819−20/C500−1
48*a*   TR POT COS IIII LIB IIII, Liberalitas stg. l. Aur: 155. Den:
       155−6/C490−1.

48*b*   P M TR P COS IIII LIB IIII, Same type. Ses: 776A/*C*492. As: 821A/*C*493

48*c*   LIBERALITAS IIII, Same type. As: 818/*C*499

49   SPQR OPTIMO PRINCIPI in oak wreath. As: 827/*C*791−3

147   The 900th anniversary of Rome, celebrated with games and a fifth donative. The type featuring the goddess Roma was struck throughout the reign. 50 Roma-std. r. or l., in several varieties.

50*a*   (No legend): Aur: 159/*C*1148−51

50*b*   TR POT COS III/I. Aur: 147−8/*C*935−8. As: 696−7/*C*892−4

50*c*   ROMA COS IIII: Den: 303/*C*696; 314/*C*697

50*d*   TR POT XIII COS IIII ROMA. Ses: 874−5/*C*690, 692. As: 883/*C*693

50*e*   TR POT XIX (or XX or XXI). COS III. Den: 273/*C*1028 (XXI). Ses: 941/*C*975 (XIX); 963/*C*1007 (XX); 979/*C*1027 (XXI)

51   MVNIFICENTIA AVG COS IIII, Elephant. As: 862−3/*C*564−6

52   − − Munificentia stg. l. As: 861/*C*563

53*a*   COS IIII LIB/ERAL AVG V, Liberalitas stg. l. Aur: 169/*C*504−5. Den: 169/*C*506.

53*b*   LIBERALITAS V COS IIII, Same type. Aur: 142/*C*507

53*c*   LIBERAL AVG V, Same type. Ses: 776/*C*508. Dup: 803/*C*509

54*a*   LIBERALITAS AVG V, Donation scene, as *47*. Ses: 775/*C*511. As: 821/*C*512

54*b*   TR POT COS IIII LIBERALITAS AVG V, Same type. Ses: 790

The celebration was prefigured by a remarkable series of coins, most of them struck between 140 and 144 (with a few repeated later in the reign), figuring scenes from ancient Roman legends. They appear here according to the time when the myth was set.

55   TR POT COS III, Janus stg. (Janus was supposedly the first king of Italy, and inventor of civilisation before he became a god. He also stands here as a symbol of the new, golden, age which the anniversary begins.) Ses: 644/*C*881. As: 693/*C*882−3

56   IVNONI SISPITAE, Juno Sospita advancing r., armed. (This Juno was the goddess of Lanuvium, the birthplace of Pius; and one of the most ancient figures in the Roman pantheon.) Ses: 608/*C*473

57*a*   (P P) TR POT COS III, Aeneas carrying Anchises and leading Ascanius by the hand. Aur: 91/*C*908. Ses: 615/*C*655.

57*b*   S C, Same type. Ses: 627/*C*761

58*a*   TR POT COS III, Sow suckling young under oak tree. (A sow with a huge progeny indicated to Aeneas the site where he founded Lavinium, the first Trojan settlement in Latium.) Ses: 722/*C*919

58*b*   COS IIII, Same type. Ses: 768/*C*450

58*c*   IMPERATOR II, Same type. As: 733/*C*450

58*d*   S C, Same type. Ses: 629/*C*775

59*a*   TR POT COS III (ITALIA), Italy std. l. on globe. Aur: 98/*C*468. Den: 85; 98/*C*466−7. Ses: 747, 789/*C*470−2

57a

62d

59*b*   ITALIA (TR POT COS II), Same type. Den: 73/*C*463. Ses: 746/ *C*464. Dup: 594/*C*465

60   (TR POT COS III) TIBERIS, the Tiber reclining l. Ses: 642–3/ *C*817–21. As: 691; 706/*C*822–4

61   TRIB POT COS III, Mars descending through the air toward sleeping Rhea Silvia. (The conception of Romulus and Remus.) Aur: 99/*C*1073. As: 694–5/*C*885–6

62   She-wolf in cave, suckling twins; various legends; some types struck late in reign.

62*a*   TR POT COS II: Den: 42a

62*b*   – – COS III: Ses: 603/*C*174–5

62*c*   – – IMPERATOR II: Ses: 718/*C*447. As: 734–5/*C*448; 997/*C*449

62*d*   – – S C: Ses: 630–4/*C*768–9, 771–4; 1060/*C*770

62*e*   – – TR POT COS III: Den: 94–6/*C*914–6. Ses: 648–50/*C*917–8

62*f*   – – TR POT COS IIII IMP III: Ses: 788

62*g*   – – TR POT XXI COS IIII: 986/*C*1046

63*a*   TR POT COS III/I, Romulus adv. r. (This type may celebrate the emperor as the new founder of Rome.) Aur: 90/*C*909–10; 149. Ses: 945/*C*611. As: 698/*C*912

63*b*   ROMVLO AVGVSTO, Same type. Ses: 624/*C*704–5. Dup: 665/*C*706

64   IMPERATOR II ANCILIA S C, Two oval shields. (The *ancilia* were twelve shields on which the safety of Rome was said to depend. They consisted of an original, which fell from heaven in the time of Numa, and eleven copies made by him, all kept in the temple of Mars.) As: 736/*C*30–2

65   IMPERATOR II IOVI LATIO S C, Jupiter stg. r. (Jupiter Latius was the ancestral god of Latium.) As: 737/*C*457

The following types are probably also to be associated with the anniversary of Rome, since they feature divinities not previously celebrated on the coinage, whose cult goes back to the earliest times, the first two supposedly founded by Romulus.

66   IOVI STATORI, Jupiter stg. front. Aur: 72/*C*458−9. Ses: 607, 773, 927/*C*460−2

67   OPI AVG, Ops std. l. Den: 77/*C*571. Ses: 612−3/*C*568−70

68   FORTVNA OBSEQVENS COS IIII, Fortuna stg. l. (Cult established by Servius Tullius.) Aur: 139/*C*389; 286a/*C*390. Den: 271/*C*386; 286a. Ses: 771/*C*388; 975 (OPSEQVENS); 1001/*C*393. Dup: 801/*C*391; 990 (OPSEQVENS); 1015/*C*395. As: 996/*C*392; 1023/*C*394

69   BONO EVENTI, Bonus Eventus stg. l. (An ancient god of agriculture.) Dup: 656A. As: 555/*C*109−10; 676−7/*C*106−7

145   Restoration of the lighthouse at Ostia.

70   ANNONA AVG FELIX, Annona stg. l. with two ships, one bearing a modius, and lighthouse in background. Ses: 757/*C*54

148   Tenth anniversary of Pius' accession, with vows for a successful continuation.

71   PRIMI DECEN/NALES (COS IIII) in oak wreath. Aur: 171/*C*669; 173; 184/*C*672. Avq: 171/*C*671. Den: 171−2/*C*667, 670, 673. Ses: 846/*C*674. As: 853/*C*675−6

72   COS IIII VOTA, Antoninus sacrificing. Aur: 170/*C*1093−4. Ses: 844/*C*1095; 856/*C*1100. Dup: 849/*C*1097; 858. As: 852/*C*1096, 1098, 1099

149   Birth of twins to Aurelius and Faustina.

73   TEMPORVM FELICITAS COS IIII, Busts of two infants on crossed cornucopiae. Aur: 185/*C*811−12. Ses: 857/*C*813. Dup: 859/*C*814

73

151   Dedication of Temple of Hadrian, the occasion for a sixth donative.

74   TR POT XIIII COS IIII (PIETAS), Octastyle temple with or without seated statues of Hadrian and Sabian. Ses: 870/*C*954−5; 873/*C*618

75 LIB/ERALITAS VI COS IIII, Liberalitas stg. l. Avq: 198/*C*513. Den: 198/*C*514. Ses: 867/*C*515

153 Seventh donative, probably to celebrate the fifteenth anniversary of the reign.

76*a* LIBERALITAS VII COS IIII, Liberalitas stg. l., Aur: 207; 229/*C*520. Den: 229/*C*520; 235/*C*522

76*b* — — Liberalitas emptying coins out of cornucopiae. Den: 228/ *C*519; 234

77 — — Antoninus stg. l., holding account-board and roll. Den: 208, 237/*C*517−18

78 — — Donation scene with Antoninus, Liberalitas and citizen. Ses: 905, 915/*C*525−6

155 Suppression of the revolt in Britain.

79 BRITANNIA COS IIII S C, Britannia std. on rock in mournful attitude. Dup: 930/*C*118. As: 934/*C*117

158 Twentieth anniversary of the reign, with vows to celebrate its completion (VOTA SOLVTA) and undertaken (VOTA SVSCEPTA) for a continuation; the occasion for an eighth donative, and for dedicating a statue of the emperor.

80 VOTA SOL DEC/ENN/AL II COS IIII, Antoninus sacrificing with bull by tripod or altar. Aur: 291−2/*C*1101, 1103, 1109, 1111. Den: 291−2/*C*1102, 1110. Ses: 792, 1062/*C*1107; 1008−9/*C*1104, 1112. Dup: 813, 1018−19, 1066/*C*1108 As: 1026−7/*C*1105

81 VOTA SVSCEP/TA DEC/ENNAL III (COS IIII), Antoninus sacrificing. Aur: 156A; 283. Den: 156A; 157/*C*1127; 283; 293−4; 306−7/ *C*1113. Ses: 793−4; 1009−11/*C*1124; 1033−4/*C*1119−20, 1123; 1063/*C*1118. Dup: 814; 1020; 1037/*C*1122. As: 1028/*C*1125; 1042/*C*1121

81   88*a*

82 SECVNDO DECEM ANNALES COS IIII S C in oak wreath. Ses: 785/ *C*779

83 VOTA VIGENNALIA COS IIII, Pius sacrificing. Aur: 295/*C*1129. Ses: 1012/*C*1128

84 VOTA SVSCEPTA VICENNAL/IA (COS IIII), Same type. Den: *BMC* p. 142

85 (P M) TR POT XXI COS IIII LIB VIII, Liberalitas stg. l. Den: 282/*C*567. Ses: 976/*C*528; 987. Dup: 991/*C*529

86   TR POT COS IIII LIBERALITAS AVG VIII, Donation scene, with Pius, attendant, Liberalitas and citizen. Ses: 791

87   COS IIII, Arched tetrastyle shrine containing statue of Antoninus holding branch and standard. Den: 285/*C*331. Ses: 974; 999/*C*332; 1029/*C*336. Dup: 989; 1014/*C*334. As: 995/*C*330; 1022/*C*333, 335; 1039/*C*337. (*RIC* 227, 269, 913, 923, 931 and 959, supposedly of earlier years, apparently all represent misreadings of the main type.)

158 or 159   Restoration of the temple of Divus Augustus.

88*a*   TEMPL/VM DIV/I AVG REST COS IIII, Octastyle temple with statues of Augustus and Livia. Aur: 143/*C*808; 289−90/*C*799; 305/*C*800. Den: 143−4/*C*809; 272/*C*802; 290/*C*804; 305/*C*801 Ses: 787/*C*810; 978/*C*803; 1003−4/*C*797, 805; 1061/*C*810. Dup: 1017/*C*807. As: 829; 1024−5/*C*798, 806; 1042

88*b*   AED/E DIVI AVG REST COS IIII, Same type. Den: 124/*C*1; 284/*C*2. Ses: 755/*C*3; 973; 998/*C*7; 998a/*C*9. Dup: 795−6/*C*4; 988/*C*5; 1013/*C*11. As: 994/*C*6; 1021/*C*10, 12

159−160   Growth of a dynasty: the children of Aurelius and Faustina (*see* Faustina II, introduction).

89   PIETATI AVG COS IIII, Faustina stg. l., holding infant Fadilla; Faustina and Lucilla stg. by her sides. Ses: 1002/*C*620; 1031/*C*621. Dup: 1035/*C*625

90   − − Faustina stg. l., holding infants Fadilla and Cornificia; Faustina and Lucilla stg. beside her. Ses: 1032/*C*626; 1045/*C*628. Dup: 1035A/*C*627; 1048/*C*629. As: 1053

161   Joint consulate of Aurelius and Verus; ninth donative.

91   CONCORD COS IIII S C, Three clasped hands. As: 1050/*C*134

92   LIBERALITAS AVG VIIII COS IIII, Donation scene with Pius, officer, Liberalitas and citizen. Aur· 312/*C*531. Ses: 1044/*C*532

93   − − Liberalitas stg. r., emptying coins from cornucopia. Den: 311/*C*530

94   CONG AVG VIIII COS IIII, Liberalitas stg. l. holding account-board and cornucopiae. Den: 308/*C*150. Ses: 1043/*C*151. Dup: 1047/*C*152

FAUSTINA the Elder

Annia Galeria Faustina, the daughter of Annius Verus who was three times consul, married Antoninus Pius by whom she had four children. Only one, Faustina, survived her. She received the title Augusta when Antoninus became emperor in 138, but died in the third year of his reign. Faustina was consecrated: a temple, a charity for poor girls, and an extensive series of coins (Antoninus *25−36*) honoured her memory.

MARCUS AURELIUS

Caesar 139/Augustus March 161–March 180

Marcus Aurelius was born in Rome in April 121 of a distinguished family, ultimately of Spanish origin; both his grandfathers had been consuls. After his father died at an early age, Marcus was raised by his grandfather and took the name Marcus Annius Verus. He soon attracted the attention of Hadrian, who supervised his education by the finest teachers of the day. At the age of fifteen, Hadrian had him engaged to the daughter of Aelius and would have intended him for the succession had he not been so young. When Aelius died, Hadrian adopted Antoninus, who was married to Marcus' aunt, and obliged him in turn to adopt Marcus, who thereupon took the name Marcus Aelius Aurelius Verus.

After the accession of Antoninus, Marcus received high honours, including membership of the priestly colleges (*1*) in 139 and the consulate (Pius *19–21*) in 140, the year he donned the *toga virilis* of manhood (*2*). In 145, he shared the consulate with his adoptive father (*3*), and while holding that office, married the emperor's daughter, Annia Galeria Faustina, the occasion for enthusiastic celebrations in Rome (*4–6*). The importance of establishing a dynasty appears in the grant of tribunician powers to Marcus on the birth of his first child, a daughter, in 146. Aurelius and Faustina had at least thirteen children, (*7,8; see* Faustina II, introduction) but only one of the sons survived infancy. During this period, Aurelius devoted himself increasingly to philosophy. In 161, while holding the consulate with his adopted brother Verus (*9–10*), he became emperor on the death of Antoninus.

Aurelius' first act as emperor was to grant full and equal powers (except the office of Pontifex Maximus) to Verus (*11–12*). To celebrate their accession, they together gave a donative to the people (*13*) and together they conducted the funeral and deification of Pius (*14–19*). Serious troubles soon began: the Parthians invaded Armenia, setting a pretender on the throne, then defeated a Roman army and pushed into Syria. The situation was exacerbated by troubles in Britain and along the northern frontier. Since the Parthian threat was the most serious, Verus set out for the East early in 162, leaving Aurelius to conduct affairs in Rome. Verus soon won a signal victory in Armenia (*20–22*) which re-established Roman control and was marked by another donative (*23*). The Romans then moved on the offensive, striking deep into enemy territory and gaining considerable glory by capturing the Parthian capital, Ctesiphon. The victory (*24–25*) produced a triumph (*26–27*) and justified another donative (*28–29*).

The year of celebration, the twentieth anniversary of Aurelius' assumption of the tribunician power (*30–31*), was fatefully marred when Verus' returning troops brought the bubonic plague from the East; it devastated the empire at the same time as Germanic tribes, the Marcomanni and Quadi, broke through the frontier and struck into Italy. The emperors responded with a long campaign which moved successfully north of the Alps into barbarian territory; these victories may have occasioned a fourth donative (*32*). The emperors finally returned to Italy early in 169, but Verus suffered a sudden stroke and died on the way to Rome. Aurelius conducted the body to the capital where he celebrated the funeral and rites of deification (*33–36*).

The emperor's stay in Rome was brief, for a new outbreak of war forced him to leave for the German frontier (*37–39*) before the end of the year. This time, he was destined to be absent continually for eight years. While Aurelius was away, the completion of ten years of his reign (as Augustus) was celebrated with the usual vows (*41–43*). The campaign of 171 brought the first victories (*44*). In the following year, the army crossed the Danube (*45*) and advanced into dangerous enemy territory, where it was twice saved by miraculous events (*46–47*). The wars brought a victory marked by lenient treatment of the conquered tribes (*48–52*). As a result, Aurelius was proclaimed imperator for the sixth time (*49–51*), and he and Commodus were both awarded the title Germanicus. Although still a child, Commodus Caesar was becoming more prominent, especially as he was now presented to the army as heir apparent (*53*). By his victories, Aurelius 'restored' Italy (*54*) and helped it to recover from the barbarian attacks.

The theatre of war now moved eastward, where the Quadi were defeated; Aurelius became imperator for the seventh time (*55*), and Faustina gained the unprecedented title *mater castrorum* (*63*; Faustina *12*) for her faithful accompaniment of the emperor on the campaigns. Another victory in 175 brought an eighth acclamation as imperator and coincided with the assumption of the *toga virilis* by Commodus, who now begins to figure more prominently on the coinage (*56* Commodus *1–9*). These victories, which included the defeat of both Germans (*58–59*) and Sarmatians (*60–61*) were extensively commemorated on the coinage and were supposed to have established peace definitively (*62*). Celebration of them, however, was delayed by the revolt of the governor of Syria, Avidius Cassius, which was soon suppressed. Aurelius continued to Syria and Egypt, but on his return, Faustina died suddenly in a village near Mount Taurus in 176. She received an elaborate funeral and was consecrated (*63–73*).

Aurelius finally returned to Rome in 177, after escaping from shipwreck (*74–78*), celebrated a triumph (*79*) and held the consulate together with Commodus, who in this year received the tribunician power and the rank of Augustus. One of these occasions provoked a seventh largesse (*80–81*). In spite of the promise of victories achieved, the wars were not over, and Aurelius had to return to the frontier in 178, public vows were undertaken for his success (*82*), but proved to be in vain, for, after making some initial gains, Aurelius died in camp in March 180, leaving Commodus, as he hoped, to pursue his policies.

Caesar, with Pius 139-161

139 Adoption as Caesar and admission to the priesthoods (*see also* Pius 3–4).

    1   PIETAS AVG, Priestly implements. Aur: 424/*C*450. Den: 424/*C*451–2. Ses: 1234/*C*454, 457, 459. Dup/As: 1240/*C*455–6, 458, 460

1   18

140 Joint consulate with Pius: *see* Pius 19–21

—— Assumption of *toga virilis* (an occasion when sacrifices were made at the shrine of Juventas at the Circus Maximus).

    2   IVVENTAS, Juventas stg. l., throwing incense on altar. Aur: 423/*C*386–7. Avq: 423/*C*388. Den: 423/*C*389. Ses: 1232–3, 1238–9/*C*390–6

145 Second consulate, shared with Pius.

    3a COS II, Aurelius in slow quadriga l. Aur: 430/*C*111

    3b S C, same type. Ses: 1246–7/*C*581–2

—— Marriage of Aurelius and Faustina, the occasion for public vows, and for dedication of an oak wreath by the Juventus (Youth), corresponding to the *corona civica* which Pius then received (*see* Pius *49, 45–46*).

    4 CONCORDIA TR POT III COS II, Concord sheltering small figures of Aurelius and Faustina. Aur: 441/*C*67

    5 VOTA PVBLICA, Aurelius and Faustina clasping hands before Concord. Aur: 434/*C*1021. Ses: 1253/*C*1022, 1024

    6 (COS II) IVVENTVS in oak wreath. Ses: 1262/*C*399. As/Dup: 1261/*C*398

149 The growing family of Aurelius and Faustina.

    7 TR POT III COS II, (PIETAS), Faustina stg. l., placing hand on head of small Faustina and holding Lucilla in her arms. Aur: 449/*C*443. Den: 449/*C*443. Ses: 1274/*C*629; 1280/*C*444

160 Further children of Aurelius and Faustina.

    8 TR POT XV COS II DESIG III (or COS III), Faustina stg., holding Fadilla and Cornificia in her arms; Faustina and Lucilla stand beside her. Aur: 487/*C*771–2; 490/*C*773. Den: 490/*C*774

161 Joint consulate with Verus (*see also* Pius *91*).
    9   TR POT XV COS III, Aurelius in quadriga. Aur: 491/*C*781, 783. Den: 491/*C*782. Ses: 1360/*C*788; 1364/*C*605. Dup: 1361
    10   TR POT XV COS III, Aurelius and Verus std. l. on platform; lictor stg. below. Ses: 820−1/*C*787

Joint reign with Verus, 161−69

−− Accession to the throne and association of Verus as co-emperor, the occasion for a donative.
    11   CONCORD/IA/E AVGVSTOR TR P XV/I COS III, Aurelius and Verus clasping hands. Aur: 7−11/*C*69−71; 41−5/*C*72−3. Den: 46. Ses: 795−7/*C*45, 47; 803/*C*64; 823−7/*C*51, 53−4. Dup: 798−800/*C*49−50; 828−9/*C*58−9. As: 801−2/*C*46, 48; 830−2/*C*52, 55−6
    12   CONCORD AVG TR P XV/I/I COS III, Concord stg. l. Den: 1−6/*C*30−32; 33−40/*C*33−36; 58−64/*C*37−43. Ses: 793−4
    13   LIB AVGVSTOR TR P XV COS III, Donation scene with Aurelius and Verus, Liberalitas and citizen. Aur: 15−17/*C*401. Ses: 806−8/*C*402, 404. Dup: 809−10/*C*405−6. As: 811/*C*403
−− Funeral and deification of Antoninus Pius. (All have *obv.*: DIVVS ANTONINVS, head r.)
    14   S C, Statue of Antoninus in quadriga of elephants. Ses: 1274/*C*766
    15   CONSECRATIO, Pyre of four tiers surmounted by quadriga. Aur: 435, 437/*C*163. Den: 436, 438/*C*164. Ses: 1266, 1268/*C*165, 167. As: 1267/*C*166
    16   CONSECRATIO, Eagle stg. on altar or globe. Den: 429−3/*C*154−8. Ses: 1262−5/*C*159−42.
    17   DIVO PIO, Pius std. l. Den: 442/*C*352
    18   DIVO PIO, Column with statue of Pius. Den: 439−40/*C*353. Ses: 1269/*C*354; 1271/*C*356. As: 1270/*C*355
    19   DIVO PIO, Square altar. Den: 441/*C*357. Ses: 1272−3/*C*358
164 Conquest of Armenia, and associated second donative.
    20   ARMEN P M TR P XVIII (OR XIX) (IMP II) COS III, Armenia std. in mournful attitude. Aur: 83−4, 86/*C*5, 11. Den: 78−82/*C*7−8; 85/*C*6;121−2/*C*9, 10
    21   P M TR P XVIII (or XIX) IMP II COS III, Victory attaching shield inscribed VIC AVG to palm tree. Aur: 88−90/*C*466−7; 127−9/*C*475
    22   VICT AVG P M TR P XVIII IMP II COS III Victory holding trophy; Armenia std. at her feet. Ses: 890−1/*C*984−5. Dup: 892/*C*986
    22A TR POT XIX IMP II COS III, Aurelius stg. l. between four standards (representing the four legions that fought in the war). Ses: 908−10/*C*804
    23   LIBERAL AVG P M TR P XIX IMP II COS III Liberalitas stg l. Dup: 893/*C*411. As: 894/*C*410

166 Celebration of victory over Parthia, with triumph and third donative to celebrate the successes of Verus in the East.

24 TR POT XX IMP IIII COS III Victory fixing shield inscribed VIC PAR to palm tree. Ses: 922, 929/*C*879; 931/*C*807; 934−5/*C*810. Dup: 932−3/*C*808−9; 936/*C*811. As: 930

25 VICT AVG TR POT XX IMP IIII COS III, Victory wearing mural crown (symbolic of the conquest of the Parthian capital), flying l., holding diadem. Ses: 941−3

26 (Legend as 24), Aurelius and Verus in quadriga. Ses: 940/*C*814

27 TR P XX/I IMP IIII COS III, Three trophies (corresponding to the three victories in Armenia, Parthia and Media). As: 947/*C*884; 955/*C*895

28*a* CONG AVG III TR POT XX IMP III COS III, Donation scene with Aurelius and Verus, prefect, official, and citizen. Ses: 914−5/*C*75−6

28*b* LIB AVGVSTOR TR P XX COS III, Same type. Ses: 917/*C*409

29*a* LIB AVG III TR P XX COS III, Liberalitas stg. l. Den: 144/*C*408

29*b* CONG AVG III TR P XX IMP III COS III, Same type. Dup: 913/*C*74.

−− Vows on completion of twenty years of reign, counted from Aurelius' assumption of tribunician power in 146.

30*a* VOTA DEC ANN SVSC TR P XX IMP IIII COS III, Aurelius sacrificing. Dup: 944/*C*1020

30*b* VOTA TR P XXI IMP IIII COS III, Same type. As: 951/*C*1019

31 VOTA PVBLICA in laurel wreath. Ses: 945/*C*1025

167 Fourth donative, perhaps to celebrate the initial victories over the Marcomanni and Quadi.

32*a* CONG AVG IIII TR P XXI IMP IIII COS III, Liberalitas stg. l. Aur: 166−7/*C*77

32*b* −− Donation scene with Aurelius and Verus, Liberalitas and citizen. Ses: 946

Sole reign, 169−177

169 Death and deification of Verus.

33 *Obv.* DIVVS VERVS, Head r. *Rev.* CONSECRATIO, Statue of Verus in quadriga of elephants. Ses: 1507−8/*C*53−4

34 *Obv.* As previous. *Rev.* CONSECRATIO, Funeral pyre. Den: 596b/*C*58. Ses: 1511−12/*C*59−60

35 *Obv.* As previous. *Rev.* CONSECRATIO, Eagle stg. on globe. Den: 596a/*C*55. Ses: 1509−10/*C*56−7

36 *Rev.* DIVVS VERVS, Head r. Ses: 1236a/*C*6

−− Beginning of the German wars: departure of the Emperor, and address to the troops, with vows for a safe return.

37 PROFECTIO AVG COS III, Aurelius on horseback; one soldier in front, three behind. Ses: 963/*C*500; 977−8/*C*502−3

38 ADLOCVT AVG COS III, Aurelius addressing troops. Ses: 973−4/
   C1

39 FORT RED (TR P/OT XXII/I IMP V), Fortuna std. l. Aur: 183−4/
   C207. Den: 185/C208; 204/C204; 205/C209; 220/C205. Ses:
   957/C211; 962/C213. Dup: 958/C212. As: 976/C206

— — Fifth donative, perhaps on departure for the wars.

40 LIBERAL AVG V COS III, Liberalitas stg. l. Den: 206/C412; 221/
   C413; 267/C412; 284/C415

171 Tenth anniversary of the sole reign of Aurelius, with vows to celebrate its completion, and in anticipation of another decade.

41 PRIMI DECENNALES COS III in wreath. Aur: 243/C491; 246/C494.
   Den: 244−5/C492−3. Ses: 1003/C495; 1005−7/C497. Dup:
   1004/C496; 1008/C498

41

45

42 VOTA SOL/VTA DECENN/ALIVM COS III, Aurelius sacrificing at tripod;
   bull at feet. Aur: 247/C1030. Den: 248/C1031. Ses: 1014/C1032;
   1016/C1034. Dup: 1015/C1033

43 VOTA SVSCEP DECENN II COS III, Aurelius sacrificing at tripod.
   Aur: 249−50/C1035. Den: 251/C1036. Ses: 1017/C1037. Dup:
   1018/C1038

— — First victories in Germany.

44 IMP VI COS III, Victory attaching shield inscribed VIC GER to
   palm tree. Aur: 256/C270. Den: 240; 257/C271. Ses: 1000−1/
   C267, 269; 1029−30/C272, 275. Dup: 1002/C268; 1031−2/
   C273−4

172 Frontier campaigns; the army crosses the Danube.

45 VIRTVS AVG IMP VI COS III, Aurelius and soldiers marching across
   bridge; boats below. Aur: 270/C999. Ses: 1047−8/C1000−1

—— Incidents in the Danubian campaigns: the siege works of the enemy destroyed by lightning; and a miraculous cloudburst which saved the Roman army, thanks to the prayers of an Egyptian priest to Mercury.

46   IMP VI COS III, Aurelius, crowned by Victory, stg. l., holding thunderbolt. Aur: 264−5/*C*308 Den: 266/*C*309

47*a*   RELIG AVG IMP VI COS I, Mercury stg. front or l. Den: 285/*C*530; 298; 308−9/*C*536−7. Dup: 1070−3/*C*531−3

47*b*   —— Statue of Mercury in tetrastyle shrine of Egyptian style. Ses: 1074−6/*C*534−5

47b

—— Defeat of the German tribes and pacification of the frontier; generous treatment of the conquered.

48   GERMANIA SVBACTA IMP VI COS III, Germania std. at foot of trophy (many varieties). Ses: 1021−4/*C*215; 1027; 1049−50/*C*217−18; 1054/*C*222. Dup: 1025/*C*216; 1052/*C*220. As: 1026; 1051/*C*219; 1053/*C*221; 1055−7/*C*223−5 1094−5/*C*226.

49   GERMANICO AVG IMP VI COS III, Trophy; German woman std. on l., German, hands bound, stg. on r. Ses: 1058−62/*C*227−9

50   IMP VI COS III, German std. at foot of trophy. Den: 277−80/*C*296−7, 300; 289−293/*C*298−9, 301;

51   VICT GERM IMP VI COS III in laurel wreath. Ses: 1090−1/*C*995−6. Dup: 1092−3/*C*997−8

52   CLEMENTIA AVG IMP VI COS III, Germania kneeling before Aurelius. Ses: 1019/*C*27

—— Presentation of Commodus to the army.

53   PROVIDENTIA AVG IMP VI COS III, Aurelius and Commodus addressing troops from platform. Ses: 1046/*C*529

173 Italy 'restored' as a result of the victories.

54   RESTITVTORI ITALIAE IMP VI COS III, Aurelius raising Italy. Ses: 1077−82/*C*538−40

174 Defeat of the Quadi, and seventh acclamation as imperator.

55   IMP VII COS III, German std. at foot of trophy. Den: 306/*C*350

175 Commodus' assumption of the *toga virilis*, and a more prominent role in government.

56   (L AVREL) COMMODVS CAES AVG FIL GERM, Head or bust. Den: 335−6/*C*1. Ses: 1153/*C*4

54   56

— — Sixth donative, either on the above occasion, or for the victories in
Germany.

57 LIBERAL/ITAS AVG VI IMP VII COS III, Liberalitas stg. 1. Aur:
317–19/*C*416. Den: 320–1/*C*417. Ses: 1147–8/*C*418–19.
Dup: 1149/*C*420

— — Victories over the Germans and Sarmatians.

58*a* DE GERM (TR P XXX/I) IMP VIII COS III P P around pile of
weapons. Aur: 337/*C*154; 362/*C*155. Den: 338; 363/*C*156. Ses:
1184/*C*163 (DE GERMANIS). Sem/Quad: 1213.

58*b* IMP VIII COS III DE GERMANIS, Same type. Ses: 1162

59 (Legend as 58*a*), two German captives std. on shields at base
of trophy. Den: 339/*C*161. Ses: 1179. Dup: 1179a–82/*C*157–
9, 162

60 DE SARMATIS (TR P XXXI) IMP VIII COS III P P, pile of weapons.
Aur: 366/*C*172. Den: 367/*C*173. Ses: 1190–1/*C*174

61 DE SARM (TR P XXX/I) IMP VIII COS III P P, Two Sarmatians,
hands bound, std. below trophy. Aur: 340/*C*164; 342; 365.
Den: 341/*C*165; 364/*C*166. Ses: 1185/*C*167. Dup:
1186–9/*C*168–71

61

63

176 Perpetual peace brought by the great victories.

    62   IMP VIII COS III PAX AETERNA AVG, Peace setting fire to a pile of weapons. Ses: 1163−4/*C*360−1. Dup: 1203/*C*364. As: 1165/ *C*362; 1202/*C*363; 1204/*C*365

—— Funeral and deification of Faustina. *Obv.* DIVA/E FAVSTINA/E PIA/E, Bust r., unless specified.

    63   MATRI CASTRORVM, Faustina std. l., holding globe with phoenix; two or three standards before her. Aur: 751/*C*159. Den: 752−3/*C*160−1. Ses: 1711−12/*C*162−3

    64   *Obv.* DIVA FAVSTINA. *Rev.* AETERNITAS, Image of Faustina enthroned between dancing girls (funeral scene with professional mourners). Ses: 1697/*C*10

    65   AETERNITAS, Image of Faustina in biga of elephants. Ses: 1698/*C*11

    66*a* *Obv.* DIVAE FAVSTINAE AVG MATRI CASTRORVM. *Rev.* CONSECRATIO, Funeral pyre surmounted by image of Faustina in biga. Aur: 748. Den: 749/*C*81. Ses: 1709/*C*80.

    66*b* —— *Obv.* DIVA AVG FAVSTINA. Den: 747/*C*77. Ses: 1707/*C*78. As: 1708/*C*79

    67*a* (No legend), Sceptre beside throne (sellisternium in honour of the goddess Faustina). Qui: 754

    67*b* CONSECRATIO, Same type, with peacock in front. Ses: 1704−5/ *C*74

    68   —— Altar (for worship of Diva Faustina). Ses: 1706/*C*76

    69*a* DIANA LVCIFERA, Diana stg. r., with a lighted torch in each hand (Diana, as Hecate, guided the soul of the deceased to the underworld). Ses: 1710/*C*90

    69*b* SIDERIBVS RECEPTA, Same type. Ses: 1715−16/*C*215−16

    70   —— Faustina in biga r. Ses: 1717/*C*217

    71   AETERNITAS S C, Victory holding torch and raising Faustina to heaven. Ses: 1699/*C*12

    72*a* CONSECRATIO, Faustina std. on flying eagle. Ses: 1701/*C*68.

    72*b* —— *Obv.* DIVA FAVSTINA AVG MATR CASTROR. Ses: 1700/*C*67.

    73   *Rev.* CONSECRATIO, Faustina std. on flying peacock. Ses: 1702/ *C*69

        Cf. also 738−754 and 1691−1718 with legend CONSECRATIO or AETERNITAS and symbolic types.

177 Return of Aurelius and Commodus to Rome, with thanks for their escape from shipwreck during the journey. The variant *Fortuna Dux* (for the normal Redux) occurs only here.

    74   TR P XXX IMP VIII COS III P P, Altar inscribed FORT REDVCI. Den: 360/*C*939

    75   FORT RED TR P XXX IMP VIII COS III, Fortuna std. l. Den: 345/ *C*210

    76   FORT DVCI TR P XXX IMP VIII COS III, Same type. Den: 343−4/*C*203

    77   FELICITATI AVG P P IMP VIII COS III, Ship with rowers r. or l.; statue of Neptune on stern. Dup: 1193/*C*189; 1198−9/*C*193−4. As: 1192/*C*188; 1194−7/*C*191−2

78   FELICITATI CAES, Ship with rowers l.; Victory or Neptune on prow. As: 1200–1/*C*195

— — Triumph of Aurelius and Commodus for German victories.

79   DE GERMA IMP VIII COS III P P, Aurelius and Commodus in slow quadriga r. Ses: 1183/*C*160

— — Seventh donative, for victories or promotion of Commodus to the rank of Augustus.

80   LIBERALITAS AVG VII IMP VIII COS III P P, Donation scene with Aurelius and Commodus, Liberalitas (and sometimes Minerva), officer and citizen. Ses: 1207–10/*C*423–6; 1211/*C*427 (legend begins LIBERAL AVGVSTOR).

80

81   Same legend (sometimes IMP VII), Liberalitas stg. Ses: 1150–1; 1205–6/*C*422; 1222. Dup: 1152/*C*421

Joint reign with Commodus, 177–180

178   Final departure of Aurelius for the frontier; vows for his success.

82   VOTA PVBLICA IMP VIIII COS III P P S, Aurelius sacrificing over tripod. Ses: 1226/*C*1026. As: 1235–6/*C*1027–8

FAUSTINA the Younger

Annia Galeria Faustina, the daughter of Antoninus Pius and Faustina the elder, married Marcus Aurelius in 145 with great celebrations (Pius *45–49*, Aurelius *4–6*). When her first child was born in 146, she received the title Augusta; she subsequently gave birth to twelve more children (*see below*), who are often celebrated on the coins struck during the reign of Antoninus (Pius *73, 89–90*; Aurelius *7–8*). Of these, only girls survived until 161 when Commodus was born. Faustina accompanied Aurelius on his campaigns; her devotion earned her the honorary title *Mater Castrorum* (*12*) in 174 after the defeat of the Quadi. She died in Cilicia while returning from the East in 176, and was greatly mourned by Aurelius, who gave her the highest posthumous honours: consecration (Aurelius *63–73*), the title Pia, and an altar erected before the temple of Venus where couples would sacrifice before marriage.

Since many of her coins feature her growing family, and show those who were alive at the time of striking, a list of its members may be helpful (names in capitals are those which appear elsewhere in their own right):

1	Annia Galeria Aurelia Faustina	146–after 161
2	T. Aelius Antoninus	147–147
3	Twins: LUCILLA	149–182
4	— — T. Aurelius Antoninus	149–149
5	T. Aelius Aurelius	152–152
6	Domitia Faustina	157–159
7	Fadilla	159–after 172
8	Cornificia	160–after 211
9	Twins: COMMODUS	161–192
10	— — Antoninus	161–165
11	M. Aurelius Verus	162–169
12	Hadrianus	*c.* 165
13	Vibia Aurelia Sabina	170–after 211

147–161 The growing family of Aurelius and Faustina.

147 1 VENERI GENETRICI, Venus stg. l., holding infant in swaddling clothes (Antoninus 2; this type celebrates the birth of a son). Aur: 512/*C*232–6

2 PVDICITIA, Pudicitia holding child in knee; another stands before (Faustina and Antoninus: 1 and 2). Ses: 382/*C*188

150 3 IVNO, Juno std. l., holding child on knee; another stands before (Faustina and Lucilla: 1 and 3). Aur: 504/*C*129

157 4 FECVNDITAS AVGVSTAE, Faustina std. r., with child on lap; two others stand beside (Faustina, Lucilla, Domitia: 1, 3 and 6). Aur: 681–2/*C*105. As: 1641

159 5 FECVNDITATI AVGVSTAE, Faustina stg. holding infant; girl stg. on either side (Faustina, Lucilla and Fadilla: 1, 3, and 7). Aur: 679–80/*C*104

5   10

6 IVNONI LVCINAE, Same type. Aur: 692–3/*C*134–5. Ses: 1649/*C*136. As: 1650/*C*137

160 7 TEMPOR FELIC, Faustina stg. between two girls and holding two infants (Faustina, Lucilla, Fadilla and Cornificia: 1, 3, 7 and 8). Aur: 718/*C*220. Den: 719/*C*221

8 FECVND AVGVSTAE, Same type. Ses: 1634–5/*C*93, 96. As: 1636–7/*C*97–8

161 9   SAECVLI FELICIT/AS, Two babies on pulvinar; stars above heads (celebration of birth of twin boys, Commodus and Antoninus: 9 and 10). Aur: 709/*C*189. Den: 509/*C*192; 710−12/*C*190−1 Ses: 1665/*C*193 As: 1666/*C*194

    10   TEMPOR FELIC, Faustina stg. l. between four girls, and holding two infants (Faustina, Lucilla, Fadilla, Cornificia, Commodus and Antoninus 1, 3, 7, 8, 9 and 10). Ses: 1673−4/*C*222, 224. As: 1675−7/*C*223, 225

162 Award of the right to travel in a carpentum in the city, on the birth of a son (Aelius: 5).

    11   SPQR, Carpentum drawn by two mules. Ses: 1385/*C*218

174 Award of title *mater castrorum*.

    12   MATRI CASTRORVM, Faustina stg. l., sacrificing over altar; three standards before her. Ses: 1659−61/*C*164−6. As: 1662/*C*167

LUCIUS VERUS

161−January 169

L. Ceionius Commodus, the son of Aelius, was born about 130, and was adopted by Antoninus Pius at the request of Hadrian when his own father died. He then assumed the name L. Aelius Aurelius Commodus. He was raised at the court and admitted to high office, but never gained the title of Caesar. He became co-emperor with full powers (including the tribunician, but not the office of Pontifex Maximus) on the death of Antoninus in 161, the year he shared the consulate with Aurelius (*1−2*). He now changed his name to L. Aurelius Verus, to show his relation to the imperial family, and was engaged to Aurelius' daughter Lucilla. The accession of the two emperors (*3−5*) was marked by celebrations and a donative.

In the very first year of the reign, war broke out with Parthia, when its king installed his chief general on the throne of Armenia and invaded Syria. Verus set out for the East (*6−8*), and organised the counter-attack (*9*) so successfully that the Romans soon won tremendous victories, comparable to those of Trajan. The Armenian capital was taken, a Roman client installed on the throne, and Verus was granted the title Armeniacus (*10−15*). Celebrations for the victory included a donative (*16*). In the next stage of the war, campaigns which began in Syria led to even more spectacular victories when the Parthians were pushed back and the Roman armies penetrated even to their capital, which they captured and burned in 165. Verus now gained the title Parthicus, and Rome acquired a new province in Mesopotamia. The final stage led to Media, where further victories justified another title, Medicus, and brought the conclusion of peace in 166 on terms highly favourable to Rome. Verus now returned to Italy (*17*) to celebrate a great triumph with Aurelius (*18−21*, coins struck over several years), the occasion for another donative (*22*).

During this war, the withdrawal of legions had weakened the northern frontier, and no sooner had the victories been celebrated than a new war began, to meet the invasions of the Marcomanni. The two emperors left Rome before the end of 166 and fought campaigns on the frontier which were rendered more difficult by the plague which Verus' troops had brought back from the East, and was now ravaging the empire. Nevertheless, they won victories which justified another donative (*23*). Aurelius and Verus returned to Rome (*24*) in 168, then set out again for Pannonia (*25*), where they won further victories. On their return, however, Verus suffered a fatal stroke in northern Italy in 169. He was consecrated by Aurelius (Aurelius *33–36*).

161 Joint consulate with Aurelius

1   COS II, Verus stg. l. Den: 457/*C*61. Ses: 1297/*C*62. Dup: 1298/ *C*63

2*a*   – – Aurelius and Verus std. l. on platform; officer stg. behind. Ses: 1299/*C*64

2*b*   TR POT COS II, Aurelius and Verus std. l. on platform; lictor stg. below (Aurelius *10*). Aur: 469/*C*177. Ses: 1307/*C*178

– – Accession to the throne with Aurelius, accompanied by donative.

3   CONCORD/IA/E AVGVSTOR (TR P II) COS II, Verus and Aurelius clasping hands (Aurelius *11*). Aur: 448/*C*23; 449–54/*C*43–7; 456/*C*51; 470–4/*C*49–50. Den: 455/*C*48. Ses: 1278–87/ *C*24–30; 1295–6; 1308–11/*C*36, 38, 40. Dup: 1292–4/*C*33; 1312–13/*C*41–2. As: 1288–91/*C*31–2,35; 1314–16/*C*37,39

3

4   CONCORD AVG (TR P) COS II, Concord std. l. Den: 444–7/*C*17–19,21. Ses: 1276–7/*C*20,22

5   LIB AVGVSTOR TR P COS II, Donation scene with emperors, Liberalitas or soldier, and citizen (Aurelius *13*). Aur: 459/*C*116. Ses: 1301–2/*C*117–18

162 Departure of Verus for the eastern front, with vows for his safe return.

6   PROFECTIO AVG TR P II COS II, Verus on horseback r. Aur: 477–80/*C*135–7. Den: 481/*C*138. Ses: 1321–3/*C*132–4. As: 1356–8/ *C*139–41

7   FORT RED TR POT II/I COS II, Fortuna std. l. Aur: 475–6/*C*86. Ses: 1317–20/*C*87–90; 1342–7/*C*91,93–6. Dup: 1341; 1348/*C*99; 1349/*C*102. As: 1350–5/*C*92,97–8, 100–1

8   FELIC AVG TR P III COS II, Ship with pilot and rowers l.; standards
    at helm; sometimes Victory at stern (several varieties).
    Ses: 1325–8/*C*69, 71–3; 1332–3/*C*76–7; 1339/*C*83. Dup: 1329–
    30/*C*70,75; 1336–8/*C*80–82. As: 1331/*C*74; 1334–5/*C*78–9;
    1340/*C*84

163 Organisation of the eastern campaigns; Verus addresses the troops.
9   ADLOCVT AVG, Verus, with soldier, on platform addressing troops.
    Ses: 1359, 1491/*C*3

164 Victories in Armenia, with installation of a new king, and a donative
in celebration.
10 REX ARMEN/IIS DAT/VS TR P IIII IMP II COS II, Verus std. l. on
    platform, with two soldiers (and officer on Æ); King Sohaemus
    stg. below. Aur: 511–13/*C*157–8, 165. Ses: 1370–2/*C*159,
    160–1; 1374–5/*C*163–4. Dup; 1373/*C*163

10   11

11 (ARMEN) TR P III/I IMP II COS II, Armenia std. l., in mournful
    attitude; standard before or trophy behind her (Aurelius *20*).
    Aur: 498–500/*C*4–5; 502–4/*C*219; 507–8/*C*7. Den: 501/*C*6;
    505–6/*C*220–1; 509/*C*8; 526/*C*255. Dup: 1366/*C*11. As: 1364–
    5/*C*9–10; 1367–8/*C*12–13
12 TR P IIII IMP II COS II, Verus riding r., thrusting spear at fallen
    Armenian. Ses: 1402–3/*C*256, 258. As: 1404–7/*C*257, 257–61
13 TR P IIII IMP II COS II, Victory attaching shield inscribed VIC AVG
    to palm tree (Aurelius *21*). Aur: 522–5/*C*247–8; 533–4/*C*267.
    Ses: 1396–9/*C*249–52. Dup: 1400–1/*C*253–4
14 VICT AVG TR P III/I IMP II COS II, Victory stg. r., holding trophy;
    Armenia at feet (Aurelius *22*). Ses: 1360–1/*C*330–1; 1408–10/
    *C*332, 334–5. Dup: 1411/*C*333
15 TR POT V IMP II COS II, Verus stg. l., between four standards
    (representing the four legions which fought in the war). (Aurelius
    *22*A). Ses: 1426–7/*C*188. Dup: 1428/*C*189
16 LIBERAL AVG TR P V IMP II COS II, Liberalitas stg. l. (Aurelius *23*).
    Dup: 1419/*C*121. As: 1416–18/*C*119–20, 122
165 Return of Verus to Rome.
17 FORT RED TR P V IMP II COS II, Fortune std. l. Dup: 1415/*C*109.
    As: 1412–14/*C*106–8
166 Celebration of eastern victories, with triumph and donative.

18 TR P V/I IMP III/I COS II, Victory attaching shield inscribed VIC
   PAR to palm tree (Aurelius *24*). Aur: 562−5/*C*276−8; 571/
   *C*292. Den: 566/*C*279. Ses: 1456−7/*C*206−7. Dup: 1436; 1458/
   *C*208. As: 1459

19 −− Parthian with hands bound std. at base of trophy. Aur:
   539/*C*272; 547/*C*285. Den: 540−2/*C*273−4; 548/*C*286. Ses:
   1429−30/*C*190−1; 1432−4/*C*193−5; 1440−4/*C*199−201;
   1447/*C*204. Dup: 1431/*C*192; 1435/*C*196; 1445/*C*202. As:
   1446/*C*203

20 TR POT VI IMP IIII COS II, Aurelius and Verus in triumphal
   quadriga l. (Aurelius *26*). Ses: 1455/*C*205

21*a* TR POT VII IMP IIII COS III, Three trophies (for victories in
   Armenia, Parthia and Media: Aurelius *27*). Dup: 1465/*C*301.
   As: 1464/*C*300

21*b* −− but TR POT VIII and captive std. below each trophy. As:
   1474−5/*C*321−2

22 LIB AVG III TR P VI COS II, Liberalitas stg. l. (Aurelius *29a*). Den:
   546/*C*123

167 Donative on initial victories over Marcommani and Quadi.
23 CONG AVG IIII TR P VII IMP IIII COS III, Liberalitas stg. l.
   (Aurelius 32a). Aur: 568/*C*52

168 Return of Verus to Rome
24 TR P VIII IMP IIII (or V) COS III, Std. Roma extending hand (or
   Victory on globe) to stg. Verus. As: 1473/*C*320; 1482/*C*324

−− Departure for the front, with vows for a safe return.
25 FORT RED TR P VIII/I IMP V COS III, Fortuna std. l. Aur: 582−5/
   *C*110; 596. Den: 586/*C*111

LUCILLA

Annia Lucilla, daughter of Marcus Aurelius and Faustina, was born in
149 (Aurelius *7*; Faustina II *3*), and was engaged to Verus on his accession
to the throne. In 164, Aurelius accompanied her as far as Brundisium,
where he saw her off to Ephesus, the site of the wedding. She and Verus
had three children; their fate is unknown. After Verus' death in 169,
Lucilla was unhappily married to an elderly senator, Pompeianus. When
Commodus came to the throne, he honoured Lucilla, but they soon fell
into dispute, and she participated in a plot against him. As a result, she
was exiled to Capri and there executed in 182.

164 Vows on marriage to Verus.
1 VOTA PVBLICA in or around laurel wreath. Aur: 790/*C*97. Den:
   791−2/*C*98−9

164−169 The growing family of Verus and Lucilla.
2 FECVNDITAS, Lucilla std. r., holding infant on her lap; a
   young girl stands by her feet. Aur: 764/*C*18; 766/*C*20. Den:
   765/*C*19

1

3   — — Lucilla std. l. or r., nursing a baby; a boy and a girl stand beside her. Ses: 1736−8/C21−3

COMMODUS

Caesar October 166/Augustus 177−December 192

Lucius Aurelius Commodus, the ninth child of Marcus Aurelius and Faustina, and the only boy to survive infancy, was born at Lanuvium in Latium (*19,68*) in August 161. His doting father provided him with the best teachers and awarded him high honours at an early age. Already made Caesar when he was five, Commodus was presented to the army at the age of ten (Aurelius *53*) and assumed his father's title of Germanicus. He was coopted into the priestly colleges in 175 and made *princeps iuventutis* (*1−4*), an occasion marked by the formal presentation of a shield and spear by the knights and by vows for a safe return from the frontier and a donative (*5−9*). Commodus participated in the honour of his father's victories (*10−13*), and set out with him for the East, whence he returned to Rome (*14−15*) in 176 to share Aurelius' triumph (Aurelius *79*) and gain the title imperator. Late in that year he received the tribunician power, which gave him a substantial role in the government and marked the commencement of his reign for the purpose of calculating subsequent anniversaries. In 177, he was consul for the first time (*16*) and was raised to full coregency with his father by the grant of the titles Augustus and *pater patriae* (*19*). He gave a donative with his father to celebrate the victories (*17−18*) and married Crispina in the same year. Soon after, he presided over public vows (*20*), no doubt for the success of the renewed war, which obliged him to set out for the front (*21*). He was thus present when Aurelius died in March 180, leaving him to become sole emperor.

On his accession, Commodus was presented to the troops, to whom he gave an address and a rich donative (*22--23*). He concluded the war with the Germans by an honourable peace, but abandoned his father's plans for further expansion and swiftly returned to Rome (*24*) where he celebrated a triumph and had Aurelius consecrated (*25−27*). Commodus began the year 181 by assuming his third consulate (*28*) and continued it by undertaking vows (*29*) for the successful completion of a first decade of rule, celebrated by a fourth donative (*30−31*).

The reign began to take a new direction in 182, when the emperor's sister Lucilla joined a conspiracy of senators against him. When this failed, Lucilla was executed, and Commodus entered upon a policy of open hostility toward the Senate, which led to a more autocratic and corrupt government dominated by favourites. His survival of the attempted assassination may have been the occasion for a fifth donative (*32–33*). Later in the same year, Crispina was executed for adultery.

Commodus assumed the consulate several times; his fourth (*34*) was in 183, a year also marked by the production of circus games (*35*) on an unknown occasion. The external situation had so far been peaceful, but a serious war broke out in Britain in 184. The swift victory of the Roman forces was celebrated on the coins of that and the following year (*36–37*) The emperor celebrated the tenth anniversary of his tribunician power with vows (*39–40*) undertaken in 185 for the continuation of his reign and completed in 186 at the end of the first decade. The anniversary (*41*) was celebrated by the institution of new games, the *Primi Decennales* (*42–43*), and was considered the beginning of a new golden age (*44*). Other vows, *vota publica* (*38*), celebrated in 184, are apparently different, representing state vows on behalf of the emperor.

The corruption of the regime was now causing widespread protests, and a detachment of troops marched on Rome demanding the deposition of the praetorian prefect Perennis. Commodus, who had heard rumours that Perennis was plotting treason, threw him to the troops to be executed, and thanked them for their loyalty (*45–46*). To counter the pretentions of Perennis, Commodus stressed the nobility of his descent from a line of emperors (*47*). A fifth consulate (*48–49*) followed in 186; soon afterwards, the deserter turned bandit chief, Maternus, led a force which approached Rome and came close to assassinating the emperor. A sixth donative (*50–52*) apparently celebrates the defeat of this threat. In the same year, Commodus created an auxiliary grain fleet based at Carthage (*53*) in case the normal supplies from Egypt failed. In 187, he received the honorific title *pater senatus* (*54–55*), especially ironic in view of his great hostility toward the fathers, and his persecution of them.

At about this time, coins appear which indicate Commodus' increasing identification of himself with Jupiter, first in the form Exsuperantissimus (or Exsuperatorius), 'the supreme' (*56*), and later with Jupiter Juvenis (*57*), 'the young', whose epithet reflects, once again, the golden age (*58*) which the emperor was bringing. On the mortal level, there were revolts in Africa in 188 and 189 whose suppression by the general Pertinax was considered a major victory (*59*); the subsequent fortification of this and other provinces brought security to the whole world (*60*)

Commodus held the consulate again (*61–62*) in 190, when he was thirty (*63*). This year saw the fall of another minister, Cleander, whose corruption had produced famine in Rome and brought the state to the verge of civil war. An outbreak of the plague (*69–70*), which afflicted all Italy, contributed to the severity of the famine. A seventh donative (*64–66*) may have been given to assure support after this crisis. Vows for a twentieth year of reign were now undertaken (*67*). The extravagance of

Commodus now began to turn to madness, as he refounded Lanuvium as a colony (*68*), not only because it was his birthplace, but because it was here that he first fought wild beasts in the arena and arrogated to himself the title of the Roman Hercules.

The emperor's growing megalomania dominated the last years of his reign. He withdrew from the normal activities of public life to devote himself to a different public role, that of hunter and gladiator in the arena. In 191, Commodus changed his name, which had become M. Aurelius Commodus Antoninus on his accession in 180, back to its original form, L. Aelius Commodus. At about the same time, he changed the names of the months to correspond to his name and titles, including Amazonius (appropriate to a gladiator), Herculeus, Romanus and Exsuperatorius, the latter reflecting the form of Jupiter with whom he identified himself. Some of the accounts of these years might seem fantastic were they not supported by the evidence of the coinage of 191–192 which shows an increasingly close association of the emperor with a range of divinities (*71–76*). The Egyptian gods Serapis and Isis (*76,80*) figure prominently as he became their particular devotee and publicly practised their cult. Commodus felt especially close to the gods who had saved him from conspiracies: the plot of Perennis had been revealed to him on the festival of Jupiter Capitolinus (*73*); the revolt of Maternus would have murdered the emperor at the festival of the Great Mother (*75*); and the empire had escaped mob violence produced by famine and the corruption of Cleander by the timely arrival of the Egyptian grain fleet – that is, Serapis (*76*) had saved Commodus.

Meanwhile, Commodus celebrated his seventh consulate (*77*) in 192 and gave his eighth donative (*78*). His megalomania was now manifested in his renaming the African grain fleet (*79*) as 'Commodiana Herculea', and adding to Alexandria and Carthage, the main sources of grain, the appellations 'Commodiana Togata'. It also appeared in his growing identification with a range of deities (*80–81*) which culminated when he triumphantly styled himself the Roman Hercules (*82–84*) for his prowess in the arena, and expected suitable divine worship. During these years, a great fire broke out in the temple of Peace, consuming it and large parts of the city. The consequent rebuilding was considered to be a new foundation of Rome, with Commodus as its founder, and Colonia Commodiana (*85*) as its name. The new foundation was celebrated by games whose magnificence was praised on the coinage (*86*), and by a donative (*87*). These, the last types of the reign, were struck preparatory to a planned great celebration on New Year's Day 193, when Commodus proposed to assume the consulate in the dress of a gladiator. This stirred such indignation even among his entourage that he was assassinated the night before he could degrade the office. His memory was swiftly execrated by the Senate.

Caesar, 166−177

175 Commodus enrolled in the priestly colleges, and made *princeps iuventutis* and thus heir to the throne. Presentation of a shield by the equestrian order, with prayers for the prince's safe return from the front. Castor here first appears on the imperial coinage in his role as patron of the equestrians. First donative for these honours.

1   PIETAS AVG, Priestly implements. Den: 613−4/*C*401−2. Ses: 1526/*C*403. As: 1538−9/*C*404−5

2   PONTIF, Knife, bucranium, apex and simpulum. As: 1514/*C*599; 1540

3   PRINC IVVENT, Commodus stg. l., trophy on r. Aur: 600/*C*605; 602; 615/*C*606. Den: 601/*C*607; 603/*C*608; 616−17/*C*609. Ses: 1518/*C*610; 1520/*C*612; 1527−9. As: 1519/*C*611; 1521−2/*C*613; 1541−2/*C*615−6

3   14

4   PRINCIPI IVVENTVTIS, Clasped hands holding eagle on prow. As: 1548−9/*C*603−4

5*a*   EQUESTER ORDO PRINCIPI IVVENT S C on shield lying on two spears. As: 1534−5/*C*105

5*b*   Same legend in oak wreath. As: 1536/*C*104

6   TR P II/I IMP II COS P P, Castor stg. l., with horse. Aur: 648/*C*760. Ses: 1578−80/*C*754

7   PRINCIPI IVVENTVTIS around altar inscribed FORT REDVCI. Aur: 618/*C*601. Den: 619/*C*602

8   LIBERALITAS AVG, Donation scene with Commodus, Liberalitas and citizen. Aur: 597/*C*292; 612. Ses: 1516/*C*293. As: 1517/*C*294

9   −−Liberalitas stg. l. Den: 598−9/*C*291

−− Victories over the Germans and Sarmatians (Aurelius *58−61*).

10*a* DE GERMANIS, Two captives std. at foot of trophy. Aur: 605. Den: 606−7/*C*77. As: 1532/*C*78

10*b* TR P II COS (P P) DE GERM same type. Aur: 632/*C*80. Ses: 1554−6/*C*81−2, 88; 1565/*C*92 1566−8/*C*83, 86. Dup: 1568/ *C*84−5

11   TR P/OT II COS (P P) DE GERM/ANIS, pile of weapons. Aur: 629; 633/*C*89. Ses: 1569−70/*C*79

12*a* DE SARMATIS, Type as *10*. Aur: 608/*C*93. Den: 609. As: 1533/ *C*94

12*b* TR P II COS (P P) DE SARM, same type. Aur: 634/*C*98. Ses: 1557/
*C*97; 1571−3/*C*99−100 Dup: 1574−5/*C*101−2

13 TR P/OT II COS (P P) DE SARM/ATIS, Type as *11*. Aur: 630, 635.
Ses: 1576−7/*C*95−6

176 Return of Commodus to Rome, after escape from shipwreck.

14 ADVENTVS CAES, Commodus on horseback r. Aur: 604/*C*1

15 FELICITATI CAES, Ship l., with pilot and rowers. (Aurelius *77−
78*). As: 1513; 1550/*C*118

177 First consulate.

16 TR P/OT (II) COS, Commodus in quadriga. Ses: 1563−4/*C*749−
50. As: 1553/*C*737

−− Second donative, together with Aurelius, probably to celebrate the
victories.

17 TR P II COS LIBERALITAS AVG (II), Donation scene, with Aurelius
and Commodus, officer, and citizen. (Aurelius *80*). Ses:
1558−61/*C*295−7

18 −− II, Liberalitas stg. l. (Aurelius *81*). Ses: 1562/*C*298

Augustus with Aurelius, 177−180

177 Honours to the goddess of Commodus' birthplace, probably in
thanks for his promotion to Augustus.

19 IVNONI SISPITAE TR P II IMP II COS P P, Juno Sospita adv. r.;
snake in front. Aur: 645. Den: 646/*C*270. Ses: 1582−3/*C*271

178 Vows, probably for success in the renewed fighting.

20*a* TR P II IMP II COS P P VOTA PVBLICA, Commodus sacrificing over
tripod (Aurelius *82*). Ses: 1584/*C*981. As: 1598/*C*982 (TR P III)

20*b* VOTA PVBLICA IMP II COS P P, as previous, with victimarius and
bull on l. Ses: 1594−5/*C*979−80

−− Departure for the northern front.

21 −− IMP III COS II P P PROFECTIO AVG, Commodus riding r.,
preceded by a soldier and followed by three others. Ses:
1613/*C*619

Sole reign, 180−192

180 First donative, on accession.

22 LIB AVG TR P V IMP IIII COS II P P, Liberalitas stg. l. Aur: 10a, b/
*C*300. Den: 10, 10a/*C*301−2

23 LIBERALITAS AVG TR P V IMP IIII COS II P P, Donation scene with
Commodus, officer, Liberalitas and citizen. Ses: 300/*C*305

−− Arrival in Rome.

24 ADVENTVS AVG IMP IIII COS II P P, Commodus riding r. Ses: 294/
*C*3

24A FORT RED IMP IIII COS II PP, Fortuna stg. l. Ses: 295/*C*165−6

— — Funeral and consecration of Marcus Aurelius. All with *obv.* DIVVS
M ANTONINVS PIVS, Bare head r.

25 CONSECRATIO, Funeral pyre surmounted by quadriga. Aur: 275/
*C*96. Den: 275/*C*97. Ses: 662/*C*98

26 — — Image of Aurelius in shrine on quadriga of elephants.
Ses: 661/*C*95

27 Eagle stg. or flying; many varieties. Den: 264–274/*C*78–84,
88, 91. Ses: 654–660/*C*85, 87, 89, 92–4. As: 663–4/*C*86, 90.

181 Third consulate.

28 TR P VI IMP IIII COS III P P, Commodus in quadriga. Ses: 306/
*C*813. As: 319/*C*814

— — Decennial vows, at end of fifth tribunician year, accompanied by
fourth donative.

29 VOTA DEC ANN SVSC TR P VI IMP IIII COS III P P, Commodus
sacrificing over tripod. Dup: 318/*C*976. As: 321/*C*974–5

30 LIB AVG IIII TR P VI IMP IIII COS III P P, Liberalitas stg. l. Den: 22/
*C*307. Ses: 309/*C*308–9

31 — —Donation scene, as type *23*. Ses: 310

182 Fifth donative, perhaps on escape from assassination.

32 LIBERAL V TR P VII IMP IIII COS III P P, Donation scene, as type 18.
Aur: 37/*C*313. Ses: 329/*C*314

33 (Same legend, but LIB), Liberalitas stg. l. Den: 36/*C*311–12

33   37

183 Fourth consulate

34 TR P VIII IMP V COS IIII P P, Commodus in quadriga. Ses: 353/
*C*869; 376/*C*910–12

— — Circus games, occasion unknown.

35 MVNIFICENTIA AVG TR P VIII/I IMP VI COS IIII P P, Elephant. As:
397/*C*377; 432/*C*378

184 Victories in Britain.

36 BRITT P M TR P VIIII IMP VII COS IIII P P, Britannia stg. l. Ses: 437/
*C*35–6

37 VICT BRIT P M TR P VIIII (or X or XI) IMP VII COS IIII P P, Victory
std. r., inscribing shield set on knee Ses: 440/*C*945; 451–2/
*C*946; 459e/*C*947

— — State vows on behalf of the emperor; occasion unknown.

38 VOTA PVBLICA TR P VIIII IMP VI COS IIII P P, Commodus sacrificing
over tripod. As: 433/*C*983

185−6   Decennial vows undertaken in 185 for continuation of rule, and completed in 186 to celebrate its first decade. The anniversary was celebrated by the institution of games called *Primi Decennales*, and considered as the beginning of a new golden age, introduced by Janus, the god of beginnings. The games were also commemorated by inserting the letters P D on the obverse below Commodus' bust: *43A*; others included in types *47*, *53* and *56*.

39   VOTA SVSC/EP DEC/EN P M TR P VIIII(or X) IMP VII COS IIII P P, Commodus sacrificing over tripod. Aur: 99*b*/*C*1002; 115. Den: 99a,c/*C*1003−4. Ses: 441/*C*988−9; 454/*C*990. Dup: 456/*C*987. As: 444a

40   SAEC FEL PM TR P X(I) IMP VII COS IIII (or V)P P, Victory stg. r., inscribing VO DE on shield attached to palm tree. Den: 113/*C*663; 136/*C*664−5. Ses: 449/*C*666−8; 472/ *C*669−70. As: 482/*C*671

41   VOT SOL DEC/EN P M TR P XI(or XII or XIII) IMP VIII COS V P P, Commodus sacrificing over tripod, victim beside. Den: 140/*C*1000; 161/*C*1001. As: 522

42   DECENNALES PRIMI ROMAE Constituti, P M TR P VIIII IMP VII COS III P P, Roma stg. l.; bundle of ears of wheat behind. Den: 96

43   PRIMI DECENN P M TR P X IMP VII COS IIII P P S C in wreath. As: 459a−b/ *C*600

43A   *Obv.* P D below bust. *Rev.* SPQR LAETITIAE C V in wreath. Ses: 551/ *C*713. As: 554/*C*400

44   P M TR P XI IMP VII COS V P P, Image of Janus in domed distyle shrine. Ses: 460/*C*489. As: 479/*C*490

185−6   Fidelity and concord of the troops, with an address by Commodus, after the execution of Perennis. The type of Nobilitas, new to the coinage, stresses the legitimacy of Commodus, who could trace his ancestry to Nerva, and was the first emperor born in the purple, in opposition to the pretentions of Perennis, who hoped to place his own son on the throne.

45   FID EXERC P M TR P X/I/I IMP VII/I COS IIII (or V)P P, Commodus addressing troops. Aur: 110b/*C*139. Den: 110/*C*140−2; 130; 148/*C*144. Ses: 468/*C*134−8

45

46   CONC MIL P M TR P XI IMP VII COS V P P, Two soldiers clasping hands before Commodus, and flanked by two other soldiers. Aur: 127/*C*59−60

47 NOBILIT/AS AVG P M TR P XI/I IMP VIII COS V P P, Nobilitas stg. l. Aur: 155/*C384*. Den: 139/*C382*; 155/*C385*. Ses: 485/*C379*; 501/*C381*. As: 489/*C383*; 509/*C386*

186 Fifth consulate.

48 P M TR P XI IMP VII COS V P P, Commodus std. l. on curule chair. Den: 124−5/*C504*−5. Ses: 463/*C506*; 475/*C943* (no P M)

49 −−Commodus in quadriga r. Ses: 464/*C510*

−− Sixth donative, probably on suppression of revolt of Maternus; with celebration of the loyalty of the urban troops.

50 LIB/ERAL AVG (VI) P M TR P XI IMP VII COS V P P, Liberalitas stg. l. Den: 132/*C280*; 133/*C316*. Dup: 478/*C318*

51 −−Donation scene, as type *23*. Den: 134/*C315*. Ses: 448/*C328* (TR P X); 471a/*C317*; 484(IMP VIII)

52 FIDEI COH P M TR P XII COS V, Fides stg. l. Ses: 496/*C125*

−− Creation of new grain fleet.

53 −− PROVID AVG P M TR P XII IMP VIIII COS V P P, Ship sailing l. or r. Aur: 158. Ses: 486−7/*C635*−7

53   56

187 Award of title *pater senatus* by the Senate.

54 PAT/ER SENAT/VS, Genius of Senate stg. l. Aur: 157/*C396*. Den: 156−7/*C397*. Ses: 502/*C398*

55 PIET/ATI SENAT/VS (P M TR P XIIII) C/OS V P P, Genius of Senate and Commodus clasping hands. Den: 194/*C408*. Ses: 549/*C410*. As: 538/*C411*

−− Increasing identification of Commodus with Jupiter, marking the introduction of a new golden age, led by Janus.

56 IOVI EXSVP/ERantissimo (P M TR P XI/I IMP VIII COS V P P), Jupiter std. l. Aur: 153. Den: 138/*C241*; 152/*C242*. Ses: 483/*C247*. Dup: 531/*C250*. As: 488/*C248*; 508/*C249*

57 IOV/I IVVEN/I (P M TR P XIIII IMP VIII COS V P P), Jupiter stg. l. Den: 173/*C259*; 187/*C260*. Ses: 499/*C252*; 525/*C253*; 542/*C256*. Dup. 532/*C255*. As: 535/*C254*

58 P M TR P XII IMP VIII COS V P P, Image of Janus in distyle shrine. Aur: 141/*C515*

188/9 Victories in Africa, with security brought by rebuilding of the defences.

59 VICT FEL/I P M TR P XIII IMP VIII (COS V P P), Victory adv. l.,

holding wreath over two shields inscribed s c set on base inscribed cos v p p. Den: 180−1/C949−50. Ses: 530/C948. As: 540

60   SEC/VR/IT ORB P M TR P XIII (IMP VIII) COS V (DES VI) (P P), Securitas std. l. Aur: 190/C696. Den: 179/C697; 190/C695. Ses: 529/C698; 545/C699

190 Sixth consulate, and wishes for Commodus' thirtieth birthday, symbolised by his Genius.

61   (P M) TR P XV IMP VIII COS VI, Commodus in quadriga. Aur: 213. Ses: 558/C559. As: 568/C560; 577/C944

62   − − Commodus std. l. on curule chair. Den: 212/C555. Ses: 557/C556

63   GEN AVG FELIC (P M TR P XV IMP VIII) COS VI, Genius stg. l., sacrificing. Aur: 227/C171. Den: 227/C172. Ses: 561/C174

− − Seventh donative, probably on fall of Cleander, with repeated thanks for the loyalty of the praetorian troops.

64   LIBERAL/ITAS AVG VII P M TR P XV IMP VIII COS VI, Liberalitas stg. l. Aur: 202b/C322. Den: 202a/C323. Ses: 563/C320

65   Donation scene, as type 23. Ses: 564/C321

66   FIDEI COH/ORTIVM (AVG) (P M TR P XV/I COS VI), Fides stg. l. Den: 199/C124; 207/C126; 220/ C127 Ses: 580/C128. As: 590/C129

− − Vows for twenty years of reign, undertaken after ten years of sole rule or fifteen of tribunician power.

67a   VOTIS XX COS VI in laurel wreath. Den: 229/C998

67b   VOT XX P M TR P XV IMP VIII COS VI S C in wreath. As: 576/C999

190 Refounding of Lanuvium, the birthplace of Commodus as a colony.

68   COLonia LANuvina COMMODIANA P M TR P XV IMP VIII COS VI, Commodus, as priest, ploughing r. Ses: 560/C39. As: 570/C40

191 Vows of thanks for salvation from the plague.

69   VOT SOL/V PRO SALute POpuli ROmani (COS VI P P), Commodus, with bull, sacrificing over tripod: Æ types add victimarius, one or two attendants and fluteplayer. Den: 262/C984. Ses: 602−3/C985−6

70a   SALUS GENeris HVMani (COS VI P P), Salus stg. l., raising kneeling figure. Den: 260/C677. Ses: 600/C678−9. As: 606/C680

70b   COS VI P P, Same type. Avq: 225/C72

− − Growing megalomania of Commodus, with close connection between him and the gods, especially in their role as protectors against plots.

71   CONC/OR/DIAE COMMODI (AVG P M TR P XVI IMP VIII COS VI), Concord stg. l. Aur: 198b/C42; 219a/C44. Den: 198/C43; 219/C45. Ses: 579/C47; 585/ C46. As: 589/C48

72   HERC COM/MODIANO P M TR P XVI COS VI, Hercules sacrificing over altar. Aur: 221/C180. Ses: 581/C177. Dup: 586/C179 As: 591/C178

73a   COS VI P P, Jupiter resting hand on Commodus' shoulder; both standing. Qui: 226/C71

73*b*   I O M SPONSOR SEC AVG (COS VI P P), Same type. Den: 255/
C239. Ses: 596/C240

73b

83

74   IOVI DEFENS SALVTIS AVG (COS VI P P), Jupiter stg. r.; seven
stars in field. Den: 256/C245. Ses: 597/C246
75   MATRI DEV/M CONSERV AVG (COS VI P P), Cybele riding on lion.
Den: 258/C354. Ses: 599/C355
76   SERAPIDI CONSERV AVG (COS VI P P), Serapis stg. Aur: 261/
C704. Den: 261/C703. Ses: 601/C705. Dup: 605/C707. As:
607/C706
192 Seventh consulate, perhaps the occasion for an eighth donative.
77   P M TR P XVII IMP VIII COS VII P P, Commodus in quadriga. Ses:
615/ C597
78   LIB AVG VIII P M TR P XVII COS VII P P, Liberalitas stg. l. Aur:
239a/C324. Den: 239/C325. As: 627/C326
Renaming and reorganisation of the African grain fleet.
79   — — PROVIDENTIAE AVG, Hercules, foot on prow, and
Africa clasping hands. Aur: 259/C642. Den: 259a/C643. Ses:
641/C644
— — Megalomania of Commodus, including a close connection with
Isis, to whom he was especially devoted, and culminating in
identification as the 'Roman Hercules'.
80   (P M TR P XVII IMP VIII) COS VII P P, Commodus, crowned by
Victory, clasping hands with Serapis and Isis over altar. Aur:

246/*C*73. Ses: 614/ *C*592−3, 595. Dup: 621/*C*594; 628/*C*74. As: 630/*C*75

81 FELIC COM P M TR P XVII COS VII P P, Felicitas stg. Aur: 238

82 HERCVLI ROMANO AVG, Hercules crowning trophy. Aur: 254/ *C*200−1. Den: 254. Ses: 640/*C*203. Dup: 643/*C*204

83 *Obv.* L AEL AVREL COMM AVG P FEL, Bust of Commodus, as Hercules, wearing lion's skin. *Rev.* HERCVLI ROMANO AVG/V, Club, bow, and quiver. Aur: 253/*C*196. Den: 253/*C*195. Ses: 639/*C*199

84 − − HERCVL/I ROMAN/O AVG/V/STO, Club in wreath. Aur: 251/ *C*188. Den: 250−2/*C*189−91. Ses: 637−8/*C*192. As: 644/ *C*193−4.

− − Refoundation of Rome as Colonia Commodiana, celebrated with splendid games and a donative.

85 *Obv.* as *83*. *Rev.* HERC ROM COND/ITORI (P M TR P XVII/I IMP VIII) COS VII P P, Commodus, as Hercules, ploughing with two oxen. Aur: 247/*C*181. Ses: 616/*C*183; *BMC* p. 845. Dup: 629/*C*182

86 MAGNIFICENTIAE AVG COS VII P P in wreath. Den: 248/*C*343. As: 631/*C*344

87 LIB AVG VIIII P M TR P XVII COS VII P P, Liberalitas stg. l. Den: 240/*C*327

CRISPINA

The grandfather of Bruttia Crispina had been consul under Antoninus Pius and her father campaigned with Marcus Aurelius in the Sarmatian wars. She was married to Commodus, the heir to the throne, after the triumph of 177, and given the title Augusta. After he became emperor, she was involved in a plot against him and exiled to Capri on the accusation of adultery. She was executed there about 183. Her coin types, which include dedications not found elsewhere, probably refer to prayers on her marriage, though they may equally indicate restoration of the respective altars in Rome.

177 Marriage with Commodus.

1 DIS CONIVGALIBVS, Lighted and garlanded altar. Aur: 280/ *C*13−14

2 DIS GENITALIBVS, Same type. Den: 281/*C*15−16

PERTINAX

January−March 193

P. Helvius Pertinax was born in 126, the son of a freedman. He had an extremely distinguished career in the army, rising to command legions and govern provinces, including Dacia, Syria, Britain and Africa. By 192, the year of his second consulate, he was recognised as one of the leading political figures of the age and was a natural choice for emperor when Commodus was murdered. Pertinax assumed office on New Year's Day 193, and attempted reforms of the finances and administration, with special attention to the poor. His efforts to establish military discipline, however, alienated the praetorians, who murdered him after a reign of three months. His death inaugurated a period of civil wars, in which Severus, who revered the memory of Pertinax, gained power and had him consecrated after an elaborate state funeral (Severus *4–5*).

193 Donative, with thanks for the liberation of the citizens from the tyranny of Commodus, and vows, on accession.
   1   LIBERATIS CIVIBVS, Liberalitas stg. l. Den: 5–6/*C28*
   2   LIB AVG TR P II COS II, Liberalitas stg. l. Ses: 18/*C25*. Dup: 25A/*C26*. As: 34/*C27*
   3   — — Donation scene with Pertinax, officer, citizen and Liberalitas. Ses: 19/*C23*. Dup: 26/*C24*
   4   VOT DECEN TR P COS II, Pertinax sacrificing. Aur: 13/*C55, 57*. Den: 13/*C56*. Ses: 24/*C58*. Dup: 31A/*C59*. As: 39
   5   PRIMI DECENNALES COS II S C in oak wreath. Dup: 28
— — Honours to the gods who presided over 1 January: Janus, the god of beginnings, and Fortuna, who had a festival on that day.
   6   IANO CONSERVAT, Janus stg. Den: 3/*C17*

6

   7   DIS CVSTODIBVS, Fortuna stg. l. Den: 2/*C14*. Ses: 15/*C15*

DIDIUS JULIANUS

March–June 193

M. Didius Severus Julianus, born in Milan in 133 of a distinguished family, was raised in the house of Domitia Lucilla, the mother of Marcus Aurelius, and rose rapidly through her influence to command legions, govern numerous provinces, and hold high office in Rome. Julianus was thus a rich, highly successful and ambitious senator when Pertinax was murdered. The praetorians, who commanded the situation, heard the claims to the empire of the prefect of the city, Sulpicianus, but chose Julianus when he offered them a higher bribe — an auction of the empire which is usually considered one of the lowest points of Roman history. Julianus was swiftly recognised by the Senate, and his wife and daughter (whose coins have no historical types), were made Augustae. He never gained popularity with the people, and was unsuccessful in his efforts to maintain the loyalty of the frontier legions, although he offered amnesty to those in revolt. As the forces of Severus neared Rome, Julianus was deserted by his followers and murdered on 1 June after a reign of sixty-six days.

193 Accession to the throne.

    1a RECTOR ORBIS, Julianus stg. l. Aur: 3/*C*14. Den: 3/*C*15. Ses: 16/*C*17. Dup: 13/*C*16

    1b — — Julianus std. l. on curule chair. Ses: 17/*C*19

Efforts to gain military support.

1

  2   CONCORD MILIT, Concord stg. l., holding standard. Aur: 1; 5/*C*1. Den: 1/*C*2. Ses: 14/*C*3, 4. Dup: 11/*C*5

PESCENNIUS NIGER

April 193−October 194

C. Pescennius Niger, born *c.* 135 in Italy, had a successful career which led him to become governor of Syria in 191. When news of the murder of Pertinax and of the hostility of the populace to Julianus arrived, Niger was proclaimed emperor in Antioch with the support of nine legions and all the provinces of the East. It was probably then that he assumed the surname Justus (though it may have been a family name). Unfortunately for Niger's cause, Severus occupied Rome and swiftly marched against him, to win decisive victories in Asia Minor. Niger fled to Antioch where he was captured and killed. His coins feature invocations to the native Syrian gods in Roman guise, as well as his surname Justus, whose connotations were quite different from those of Severus'; both parties issued propaganda featuring their names.

193 Invocations of the Syrian gods: the Tyche and Apollo of Antioch, and the Zeus of Heliopolis, in Roman guise. The coins with Fortuna/ Tyche also represent prayers for a safe arrival in Rome.

    1a FORTVNAE RED/V/CI, Fortune std. l., with her attributes or those of Pax or Concordia. Den: 20−6/*C* 23−4, 26, 28

    1b Fortuna stg. l., with her attributes or those of Felicitas or Aequitas. Den: 28−30/*C*25−7

2   APOLLINI SANCTO, Apollo (worshipped in Daphne, the suburb of Antioch) stg. l. Den: 2/*C*3

3   IOVI PRAES ORBIS (Jupiter, Ruler of the World, with a title appropriate to Zeus, the patron of Heliopolis in Syria). Den: 43/*C*54

4   MINER VICTRIS, Minerva stg. l. (perhaps an appeal to Athena Nikephoros, the patron goddess of Pergamum, in Niger's domains). Den: 59−61A/*C*53−4

— — The surname of Niger, representing the justice of his cause.

5   IVSTI AVG, Two capricorns supporting shield decorated with seven stars. Den: 44/*C*42

5

6   VICTOR IVST AVG, Victory adv. l. Den: 81/*C*76−8

CLODIUS ALBINUS

Caesar April 193/Augustus Autumn 195 − February 197

D. Clodius Septimius Albinus, born of a distinguished family in Hadrumetum in Africa, commanded armies under Commodus and became governor of Britain before 193. Since he was a viable candidate for the throne after the death of Pertinax, and highly popular in the Senate, Severus made him an ally by giving him the title of Caesar and adopting him as his heir, soon after his occupation of Rome. Severus was thus left free to deal with Niger, whom he defeated in 194, the year of Albinus' second consulate. Relations between Augustus and Caesar then began to deteriorate, for it was apparent that Severus intended to promote his own sons rather than Albinus. Therefore, late in 195, Albinus was proclaimed emperor at Lugdunum, which became the main base of his power. Severus, refusing to recognise this rank, marched into Gaul where he defeated and killed Albinus in 197.

193 Appointment as Caesar, by the foresight of Severus.

    1   PROVID AVG COS, Providentia stg. l. Aur: 1/*C*57. Den: 1/*C*55−6, 58

194 Celebration of origin, with honours to the god of Hadrumetum.

    2   SAEC/VLO FRVGIF/ERO COS II, Saeculum Frugiferum stg. l. Aur: 9/*C*70. Den: 8/*C*65; 12/*C*67 (no cos II). Ses: 56/*C*71

    2*b*   Saeculum Frugiferum stg. l., flanked by sphinxes. Aur: 10/*C*68

— — Vows for Severus' success against Niger.

    3 FORT REDVCI COS II, Fortuna std. l. Aur: 5/*C*28−9. Den: 5/*C*30. Ses: 53/*C*32−3. Dup/As: 59/*C*34

195−7 Honours to Lugdunum, Albinus' base.

    4 GEN LVG COS II, Genius of Lugdunum stg. front. Aur: 24. Den: 23/*C*40−1

197 Vows for Albinus' safe arrival in Rome (as emperor, after defeating Severus).

    5 FORTVNAE REDVCI COS II, Fortuna std. l. As: 64

SEPTIMIUS SEVERUS

April 193−February 211

L. Septimius Severus was born in the North African city of Leptis Magna in 145. Thanks to good connections, he rose rapidly, entering the Senate in 169, and rising to command a legion in Syria under Marcus Aurelius. He was dismissed from office by Commodus, but soon restored to favour and made governor of Gallia Lugdunensis in 187. At this time his wife died, and Severus married Julia Domna, daughter of the priest of the Sun-god of Emesa. The reign of Pertinax saw him governor of Upper Pannonia, in command of three legions.

When the news of the murder of Pertinax reached the frontier, the Pannonian troops proclaimed Severus Emperor. He immediately gained the full support of the sixteen legions (*1*) stationed along the Rhine and Danube, the largest of the imperial armies and the closest to Rome. When the legions of Britain favoured their own commander Albinus, Severus neutralized the threat by offering his potential rival the rank of Caesar. Severus then assumed the name of Pertinax, and claimed to be his avenger, thereby gaining the support of the Senate and the people of Rome. By the time news of his departure reached the capital, Severus was already in Italy; Julianus, deserted by his supporters, was killed on 1 June and Severus captured the throne without a battle. He entered Rome with his army, gave a conciliatory speech to the Senate (whose support he still needed), and a donative to the people (*2−3*). He also celebrated a state funeral for the consecration of Pertinax (*4−5*). In his initial propaganda, he stressed his African origin and invoked the help of his native gods (*6−7*) against Pescennius Niger, who had been proclaimed emperor by his troops in Syria. Severus assumed the consulate for 194 with Albinus, and set out for the East (*8*), spending less than a month in Rome.

Swift victories in Asia Minor left the East open to Severus and caused Niger to flee eastward, only to be captured and executed. Severus then moved against Niger's allies, the Osrhoeni, the Adiabeni and the Arabs, who lived beyond the imperial frontier (*9−10*). In a long campaign in 195, he defeated the Parthians, who also had supported Niger, and annexed a new province, Mesopotamia. During the war, Severus announced his adoption as the son of Marcus Aurelius (*13*) and consequently changed the name of his own son Bassianus, whom he had named Caesar in 196 (*14*), to Marcus Aurelius Antoninus. This provoked a break with Albinus, whose title of Caesar was now worthless. Albinus was proclaimed Emperor by his troops, and a new civil war began.

Late in 196, Severus returned briefly to Rome (*15*), celebrated his victories by a donative (*16*) and marched (*17–20*) against Albinus who was defeated and killed near Lugdunum in 197. When he returned to the capital, Severus behaved harshly toward the Senate, executing many who had sided with his rivals, and praising the great persecutor of senators, Commodus, whose deification (*21*) he ordered, a logical act since the two had become brothers by adoption. Then, after entertaining the Roman populace with games (*22*), he set out (*23*) once again for the East.

While Rome was torn by civil war, the Parthians had attempted to regain Mesopotomia. Late in the summer of 197 Severus moved against them, marching deep into the heart of enemy country. His forces captured and looted Ctesiphon, the Parthian capital, in January 198, a great victory (*24–30*) which was considered the suitable occasion for confirming the dynasty he had founded: Antoninus was appointed Augustus, his younger brother Geta Caesar (*31–42*), and vows were celebrated (*35–36*). Severus then returned to Roman territory and made peace with Parthia in 199. From the East the imperial party proceeded to Egypt, then Syria, where Severus and Antoninus assumed the joint consulate (*50*) for 202.

The visit to Egypt (*44*) brought new interest in the local religion and new tolerance for its gods, whose worship had been forbidden within the *pomoerium* of Rome. As a result, temples of Isis and Serapis (*74*) were built and the Egyptian gods entered into the propaganda of the imperial dynasty, with Severus being identified with Serapis (many of his obverses show him with the long locks of the god on his forehead) and Antoninus with the young Horus (Domna *6*). Later in 202, the emperors finally returned to Rome, where Severus' great building programme (*45–48*) had begun, and an equestrian statue (*49*) had been dedicated to him. Severus' return (*51–56*) coincided with the decennalia of his reign (*58–60*) and thus became the occasion for magnificent celebrations, a donative (*57*) and a triumph. This year also saw the wedding of Antoninus and Plautilla, daughter of the praetorian prefect Plautianus.

Severus spent most of the next five years in Italy. In 203, he received a permanent monument of victory, the great arch (*61*) which bears his name in the Roman Forum, and in the following year celebrated the Secular Games (*63–68*). These inaugurated a new era and were the occasion for a public holiday lasting a month. The rites began at midnight on 1 June 204 with sacrifices and prayers to the Fates on the banks of the Tiber; ceremonies, games and a donative (*69–71*) followed, all presided over by Severus and his sons. The sons thereupon assumed the consulate (*73*) for 205, the first year of the new *saeculum*. During these years, Severus enriched Rome with many buildings, and made grants to

Carthage (*62*) and the cities of Italy (*72*). He celebrated the fifteenth anniversary of his reign in 207 with games (*75*) and vows (*76–77*) and apparently visited Africa (*78–79*) in the same year.

Severus' final campaign began in 208, when he and his family left Rome (*80–81*) after receiving reports of incursions of northern tribes into Britain. The emperors undertook a massive campaign which led Roman forces far up the east coast of Scotland, apparently with the aim of bringing the whole island under their control. The Firth of Forth was bridged (*82*), and the Tay crossed by a bridge of boats: archaeology reveals the extent of the campaign and the network of forts which supported it. These victories led to a treaty in 209 by which much territory was gained: as part of the celebration (*86–93*), Geta was raised to the rank of Augustus (*83*), and a donative (*84–85*) was given. A revolt the following year led to a new campaign, but this proved abortive when Severus, worn out by his exertions and embittered by the quarrels between his sons, died at York in 211, before he could return to Rome (*94–95*).

The Civil Wars, 193–197

193 Loyalty of the legions supporting Severus. LEG (as below) TR P COS, Legionary eagle between two standards. All are denarii unless specified.

   1a   I ADIVT: 2/*C256*
   1b   I ITAL: 3/*C257*
   1c   I MIN: Aur: 4/258. Den: 4/259
   1d   II ADIVT: 5/*C260*
   1e   II ITAL: 6/*C261*
   1f   III ITAL: 7/*C262*
   1g   IIII FL: 8/*C264*
   1h   V MAC: 9/*C265*
   1i   VII CL: 10/*C266*
   1j   VIII AVG: Aur: 11. Den: 11/267; 357
   1k   XI CL: 12/*C268*
   1l   XIII GEM: 13/*C269*
   1m   XIIII GEM M V: Aur:14/*C271*; 358; 397/*C273* Den: 14/*C272*; 397/*C274*. Ses: 652/*C275* (adds P M TR P COS).
   1n   XXII: 15/*C276*
   1o   XXII PRI: 16/*C277*
   1p   XXX VLP: 17/*C278*

— — First donative, on accession.

   2a   LIBER/AL AVG (TR P COS), Liberalitas stg. l. Aur: 18/*C280*; 400. Den: 18/*C281*; 27; 398; 399/*C282*; 400/*C283*; 401/*C287*; 442/*C279*; 455 Ses: 653/*C284*
   2b   LIBERA/L AVG, Liberalitas std. l. Aur: 400. Den: 401–3/*C287*
   3   LIBERAL AVG TR P COS (II), Donation scene with Severus, officer, Liberalitas and citizen. Ses: 654/*C285*; 662/*C286*

1*f*   6

—— Consecration of Pertinax.
  4   —— *Obv.* DIVVS PERT PIVS PATER, Bare head r. *Rev.* CONSEC-
         RATIO, Funeral pyre. Aur: 24B/*C*11. Ses: 660C/*C*12
  5   Eagle on globe. Aur: 24A/*C*7. Den: 24A/*C*6. Ses: 660B/*C*8,9.
         As: 660B/*C*10 (PERTIN)
194 Celebration of Severus' native country.
  6   —— AFRICA, Africa stg. r. Ses: 668/*C*26; 676/*C*28−9. Dup:
         680/*C*30
—— Honours to Hercules and Liber, the patron gods of Severus' home,
    invoking their aid against Niger.
  7   DIS AVSPICIB TR P II COS II P P, Hercules and Liber (Bacchus)
         stg. Aur: 25/*C*113; 31/*C*114. Den: 31/*C*115. Ses: 661/*C*118;
         666/*C*116; 669/*C* 119−20. As: 666/*C*117
—— Departure to campaign against Niger: vows for safe return.
  8*a*   FORTVNAE REDVCI (variously abbreviated), Fortuna std. l. Den:
         380−1/*C*180; 386/*C*177; 387; 450; 451/*C*168; 452/*C*172
  8*b*   —— Fortuna stg. l. Den: 376−8; 382−4; 385A; 388/*C*159;
         439/*C*156; 440/*C*161; 448−9/*C*160; 453/*C*157
  8*c*   —— Fortuna stg. l., sacrificing. Den: 385/*C*185; 437A
195 Victory over Pescennius Niger, commemorated as triumphs over his
    allies, the Arabs, Adiabenians and Parthians.
  9*a*   ARAB ADIABENIC, Victory advancing l. Den: 466/*C*52
  9*b*   ARAB ADIAB COS II P P, Same type Aur: 41; 64/*C*49. Den: 58/
         *C*48; 63A; 64/*C*50; 76/*C*51; 346
  9*c*   (PAR) AR AD TR P VI COS II P P, Same type. Den: 494A; 495−6/
         *C*360−1, 369
 10*a*   AR AD TR P VI COS II P P, Two captives std. back to back below
         trophy. Den: 494*b*
 10*b*   PART ARAB PART ADIAB COS II P P, Same type. Aur: 55/*C*364.
         Den: 62/*C*363; 63/*C*365. Ses: 690/*C*366−7. Dup: 696/*C*368
—— Types probably connected with the campaign against Niger. The
    imperial title 'iustus' appropriates that which Niger regularly used.
 11   VICTOR SEVER (C) AUG, Victory advancing l. Den: 428−9/
         *C*749−50
 12   VICTOR IVST AUG (II COS), Same type. Den: 362/*C*738; 362A;
         427A/*C*739−40

— — Severus announces his 'adoption' into the Antonine house as 'Son of the Divine Pious Marcus'.

13   DIVI M PII F P M TR P III COS II P P, Types as follow:
  a Mars adv. l.: Aur: 65/*C*123
  b Victory adv. l.: Aur: 66
  c Felicitas stg. l.; Ses: 701/*C*124. Dup: 712/*C*125
  d Roma stg. l., crowning Severus: Ses: 702/*C*128
  e Roma std. l.: Ses: 686/*C*126; 700/*C*127; 702A

196 Antoninus named Caesar (*see also* his early issues).
14   SEVERI AVG PII FIL, Bust of Antoninus r. Aur: 72
— — Return to Rome after victory over Niger.
15   — — ADVENTVI AVG FELICISSIMO, Severus riding r., sometimes preceded by soldier leading horse. Aur: 73−4/*C*5−6. Ses: 718−9/*C* 7−8. As: 731/*C*9

15

— — Donative to the people to celebrate victory.
16   LIBERALITAS AVG. II, Liberalitas stg. l. Aur: 81/*C*289; Den: 81
196/7 Campaign against Clodius Albinus: prayers for victory; departure of Severus; and vows for a safe return.
17   VOTA PVBLICA, Severus sacrificing at altar. Aur: 96/*C*776. Den: 96/*C*777. As: 736/*C*778
18   — — Severus and Antoninus sacrificing. Ses: 730/*C*782−3
19   PROFECTIO AVG, Severus on horseback r. Den: 91/*C*578. Ses: 728/*C*581
20*a* FORT/VNAE REDVC/I, Fortuna std. l. Aur: 78. Den: 78; 478/*C*166; 479/*C*170; 479A. Ses: 703/*C*189−90; 720/*C*191, 193. As: 732/*C*192
20*b* — — Fortuna stg. l. Den: 477/*C*164; 477A
20*c* — — Fortuna stg l., sacrificing. Den: 264A

Sole reign, 197−198

197 Consecration of Commodus, the adoptive brother of Severus.
21   *Obv.* M COMM ANTO AVG PIVS FEL, Head r. *Rev.* CONSECRATIO, Eagle stg. on globe. Den: 72A/*C*6
— — Games to celebrate victory over Albinus.

22 MVNIFICENTIA AVG, Elephant walking r. Den: 82/*C*348; 100/*C*349.
Ses: 721/*C*350−1; 737/*C*352

—— Departure for the East, to campaign against Parthia.

23 PROFECTIO AVG, Type as 19. Aur: 106/*C*579. Den: 106/*C*580;
494. Ses: 740A; 746

198 Victories in the war against Parthia, an abundant series struck over
several years. The greatest achievement of the war was the capture
of Ctesiphon in 198 for which Severus gained the title 'Parthicus
Maximus'. The coins claim that the emperor has 'anchored' peace
and that the victory is to be eternal.

24*a* VICT/ORIA PARTH/ICA MAX/IMA, Victory advancing l. Aur: 195B;
295/*C*743; 297/*C*747. Den: 295/*C*744; 296/*C*746; 297

24*b* VICT PARTHICAE, Victory adv. l., captive at feet. Aur: 142.
Den: 121/*C*742; 142/*C*741; 514

25 P M TR X P COS III P P, Victory advancing r., holding shield
inscribed VIC PAR. Aur: 183/*C*458

26*a* PART MAXIMVS COS II P P, Two captives std. below trophy. Aur:
512

26*b* PART MAX P M TR P VIII (or X) (COS III P P), Same type. Den: 153;
176/*C*370; 184−5/*C*372−3

27 VICT PARTHIC AVGG P M TR P VIIII, Victory running r. Ses: 754

28 VIC PAR MAX AVG, Victory in fast biga, r. As: 828

29 FVNDAT/OR PACIS, Severus stg. l. Aur: 160/*C*202. Den: 128/
*C*207; 129/*C*204; 160/*C*203; 265/*C*205

30 VICT AETERNAE, Victory flying l. Den: 141/*C*672

Joint reign of Severus and Antoninus, 198−209

—— Proclamation of Antoninus as Augustus, and Geta as Caesar after
the capture of Ctesiphon; with decennial vows on the accession of
Antoninus.

31 *Obv.* IMPP INVICTI PII AVGG, Jugate busts of Severus and
Antoninus. *Rev.* VICTORIA PARTHICA MAXIMA, Victory advancing
l. Aur: 311/*C*8. Den: 311/*C*9

31

32 SAECVLI FELICITAS, Busts of Antoninus and Geta, vis-à-vis.
Aur: 513

33 IMPERII FELICITAS, Busts of Severus and Geta vis-à-vis. Aur:
98/*C*1

34   L SEPTIMIVS GETA CAES, Bust of Geta. Den: 132; 506/*C*4

35   VOTIS DECENNALIBVS in oak wreath. Aur: 520/*C*797. Den: 520/*C*798

36   — — Severus sacrificing at altar. Den: 519/*C*796

198–202   and later: Proclamation of the new dynasty, an abundant series which features the imperial family, especially the new Augustus, Antoninus and Caesar, Geta. The largest issue announces the 'Eternity of the Empire' — the stability which the dynasty would bring.

37   CONCORDIAE AETERNAE, Jugate busts of Severus and Julia. Den: 522

37A   IVLIA AVGVSTA, Bust r. Aur: 161/*C*1. Den: 161/*C*2; 273/*C*3

38   *Obv.* FELICITAS PVBLICA, Busts of Severus and Julia vis-à-vis. *Rev.* PERPETVA CONCORDIA, Busts of Caracalla and Geta vis-à-vis. Aur: 312/*C*7

39   FELICITAS SAECVLI, Bust of Julia facing between Antoninus and Geta. Aur: 159; 175/*C* 1; 181/*C*2,4,5, Den: 181/*C*3, 6

40*a*   AETERNIT IMPERI, Busts of Antoninus and Geta facing each other. Aur: 155; 174; 178A. Den: 174; 178A; 250–2/*C*l, 6–7

40*b*   — — Busts of Severus and Antoninus vis-à-vis. Den: 250/*C*1

40   49a

41*a*   ANTONINVS AVGVSTVS, Bust r. Aur: 157/*C*2. Den: 157; 521/*C*3

41*b*   ANTONINVS AVG PON TR P III (or v), Same type. Den: 179/*C*5; 521/*C*4

41*c*   ANTONINVS PIVS AVG, Same type. Den: 180, 180A

42   P SEPT/IMIVS GETA CAES (PONT), Bust r. Den: 164; 281

200   Severus sets out for Rome from the East; with prayers for his safe return

43   PROFECT/IO AVG/G (FEL), Severus on horseback r. Aur: 165. Den: 138/*C*576; 165/*C*577. Ses: 752/*C*583

43*a*   VOTA PVBLICA, Severus sacrificing over altar. Aur: 149/*C*779. Den: 172/*C*780

— —   Visit to Egypt

44   P M TR P VIII COS II P P, Nile reclining l., attended by the Four Seasons. As: *Clay (1970)* 71

201   and later. Rebuilding programme in Rome.

45   RESTITVTOR/I VRBIS, Severus sacrificing. Aur: 167–8/*C*598; 611;

289/*C*601. Den: 140/*C*600; 167–8/*C*599; 612; 289/*C*602; 512A. Qui: 140A. Dup: 755/*C*603

46 — — Roma std. r. Aur: 288/*C*605. Den: 288/*C*606. As: 825/ *C*607–8

47 — — Bust of Roma r. Aur: 290

48 — — Severus stg., facing std. Roma; altar between. As: 757/ *C*610

— — Dedication of an equestrian statue of Severus.

49*a* SPQR OPTIMO PRINC, Severus on horseback l. Aur: 169/*C*653. Den: 415/*C*652

49*b* — — OPTIMO PRINC SPQR P M TR P VIII. Ses: *Hill* (*1964*) 525A

202 Joint consulate of Severus and Antoninus.

50 AVGVSTI COS, Severus and Caracalla seated side by side on platform; behind, officer; in front, soldier holding spear. As: 822/*C*54

— — Return of Severus to Rome, with sacrifice of thanks to Fortune and a third donative to the people.

51 ADVENT AVGG, Severus, Antoninus and Geta galloping r. Aur: 177/*C*2

52 ADVENTVS AVGVSTOR, Galley with rowers l. Aur: 178

53 ADVENT AVGG, Severus on horseback l., preceded by soldier on foot. Den: 248/*C*1

54 FORTVNA REDVX, Severus sacrificing over tripod, in front of Fortuna std. l. Aur: 188/*C*183

55 — — Fortuna stg. l. Aur: 187/*C*178. Den: 264/*C*181. Qui: 264/ *C*179. As: 824/*C*184

56 FORTVNAE REDVCI, Fortuna stg. l. Den: 264A

57 LIB AVG III P M TR P X COS III P P, Liberalitas standing l. Den: 182/*C*291

— — Tenth anniversary of the reign, with sacrifices for its successful conclusion, and in hopes of another decade.

58 VOTA SOLVT DEC COS III, Three figures sacrificing over tripod; bull at side Den: 307/*C*785

59 VOTA SVSC DEC P M TR P X COS III P P, Severus sacrificing. Den: 186/*C*786

60 VOTA SVSCEP DECEN S C, Severus with three companions sacrificing over altar in front of hexastyle temple; before him, two men and a victimarius with a bull; fluteplayer behind altar. As: 832/*C*787

— — Triumph for the Parthian victories, commemorated by a monumental arch in the Forum, completed in 204 and still standing.

61*a* COS III P P, Triumphal arch of Severus. Den: 259/*C*104

61*b* ARCVS AVGG S C, same type. As: 764/*C*53

203 Special favour to Carthage, capital of Severus' native province, probably consisting of an aqueduct.

62 INDVLGENTIA AVGG IN CARTH, Dea Caelestis (goddess of Carthage) riding a lion over waters gushing from a rock. Aur:

61   62

193/*C*224; 266/*C*227; 267/*C*217. Den: 266/*C*222; 267; 267A/
*C*219; 267B. Ses: 763/*C*225; 763A/*C*220. As: 759; 759A/*C*218;
766/*C*226; 766A/*C*221

204 Celebration of the Secular Games, with sacrifices, games and a
donative. Bacchus and Hercules, the patron gods of Severus' home,
were given a prominent role in the celebrations. The sacrifice depicted
took place on the second night of the festival, on the banks of the
Tiber, and honoured the goddess of birth and Tellus. The most
spectacular of the festivals involved the display of a ship filled with
wild beasts in the arena.

63   COS III LVDOS SAECVL FEC, Bacchus and Hercules standing facing
each other. Aur: 257/*C*108. Den: 257/*C*109. Ses: 763B/*C*110.
As: 765

67a

64   DI PATRII, Same type. Ses: 762/*C*112
65   COS III LVD SAEC FEC S C on column; Bacchus and Hercules as
previous As: 764A/*C*106
66   — — Severus sacrificing over altar, facing Hercules, victimarius
with pig, fluteplayers and Bacchus; in front, Tellus reclining.
Ses: 761/*C*105
67*a*   SACRA SAECVLARIA, Severus and Antoninus sacrificing over
altar; Pietas (Concordia?) behind; musicians on either side;
Tellus reclining in front l.; canopy or temple in background.
Aur: 293/*C*623. Den: 293A. Ses: 816/*C*624−5. As: 826a
67*b*   (Same legend), similar but no musicians or Tellus; temple in
background. As: 826b/*C*626
68   LAETITIA TEMPORVM, Vessel with sail raised and gangway to
ground; below, bird, lion, two tigers, stag, bull, tiger; above,
four quadrigae, two on each side of ship. Aur: 274/*C*254.
Den: 274/*C*253

68   91

69   LIBERALITAS AVGG IIII, Liberalitas stg. l. Den: 276/*C*293. As: 767/*C*294

70   FELICITAS SAECVLI, Donation scene with Severus, Antoninus and Geta, officer and citizen who dips hand in urn. Ses: 815/*C*138. As: 823/*C*139

71*a*   SAECVLI FELICITAS COS III P P, Felicitas standing l., emptying fruit out of fold of dress with r. hand and holding cornucopia in l.; three figures r. and l., running up to catch fruit. Aur: 293B. As: 827/*C*635

71*b*   — — Felicitas stg. l., emptying cornucopiae into hands of two people; behind, three others await the distribution. Aur: 327/*C*634

— — Special beneficence to Italy, consisting of a free supply of oil to Rome and other cities.

72   INDVLGENTIA AVGG IN ITALIAM, Italia std. l. Den: 268/*C*228

205 Joint consulate of Antoninus and Geta, celebrated by fifth donative to the people.

73   LIBERALITAS AVGG V, Liberalitas stg. l. Aur: 277/*C*295. Den: 277/*C*296

206 Introduction of the worship of the Egyptian gods into the city by Antoninus.

74   IOVI SOSPITATORI, Image of Jupiter-Serapis in distyle shrine (probably in the palace). Den: 271/*C*245

207 Fifteenth anniversary of the reign of Severus, and tenth of Antoninus, celebrated by games and the undertaking of vows for the completion of 20 years.

75   COS III P P, Stadium of Domitian with spectators and combatants within. Aur: 260/*C*571

76   VOTA SVSCEPTA XX, Severus and Antoninus sacrificing over altar; fluteplayer in background. Aur: 309/*C*793. Den 309/*C*794

77*a*   VOTA SVSCEPTA XX COS III P P, Severus sacrificing; fluteplayer behind; on r., victimarius about to sacrifice bull. Den: 310

77*b*   VOTA SVSCEPTA XX, Severus sacrificing over tripod; lictor in front, fluteplayer behind. Ses: 821/*C*795

77*c*   — — Severus sacrificing. Den: 308/*C*791. Dup: 821/*C*792

– – Imperial visit to Africa, with honours to the Punic god of healing, equivalent to Aesculapius.

78*a*   AFRICA, Africa stg. r., lion at feet. Den: 253/*C*25

78*b*   P M TR P XV COS III P P, Same type. Den: 207/*C*493; 207A

78*c*   AFRICA, Africa reclining l. Den: 254/*C*31

79   P M TR P XV COS III P P, Statue of Aesculapius stg. between two snakes in distyle shrine. Aur: 205/*C*484. As:775/*C*485

208 Departure for the British front, with vows and first operations, featuring construction of a bridge, perhaps over the Firth of Forth.

80   VOTA PVBLICA, Severus sacrificing over altar. Den: 306/*C*781. As: 831

81   P M TR P XVI PROF AVGG, Severus riding r., preceded by foot soldier. Den: 225A. Ses: 780/*C*574 (two soldiers behind)

82   P M TR P XVI COS III P P, Bridge with portico of four columns at each end; boat below. Aur: 225/*C*521. As: 786/*C*523

209 Proclamation of Geta as Augustus, with a donative.

83   CONCORDIA AVGVSTORVM, Antoninus and Geta holding victory between them. Aur: 255; 330A

84   LIBERALITAS AVG VI, Liberalitas stg. l. Aur: 278/*C*297. Den: 278/*C*298

85   – – Donation scene with Severus, Antoninus and Geta, officer, Liberalitas and citizen. Aur: 279/*C*300

209–211 Celebration of victories in Britain.

86*a*   VICTORIAE BRIT, Victory advancing l. or r. Aur: 334. Den: 332/*C*727; 333/*C*728

86*b*   P M TR P XIX COS III P P VICT BRIT, Same type. Den: 247/*C*722

87   VICTORIAE BRIT, Victory std l., inscribing shields set on knees. Den: 335/*C*731

88*a*   – – Victory attaching shield to palm tree. Den: 336/*C*730. Dup: 834/*C*735. As: 837A/*C*734

88*b*   – – Same type, but tree with shield attached Den: 302A; 337/*C*729

88*c*   VICTORIAE BRITTANNICAE, Victory stg. r., foot on human head, inscribing shield set on palm. Dup: 834/*C*735. As: 837A/*C*734

89   – – Victory leading captive and holding trophy. Aur: 302/*C*726. Den: 302

90   VICTORIAE BRITTANNICAE, Victory r., holding trophy; std. captive at each side. Ses: 819/*C*737. Dup: 809/*C*725. As: 812/*C*724; 837/*C*736

91   – – Two Victories fixing shield on palm; two captives at feet. Ses: 808; 818/*C*732

210 Severus addresses troops after victory.

92   P M TR P XVIII COS III P P, Severus stg. between two soldiers, std. captive to l.; soldiers holding standards in background. Ses: 799/*C*558

93   – – Severus, Antoninus and Geta on platform, addressing officer and two soldiers. Ses: 800/*C*559

211 Vows for Severus' return and celebration of the event, which he did not live to accomplish.

94*a* TR P XIX COS III P P FORT RED, Fortuna stg. l. Den: 247A. As: 810/*C*155

94*b* FORTVNAE REDVCI, Same type. As: 836/*C*194

95 ADVENTVS AVGVSTI, Severus on horseback. Den: 249/*C*15; 330/ *C*14

JULIA DOMNA

Augusta, 193−217

Julia, daughter of Bassianus, the high priest at Emesa in Syria, married Severus while he was governor of Gallia Lugdunensis, from 185 to 187. The marriage was an especially desirable one since her horoscope foretold that her husband would become emperor. Soon after giving birth to two sons, Antoninus and Geta, she fulfilled this destiny and as empress exercised considerable influence over Severus. She also had two daughters: her fertility (*1*) thus assured continuity of the dynasty from the beginning of the reign. She frequently travelled with Severus on his campaigns and so was honoured with the title *Mater Castrorum* (*2*) in 195, just as Faustina the Younger had been for the same reason. When both her sons became Augusti in 209 with the promotion of Geta, she received the additional title *Mater Augustorum* (*9*). To these, the Senate added the more grandiose and unparalleled *Mater Senatus* and *Mater Patriae* (*10*) after the accession of Antoninus. Julia naturally figured in the imperial propaganda which identified the dynasty with the Egyptian gods, and Antoninus, in particular, with Horus (*6*; Caracalla *87*).

Although Antoninus had long been favoured by Julia, his actions brought horror to her when in February 212 Geta, who had been summoned to her rooms on a pretext, was murdered in her arms. Nevertheless, for the next few years she continued to play a major role in the imperial administration, and in public works, as evidenced by her restoration of the temple of Vesta (*11−12*; Caracalla *83*).

Julia accompanied Antoninus on his eastern campaign, but stayed in Antioch as he advanced to the front and his death. When the news of his murder reached her, she contemplated suicide, but was well treated by Macrinus, who, however, soon banished her to Rome to avoid potential trouble. She starved herself to death there in 217. She was consecrated by her great-nephew Elagabalus when he became emperor (Elagabalus *6−7*).

194 The family of Severus and Julia, the future dynasty.

1 FECVNDITAS, Julia stg. l., holding a child on l. arm, with two others stg. beside her. Den: 550/*C*39

195 Award of title *Mater Castrorum*.

    2*a*   MATER (or MATRI) CASTRORVM, Julia sacrificing at altar; three standards on l. Aur: 563. Den: 563; 567/*C*134. Ses: 860/*C*135. Dup/As: 880/*C*120; 884/*C*136

    2*b*   MATRI CASTRORVM, Julia std. l.; standards on l. Aur: 569/*C* 133. Den: 568−69/*C*131−2

198−202 Proclamation of the new imperial dynasty: *See also* Severus *37−41*.

    3   AETERNIT IMPERI, Busts of Severus and Antoninus facing each other. (Severus *40b*). Aur: 539, 540/*C*1. Den: 539−541/*C*2−3

    4*a*   ANTONINVS (PIVS) AVG PON/T TR P IIII (or V), Bust r. (Severus *41b*). Aur: 543. Den: 542

    4*b*   ANTONINVS PIVS AVG (BRIT), Same type (Severus *41a*). Den: 544−5/*C*1−2

    5   CONCORDIA FELIX, Severus and Julia clasping hands. Den: 547/*C*23

202 Acceptance of Egyptian cults and identification of the dynasty with the Egyptian gods.

    6   SAECVLI FELICITAS, Isis suckling Horus. Aur: 577; 645/*C*177. Den: 577/*C*174; 645. Ses: 85/*C*176

    6   10*a*

202/5 Birth of a child to Antoninus and Plautilla.

    7   PIETAS AVGG, Plautilla stg. l., holding infant (Plautilla *3*). Den: 642

204 The new golden age, introduced by the dynasty and celebrated by the Secular Games, with an implied parallel between the empress and Terra.

    8   FECVNDITAS, Terra reclining l. under tree, resting hand on star-spangled globe over which the Four Seasons play. Aur: 549/*C*34. Den: 549/*C*35

209 Award of title *Mater Augustorum*.

    9   MATER AVGG, Julia as Cybele (the Mother of the Gods) in quadriga of lions. Aur: 526/*C*116. Den: 526/*C*117

211 or later. Award of more grandiose titles, 'Mother of the Senate and of the Country'.

    10*a*   MAT AVGG MAT SEN M PATR, Julia stg. l. Aur: 380. Den: 380/*C*114

    10*b*   −− Julia std. l. Aur: 381/*C*110. Den: 381/*C*111. Ses: 588/*C*112. Dup/As: 601/*C*113

214 Restoration of the temple of Vesta in the Forum.

    11   VESTA, Four Vestals and two children sacrificing before round temple of Vesta (Caracalla *83*). Aur: 392/*C*232. Ses: 594/*C*233, 235

    12*a* — — Vesta std. l. Den: 391/*C*226. Ses: 593/*C*228

    12*b* — — Vesta stg. l. Den: 390/*C*230

CARACALLA

Caesar 196/Augustus June 198–April 217

Julius Bassianus, named for his maternal grandfather, was born to Severus and Julia Domna at Lugdunum in April 188. When Severus announced his adoption into the family of Marcus Aurelius in 195, he changed his son's name to Marcus Aurelius Antoninus, by which he was always officially known. In 196, in preparation for the war against Albinus, Severus made Antoninus Caesar (*1–3*), and two years later proclaimed him Augustus (*4–7*) after the great victory over the Parthians at Ctesiphon (*8–11*). While Severus was alive, Antoninus shared in the government; consequently, his coinage (*12–13*, *25–39*) reflects the major events and activities of Severus' reign. He was consul (*14*) with his father in 202, and with Geta in 205 (*40–43*). His first consulate saw his marriage (*21–24*) to Plautilla, daughter of the all-powerful praetorian prefect Plautianus. Antoninus and Geta both took part in the campaigns in Britain (*51–52*) and when Severus died there in February 211, his sons become joint Augusti without opposition.

The new emperors abandoned any further wars in Britain and returned to Rome (*64–67*), where their arrival was the occasion for a donative. The consecration of Severus (*68–71*) and the British victories (*56–63*, *72*) were celebrated, and Julia Domna was honoured with new titles. Relations between the brothers, long since strained, now reached an open hostility which culminated in the murder of Geta in February 212 and the slaughter of his partisans. Antoninus made sure of the support of the praetorians by a special donative (*73*) to celebrate his escape from the 'conspiracy' of Geta. Soon afterwards, he issued the law which granted universal Roman citizenship, an event of great importance hardly noted by the historians and absent from the coinage.

In February 213, after assuming a fourth consulate (*74*), and rebuilding the Circus Maximus (*75–76*), Antoninus set out for the German frontier (*77*) where a series of campaigns led to a substantial victory (*78–81*) over the Alemanni. It was during these wars that the emperor adopted the German hooded cloak, the *caracallus*, which gave him the nickname Caracalla, by which he is generally known, although it never formed part of his official nomenclature. An eighth donative (*82*) celebrated the victories. Soon afterwards, Antoninus joined his mother in rededicating the temple of Vesta (*83*), rebuilt after its destruction in the fire of 191.

The most ambitious campaign began in 214, when the emperor and his army set out for the East. He travelled via the northern frontier, where he won further victories over the German tribes, the occasion for a ninth donative (*84–85*). Antoninus then crossed into Asia, visited Troy and Pergamum, where he sought relief from chronic illness at the famous shrine of Aesculapius (*86*), and spent the winter in Nicomedia. The next year saw, not the major war against Parthia, but an unsuccessful campaign in Armenia, and the visit of the emperor to Alexandria (*87*), where he proceeded to massacre the citizens because of the ridicule they heaped on him. He spent the winter in Alexandria, returning to Antioch, his headquarters for the Parthian war, in the spring. The greatest monument of the age, the Baths of Caracalla in Rome, was finished in this year (it does not appear on the coins), and a major reform in the coinage was made, with the introduction of the antoninianus.

The eastern war began in earnest in 216, when the Romans captured the kings of Osrhoene and Armenia, and the army advanced far to the east, and crossed the Tigris, without meeting any real opposition. This campaign justified celebration of a victory (*88*) which coincided with the twentieth anniversary of the reign (*89*). In the following year, a large Parthian army took to the field, and Antoninus moved to Edessa to meet them. By this time, however, his extravagances and cruelties had earned him such universal hatred that a conspiracy led by the praetorian prefect Macrinus was formed. In April 217, during an excursion to the temple of the Man at Carrhae, as the emperor stopped by the side of the road to relieve himself, he was ignominiously murdered by the conspirators.

Caesar, 196–198

196 Appointment of Antoninus as Caesar and *princeps iuventutis*. (*See also* Severus *14*.)

   1 SEVERI AVG PII FIL, Priestly implements. Aur: 3/*C*582. Den: 4/*C*587; 15/*C*588. Ses: 400/*C*535; 404/*C*586

   2 DESTINATO IMPERAT, Same type. Den: 6/*C*53

   3 PRINCIPI IVVENTVTIS, Antoninus stg. l. Aur: 13/*C*504. Den: 13/*C*505; 329/*C*505; 38A (struck 199–200, as Augustus). Ses: 398/*C*546–7

Augustus with Severus, 198–209

198 Proclamation of Antoninus as Augustus and Geta as Caesar, with celebration of the foundation of a dynasty. Types struck for several years. (*See* Severus *31–42*.)

   4*a* SEVERI AVG PII FIL, Antoninus holding Victory; captive at feet. Aur: 45/*C*589. Den: 45/*C*590. Ses: 411/*C*591. Dup: 413/*C*592

4*b*   IVVENTA IMPERIL, Same type Aur: 20. Den: 20/*C*115; 24B.
5   P SEPT GETA CAES PONT, Bust r. Aur: 17/*C*4; 38/*C*1; 53/*C*6. Den: 29B/*C*5; 38/*C*2; 62/*C*7
6   CONCORDIAE AETERNAE, Jugate busts of Severus and Domna r. Aur: 36/*C*4; 52/*C*1; 59/*C*2

6   9

7   — — Antoninus and Geta stg., clasping hands. Aur: 61
8   SAECVLI FELICITAS, Busts of Antoninus and Geta facing each other (Severus *32*). Aur: 25A/*C*8
9   AETERNIT IMPERI, Busts of Antoninus and Severus facing each other (Severus *40b*). Den: 32/*C*2

198 Celebration of victories over Parthia.
10*a*   VICT/ORIA PART/HICA MAX/IMA, Victory l., holding wreath and palm (Severus *24a*). Aur: 78−9/*C*662; 144/*C*660. Den: 144/*C*658; 145/*C*661; 168A
10*b*   VICTORIAE PARTHICAE, Victory advancing l., holding trophy; captive at feet (Severus *24b*). Aur: 49A; 353
11   PART MAX PONT TR P IIII (or V) (COS), Two captives std. beside trophy (Severus *26*). Aur: 55/*C*176. Den: 54/*C*175; 55/*C*177; 63−5/ *C*178−9 (TR P V); 346/*C*177
12   P MAX TR P IIII COS, Antoninus sacrificing over altar. Den: 344/ *C*183
13   VIRTVS AVGG PONT TR P IIII, Antoninus crowning trophy beside which sit two captives with hands bound. Ses: 409/*C*671

201 and later. Rebuilding programme of Severus in Rome.
14   RESTITVTOR VRBIS, Antoninus stg. l., sacrificing (Severus *45*). Aur: 142/*C*548. Den: 41/*C*553
15   — — Roma std. l. (Severus *46*). Aur: 166−7/*C*549. Den: 166/ *C*549; 228/*C*551. Ses: 461/*C*552. As: 475/*C*550

202 Joint consulate of Severus and Antoninus.
16   AVGVSTI COS, Severus and Antoninus std. on platform; officer behind, lictor in front (Severus *50*). Aur: 73A/*C*16. As: 422A/ *C*17

— — Return of the emperors to Rome, with vows of thanks and celebration of the fifth anniversary of Antoninus' reign.
17   ADVENT AVGG, Severus, Antoninus and Geta galloping on horseback (Severus *51*). Aur: 56/*C*2
18   ADVENT/VS AVGVSTORVM (or AVGG), Galley with crew and passengers (Severus *52*). Aur: 57−8. Den: 120−1/*C*3, 8
19   FORTVNA REDVX, Fortuna stg. l. (Severus *55*). Den: 37

21

20*a* VOTA SVSC DEN PON TR P V COS, Antoninus sacrificing. Den: 68/
*C*686

20*b* VOTA SVSCEPTA X, Same type. Den: 150/*C*688; 179/*C*689. As:
478/*C*691

— — Marriage with Plautilla.

21 CONCORDIA FELIX, Antoninus and Plautilla stg., clasping hands.
Aur: 123/*C*22 (with Concordia in background). Den: 124/*C*23

22 CONCORDIAE AETERNAE, Same type. Aur: 60/*C*26

23 PROPAGO IMPERI, Same type. Aur: 67/*C*524

24 PLAVTILLA AVGVSTA, bust r. Aur: 163A. Den: 139/*C*3

202 Triumph for Parthian victories, with construction of the Arch of
Severus in the Forum, dedicated in 204.

25 PONTIF TR P VII COS, Antoninus in triumphal quadriga l. Aur:
77/*C*418

26 VICTORIAE, Two Victories flying, holding shield inscribed AVGG;
Antoninus stg. above; two captives below. Den: 146/*C*619

27 VICTORIA AVGVSTORVM, Severus and Genius of the Senate holding Victory and accompanied by soldiers; two captives std.
below. Ses: 418B

28*a* COS II, Triumphal arch of Severus (Severus *61a*). Den: 87A,
212A

28*b* ARCVS AVGG, Same type (Severus *61b*). As: 419/*C*15

203 Generosity of the emperors to Carthage, with measures to ensure
the water supply.

29 INDVLGENTIA AVGG IN CARTH, Dea Caelestis riding lion over
water gushing from rock (Severus *62*). Aur: 130–1/*C*96. Den:
130/*C*97. Ses: 415/*C*98; 418A. Dup: 415/*C*99. As: 415/*C*101;
471/*C*101

204 Celebration of the Secular Games, with honours to Bacchus and
Hercules, sacrifices, games and a donative.

30 COS LVDOS SAECVL FEC, Bacchus and Hercules stg. facing each
other (Severus *63*). Aur: 74/*C*51. Den: 74/*C*50. As: 421/
*C*52

31 DI PATRII, Same type (Severus *64*). Aur: 76/*C*55. As: 422/*C*56

32 COS LVD SAEC FEC on column between Bacchus and Hercules
(Severus *65*). As: 420/*C*49

33 COS II, Hercules between Pinarius and Potitius at banquet
served by two slaves (a legend: Pinarius and Potitius were the
hosts of Hercules when he came to the Palatine before the
foundation of Rome. The type may allude to the imperial
banquet which took place on the first day of the festival). As:
430/*C*39

34   COS LVD SAEC FEC, Antoninus sacrificing at altar; facing him,
      Bacchus, Hercules and victimarius with pig; on l., Tellus re-
      clining; fluteplayer in background (Severus *66*). Ses: 418/*C*48

35   SACRA SAECVLARIA, Severus and Antoninus sacrificing; Concordia
      behind; musicians on either side; Tiber reclining on l.; temple
      in background (Severus *67*). Ses: 462/*C*555−6

36   LAETITIA TEMPORVM, Ship in circus between four quadrigae;
      cock and bear on l.; bull and tiger on r.; lion and two tigers
      below (Severus *68*). Aur: 133/*C*117. Den: 157/*C*118

37   FELICITAS SAECVLI, Severus, Antoninus and Geta std. on plat-
      form; officer(s) or Liberalitas behind; below, citizen(s) receiving
      gifts (Severus *70*). Aur: 128/*C*67. As: 469−70/*C*68−9

38   LIBERALITAS AVGG IIII, Liberalitas stg. l. (Severus *69*). Den:
      135/*C*122. As: 416/*C*123

— — Grant of free olive oil to the cities of Italy.

39   INDVLGENTIA AVGG IN ITALIAM, Italy std. l. (Severus *72*). Den:
      132/*C*103

205 Joint consulate with Geta, celebrated by a donative.

40   IMP ET CAESAR AVG FILI COS, Antoninus and Geta std. on plat-
      form; Concordia between. Den: 75/*C*93

41   COS II, Antoninus in quadriga r. Aur: 87/*C*37. Den: 87/*C*38

42   LIBERALITAS AVGG COS II, Donation scene with Severus and
      Antoninus, officer and soldier. As: 430A/*C*126

43   LIBERALITAS AVGG V, Liberalitas stg. l. (Severus *73*). Aur: 136.
      Den: 136/*C*124

206 Introduction of the worship of the Egyptian gods into the city by
Antoninus.

44   IOVI SOSPITATORI, Image of Jupiter-Serapis in distyle Shrine
      (Severus *74*). Aur: 156. Den: 156/*C*108. As: 472/*C*109

44   47

207 Victories of Antoninus on the Danube.

45*a* PONTIF TR P X COS II, Antoninus stg. between river-god and two
      captives. Den: 96/*C*441

45*b* VIRTVS AVGG, Same type. Den: 175/*C*670

207/8 Tenth anniversary of the reign of Antoninus; payment of first
decennial vows and undertaking of second.

46*a* VOTA SOLVTA DEC COS III, Antoninus sacrificing over tripod;
      victimarius and bull on l.; flute-player behind. Aur: 205/*C*683.
      Den: 205/*C*684

46*b*   PONTIF TR P XI COS III, Same type. Aur: 105/*C*452. Den: 105/ *C*453

46*c*   (Legend as *46a*), Antoninus sacrificing; bull by altar. Den: 204/*C*682

46*d*   VOT SOL DEC PONTIF TR P XI COS III, Type as *46a*. As: 441A/ *C*685

47   VOTA SVSCEPTA XX, Antoninus sacrificing. Den: 180/*C*692

48   — — Severus and Antoninus sacrificing; flute-player in background (Severus *76*). Den: 181/*C*693

208   Second joint consulate of Antoninus and Geta.

49   PONTIF TR P XI COS III, Antoninus and Geta std. on platform with Severus stg. between them. Aur: 106/*C*455. Den: 106/ *C*456

50   — — Antoninus in quadriga. Aur: 103. Den: 104/*C*451

— — Departure for the British campaign, with vows.

51*a*   PROF (AVGG) PONTIF TR P XI/I COS III, Antoninus on horseback, sometimes with captive before. Den: 107−8/*C*510−1. Ses: 431; 432/*C*515. Dup: 446/*C*522. As: 438−440/*C*517−8; 449/ *C*521

51*b*   — — Antoninus on horseback accompanied by foot soldiers (Severus *81*). Ses: 433/*C*516; 445/*C*519

52   VOTA PVBLICA, Antoninus sacrificing (Severus *80*). Den: 178/ *C*680

Joint reign with Severus and Geta, 209−211

209   Proclamation of Geta as Augustus, celebrated by a donative.

53   CONCORDIA AVGVSTORVM, Antoninus and Geta holding Victory between them (Severus *83*). Aur: 152

54   LIBERALITAS AVGG VI, Donation scene with Severus, Antoninus and Geta, officer, Liberalitas and citizen (Severus *85*). Aur: 159/*C*127

55   LIBERALITAS AVG VI, Liberalitas stg. (Severus *84*). Den: 158/ *C*128

209−211   Victories in Britain celebrated with vows of thanks.

56   VICTORIAE BRIT/TANNICAE, Victory std., shield on knee, holding palm. Aur: 174/*C*633. Dup: 516/*C*635. As: 521/ *C*634

57   VICTORIA/E BRIT, Victory advancing l. (Severus *86a*). Den: 173/*C*631; 231/*C*632. Qui: 230

58*a*   VICTORIAE BRIT, Victory dragging captive and holding trophy (Severus *89*). Aur: 172/*C*628

58*b*   — — Victory holding trophy. Den: 172A; 231A/*C*629

59*a*   VICT BRIT P M TR P XIIII COS III P P, Victory stg., inscribing shield set on palm. Ses: 484. Dup: 487/*C*644; 490/*C*642

59*b*   VICTORIAE BRITANNICAE, Same type. Dup: 467/*C*637. As: 522/*C*636

60 VICTORIAE BRITTANNICAE, Two victories setting shield on palm; two captives at foot (Severus *91*). Ses: 465/*C*638

61*a* — — Victory stg. l. erecting trophy; on r., woman with mural crown (Britannia, or York) stg. and captive std. Ses: 464/*C*639

61*b* VICT BRIT P M TR P XIIII COS III P P, Same type. Ses: 483/ *C*640−1

62 PONTIF TR P XIII COS III, Antoninus raising kneeling woman with turreted crown (restoration of Britain after the wars). Aur: 119/*C*488

72

63 VOTA PVBLICA, Antoninus sacrificing, with bull. Ses: 513/ *C*677. Dup: 517/*C*679. As: 523/*C*678

Joint reign with Geta, 211−212

211 Return of the emperors to Rome, with a donative and vows of thanks for a safe return.

64 ADVENTVS AVGVSTI, Antoninus on horseback. Den: 212/*C*7

65 LIB AVGG VI ET V, Donation scene with Antoninus, Geta, Liberalitas and citizen. Aur: 215/*C*130. Den: 215/*C*131. Ses: 509/*C*132

66 LIBERALITAS AVG VI, Liberalitas stg. l. Den: 216−7/*C*129

67*a* P M TR P XIIII COS III P P FORT RED, Fortuna std. l. Aur: 190. Den: 190/*C*89. Ses: 479/*C*85. Dup: 485/*C*87−8. As: 488−9/ *C*86

67*b* — — Fortuna stg. l. Den: 189/*C*84

— — Funeral and consecration of Severus. All have *Obv.:* DIVO SEVERO PIO, head r. and *Rev.*CONSECRATIO.

68 Pyre surmounted by quadriga. Aur: 191F/*C*88. Den: 191F/ *C*89. Ses: 490B/*C*90 (DIVO SEPTIMIO SEVERO)

69 Eagle carrying Severus into the sky. Ses: 490A/*C*83

70 Eagle on thunderbolt. Den: 191A-D/*C*81−2, 84, 86

71 Wreath on throne, stool below (*sellisternium* for the god Severus). Den: 191E/*C*87

— — Games to celebrate victories in Britain.

72 P M TR P XIIII (or XV) COS III P P, Elephant r. or l. Den: *Hill (1964)* 1345; 199/*C*208. Ses: 491/*C*209. Dup: 442B. As: 495/ *C*210

71

77

Sole reign, 212–217

212 Donative to celebrate Antoninus' escape from the 'conspiracy' of Geta.

    73   LIBERALITAS AVG VII, Liberalitas stg. l. Den: 218/*C*133

213 Assumption of fourth consulate.

    74   P M TR P XVI IMP II COS IIII P P, Antoninus in quadriga, crowned by Victory. Aur: 210/*C*232 (no Victory). Ses: 499/*C*233. As: 506/*C*234

— — Rebuilding of the Circus Maximus, with games.

    75   P M TR P XVI (IMP II) COS IIII P P, Circus Maximus. Aur: 211B. Ses: 500/*C*236–7

    76   — — Elephant r. Aur: 211A/*C*231. Den: 211A/*C*230; 250A

— — Departure for campaigns in Germany.

    77   PROFECTIO AVG, Antoninus stg., holding spear; two standards or standard-bearer behind. Den: 225/*C*508; 226/*C*509

— — Victories in Germany, with address to the troops and a donative.

    78   VICTORIA GERMANICA, Victory advancing r. Aur: 237/*C*645; 316. Den: 237/*C*646

    79   P M TR P XVII IMP III COS IIII P P, German kneeling before std. Roma. Dup: 530/*C*265–6. As: 533/*C*264

    80   — — Victory stg. l., holding trophy; suppliant captive at feet. As: 534/*C*268

    81   — — Antoninus on platform with officers, addressing troops. Ses: 525/*C*273–5

    82   LIBERALITAS AVG VIII, Liberalitas stg. l. Den: 219/*C*134; 220; 305/ *C*135. Ses: 510/*C*136.

214 Restoration of the temple of Vesta in the Forum by Julia Domna,

    83   P M TR P XVII/I COS IIII P P, Antoninus, with group of priests, Vestals and children (variously composed, and sometimes including Julia) sacrificing in front of round temple of Vesta. Aur: 249–50/*C*249–50; 271–2

— — Ninth donative, after further victories on the frontier.

    84   (P M TR P XVII IMP II COS IIII P P) LIB/ERAL AVG VIIII, Donation scene with Antoninus, lictor, Liberalitas and citizen. Aur: 303/ *C*138. Ses: 527/*C*137

    85   LIBERAL AVG VIIII, Liberalitas stg. l. Den: 302/*C*139

— — Visit of Antoninus to Pergamum to seek a cure from the famous shrine of Aesculapius.

86   P M TR P XVIII COS IIII P P, Antoninus and togate figure sacrificing before tetrastyle shrine containing image of Aesculapius with Telesphorus. Aur: 270/*C*317–18

215 Imperial visit to Alexandria.

87   P M TR P XVIII (IMP III) COS IIII P P, Isis presenting ears of wheat to Antoninus who stands in the guise of Horus, with his foot on a crocodile. Aur: 257/*C*319. Ses: 544/*C*334

216 Campaign against Parthia, considered a victory, coinciding with the twentieth anniversary of the reign.

88   VICT PARTHICA, Antoninus holding Victory, between seated captives. Ant: 315. Den: 315/*C*657

89   – – Victory std. r., inscribing VO XX on shield; quiver and trumpet in exergue. Ant: 314. Den: 314/*C*656

PLAUTILLA

Augusta, 202–205

Fulvia Plautilla was the daughter of Plautianus, the fellow-countryman and praetorian prefect of Severus, who had acquired such wealth and influence that he could marry his daughter to Antoninus, the heir to the throne. The wedding was celebrated with great festivity in 202, the year of Severus' decennalia. Antoninus, however, being forced into the marriage, always hated Plautilla, and when her father fell from favour and was murdered in 205, she was exiled to the Lipari islands. When Antoninus became emperor in 211, one of his first acts was to have her murdered. Type *3*, which also appears on the coinage of Julia Domna, apparently indicates that the imperial couple had a child, who is unknown to history.

202 Wedding of Antoninus and Plautilla.

1*a*   CONCORDIAE AETERNAE, Antoninus and Plautilla clasping hands. Aur: 361/*C*9. Den: 361/*C*10

1*b*   CONCORDIA FELIX, Same type. Den: 365/*C*12

2   PROPAGO IMPERI, Same type. Aur: 362/*C*22. Den: 362/*C*21. Ses: 578A

2

3   PIETAS AVGG, Pietas stg. l., holding infant. Aur: 367/*C*15. Den: 367/ *C*16. Dup/As: 581/*C*18–19

GETA

Caesar June 198/Augustus 209—February 212

Publius (or Lucius) Septimius Geta was born to Severus and Domna in Rome in May 189. While still a child, he accompanied the emperor on his eastern campaign and was proclaimed Caesar (*1—3*) after the capture of Ctesiphon. He also became *princeps iuventutis*, and so remained for most of the reign of Severus. During the time, he played an insignificant role in the government of the empire, although he received the honour of two consulates (*16—21, 23—26*) with his brother Antoninus in 205 and 208. In 209, after the first victories in the British campaign, in which he participated, he was raised to the rank of Augustus (*28—29*), becoming co-emperor with Severus and Antoninus. It is especially from this time that the enmity between the brothers flared into open hostility. The extensive coinage featuring Concord of the Emperors (*28, 36—38*) refers to this hostility and expresses the hopes of the state.

When Severus died, the brothers, now co-emperors (*36—38*), escorted his body back to Rome and there celebrated his funeral and consecration. Their mutual hatred, however, grew to such an extent that they lived in separately walled parts of the palace and contemplated dividing the empire. Geta, who seems to have been of a more agreeable disposition, was attracting a substantial following when Antoninus solved the problem by having him murdered in their mother's arms in February 212.

Because of Geta's youth and his short reign, the great majority of his coinage reflects that of Severus and may be considered as part of his dynastic propaganda rather than as an independent series. Similarly, most of his issues as Augustus follow the types of Caracalla.

Caesar, 198—209

198 Proclamation as Caesar, with celebration of the new dynasty.
1 SEVERI AVG PII FIL, sacrificial implements (Caracalla *1*). Aur: 3/ C187. Den: 3/C188; 107/C189. Ses: 110. Dup/As: 110A/C191
2 PRINC IVVENT/VT IS, Geta stg. l. (Caracalla *3*). Aur: 16a/C156. Den: 15—18/C157, 159; 106. Ses: 113A
3 CASTOR, Castor stg. l. (Castor figures here as the patron of the equestrian order, which was headed by the *princeps iuventutis*). Aur: 6/C11. Den: 6/C12. Qui: 6/C13. Ses: 111/C15. Dup/As: 116/C16

3

17

4   FELICITAS TEMPOR, Felicitas and Geta clasping hands. Den: 94/ *C*49; 97/*C*47

5   CONCORDIAE AETERNAE, Jugate busts of Severus and Julia Domna (Severus *37*). Aur: 7

6   AETERNIT IMPERI, Busts of Severus and Antoninus facing each other (Severus *40b*, Caracalla *9*). Den: 5/*C*1

— — Celebration of victories over Parthia.

7   VICT AETERN, Victory flying l. (Severus *30*). Den: 101/*C*206

8   VICTORIAE AVGVSTORVM, Antoninus and Geta holding globe; between them, Victory stg. over altar, captive at feet. Ses: 115/*C*217. Dup/As: 123/*C*218

201 and later. Rebuilding of Rome.

9   RESTITVTORI VRBIS, Severus sacrificing (Severus *45*). Den: 53/ *C*174

10   — — Rome std. l. (Severus *46*). Den: 52/*C*172. Dup/As: 142/ *C*173

202 Donative on return of the emperors to Rome.

11   LIBERALITAS AVGVSTORVM, Liberalitas stg. l. Den: 11/*C*73. Ses: 113/*C*74

204 Celebration of the Secular Games, with honours to Liber and Hercules, games and a donative.

12   DI PATRII, Liber (Bacchus) and Hercules stg. facing (Severus *64*). Ses: 112/*C*32. Dup/As: 117/*C*33

13*a*   SAECVLARIA SACRA, Severus and Antoninus sacrificing over altar before temple; Concordia behind; musicians on either side; Tiber reclining on l. (Severus *67a*; Caracalla *35*). Ses: 131/ *C*180

13*b*   — — Similar, but without Concord and musicians (Severus *67b*). Ses: 137/*C*179. Dup/As: 132/*C*177

14   LAETITIA TEMPORVM, Ship in circus between four quadrigae; animals on both sides and below (Severus *68*; Caracalla *36*). Den: 43/*C*67

15   FELICITAS SAECVLI, Donation scene with Severus, Antoninus and Geta, officer and citizen (Severus *66*, Caracalla *37*). Dup/ As: 126/*C*41

15   LIBERALITAS AVGG IIII, Liberalitas stg. l. (Severus *69*, Caracalla *38*). Dup/As: 119

205 First consulate of Geta, shared with Antoninus; and attendant vows.

16   IMP ET CAESAR AVG FILI COS, Concordia stg. between std. Antoninus and Geta (Caracalla *40*). Den: 42/*C*64

17   COS, Geta in quadriga (Caracalla *41*). Den: 28/*C*28

18   PRINC IPI IVVENT COS, Severus, Antoninus and Geta on horseback galloping r. Aur: 37/*C*161. Den: 37/*C*162. Ses: 124–5A/*C*164, 166. Dup/As: 130/*C*165, 167

19   — — Geta stg. l. before trophy. Ses: 125/*C*163

20   — — Five horsemen galloping r. Dup/As: 131/*C*169

    21   VOTA PVBLICA, Geta sacrificing over tripod. Aur: 24−5/*C*235; 38/*C*229. Den: 24/*C*231; 26/*C*228; 38/*C*230. Dup/As: 133

206 Introduction of the worship of the Egyptian gods into the city by Antoninus.

    22   IOVI SOSPITATORI, Image of Jupiter-Serapis in distyle shrine (Severus *74*, Caracalla *44*). Ses: 136/*C*66

208 Second joint consulate with Antoninus.

    23   PONTIF COS II, Severus std. on platform between Antoninus and Geta (Caracalla *49*). Aur: 65/*C*125. Den: 65/*C*126

    24   −− Geta in quadriga l. or r. (Caracalla *50*). Aur: 63/*C*121. Den: 63/*C*122; 66 (PONTIFEX)

    25   −− Geta stg. l. Den: 61/*C*117

    26   −− Geta sacrificing. Den: 62/*C*119

−− Departure for the British front, with vows.

    27   VOTA PVBLICA, Geta sacrificing over tripod, by which stands bull (Caracalla *52*). Den: 57/*C*227 (no bull). Ses: 187/*C*232. Dup: 188/*C*234. As: 192/*C*233

Augustus with Severus and Antoninus, 209−211

209 Proclamation of Geta as Augustus, with a donative and emphasis on the desired harmony between the imperial brothers.

    28*a* CONCORDIA/E AVGG, Antoninus and Geta clasping hands (*cf.* Severus *83*, Caracalla *53*). Aur: 73/*C*24; 86/*C*23. Den: 85/*C*17 (CONCORDIA only)

    28*b* CONCORDIA AVGVSTORVM, Antoninus and Geta sacrificing over altar; Pietas between. Ses: 164

    28*c* CONCORDIAE AVGG, Antoninus and Geta clasping hands over altar, each crowned by Victory. Ses: 165/*C*26

    28*d* −− Antoninus and Geta clasping hands, one crowned by Apollo, the other Victory. Ses: 184/*C*25

    29   LIBERALITAS AVG VI, Liberalitas stg. l. (Severus *84*, Caracalla *55*). Aur: 44. Den: 44/*C*69

209−211 Celebration of victories in Britain, with address to the troops.

    30   VICTORIAE BRIT, Victory advancing l. or r. (Severus *86a*; Caracalla *57*). Den: 91/*C*220; 92/*C*219

    31*a* VICTORIAE BRITTANICAE, Victory std. l., inscribing shield set on knees (Severus *87*) Ses: 166/*C*221. As: 191

    31*b* VICT BRIT TR P III/I COS II, Same type. Ses: 172/*C*210; 180. As: 178/*C*211

    32   VICTORIAE BRITTANICAE, Two victories attaching shield to palm; two captives at foot (Severus *91*; Caracalla *60*). Ses: 167/*C*224

    33   −− Victory erecting trophy; on r., Britannia with hands tied and captive at feet (Caracalla *61a*). Ses: 186/*C*223

31b

34 PONTIF TR P II COS II, Severus, Antoninus and Geta on platform addressing officer and two soldiers. (Severus *93*). Ses: 159/*C*147

35 PONTIF (TR P II/I) COS II, Antoninus and Geta accompanied by three soldiers facing std. captive. Ses; 147/*C*127; 151/*C*128; 157/*C*146; 169/*C*154

Augustus with Antoninus, 211−212

211 Accession to supreme power, with Antoninus; vows for the reign. These types probably also celebrate the victories in Britain.

36 PONTIF TR P II COS II, Antoninus and Geta stg. l., facing Victory. Ses: 158

37 −− Antoninus and Geta clasping hands, crowned by Liber and Hercules. Ses: 155/*C*143

38 −− Antoninus and Geta sacrificing; fluteplayer behind. Ses: 156/*C*145; 170 (TR P III)

−− Return of the emperors to Rome, the occasion for a donative − the sixth of Antoninus and fifth of Geta − and vows of thanks.

39 ADVENTVS AVGVSTI, Geta on horseback (Caracalla *64*). Den: 84/*C*3. Ses: 182

40 LIBERALITAS AVGG VI ET V, Donation scene with Antoninus, Geta, Liberalitas and citizen. (Caracalla *65*). Aur: 87/*C*70. (V ET VI). Ses: 185/*C*71. As: 190/*C*72

41 LIBERALITAS AVG V, Liberalitas stg. l. (Caracalla *66*). Den: 88−9/*C*68

42 FORT RED TR P III/I COS II, Fortuna std. l. (Caracalla *67a*). Aur: 76/*C*58. Den: 76/*C*59; 77/*C*62; 93A. Ses: 168/*C*52. Dup: 173/*C*61. As: 175/*C*53−4; 176/*C*60

−− Games to celebrate victories in Britain.

43 TR P IIII COS II P P, Elephant (Caracalla *72*). Ses: 179. As: 181/*C*204

MACRINUS

April 217 – June 218

Marcus Opellius Macrinus, born in Mauretania in North Africa in about 265, was a distinguished lawyer who rose to become praetorian prefect under Caracalla. He was involved in the plot which deposed the hated emperor, and was promoted to be his successor after a short delay. On his accession (*1*), he added the name Severus to his own and Antoninus to that of his son Diadumenian, in order to proclaim a (fictitious) connection with the previous dynasty and to ensure the support of the troops, who had greatly favoured Caracalla. He carried on the Parthian war inconclusively, finally agreeing to pay a large tribute in exchange for peace; this settlement was styled a victory (*3*). His lack of military success, combined with the need for economy, stirred disaffection in the army, while the Senate and people of Rome came to regard him as an ineffective nonentity. To maintain support in the army, he proclaimed his son Diadumenian Augustus, the occasion for a donative (*4–5*), but such measures had no effect as the troops revolted in favour of Elagabalus. Macrinus' forces were soon defeated and he fled westward, only to be captured and executed in Asia Minor. He was the first emperor of equestrian rank, and the first to come from Mauretania.

The coinage of this brief reign offers only one peculiarity. When Macrinus was proclaimed, the Senate granted him the rank of consul, but he did not actually assume the office until 1 January 218. At that time, he correctly refused to have the first period recognised as a consulate, choosing to be designated as 'cos' rather than 'cos II'. The officials at the mint in Rome, however, naturally put 'cos II' on the coins until word of the emperor's choice reached them. The coinage therefore presents the anomaly of showing the first consulate after the second (*2*).

217 Vows on accession. All with symbolic types and inscribed VOTA PVBLICA P M TR P.

    1a   Securitas std. l. before altar. Aur: 12/*C*152. Den: 13/*C*153. Ses: 132/*C*154. As: 133/*C*155

    1b   Felicitas stg. l. Ant: 7. Den: 6/*C*147. Dup: 127/*C*148

    1c   Fides stg. l., holding standards. Ant: 9/*C*145. Den: 8/*C*144. Dup: 128/*C*146. As: 129

    1d   Salus std. l. Ant: 11/*C*149. Den: 10/*C*150. Dup: 130. As: 131/*C*151

    1e   Jupiter stg. l, with small figure of Macrinus at feet. Den: 5/*C*142. Ses: 126/*C*143

218 First (second) consulate.

    2   PONTIF MAXIM TR P II COS (II) P P, Macrinus in quadriga crowned by Victory. Aur: 47/*C*104; 48. Den: 36/*C*88. Ses: 160/*C*105. Dup: 161. As: 152–3/*C*106–7

— — Conclusion of peace with Parthia, called a victory.

    3a   VICT PART P M TR P II COS II P P, Victory flying r. between two shields. Aur: 50/*C*138

2

3*b* — — Victory walking r. Den: 49/*C*137
3*c* — — Victory stg., inscribing shield. Ses: 164/*C*139. Dup: 165/
    *C*141. As: 166/*C*140
3*d* VICTORIA PARTHICA, Type as *3a*. Aur: 98
3*e* — — Type as 3*b*. Den: 96−7/*C*134−5
3*f* — — Type as 3*c*. Ses: 209/*C*133
— — Donative on promotion of Diadumenian to Augustus.
    4 LIBERALITAS AVGVSTI, Donation scene with Macrinus and
       Diadumenian, Liberalitas, officer and citizen. Aur: 79/*C*43.
       Ses: 194/*C*44
    5 LIBERALITAS AVG, Liberalitas stg l. Den: 78/*C*41. Ses: 193/*C*42

DIADUMENIAN

Caesar April 217/Augustus May−June 218

Marcus Opellius Diadumenianus was a child of nine when he was made
Caesar by his father and given the name of Antoninus (i.e. Caracalla) to
advertise continuity with the previous dynasty. A year later, after the
revolt of troops favourable to Elagabalus; he was raised to the rank of
Augustus, in an effort to gain support by providing the occasion for a
donative. This proved of no avail and, on the defeat of his father, he
attempted to flee to the Parthians, but was captured and killed.

217 Proclamation as Caesar.
    1 PRINC IVVETVTIS, Diadumenian stg. l. in military dress; on r.,
       two standards (several variations). Aur: 101/*C*2; 103/*C*5. Avq:
       110/*C*16. Ant: 106/*C*11. Den: 102/*C*3; 104−5/*C*6; 107−9/*C*12,
       14; 112/*C*18. Qui: 111/*C*17. Ses: 211/*C*7; 214−15/*C*15. As: 212/
       *C*8−9; 213; 216−17/*C*13

ELAGABALUS

May 218−March 222

The son of Julia Soaemias, grandson of Julia Maesa and thus great-
nephew of Severus, Varius Avitus, also called Bassianus, was the hereditary
high-priest of the sun-god Elagabalus at Emesa in Syria. When Macrinus
proved to be ineffectual and parsimonious, the disaffected troops were
easily swayed by the bribes and propaganda of Maesa and Soaemias to

support the young priest, especially when the royal ladies revealed that he was the illegitimate son of their hero, Caracalla. He took the name Marcus Aurelius Antoninus (by which he was always officially known and which alone appears on the coins) to advertise his parentage and was saluted Augustus by the troops at Emesa. After a short campaign, Macrinus was defeated and the new Antoninus assumed supreme power at the age of fourteen.

On his accession, Elagabalus took the title of consul, paid vows and a donative (*1*−*2*), celebrated his victory (*3*) over Macrinus and consecrated Caracalla and Julia Domna (*4*−*7*). This activity was part of the advertisement of his legitimacy as a member of the dynasty of Severus (*8*−*9*). He then proceeded to Nicomedia for the winter, giving a taste of the new regime by his extravagances and addiction to the strange rites of his god. He there assumed the consulate which he called his second (*10*), though the first was never officially recognised, while the Senate celebrated vows for his safe arrival in Rome (*11*). In July 219, Elagabalus and his train reached Rome, whose populace received a donative in celebration (*12*−*14*). The emperor now indulged his whims and passions (all unnatural), establishing a regime which soon became notorious for its extravagance and corruption. He devoted special effort to promoting the cult of his god, who was represented by a sacred stone kept in his temple in Emesa, by bringing the stone to Rome and building grandiose temples to Elagabalus in the city. Each year, walking backward in reverence, he led the stone mounted on a chariot in solemn procession (*23*−*24*). As a result, posterity has given the name of the god to the emperor. Even more shocking to the Romans, the emperor married a Vestal virgin, Aquilia Severa (*20*), on the grounds that this represented a marriage between his god and the most sacred cult in Rome. He soon replaced her with Annia Faustina (*21*), but returned to her a few months later. He had previously been married to Julia Paula (*see* her coins).

For a time, Elagabalus placated the people with numerous festivals (*19*), gifts and entertainments, but eventually the troops and public became disgusted. Julia Maesa, realising that drastic action was necessary to save the dynasty, persuaded the emperor to adopt his cousin Alexander (*18*−*19*) and name him Caesar in 221. When he regretted this action, and began to plot against Alexander in 222, the troops rose in revolt and murdered him together with his mother Soaemias. His body was thrust down a sewer after suffering unparalleled indignities.

The period was generally one of peace; its greatest interest, clearly reflected in the coins (*23*−*26*), lies in the religious developments, with the introduction and extravagant display of the new cult and its priest, the emperor.

218 Vows on accession, with first donative.
    1 VOTA PVBLICA, Elagabalus sacrificing. Den: 202−3/C306
    2 LIBERALITAS AVG/VSTI, Liberalitas stg. l. Den: 97/C78. Ses: 352
− − Celebration of victory over Macrinus, stressing the emperor's new dynastic name.

3 VICTOR ANTONINI AVG, Victory running r. Aur: 151/*C*292; 154/*C*288. Ant: 152/*C*294; 155. Den: 153/*C*293; 156/*C*289; 157A. Qui: 157/*C*290. Ses: 377/*C*297. Dup: 375/*C*295. As: 376/*C*296

— — Consecration of Caracalla and Julia Domna.

4 *Obv.* DIVO ANTONINO MAGNO, Head r. *Rev.* CONSECRATIO, Funeral pyre surmounted by quadriga. Ses: *Alex.*719/*C*34

5 — — Eagle on globe. Den: *Alex.*717/*C*32. Ses: *Alex.*718/*C*33

6 *Obv.* DIVA IVLIA AVGVSTA, Bust r. *Rev.* CONSECRATIO, Peacock walking l. Den: *Alex.*715/*C*24

7 — — Peacock bearing Julia aloft. Ses: *Alex.*716/*C*25

— — Advertisement of connection with the Severan family.

8 IVLIA SOAEMIAS AVG, Bust r. Den: 207/*C*1

9 IVLIA MAESA AVG, Bust r. Den: 208/*C*1

— — Assumption of the consulate in Nicomedia.

10*a* CONSVL II P P, Elagabalus in quadriga l. Aur: 170/*C*25

10*b* TR POT II COS II P P, Same type. Aur: 174/*C*284

10*c* PONTIF MAX TR P II COS II P P, Same type, but emperor crowned by victory. Aur: 26A. Ses: 296/*C*234. Dup: 297. As: 298/*C*235−6

— — Prayers for a safe return to Rome.

11*a* FORTVNA REDVX, Fortuna std. l. Den: 81/*C*47; 189

11*b* FORTVNAE REDVCI, Fortuna stg. l. Den: 83−83A/*C*50. Qui: 84/*C*51. Ses: 348/*C*52. As: 349/*C*53

219 Arrival in Rome, the occasion for a second donative.

12 ADVENTVS AVG/VSTI (TR P III), Emperor on horseback. Aur: 57/*C*4−5. Den: 184/*C*2. Ses: 340/*C*6. As: 299/*C*3; 341−2/*C*7

12   26c

13 P M TR P II COS II P P LIB/ERAL/ITAS AVG II, Donation scene with Elagabalus, Liberalitas and citizen. Aur: 9−10/*C*74−5. Ses: 288/*C*83; 290/*C*76. As: 287/*C*77; 291

14 LIBERALITAS AVG/VSTI II, Liberalitas stg. l. Den: 98−100/*C*80, 82; 102/*C*79. Qui: 101/*C*81. Ses: 353/*C*84. As: 354/*C*85

220 Third consulate, apparently the occasion for a donative.

15 P M TR P III/I COS III P P, Elagabalus in quadriga l. Aur: 35/*C*171, 173; 180/*C*210. Den: 36/*C*180 (with Victory behind emperor). Ses: 308/*C*173; 313/*C*179; 316/*C*240; 331/*C*211. Dup: 309/*C*175. As: 310−2/*C*174, 176−7; 317/*C*241

16 — — Elagabalus std. l. on curule chair. Aur: 33−4/*C*165−7. Ses: 315/*C*239

17   LIBERALITAS AVG/VST III, Liberalitas stg. l. Den: 103/*C*86. Ses: 354A

221   Adoption of Alexander, the occasion for a donative and perhaps for games (the date of type *19* is uncertain; Elagabalus is reported to have held many festivals).

18   LIBERALITAS AVG IIII, Liberalitas stg. l. Den: 104/*C*88

19   MVNIFICENTIA AVG, Elephant r. As: 365/*C*118

— —   Marriage with the Vestal, Aquilia Severa (*see also* her coins).

20   IVL AQVIL SEV AVG Bust r. Aur: 205/*C*1

— —   Marriage with Annia Faustina (*see also* her coins).

21   ANNIA FAVSTINA AVGVSTA, Bust r. Aur: 206/*C*1

222   Fourth consulate.

22   P M TR P V COS IIII P P, Elagabalus in quadriga l. Aur: 54, 182/*C*217. Den: 55, 183/*C*218. As: 337−8/*C*219−21

219−222   Religious types, with the procession of the sacred stone of Elagabalus, and with specific identification of the emperor as his priest.

23   CONSERVATOR AVG/VSTI, Stone of Emesa surmounted by eagle and four parasols in quadriga. Aur: 61/*C*16, 18; 64. Den: 62/*C*17

24   SANCT DEO SOLI ELAGABAL, Same type. Aur: 143/*C*265; 196A. Den: 144/*C*266; 195−7/*C*267−9

25   COS III P P, Sacred stone adorned with stars and eagle. Den: 176/*C*26

26*a*   INVICTVS SACERDOS AVG, Elagabalus sacrificing over altar or tripod; some varieties have bull behind. Aur: 86/*C*59. Den: 87/*C*58; 88, 191/*C*61, 62. Ses: 350/*C*64. As: 351/*C*65

26*b*   SACERD DEI SOLIS ELAGAB, Same type (no bull). Den: 131/*C*246; 134−5/*C*249, 252; 194/*C*246; Qui: 132−3B/*C*247−8. Ses: 369/*C*253. Dup: 370−1/*C*251

26*c*   SVMMVS SACERDOS AVG, Same type. Den: 146−7/*C*276−7; 200.

JULIA PAULA

The wedding of Elagabalus and Julia Cornelia Paula, his first wife, was celebrated with games in the summer of 219. He put her aside at the end of the next year, and she retired to private life.

219   Marriage to Elagabalus.

1   CONCORDIA AETERNA, Elagabalus and Julia clasping hands; Concord stands between them. Aur: 215/*C*13. Ses: 386/*C*14. As: 387/*C*15

AQUILIA SEVERA

Elagabalus scandalised Rome by taking Julia Aquilia Severa, a Vestal virgin, as his wife at the end of 220, and claiming that the highest priest should marry a Vestal so that they could have divine children. He divorced her in the following summer, but took her back by the end of 221 and remained married to her until his death.

220 Marriage to Elagabalus.
   1 CONCORDIA, Elagabalus and Aquilia clasping hands. Den: 228/*C*6

ANNIA FAUSTINA

Annia Faustina, a descendant of Marcus Aurelius was married to Elagabalus for a new months in the second half of 221. He then returned to Aquilia Severa.

221 Marriage to Elagabalus.
   1 CONCORDIA, Elagabalus and Annia clasping hands. Den: 232/*C*1.
     Ses: 399/*C*2

JULIA SOAEMIAS

Soaemias, the daughter of Julia Maesa and wife of a prominent senator, and mother of Elagabalus whom, she alleged, she had conceived from adultery with Caracalla, a notion in accord with her reputation. During her son's reign (Elagabalus 8), she is supposed to have participated in the government, and to have tolerated his excesses. She was murdered together with him.

218/222 Honours to the goddess of Syria, Atargatis, in Roman guise.
   1 VENVS CAELESTIS, Venus stg. l., sometimes with child. Aur:
     240/*C*9. Ant: 245/*C*17. Den: 241/*C*8; 243/*C*14. Qui: 242/*C*10;
     244/*C*15. Ses: 402/*C*11; 406/*C*18. Dup: 403/*C*12; 405/*C*13;
     407/*C*19. As: 404/*C*12; 408/*C*20

JULIA MAESA

Maesa, daughter of Bassinaus, the high priest of Emesa and sister of Julia Domna, married Julius Avitus, an ex-consul, and gave birth to Soemias and Mamaea, both mothers of future emperors. She lived at court with her sister during the reigns of Severus and Caracalla, but returned to the East by order of Macrinus. She stayed in Emesa, where she used her vast wealth to suborn the troops in favour of her grandson Elagabalus. She had considerable influence during his reign, but finally could not control his excesses and was instrumental in having his cousin Alexander promoted to Caesar. She died in 226 and was consecrated (Alexander *11−12*; *see also* Elagabalus *9*).

218/222   Celebration of Maesa's family, combined with prayers for a safe return to Rome. The two children of types *1* and *2* are no doubt Maesa's grandchildren, Elagabalus and Alexander, while the single child of *3* is probably Alexander, to indicate a coin struck during his reign, after the disgrace of his cousin.
1   FORTVNAE REDVCI, Fortuna (or Fecunditas) stg. l.; child stg. at each side. Den: 252/*C*14
2   TEMPORVM FEL, Felicitas std. l. between two children. Den: 274/*C*51
3   FECVNDITAS AVG/VSTAE, Fecunditas stg. or std., extending her hand to a child. Den: 249/*C*8. Qui: 250/*C*10. Ses: 410/*C*11. As: 311/*C*12

SEVERUS ALEXANDER

Caesar July 221/Augustus March 222-March 235

Alexianus, the son of Julia Mamaea and grandson of Julia Maesa, and thus great-nephew of Severus and cousin of Elagabalus, was born in Phoenicia in October 208. He was raised in Syria and accompanied his cousin to Rome when he became emperor in 218. In 221, when the regime of Elagabalus was in danger of collapse, Maesa ensured that Alexianus was adopted and made Caesar *(1−2)* in order to preserve the dynasty; he thereupon took the name Marcus Aurelius Alexander. In 222, the two rulers were joint consuls *(3)*, but Elagabalus, led by suspicion and jealousy, attempted to have his cousin killed. The troops then rioted, forcing the emperor to name Alexander as co-ruler.

On the murder of Elagabalus, Alexander was swiftly recognised as emperor by the troops, to whom he gave the customary donative *(4−6)*, and assumed the name Severus to advertise his membership of the dynasty (of which, as it turned out, he was the last). Since he was only thirteen at the time, he remained under the guidance of his mother, whose influence increased, especially after the death and consecration of Maesa *(11−12)* in 225.

Under Alexander, the situation in Rome returned to normal. The sacred stone was sent back to Emesa, and the temple to the god Elagabalus was re-dedicated to Jupiter Ultor *(7−9)* in 224. Rome saw much construction at this time: the Colosseum was rebuilt *(7)* in 223, and a monumental Nymphaeum *(15)* was erected at the end of the Julian aqueduct in 226. In 225, Alexander married Orbiana, daughter of a man who for a time rose to the rank of Caesar. On his fall in 227, however, she was banished to Africa; the jealousy of Mamaea doubtless contributed to the exile. Issues of 229 commemorate a reform of the coinage (*19—20*) whose nature has not been determined; it apparently involved the gold coins.

During these years, events which were to prove fateful for the Romans were taking place in the East. Artaxerxes (Ardeshir), the Sassanian prince of Persis, defeated the Parthian Artabanus in 227 to become ruler of Persia and founder of a new, better organised and more aggressive dynasty. He soon made claims to Roman territory and began a policy of active expansion. In 230 his forces crossed the Euphrates and over-ran Mesopotamia; some bands penetrated into Syria and Asia Minor. Alexander and his mother therefore spent the winter in Antioch, where attempts to negotiate a peace failed. In the indecisive campaign which followed in 232, Roman territory was regained, and a victory (*23— 24*) could be claimed. It coincided with the tenth anniversary (*23—25*) of the reign. In 233, Alexander returned to Rome to celebrate a triumph with a donative (*26—28*) to the people.

During the Persian campaign, when troops had been withdrawn from the Rhine and Danube frontier, the German tribes had attacked Roman territory. In 234, therefore, Alexander and Mamaea set out for the front in Germany. Although the Roman forces crossed the Rhine and won a notable victory, the troops, dissatisfied with the regime of Mamaea, murdered the emperor and his mother, and proclaimed Maximinus in March 235.

221 Proclamation as Caesar.
    1 PIETAS AVG, Priestly implements.
       Den: 3/*C*198. Ses: 383/*C*199.

          1   16

    2 PRINC IVVENTVTIS, Alexander stg. 1. in military dress; two stan-
       dards on r. As: 386/*C*485
222 First consulate.
    3 PONTIFEX COS, Alexander in quadriga r. Ses: 384/*C*458. As: 385/
       *C*459

Augustus, 222—235

—— Accession to the throne, with consular procession and a donative.

4   P M TR P COS P P, Alexander in quadriga l. Aur: 16/*C*225. Den: 17/*C*226.

5   LIBERALITAS AVG/VSTI, Liberalitas stg. l. Aur: 147/*C*107; 149/*C*110. Den: 148/*C*108; 281–3/*C*143. Ses: 564/*C*111. Dup: 565/*C*112

6   – – Donation scene with Alexander, Liberalitas and citizen. Aur: 150/*C*113. Ses: 566/*C*114

223 Rebuilding of the Colosseum, which had been struck by lightning in 217.

7   PONTIF MAX TR P II COS P P, The Colosseum; Emperor and one other figure sacrificing on r. before shrine; another shrine on r.; combat within Colosseum. Ses: 410/*C*468. As: 411/*C*469

224 Dedication of temple to Jupiter Ultor, the occasion for a second donative.

8   IOVI VLTORI (P M TR P III COS P P), Hexastyle temple in colonnaded courtyard. Den: 146/*C*101. Ses: 412/*C*103

9   IOVI VLTORI, Jupiter std. l. Aur: 142/*C*94. Den: 143/*C*97; 144/*C*95; 203. Qui: 145/*C*96

10   LIBERALITAS AVG/VSTI II, Liberalitas stg. l. Aur: 152/*C*117. Den: 153/*C*118. Ses: 567/*C*122. Dup: 568/*C*124. As: 569/*C*123

225 Funeral and consecration of Julia Maesa.

11   *Obv.* DIVA MAESA AVG/VSTA, Bust r. *Rev.* CONSECRATIO, Funeral pyre in three storeys surmounted by a quadriga. Den: 379/*C*5. Ses: 712; 713/*C*6 (IVLIA MAESA AVG)

12   Maesa borne aloft on a peacock or eagle. Den: 377–8/*C*2–3. Ses: 714/*C*4

226 Second consulate, with third donative.

13   P/ONTIF M/AXIM TR P V COS II PP, Alexander in quadriga l. or r. Aur: 56/*C*294. Den: 56A. As: 448/*C*295; 452/*C*478

14   LIBERALITAS AVG/VSTI III, Liberalitas stg. l. Den: 154/*C*128. Ses: 573/*C*129. As: 574/*C*130

– – Construction of the Nymphaeum.

15   P M TR P V COS II P P; Elaborately decorated nymphaeum. Aur: 58/*C*298. Den:/*C*297. Ses: 449/*C*303; 453/*C*480. As: 450/*C*300, 302

229 Third consulate, with fourth donative.

16   P M TR P VIII COS III P P, Alexander in quadriga r. Aur: 98. Den: 99/*C*376. Ses: 495–6/*C*377, 381. Dup: 497/*C*380. As: 498/*C*378–9

17   LIBERALITAS AVG/VSTI IIII, Liberalitas stg. l. Aur: 204/*C*132. Den: 205/*C*133. Qui: 206/*C*134

18   Donation scene with Alexander, officer (and soldier), Liberalitas and citizen. Ses: 578/*C*139. As: 579/*C*140

– – Reform of the coinage, nature uncertain.

19   RESTITVTOR MON, Alexander stg. l. Dup: 601/*C*516–17

20   MON RESTITVTA, Moneta stg. l. Dup: 589/*C*180

231 The Persian war: departure for the front, with an address to the troops.

21*a* PROFECTIO AVG/VSTI, Alexander on horseback. Den: 210/*C*488.
As: 595/*C*489—90; 639/*C*491

21*b* — — but emperor preceded by Victory. Ses: 596/*C*492; 640/
*C*493

22 ADLOCVTIO AVGVSTI, Alexander on platform with officers addressing three soldiers. Ses: 544/*C*3, 4

— — Victory in the Persian war, coinciding with the tenth anniversary of
the reign; vows for a second decade.

23*a* VICTORIA AVGVSTI, Victory stg. r., inscribing VOT X on shield
attached to palm tree. Aur: 217/*C*565. Den: 218—19/*C*566.
Ses: 616/*C*567. As: 617/*C*568.

23*b* P M TR P VIIII COS III P P, Same type. Ses: 505/*C*398. As: 506/
*C*396

23*a*

24 Alexander std. l., crowned by Victory and facing Virtus who
rests hand on shield inscribed VOT X set on cippus. As: 410/
*C*468

25 VOTIS VICENNALIBVS (COS III P P) in wreath. Aur: 260/*C*595.
Den: 261/*C*596. Ses: 654

233 Triumph for Persian war, with fifth donative.

26 P M TR P XII COS III P P, Alexander in quadriga. Aur: 121/*C*445

27 LIBERALITAS AVGVSTI V, Liberalitas stg. l. Ses: 533/*C*144

28 — — Donation scene with Alexander, officers and soldier,
Liberalitas and citizen. Ses: 534/*C*145

ORBIANA

Gneia Seia Herennia Sallustia Barbia Orbiana was the daughter of
Sallustius Varius Macrinus, a shadowy figure who became Caesar under
Alexander when or after his daughter and the emperor were married in
225. When he fell from power and was executed in 227, Orbiana was sent
into exile. No details of her life are known.

225 Marriage with Alexander.

1*a* PROPAGO IMPERI, Alexander and Orbiana clasping hands. Den:
323/*C*10

1*b* CONCORDIA AVGVSTORVM, Same type. Ses: 657/*C*6

JULIA MAMAEA

Julia Avita Mamaea, the daughter of Julius Avitus and Julia Maesa, married a Syrian procurator by whom she had a son, Alexianus. Her relations with Caracalla, however, were such that her mother Maesa could claim in her propaganda that the child was actually the offspring of the emperor. Mamaea actively protected Alexianus against the plots of his cousin Elagabalus, and when he succeeded to the throne, she assumed a dominant role. With the title Augusta, she virtually ran the government, being recognised as Alexander's equal in most matters. Although she received high honours, and was even called *Mater Castrorum*, she was unpopular with the troops, who objected to her dominant role, and murdered her with her son in 235. She appears frequently on medallions, her bust conjoined with that of her son.

222/235   Family of Mamaea, with Alexander represented as a child.
     1*a*   FECVND/ITAS AVGVSTAE, Fecunditas stg. l., extending hand to child. Den: 331/C5. Ses: 668/C8. As: 669/C9
     1*b*   ――Fecunditas std. l., holding hand of child. Den: 332/C6. Qui: 333/C7

MAXIMINUS

March 235–May 238

C. Julius Verus Maximinus was a half-Romanised native of Thrace who enrolled in the army under Severus and rose through the ranks to become prefect in charge of new recruits during the reign of Alexander. He was extremely popular with the troops, who proclaimed him emperor when they mutinied and killed Alexander (*1–2*).

Maximinus then in turn named his young son Maximus as Caesar, and assumed the consulate (*3–5*) for 236. In spite of his bloodthirsty behaviour toward his enemies, and particularly the Senate, he kept the favour of the army by conducting extremely successful campaigns in Germany (*9–11*) and along the Danube. The demands of the wars, however, produced an increase in taxes, which gave rise to a series of revolts. The most serious, that of the Gordiani in Africa, though soon repressed, provoked the alienation of the Senate and people of Rome from Maximinus, who was formally deposed and declared a public enemy. When the news reached the frontier, Maximinus and the army set out to reduce the capital to submission. On the way he was detained by the strong defence of Aquilea in northern Italy, and after a long and unsuccessful siege there, he and his son were murdered by the troops after a reign of three years during which they never saw Rome.

235   Accession to the throne, with decennial vows.
     1   P M TR P P P, Maximinus stg. l. between two standards. Aur:

1/*C*44. Den: 1/*C*46. Qui: 1/*C*45. Ses: 24/*C*48 Dup: 25/*C*50. As: 26/*C*49

2   VOTIS DECENNALIBVS in wreath. Den: 17/*C*117. Ses: 75/*C*118. Dup: 76/*C*120. As: 77/*C*119

2   7

236   Consulate, with a donative.

3   P M TR P II COS P P, Maximinus, crowned by Victory, in quadriga l. Ses: 27–8/*C*53. As: 29/*C*54

4*a*   LIBERALITAS AVG/VSTI, Donation scene with Maximinus, officer, Liberalitas and citizen. Aur: 9/*C*23

4*b*   — — same type, but two soldiers with emperor and five more below platform. Ses: 48/*C*24; 51 (AVGSTI); 52/*C*25

5   — — Liberalitas stg. l. Den: 10/*C*19. Ses: 49/*C*21; 53/*C*26. Dup: 50/*C*22. As: *BMC*49

— — (Date uncertain). Death and consecration of Paulina, wife of Maximinus. All have *obv.* DIVA PAVLINA, Bust r.

6   CONSECRATIO, Paulina borne aloft by peacock. Aur: 2. Den: 2/*C*2. Ses: 3/*C*3

7   — —Peacock facing. Den: 1/*C*1

8   — —Diana in biga r. Ses: 4/*C*4

236–8   Victories in Germany.

9   VICTORIA GERM/ANICA, Victory stg. 1., captive at feet. Aur: 23/*C*106. Avq: 23/*C*105. Den: 23/*C*107. Qui: 23/*C*108. Ses: 90/*C*109. Dup: 72; 91/*C*111. As: 73; 92/*C*110

10   — — Maximinus, crowned by victory, stg. 1., captive at feet. Ses: 70/*C*113; 93/*C*114. Dup: 71. As: 71; 94/*C*115

11   VICTORIA AVGVSTORVM, Maximinus and Maximus holding image of Victory; between, two std. captives; behind, soldier on either side. Ses: 89/*C*104

PAULINA

Nothing is known of Maximinus' wife Paulina, whom he consecrated (Maximinus 6–8). She may have died before he came to the throne.

MAXIMUS

Caesar 236—May 238

Little is known about C. Julius Verus Maximus, who was appointed Caesar by his father in 236, stayed on the frontier with him, and suffered the same fate.

236 Appointment as Caesar and *princeps iuventutis*.
    1*a* PRINC/IPI IVVENTVTIS, Maximus stg. l.; two standards behind. Aur: 5. Den: 3/10. Qui: 3. Ses: 9/*C*12; 13/*C*14. Den: 10/*C*13; 14a/*C*15. As: 10; 14
    1*b* Maximus stg. l. holding globe. Den: 4
    2   PIETAS AVG, priestly implements. Den: 1—2/*C*1, 3. Ses: 6/*C*5; 8/*C*9; 11/*C*7. Dup: 7/*C*6; 12. As: 7; 12

GORDIAN I

March—April 238

M. Antonius Gordianus Sempronianus Africanus was born about 159, of a distinguished aristocratic family which had large landholdings in North Africa. He rose through public offices to become consul in 222. When the pressure of taxation to support the wars of Maximinus drove the Africans to revolt, they proclaimed the reluctant Gordian emperor. He associated his son, also called Gordian, in the rule, easily occupied Carthage, and sent news of his proclamation to Rome. The Senate willingly accepted the Gordiani as emperors and condemned Maximinus. The governor of Numidia, however, remained loyal to Maximinus, marched on Carthage (which had no regular troops) and defeated the younger Gordian, who was killed. When his father received the news, he hanged himself. The revolt had lasted about three weeks.

238 Accession to imperial power.
    1   P M TR P COS P P, Gordian, togate, stg. l. Den: l/*C*2. Ses: 7—8/*C*3

1

GORDIAN II

Son and co-ruler with his father, Gordian I. His coinage contains no historical types.

BALBINUS and PUPIENUS

April–July 238

When the news of the defeat of the Gordians reached Rome, the Senate, which could no longer retreat from active opposition to Maximinus, appointed two of its own members to serve as joint emperors with equal powers, a situation reminiscent of the ancient consuls of the Republic. Both were senior senators of some distinction. D. Caelius Calvinus Balbinus, born about 178 to an old aristocratic family, had twice been consul and had governed several provinces, while his colleague, M. Clodius Pupienus Maximus, had held important military posts as well as the consulate and had been prefect of the city. No sooner were they installed (*1–2*) than they had to face a popular revolt in favour of the family of the Gordians; as a result, the young Gordian III was associated in their rule as Caesar, the occasion for a joint donative (*3–4*) and the consecration of the Gordiani (not commemorated on the coinage). Pupienus now marched north to organise the resistance against Maximinus, while Balbinus attempted to regulate affairs in Rome, which suffered from a violent and destructive conflict between the populace and the praetorians. When Maximinus was killed, Pupienus returned to Rome, to be greeted enthusiastically by the populace. The two emperors ruled with justice and were popular with the Romans, but hostility between the regular troops and the praetorians, combined with their mutual jealousy (*5–6*) brought about their downfall. When Pupienus was attacked by the praetorians, Balbinus hesitated to send a force to his aid, and as a result both were murdered after a reign of three months.

The co-emperors issued common coinage, using the same types and dies. Much of it celebrates, with wishful thinking, the mutual trust and affection whose absence led to their downfall, while Pupienus adds their unique character as senior members of the Senate.

BALBINUS

238   Announcement of accession, with decennial vows.
1   P M TR P COS II P P, Balbinus stg. l. Den: 5/*C*20. S: 16/*C*21. Dup: 17/*C*22
2   VOTIS DECENNALIBVS in wreath. Ses: 20/*C*33. Dup: 21/*C*34
– –   Donative, on adoption of Gordian III.
3   LIBERALITAS AVGVSTORVM, Liberalitas stg. l. Den: 3/*C*10. Ses: 15/*C*11
4   – – Donation scene with Balbinus, Pupienus and Gordian III, a soldier, Liberalitas and citizen. Ses: 14/*C*13
– –   Advertisement of the cooperation between the emperors.
5*a*   CONCORDIA AVGG, Clasped hands. Ant: 10/*C*3
5*b*   FIDES MVTVA AVGG, Same type. Ant: 11/*C*6

5*c* PIETAS MVTVA AVGG, Same type. Ant: 12/*C*17

Balbinus 5*a*

PUPIENUS

238 Announcement of accession, with decennial vows.
  1   P M TR P COS II P P, Pupienus stg. l. Den: 5/*C*29. S: 15/*C*30
  2   VOTIS DECENNALIBVS in wreath. Ses: 18/*C*44. Dup: 19
  Donative on association of Gordian III in power.
— — 3   LIBERALITAS AVGVSTORVM, Liberalitas stg. l. Den: 3/*C*14. Ses:14/
       *C*15
— — 4   Donation scene, as Balbinus *4*. Ses: 13/*C*18
— — Advertisement of the mutual affection of the Augusti, and of their
       role as senior senators.
  5*a*   AMOR MVTVVS AVGG, Clasped hands. Ant: 9/*C*1, 2
  5*b*   CARITAS MVTVS AVGG, Same type. Ant: 10/*C*3, 4
  6   PATRES SENATVS, Same type. Ant: 11/*C*19, 21

Pupienus 6

GORDIAN III

Caesar April 238/Augustus July 238—March 244

M. Antonius Gordianus, the grandson of Gordian I and nephew of
Gordian II, was raised to the rank of Caesar in 238 by a popular demon-
stration and associated with Balbinus and Pupienus, the occasion for a
donative (*1—2*; Balbinus and Pupienus *3—4*) to the people. When they
were killed, he became Augustus at the age of thirteen, and undertook
the optimistic decennial vows (*3*) which had now become customary at the
beginning of reigns, although they rarely lasted that long. He assumed the
consulate (*4—6*) in 239, perhaps the occasion for another donative (*7—8*).

The reign was marked by serious external and internal problems: the Goths and Carpi attacked the northern frontier and revolt broke out in Africa. It was probably the suppression of the latter which produced the third donative (*9*). In 241, during the second consulate (*10–12*) of Gordian, Timesitheus, whose distinguished career had given him experience in all aspects of imperial administration, was raised to the rank of praetorian prefect, and the emperor married his daughter Tranquillina, the occasion for a fourth donative (*13–14*). Timesitheus effectively directed the empire for the next three years with considerable success.

Sapor (Shapur), the Sassanian king invaded Syria in 241, provoking a major Roman campaign (*15–16*) which began early the next year. Gordian and Timesitheus set out from Rome via the northern frontier, where they defeated the Carpi, then crossed into Asia. In 243 the Romans won signal victories (*17–18*) against the Persians and pushed far into Mesopotamia. They planned to advance toward Ctesiphon, when Timesitheus suddenly died, succumbing either to disease or to the ambition of his successor Philip. Early in the following year, when the Roman army had reached Dura on the Euphrates, Philip, who had won support among the troops, had Gordian murdered and became emperor.

Caesar, 238

238 Appointment as Caesar, with donative.
   1   PIETAS AVGG, Priestly implements. Den: 1/*C*182. Ses: 3/*C*183
   2   LIBERALITAS AVGVSTORVM, Liberalitas stg. l. Ses: 2/*C*128

Augustus, 238–244

—— Decennial vows, on accession.
   3   VOTIS DECENNALIBVS in wreath. Aur: 14/*C*409. Ses: 263/*C*410. As: 264/*C*411
239 First consulate, with second donative.
   4   P M TR P II/I COS P P, Gordian sacrificing. Aur: 43/*C*209; 59; 73/*C*214. Ant: 37/*C*210; 54/*C*212; 68/*C*216; 169/*C*187 (P M TRI P CON P P). Qui: 46; 77/*C*228. Ses: 271/*C*211; 280/*C*213; 291–2/*C*217, 229. Dup: 292. As: 292/*C*230
   5   —— Gordian in quadriga r. or l. Ant: 50B, 173/*C*220. Ses: 276/*C*221. As: 276/*C*222; 284
   6a —— Gordian, crowned by Victory, std. l. on curule chair receiving branch from Pax. Ant: 50C, 175/*C*223.
   6b P M TR P III COS P P, Gordian std. l. on curule chair. Ant: 82. Ses: 294/*C*231. Dup: 294/*C*232. As: 294
   7   LIBERALITAS AVG/VSTI II, Liberalitas stg. front. Aur: 42/*C*129; 58.

Gordian III 4

Ant: 36/*C*130; 53/*C*133; 66/ *C*132. Den: 45/*C*131. Ses: 269/ *C*136; 279/*C*134; 289. Dup: 269; 270/*C*140; 279/*C*135. As: 270/ *C*139

8 Donation scene with Gordian, officer, soldier and citizen. Dup: 275

240 Third donative, on suppression of revolt in Africa.

9 LIBERALITAS AVG/VSTI III, Liberalitas stg. front. Ant: 67/*C*142. Ses: 283; 290/*C*143: Dup: 283; 290/*C*145. As: 290/*C*144

241 Second consulate.

10 P M TR P IIII COS II P P, Gordian, crowned by Victory, in quadriga, preceded by soldiers (on *Aur* only). Aur: 135/*C*259. Ant: 139/*C*258. As: 320

11 – – Gordian stg. r. (type repeated in following years). Aur: 105/*C*252. Ant: 91/*C*242; 92/*C*253. Den: 115/*C*243 Ses: 308, 308A/*C*277. Dup: 308. As: 308A/*C*278

12 – – Gordian sacrificing. Ant: 137A/*C*246. Den: 139A/*C*247

– – Fourth donative, apparently on Gordian's marriage.

13 LIBERALITAS AVG III, Liberalitas stg. 1. Ant: 137/*C*147. Ses: 316/*C*148. Dup: 316/*C*149. As: 316

14 LIBERALITAS AVGVSTI IIII, Donation scene with Gordian, two officers, Liberalitas and citizen. Ses: 317/*C*150. As: 317/*C*151

242–4 The Persian war: vows for a safe return, address to the troops and announcement of a personal and lasting victory.

15 FORT/VNA REDVX, Fortuna std. 1. Aur: 160–1/*C*96. Ant: 143– 4/*C*97–8. Ses: 331/*C*99 As: 331/*C*100–1

16 ADLOCVTIO AVGVSTI, Gordian, on platform, addressing three soldiers. Ses: 313/*C*13–14

17 VICTORIA GORDIANI AVG, Victory running r. Ant: 219/*C*380

18 VICTOR/IA AETER/NA, Victory leaning on shield, captive at feet. Ant: 154–6/*C*348–9, 353. Ses: 337/*C*351; 338/*C*354. As: 337/*C*352, 350; 338/*C*355

TRANQUILLINA

Little is known of Furia Sabinia Tranquillina, the daughter of the powerful praetorian prefect Timesitheus, who married Gordian III in May 241. Her fate after his murder is unknown.

241 Marriage with Gordian.
   1 CONCORDIA AVGVSTORVM, Gordian and Tranquillina clasping hands.
      Ant: 250/*C*4. Ses: 341/*C*5. Dup: 341/*C*6. As: 341/*C*7

PHILIP I

February/March 244−September/October 249

M. Julius Philippus was born about 204 in the Roman province of Arabia. His career led him to become second in command, after the praetorian prefect Timesitheus, of the Roman forces sent against Persia under Gordian III. When the prefect was killed, Philip succeeded to his office, and rose to supreme power when Gordian in turn was removed early in 244. He was acclaimed by the troops, to whom he gave a donative (*1−2*), and told the Senate that Gordian had died of disease. The usual vows were celebrated (*3*), and, as an ostensible sign of piety, he arranged for the funeral and consecration of the late emperor (not celebrated on the coins).

After settling the terms for an honourable peace with the Persians (*4−5*), he returned along the northern frontier to Rome, where his arrival in July 244 was celebrated by a donative (*6−7*) to the people. Like many of his predecessors, he planned to found a dynasty (*8−9*); he therefore gave special honours to his wife Otacilia Severa and raised his young son, also called Philip, to the rank of Caesar. During 245, when the emperor was holding his first consulate (*10*), the German tribe of the Carpi attacked the frontier provinces and engaged the Romans in a long campaign, which was only concluded in 247 when Philip was consul (*11*) jointly with his son. After his victory (*12*), Philip returned in triumph to Rome, and raised the younger Philip to be full co-ruler, or Augustus, the occasion for a third donative (*13−15*).

The greatest event of the reign, widely featured on the coinage, was the thousandth anniversary of the foundation of Rome (*16−26*), whose celebration began on 21 April 248. This auspicious event, considered as the beginning of a new age, was celebrated with magnificent festivals and Secular Games featuring a great array of exotic animals brought from the East.

The next year, however, saw the beginning of the revolt of Pacatian on the Danube, and of a major Gothic irruption which was to have disastrous effects. Philip did not live to see the results, however, for, after making vows for a safe return from the frontier (*27*), he set out against Decius who had been proclaimed emperor by the legions on the Danube. The two armies met at Verona where Philip was defeated and killed.

244 First donative, on proclamation as emperor, with vows.
1 LIBERALITAS AVG/G, Liberalitas stg. l. Ant: 37A. Ses: 177—8/ C83. As: 178.
2 — — Donation scene with Philip I and II, soldiers, Liberalitas and citizen. As: 179/C85
3 VOTIS DECENNALIBVS in wreath. Ant: 53A. Ses: 195/C246. Dup: 195/C248. As: 195/C247
— — Peace established with the Persians, and supposed to be enduring.
4 PAX AETERN/A, Pax stg. or running l. Aur: 40. Ant: 40/C103; 41—2/C102, 109. Ses: 184/C105, 108; 185/C110. Pup: 184/C107; 185/C111. As: 184/C106; 185
5 PAX FVNDATA CVM PERSIS, Pax stg. l. Ant: 69/C113; 72/C114

5

— — Arrival in Rome, with donative to the people.
6 ADVENTVS AVGG, Philip on horseback r. Ant: 26/C3; 81/C4. Den: 26/C5. Ses: 165/C6
7a LIBERALITAS AVG/G II, Liberalitas stg. l. Aur: 38/C86. Ant: 38/ C87. Ses: 180/C88. As: 180/C89
7b M IVL PHILIPPVS AVG M IVL PHILLIPPVS N C, Busts of Philip I and Philip II vis-à-vis. *Rev.* As previous. Ant: 56/C8
244 and later: establishment of a dynasty.
8 MARCIA OTACILIA SEVERA AVG, Bust r. Aur: 64/Cl. Ant: 39/C2. As: 196/C3—4
9a PIETAS AVGG, Busts of Otacilia and Philip II vis-à-vis. Ant: 43/ C4. Den: 43/C5
9b DE PIA MATRE PIVS FILIVS, Same type. Ant: *30/C1*
245 First consulate of Philip.
10 P M TR P II COS P P, Philip std. l. on curule chair. Aur: 2/C119. Ant: 2/C120. Ses: 148a/C121. As: 148/C122
247 Second consulate.
11 P M TR P IIII COS II P P, Type as previous. As: 151/C142—3
— — Victory over the Carpi.
12 VICTORIA CARPICA, Victory running r. Ant: 66/C238
— — Promotion of Philip II to the rank of Augustus, with third donative.
13 IMP (M IVL) PHILIPPVS AVG, Bust of Philip II r. Ant: 68/C4. Ses: 197/C5. Dup: 197/C7. As: 197/C6
14 LIBERALITAS AVGG III, Liberalitas stg. l. Ses: 181/C92
15 — —Philip I and II std. on curule chairs. Ses: 182. As: 182
247—248 Celebration of the thousandth anniversary of Rome, with

Secular Games, and honours to Roma Aeterna, worshipped in the temple founded by Hadrian.

16   ROMAE AETERNAE, Rome std. l. Aur: 44/*C*168. Ant: 44, 45/*C*169−70; 65/*C*171; 85/*C*167

17*a* SAECVLVM NOVVM, Temple of Roma Aeterna, with cult image. Aur: 25. Ant: 25/*C*198; 86/*C*200

17*b* SAECVLARES AVGG, Same type. Ses: 163/*C*202; 164/*C*201 Den: 163/*C*204. As: 163/*C*203

17   22

18*a* Low column inscribed cos III. Aur: 24/*C*191. Ant: 24/*C*193. Qui: 24/*C*192. Ses: 162/*C*195. Dup: 162/*C*197. As: 162/*C*196

18*b* MILIARIVM SAECVLVM, Same type. Ses: 157/*C*95−6. Dup: 157/*C*97

19   AETERNITAS AVGG, Elephant walking l. Ant: 58/*C*17. Ses: 167/*C*18. Dup: 167/*C*20, 21. As: 167/*C*19

20   SAECVLARES AVGG, Two lions stg. facing each other. Aur: 14

21   − − Lion walking r. or l. Ant: 12−13/*C*172−3. Ses: 158/*C*176

22   − − Wolf and twins. Ant: 15−16/*C*177−8. Ses: 159/*C*179

23   − − Gazelle walking l. Ant: 17/*C*186

24   − − Antelope walking l. Ant: 18; 21−2/*C*188−9. Ses: 161/*C*190

25   − − Goat walking l. Ant: 23/*C*187

26   − − Stag walking r. Ant: 19/*C*182; 20/*C*185. Ses: 160/*C*183. As: 160/*C*184

249 Vows for a safe return from campaign.

27   FORTVNA REDVX, Fortuna std. l. Aur: 63/*C*66. Ant: 63/*C*65. Ses: 174/*C*67. As: 174/*C*68

OTACILIA SEVERA

Augusta, 244−249

Little is known of Marcia Otacilia Severa, who married Philip I before he became emperor, and was the mother of Philip II. When her husband assumed the throne, she was awarded the title of Augusta, soon followed by those of *Mater Castrorum*, and *Mater*

Senatus et Patriae; these appear in inscriptions, not on the coins. She was apparently killed at the same time as her son.

244 and later: proclamation of the new dynasty.
    1   PIETAS AVGSTORVM, Busts of Philip I and II vis-à-vis. Ses: 212/ C2. As: 212/C3

247–248 Millenary of Rome, with Secular Games.
    2   SAECVLVM NOVVM, Temple of Roma Aeterna (Philip *17a*). Aur: 118/C71
    3*a* SAECVLARES AVGG, Low column (Philip *18a*). Aur: 117/ C67. Ses: 202/C68. Dup: 202/C70 As: 202/C69
    3*b* MILIARIVM SAECVLVM, Same type (Philip *18b*). Ses: 199/ C25. Dup: 199/C27 As: 199/C26
    4   SAECVLARES AVGG, Hippopotamus stg. r. Aur: 116/C62. Ant: 116/C63–4. Ses: 200/C65

4

    5   — — Gazelle walking l. (Philip *23*). Ses: 201/C66

PHILIP II

Caesar 244/Augustus 247–249

M. Julius Severus Philippus was only about seven when he was made Caesar (*1*) on his father's accession. At that time, he also assumed the customary rank of *princeps iuventutis*, a title he maintained while Augustus. His coins reflect the types of his father, with whom he shared the consulate in 247 and 248. In 247, he was raised to the rank of Augustus (*6–8*) and celebrated the Secular Games (*9–12*). When his father went to campaign against Decius, the younger Philip remained in Rome, where he apparently held out until November 249. During this time, he gave a donative to the troops in the hope of securing support against Decius.

244 Proclamation as Caesar and *princeps iuventutis*.
    1   PRINCIPI IVVENT/VTIS, Philip II stg. l. Aur: 216/C52; 218/C46; 220/C60. Ant: 216/C54; 217/C58 (accompanied by soldier); 218/ C48; 219/C57; 220/C61. Den: 216/C53; 218. Qui: 218/C47. Ses: 255–8/C49, 55, 62, 65. Dup/As: 255–6/C56, 50; 258/C63–4

—— 'Eternal' peace established with the Persians.

    2   PAX AETERNA, Pax stg. 1. (Philip *4*). Ses: 268/*C*25, 27. As: 268/ *C*26, 28

—— Donative on return to Rome.

    3   LIBERALITAS AVGG II, Philip I and II std. on curule chairs. Ses: 266/*C*16

244 and later; announcement of the new dynasty.

    4   PIETAS AVGVSTORVM, Busts of Philip I and II vis-à-vis. Dup/As: 260/*C*1

    5   CONCORDIA AVGVSTORVM, Busts of Philip II and Otacilia vis-à-vis (Philip *9a*). Dup/As: 261/*C*3

247 Proclamation of Philip II as Augustus, with donative and decennial vows.

    6   AVG PATRI AVG MATRI, Type as *5*. Ant: 229/*C*1

    7   LIBERALITAS AVGG III, Type as *3* (Philip *15*). Ant: 230/*C*17. Ses: 267/*C*18

7

    8   VOTIS DECENNALIBVS in wreath. Ses: 269/*C*91. As: 269/*C*90

247–248 Millenary of Rome, with Secular Games.

    9   ROMAE AETERNAE, Rome std. 1. (Philip *16*). Ant: 243/*C*7

   10   SAECVLVM NOVVM, Temple of Roma Aeterna (Philip *17a*). Ant: 244/*C*8

   11   SAECVLARES AVGG, Low column inscribed COS II (Philip *19a*). Aur: 225/*C*77. Ses: 265/*C*78. Dup: 265/*C*80. As: 265/*C*79

   12   —— Goat walking 1. (Philip *25*). Ant: 224/*C*72. Ses: 264/*C*73. As: 264/*C*74

249 Fourth donative, to rally support against Decius.

   13   LIBERALITAS AVGG IIII, type as *3*. Ant: 245/*C*19

PACATIAN

249

Ti. Claudius Marinus Pacatianus, who came from a senatorial family, was an officer in Moesia or Pannonia on the Danube frontier when the troops proclaimed him emperor early in 249. Philip sent an army under Decius to suppress the revolt, but Pacatian was killed by his own soldiers before a battle could be fought. He optimistically claimed to be presiding over the beginning of a new age, since the first year of the *saeculum* which started with the millenary of Rome fell during his usurpation.

249   The thousand and first year of Rome.
    1   ROMAE AETER AN MILL ET PRIMO, Roma std. l. Ant: 6/C7
— —   Vows for a safe arrival in Rome.
    2   FORTVNA REDVX, Fortuna std. l. Ant: 4/C5

JOTAPIAN

Usurper in the East: no historical types.

SILBANNACUS

Usurper, apparently in the reign of Philip: no historical types.

DECIUS

July 249–June 251

C. Messius Quintus Traianus Decius was born in the Danubian province of Pannonia. He sprang from a family of landowners and married a woman from the Italian aristocracy. He rose to become consul and was prefect of the city under Philip when news arrived of the revolts of Pacatian and Jotapian. Philip persuaded Decius to undertake the defence of the critical Danube area, where he arrived after the fall of Pacatian, and had to face a major inroad of the Goths. When he was successful in driving them back, his troops, despite his objections, proclaimed him emperor in July 249. After attempting to reach an accommodation, Decius led his forces on Italy, and defeated and killed Philip at Verona.

Decius, perhaps as a sign of his triumph, added the name of Trajan to his own, and on his arrival (*1*) in Rome, celebrated the now customary decennial vows and gave a donative (*2–4*). The new emperor evidently took pride in his origins and in the support of the legions of the Danube; his coinage (*5–9*) extensively commemorates that area.

Decius was destined to spend much of his reign in the Balkans, for the Goths invaded Dacia and Moesia in overwhelming force in 250. In reply, Decius created his elder son Herennius Caesar (*10–13*) and sent him at the head of an army. He soon followed in person and managed to gain one major victory, but most of the campaign was unsuccessful. During the summer, he made his second son Hostilian Caesar, thus expanding the imperial college and creating a line of succession (*10–12*).

The opening campaigns of 251 saw a significant victory (*14*), but it was soon dwarfed by the magnitude of the disaster in June, when the emperor,

Herennius and most of the army fell into a Gothic ambush and were destroyed. The reign of Decius is best known for this unparalleled catastrophe and for the extensive but unsuccessful persecution of the Christians. The latter effort was part of a policy which stressed the values of the state religion. It is reflected in the curious series of antoniniani celebrating the deified emperors, perhaps in connection with the new age which began in 248; but the coins (*15*) pose many problems of interpretation.

249 Arrival in Rome, with decennial vows and first donative.
    1   ADVENTVS AVG, Decius on horseback l. Aur: 1/*C*5; 11/*C*3. Ant: 1/*C*6; 11/*C*4; 34. Ses: 111/*C*7. As: 111/*C*8
    2   VOTIS DECENNALIBVS in wreath. Ant: 30/*C*129. Ses: 110/*C*130−1. As: 110c/*C*132
    3   LIBERALITAS AVG, Liberalitas stg. l. Aur: 19. Dup: 120/*C*72. As: 120/*C*71
    4   − − Donation scene with Decius, officer, Liberalitas and citizen. Ses 106/*C*76; 121/*C*75
− − Celebration of the Danube provinces, home of Decius, and of their armies which put him in power.
    5*a* GENIVS EXERC/ITVS ILLVRICIANI, Genius stg. by standard. Aur: 3; 4/*C*62; 16/*C*48. Ant: 3/*C*50; 4/*C*63; 16/*C*49; 17/*C*56; 18/*C*64; 39/*C*51, 57. Den: 16. Qui: 17/*C*58. Ses: 103−5/*C*52, 59, 65, 67; 117−9/*C*53, 66. Dup: 105/*C*68; 117/*C*55; 118/*C*61. As: 117/*C*54; 118/*C*60
    5*b* GEN ILLVRICI, Same type, no standard. Aur: 15. Ant: 9/*C*45; 15/*C*46; 38/*C*43−4. Ses: 116/*C*47

                     5*a*   9

    6   EXERCITVS INLVRICVS, Fides (?) stg. l., holding standard in each hand. Ses: 102/*C*37. As: 102/*C*38
    7*a* PANNONIAE, Two Pannonias stg. front. Aur: 21−2/*C*85. Ant: 21/*C*86; 23−5. Ses: 124/*C*87−9. Dup: 124/*C*89. As: 124/*C*88
    7*b* Two Pannonias clasping hands. Ant: 26/*C*81; 41/*C*82−3
    8   − − Pannonia stg. front. Ant: 5/*C*79; 20/*C*80
    9   DACIA (FELIX), Dacia stg. l. Aur: 2/*C*12; 14/*C*31; 37/*C*30. Ant: 2/*C*13; 12/*C*16; 13−14/*C*27, 34; 35−7/*C*15, 25−6, 32−3. Qui: 12/*C*17; 35/*C*14. Ses: 101/*C*21−2; 112−14/*C*18, 28, 35. Dup: 101/*C*24; 112/*C*20. As: 101/*C*23; 112/*C*19; 113/*C*29; 114/*C*36

250 Proclamation of Herennius and Hostilian as Caesars and establishment of a dynasty; the promotion of Herennius was celebrated with a second donative (not numbered on the coins, but distinguished from the first by legend and type).

   10   CONCORDIA AVGG, Bust of Herennia Etruscilla facing those of Herennius and Hostilian. Ant: 31/*C*1. Ses: 131/*C*1
   11   PIETAS AVGG, Busts of Herennius and Hostilian vis-à-vis. Ant: 32
   12   LIBERALITAS AVG, Donation scene with Decius, Herennius, officer, Liberalitas and citizen. 2Ses: 122/*C*74
   13   LIBERALITAS AVGG, Liberalitas stg. l. Dup: 123
251   Victory over the Goths.
   14   VICTORIA GERMANICA, Decius on horseback, preceded by Victory. Ant: 43/*C*122
249/51   Celebration of the state religion, as represented by the deified emperors. All are antoniniani.
   15   *Obv.* Radiate head r. *Rev.* CONSECRATIO, Eagle (a) or Altar (b).
      a   DIVO AVGVSTO: (a) 77/*C*577; (b): 78/*C*578
      b   DIVO VESPASIANO: (a): 79/*C*651; (b): 80/*C*652
      c   DIVO TITO: (a): 81/*C*404; (b): 82/*C*405−6
      d   DIVO NERVAE: (a): 83/*C*152; (b): 84/*C*153
      e   DIVO TRAIANO: (a): 85/*C*666; (b): 86/*C*664
      f   DIVO HADRIANO: (a): 87/*C*1509; (b): 88/*C*1510
      g   DIVO PIO: (a): 89/*C*1188; (b): 90/*C*1189
      h   DIVO MARCO (ANTONINO): (a): 91/*C*1056−7; (b): 92/*C* 1058−9
      i   DIVO COMMODO: (a): 93/*C*1009; (b): 94/*C*1010
      j   DIVO SEVERO: (a): 95/*C*799; (b): 96/*C*800
      k   DIVO ALEXANDRO: (a): 97/*C*599; (b): 98/*C*598

HERENNIUS ETRUSCUS

Caesar 250/Augustus May−June 251

C. Herennius Etruscus Messius Decius, the elder son of Decius, was made Caesar in the spring of 250. As such, he commanded the first army which was sent against the Goths, and subsequently assisted his father in the major campaigns, during which he was raised to the rank of Augustus. A month later, he and his father were killed in battle.

250   Proclamation as Caesar (*see also* Decius *10−12*).
   1   PRINCIPI IVVENTIVTIS, Herennius stg. l. in military dress. Aur: 147−8/*C*25, 32. Ant: 147−8/*C*26, 33. Qui: 147/*C*27. Ses: 171−3/*C*28, 31, 34. Dup/As: 170−1/*C*29
   2   PIETAS AVGVSTORVM, Priestly implements. Ant: 143/*C*14. Ses: 168/*C*15. Dup/As: 168

2

— — Honours to the native province of the imperial family.
3 PANNONIAE, Pannonia stg. front (Decius *8*). Ant: 158/*C*9
251 Proclamation as Augustus, with decennial vows.
4 VOTIS DECENNALIBVS in wreath. Ant: 155/*C*42
— — Victory over the Goths.
5 VICTORIA GERMANICA, Victory running r. Ant: 154/*C*41

HOSTILIAN

Caesar 250/Augustus May (?)—November 251

C. Valens Hostilianus Messius Quintus, the younger son of Decius, was appointed Caesar in the summer of 250. He was left behind in Rome when his father and brother led the war against the Goths, and became emperor when they were killed. It is not clear whether he assumed the title Augustus at this point, or had already been awarded it together with Herennius. Trebonianus Gallus, who had been proclaimed by the troops, and was marching on Italy, reached an accommodation with Hostilian by which he would adopt the younger man and both reign as Augusti. This continued until Hostilian died of the plague which was ravaging the empire, in November 251.

250 Proclamation as Caesar (*see also* Decius *10−11*).
1 PRINCIPI IVVENTVTIS, Hostilian stg. l. in military dress. Aur 181/ *C*33; 183/*C*37. Ant: 181−3/*C*34, 36, 38−9. Qui: 183. Ses: 216/ *C*35; 218/*C*41. Dup/As: 217−18.
2 PIETAS AVGVSTORVM, Priestly implements. Ses: 212/*C*26
— — Celebration of the native province of the imperial family.
3 PANNONIAE, Pannonia stg. front. (Decius *8*).
Ant: 195/*C*17
— — Victory over the Goths.
4 VICTORIA GERMANICA, Victory running r. (Herennius *5*). Ant: 185/*C*70
251 Proclamation as Augustus, with decennial vows.
5 VOTIS DECENNALIBVS in wreath. Ant: 155/*C*42
— — Honours to the patron goddess of Hostilian's colleague Gallus.
6 IVNONI MARTIALI, Image of Juno in distyle temple. Ant: 190/*C*8; 202A/*C*9

TREBONIANUS GALLUS

June 251–May 253

C. Vibius Trebonianus Gallus, born in Perugia of an old Etruscan family, had served as senator and consul before becoming legate of Moesia in 250. He commanded the reserve force at the battle which proved fatal for Decius, and was there proclaimed emperor by the troops. After making a treaty with the Goths, he arranged an accommodation with Hostilian, the surviving son of Decius, by which both would reign as Augusti, while Gallus' son Volusian became Caesar. Gallus then arrived in Rome where he celebrated the usual vows (*1–2*), and reigned with Hostilian until the latter died of the plague in November 251. Volusian was then proclaimed Augustus; in his place (*3*); this was probably the occasion for the sole recorded donative (*4*). The reign was marked by a devastating plague (*6–7*) and disastrous attacks of the Persians and Goths. Disturbances caused by the latter provoked the legions of the Danube to proclaim their commander Aemilian, Augustus in 253. The rebel led his forces on Italy, but before a battle could be fought, Gallus and his son were murdered by the soldiers in May 253.

251 Arrival in Rome, with decennial vows.
　　1　ADVENTVS AVG/G, Gallus on horseback l. Aur: 14–5/*C*1. Ant: 79/*C*2.
　　2　VOTIS DECENNALIBVS in wreath. Ant: 49/*C*136. Ses: 127/*C*137. Dup: 127. As: 127/*C*138
— — Proclamation of Volusian as Augustus, with donative.
　　3　IMP C C VIB VOLVSIANVS AVG, Bust r. Ant: 68/*C*6
　　4　LIBERALITAS AVGG, Liberalitas stg. l. Ant: 36/*C*56. Ses: 113/*C*57
252 Second consulate.
　　5*a*　P M TR P IIII COS II, Gallus stg. l. Aur: 1/*C*92. Ses: 99/*C*94
　　5*b*　— —Gallus sacrificing. Ses: 100/*C*96
— — The plague: invocation of Apollo and of Juno Martialis, the goddess of Gallus' native Perusia.
　　6　IVNONI MARTIALI, Image of Juno in distyle temple. Ant: 54/*C*49. Ses: 109–12/*C*50, 52, 54. As: 110/*C*51

　　　　　　　　　6　　　　　　　　　　　　　　　　7

　　7　APOLL/O SALVTARI, Apollo (as the healing god) stg. l. Ses: 103–4/*C*21

VOLUSIAN

Caesar June 251/Augustus November 251—April 253

C. Vibius Afinius Gallus Veldumnianus Volusianus, born about 230, was made Caesar when his father Gallus became emperor. On the death of Hostilian, he was raised to the rank of Augustus. He was killed by the troops together with his father before the imminent battle with Aemilian.

251 Proclamation as Caesar, with decennial vows.
    1   PRINCIPI IVVENTVTIS, Volusian stg. l., in military dress. Aur: 129—30/*C*98—9. Ant: 134/*C*100. Ses: 241—2/*C*103
    2   VOTIS DECENNALIBVS in wreath. As: 243/*C*141
—— Promotion to Augustus, with donative.
    3   LIBERALITAS AVGG, Liberalitas stg. l. (Gallus *4*) Ant: 178/*C*49. Ses: 254/*C*50. As: 254/*C*51
252 Invocation of Juno and Apollo for help against the plague.
    4   IVNONI MARTIALI, Image of Juno in distyle shrine (several varieties). Aur: 155—6/*C*40. Ant: 131—2/*C*47; 171—7/*C*39, 43—5, 48 Ses: 252—3/*C*41, 46. As: 252—3/*C*42
    5   APOLL/O SALVTARI, Apollo stg. l. S: 247—8/*C*15. As: 248/*C*16
253 Second consulate.
    6*a*   P M TR P IIII COS II, Volusian sacrificing (Gallus *5b*). Aur: 138—9/*C*93. Ant: 141/*C*94—5
    6*b*   —— Volusian stg. l. (Gallus *5a*). Ant: 140/*C*92

AEMILIAN

April—July 253

M. Aemilius Aemilianus had succeeded Gallus as governor of Moesia in 251, and there, after major victories over the Goths, was proclaimed emperor by his troops in the spring of 253. He marched on Rome and gained supreme power without a battle when Gallus was slain in a mutiny. Troubles were far from over, however, and Aemilian felt the need to call on Valerian, the commander of the Rhine provinces for help. He in turn was proclaimed emperor, and marched on Italy, where Aemilian was killed by his own troops before fighting a battle, after a reign of about three months.

253 Announcement of accession and decennial vows.
    1   P M TR P/OT (I) P P Aemilian sacrificing. Ant: 7/*C*32; 16—18/*C*33—4. D: 36A
    2   VOTIS DECENNALIBVS in wreath. Ant: 13/*C*64. Ses: 42/*C*65; 54/*C*67. Dup: 42; 54/*C*68. As: 42/*C*66

URANIUS ANTONINUS

Spring – Winter 253

When the Persians invaded Syria early in 253, one army moved on Antioch, where it gained great success, and another attacked the strategic site of Emesa. The people of this city entrusted their defence to their traditional ruler, the priest of the sun-god Elagabalus. A distant relative of Septimius Severus, he was proclaimed emperor and assumed the name L. Julius Aurelius Sulpicius Uranius Severus Antoninus. He successfully defended the city and drove back the Persians. Late in 253 or early in 254, when the forces of Valerian arrived and took control of Antioch, he either abdicated the imperial power or was removed from it. His coins feature the worship of the sun-god, whose sacred stone, transported to Rome by Elagabalus, had been returned to Emesa to remain to object of sacred devotion. The coins reflect types of Elagabalus, who had headed the same cult.

253 Prayers for a successful return from battle.
    1   FORTVNA REDVX, Fortuna std. l. Aur: 4
– – Advertisement of the cult of Elagabalus, with revival of types of the emperor Elagabalus.
    2   CONSERVATOR AVG, Draped and ornamented stone of Emesa. Aur: 1/C1

2

    3   Sacred stone and parasols on quadriga. Aur: 2/C2
    4   SOL ELAGABALVS, Altar with parasols and candelabra; on l., eagle on sacred stone. Aur: 8

VALERIAN

September 253–June 260

P. Licinius Valerianus, born before 200 of a distinguished family, was suffect consul in 238, when he supported the revolt of the Gordians, and held high civil and military office in the government of Decius. In 253, Trebonianus Gallus called on Valerian, then commanding on the northern frontier, to send troops against the rebel Aemilian, but when the emperor was defeated and killed, Valerian's troops proclaimed him emperor. On this news, Aemilian was killed by his own men, and

Valerian was recognised by Senate and army in September 253. He immediately marched to Rome and appointed his son Gallienus as co-ruler; their joint accession was the occasion for vows (*1–2*).

The problems which beset the empire, with massive attacks from all quarters, compelled Valerian to divide the imperial authority. Leaving Gallienus in charge of the West, he set out for the eastern frontier to meet the Persian threat early in 254. Before departing, he celebrated the consecration of Mariniana (*3–4*) and the promotion of Salonina to Augusta, the occasion for a donative (*5*). By this time, the Persians had overrun Syria and captured Antioch. Although Valerian arrived too late to save the city, he did restore it, and suppressed the rebellion of Uranius Antoninus. These accomplishments gained him the title 'Restorer of the Orient' and the more extravagant 'Restorer of the Human Race' (*6–7*). The chronology of the following years, when Valerian was fighting almost constantly against the Persians, is difficult to establish; the sequence of events and interpretation of the coinage, therefore, are often very uncertain. In 255, the emperors assumed a joint consulate (*8–9*) and gave a new donative (*10*). The Goths compounded the problems in the East by attacking Asia Minor, and plague (*11*) struck the army. Gallienus, meanwhile, was winning victories on the northern frontier which are celebrated in the coinage of his father (*12*).

In 256, a third donative (*13–14*) was given when the emperors proclaimed Cornelius Valerianus, son of Gallienus, as Caesar in an effort to strengthen the imperial house. In the following year, when the emperors again shared the consulate (*15–17*), Valerian won a signal victory against the Persians (*18–19*), while Gallienus made considerable progress in Germany (*20*). His successful campaigns were reflected in dedication of a statue to Jupiter Victor (*21*; *cf* Gallienus *22*). All these victories seemed to justify the title 'Restorer of the World' (*22–23*). Campaigns against the Persians continued, marked in 259 by a victory near Edessa, but they culminated in disaster. In June 260, the Roman world saw the considerable humiliation of Valerian taken captive by the Persians. He was never released, but died in Persia under unknown circumstances.

253 Accession of Valerian, with decennial and popular vows.

    1 VOTA ORBIS, two Victories affixing shield inscribed SC to palm tree. Ant: 294–6/C279–81

    2 VOTIS DECENNALIBVS in laurel wreath. Ant: 139. Ses: 184/C283. Dup: 188. As: 206/C284

—— Consecration of Mariniana, who apparently died before Valerian became emperor.

    3 *Obv.* DIVAE MARINIANAE, veiled bust r. *Rev.* CONSECRATIO, peacock looking or walking l. or r. Aur: 1/C1. Ant: 3–5/C2–6, 11. Ses: 9/C7; 10/C12. Dup: 11/C8, 10.

    4 *Obv.* As previous. *Rev.* CONSECRATIO, peacock carrying Mariniana to heaven. Aur: 2/C13. Ant: 6/C14. Qui: 8/C17. Dup: 12/C15

3   7

— — Donative on promotion of Salonina (Gallienus' wife) to be Augusta.

    5   LIBERALITAS AVGG, Liberalitas stg. l. Aur: 42/*C*104. Ant: 98/ *C*105, 109

— — Suppression of revolt of Uranius Antoninus and restoration of Antioch.

    6   RESTITVT ORIENTIS, Oriens presenting wreath to Valerian. Ant: 286/*C*188

    7   RESTITVT(I) GENER HVMANI, Valerian walking r., holding globe. Aur: 220/*C*179

255 Joint consulate of Valerian and Gallienus, with donative (not distinguished by number).

    8   P M TR III COS III P P, Valerian sacrificing. Aur: 29/*C*161−2

    9*a*   (Same legend), Valerian stg. l., holding globe and sceptre. Ant: 142b/*C*163

    9*b*   P M TR P V COS III, same type. Ant: 142c/*C*166. As: 189/*C*168

    10*a*   LIBERALITAS AVGG, Liberalitas stg. l. Aur: 43. Ant: 99−100/ *C*107−8. Ses: 164−5/*C*110. Den: 185/*C*112. As: 196/*C*111

    10*b*   (Same legend), Liberalitas std. l. Ant: 101/*C*113−14

— — Prayers to Apollo, in his role of averter of the plague, then afflicting the army.

    11   APOLL SALVTARI, Apollo stg. l. Ant: 76/*C*28

— — Victories of Gallienus in Germany.

    12   VICTORIAE AVGG IT GERM, Victory stg. l., captive at feet. Ant: 129−30/*C*242−3

256 Third donative, on the proclamation of Valerian II as Caesar.

    13*a*   LIBERALITAS AVGG III, Emperors std. l. on curule chairs; prefect behind. Aur: 45/*C*124

    13*b*   As previous, but emperors std. on platform. Ant: 105/*C*86

    14   LIBERALITAS AVGG III, Liberalitas stg. l. Aur: 44/*C*118. Ant: 104. Ses: 167−8/*C*121−2. As: 197/*C*123

257 Joint consulate of Valerian and Gallienus.

    15   FELICIT AVGVSTORVM, Valerian, Gallienus and Valerian II in triumphal car; soldier on each side. Ses: 156/*C*60

    16   P M TR P V COS IIII P P, Emperors stg. face to face. Ant: 277/ *C*169−70

    17   (Same legend), Valerian stg. l., holding globe. Ses: 151/*C*167

— — Victories over the Persians (here called by their antique name Parthians) and Germans, celebrated by dedication of a statue to Jupiter Victor, and apparent restoration of universal peace.

18 VICTORIA PARTHICA, Victory presenting wreath to emperor. Ant: 291/*C*256

19 VICT PART(ICA), Victory stg. or running r. or l., sometimes with captive at feet. Ant: 22/*C*(v.II)12−13; 262/*C*255

19

20 VICTORIA GERM(ANICA), Type as previous. Ant: 132/*C*245, 248; 263−5/*C*251−4. Ses: 181/*C*246, 249. As: 203/*C*247, 250

21 GALLIENVS CVM EXER SVO, Statue of Jupiter, base inscribed IOVI VICTORI. Ant: 7−8/*C*77−8

22 RESTITVTOR(I) ORBIS, Valerian raising kneeling Orbis Terrarum. Aur: 50/*C*181. Ant: 116−18/*C*183−5, 187. Ses: 171−2/*C*186

23 (Same legend), Valerian std. l. eagle at foot. Ant: 119/*C*180

MARINIANA

Nothing is known of this empress, who appears to have been the daughter of Egnatius Marinianus, governor of Moesia. She may have died before her husband Valerian became emperor, or shortly after. For her coins, *see* Valerian *3−4*.

GALLIENUS

P. Licinius Egnatius Gallienus, born in Milan in 218, was in Rome in 253 when he was made co-emperor by his father Valerian; their accession was celebrated with vows (*1−2*). Gallienus entered his first consulate (*3*) in 254 and gave a donative jointly with his father on the consecration of his mother Mariniana and the promotion of his wife Salonina to be Augusta (*4*). Gallienus, left in charge of the West, spent most of his reign meeting the threats of the Germanic tribes along the northern frontier, from Gaul to the Black Sea. When he and Valerian parted in 254, Gallienus advanced to the Danube where he fought a series of campaigns, whose details and chronology are obscure. The concurrent victories of Valerian (*5−6*) are celebrated on Gallienus' coinage.

The two emperors gave a donative (*7−8*) when they jointly entered the consulate in 255, a year marked by two major victories (*9*) over the Germans. The promotion of Valerian II in 256 justified a third donative (*10−11*); that year saw another significant victory (*12*) in the north.

During his next consulate (*13*) in 257, Gallienus finally pacified the Danube region. His victories (*14–17*), extensively celebrated in the coinage, coincided with the successes of Valerian (*18–19*) in the East. With peace established on the Danube, Gallienus was free to move against the threats in the West. He established his base at Cologne and swiftly won victories which restored peace to Gaul (*20*) and helped to protect Italy (*21*) from attack. These justified dedication of a statue to Jupiter Victor (*22*; cf. Valerian *21*). In 258, however, his eldest son, Valerian II, who had been Caesar since 256 and involved in operations on the northern front, died and was consecrated (*23–26*). The constant wars in the north culminated in the destruction of the Alemanni at Milan in 259, celebrated as Gallienus' fifth victory (*27*).

The effect of these successes was annihilated by the defeat and capture of Valerian in 260, which brought widespread anarchy. The revolt of Postumus deprived the empire of its western provinces, but those of Ingenuus and Regalianus in the Danube region were suppressed by the end of 260. These were considered the sixth and seventh victories of Gallienus and, together with the defeat of the Alemanni, were celebrated by coins which honoured the legions loyal to Gallienus (*28–29*). The meaning and dating of this remarkable series are much debated; they are probably to be associated with the military reforms of Gallienus and his creation of a new cavalry army based on Milan where they were struck.

After restoring imperial control over the Danube region Gallienus returned to Rome (*30*), where he celebrated his victory over Regalian (*31–33*) and entered the consulate (*34–35*) for 261. At this time, he decided to make a new beginning and a break with the past associated with the disaster of Valerian. Types of Janus (*36*), the god of beginnings, and reference to Falerii (*37*), the ancestral home of Gallienus' mother, reflect this policy, as does the practice of renumbering the emperor's victories to count only those which he could claim entirely for himself, beginning with the defeat of the Alemanni in 259. Consequently, the defeat of Regalian was celebrated as both the third and seventh of Gallienus. (This generally accepted interpretation is open to serious objections; the problem of these victories, like so many others in this coinage, is not yet resolved.)

Early in 261, Gallienus moved to Milan (*38*) where he supervised army reforms and organised defence against the revolt of the Macriani in the Balkans. By the end of the year Macrianus, with his sons Macrianus and Quietus, had been suppressed (*46–47*), the latter with the help of Odenathus of Palmyra who, as ally of the Romans, inflicted a severe defeat on the Persians. By August, when Gallienus celebrated the tenth anniversary (*39–40, 42*) of his reign with festivals and a donative (*41*), the external situation was relatively stable, thanks to the troops, whose loyalty was consequently celebrated (*43–45*). Gothic attacks soon resume on the Balkan frontier, however, and Gallienus established a mint at Siscia (*48–49*), which he made his base of operations in 263.

By the end of 264, the emperor was ready to move against Postumus.

He gained initial success and advanced far into Gaul before he was wounded (*51*) and withdrew, entrusting the campaign to Aureolus, who pursued it with such diffidence that the anticipated victory (*50*) never took place. Once again Gallienus was called to the Balkans, and after visiting the frontier, he spent the winter in Athens and was initiated into the Eleusinian mysteries. Meanwhile, temporary peace (*52*) was established in the East. In 266, when Gallienus held his seventh consulate (*53*), he visited Rome, but soon had to return to the Danube, where he inflicted such a severe defeat on the Heruli that universal peace (*54*) seemed to be at hand. However, it was not long before the Goths overran Greece and Asia Minor, drawing Gallienus once again to the East. Before he could make any progress, he was forced to return to the west by the revolt of Aureolus, which was considered a serious threat (*56–63*), especially as it was supported by Postumus. The emperor travelled through Siscia (*55*) to Milan, where he blockaded the usurper through the winter, but fell victim to a conspiracy in August 268.

Joint reign with Valerian: 253–260

253 Vows on accession.
    1   VOTA ORBIS, two Victories attaching shield inscribed SC to palm tree (Valerian *1*). Ant: 459–60/*C*1335–6

1   12

    2   VOTIS DECENNALIBVS in wreath (Valerian *2*). Ses: 250/*C*1342. Dup: 258/*C*1344
254 First consulate.
    3   P M TR P II COS P P, Gallienus sacrificing. Ant: 287/*C*798
—— Consecration of Mariniana and promotion of Salonina, celebrated by a donative.
    4   LIBERALITAS AVGG. Liberalitas stg. l. (Valerian *5*). Ant: 147/*C*570
—— Victories of Valerian in the East.
    5   RESTITVT ORIENTIS, Oriens presenting wreath to Valerian (Valerian *6*). Ant: 448/*C*902–3
    6   RESTITVT GENER HVMANI, Valerian walking r., holding globe (Valerian *7*). Ant: 296/*C*901
255 Joint consulate of Valerian and Gallienus, celebrated by donative (not numbered).
    7*a* LIBERALITAS AVGG, Liberalitas stg. l. (Valerian *10a*). Ant: 433–

4/C567−9; 385/C566. Ses: 220−2/C572−4. Dup: 255. As: 270−1/C575−6

7*b* (Same legend), Liberalitas std. l. (Valerian *10b*). Ant: 149

8 (Same legend), Emperors std. on curule chairs; Liberalitas stg. behind. Ant: 150

−− Second major victory of Gallienus on the German frontier.

9 VICTORIAE AVGG IT GERM, victory stg. l. (Valerian *12*) Ant: 178−9/C1198−9

256 Third donative, on proclamation of Valerian II as Caesar.

10 LIBERALITAS AVGG III, Emperors std. l. on curule chairs; citizen stg. behind. (Valerian *13*) Aur: 84/C583; 431

11 (Same legend), Liberalitas stg. l. (Valerian *14*) Aur: 82−3/C577−8. Aur: 151/C584; 386. Ses: 223; 420/C580. As: 272/C582

−− Third German victory.

12 GERMANICVS MAX TER, Trophy between two captives. Ant: 141/C307

257 Third Consulate

13 P M TR P V COS III P P, Gallienus stg. l. Ses: 201/C809. As: 259/C811

−− Celebration of victories on the Danube.

14*a* VICT/ORIA GERM/ANICA (sometimes GM), Victory walking l. or r., sometimes, captive at feet (many varieties). (Valerian *19*). Aur: 2/C1046; 3/C1057; 95−7/C1158−9. Ant: 39−45/C 1048−54, 1056, 1059−61; 173−5/C1160−64; 176/C1185−7; 177/C1175, 1178, 1189; 180; 404/C1045; 406/C1165. Qui: 62−3/C1058; 194−6/C1166, 1186. Ses: 245/C1167, 1169; 429−30/C1171−2. As: 283−4/C1168.

14*b* −− Victory on globe between captives. Ant: 46−52/C1062−3, 1065−7, 1176, 1179, 1181; 180*a*. Qui: 61/C1064

15 −− Victory presenting wreath to Gallienus. Ant: 451−2/C1173−4

16 −− Victory crowning Gallienus. As: 285/C1184

17 GERMANICVS MAXIMVS, Trophy between captives. Ant: 142

−− Celebration of victories of Valerian.

18 VICTORIA PART, Victory presenting wreath to Valerian (Valerian *18*). Ant: 453/C1192

19 RESTITVTOR ORBIS, Valerian raising kneeling female (Orbis Terrarum) (=Valerian *22*). Aur: 91/C910. Ant: 164−5/C911. Ses: 234−6/C913−5

−− Victories of Gallienus on the Rhine; restoration of peace in Gaul and security for Italy.

20 RESTIT/VTOR GALLIAR/VM, Gallienus raising kneeling Gaul. Ant: 27−35/C895−8, 900, 904−9

21 SALVS ITAL, Salus offering fruits to Gallienus. Ant: 400/C943

22 IOVI VICTORI, Statue of Jupiter on base inscribed IMP CES. Ant: 21−3/C397−400.

258 Death and consecration of Valerian II. All have *obv*. DIVO CAES VALERIANO (or DIVO VALERIANO CAES), Bust r.

20 28a

23 CONSECRATIO, Eagle l. or r. Ant: 7. Ant: 3/*C*2, 4; 27/*C*7−9. Qui: 31/*C*10

24 — — Eagle bearing Valerian to heaven. Ant: 9/*C*5. Dup: 41/ *C*11. As: 42

25 — — Altar. Ant: 24−6/*C*12−14

26*a* — — Effigy of Valerian in biga on funeral pyre. Ant: 28/*C*15. Ses: 35/*C*17. As: 43/*C*18

26*b* — — Funeral pyre. Ant: 10/*C*6

259 Crushing defeat of the Alemanni at Milan.

27 GERMANICVS MAX V, Trophy between captives. Ant: 17−19/*C* 308−14; 382−3/*C*306. (GERMANICVS MAXIMVS). Qui: 60/*C*315.

260 Defeats of Ingenuus and Regalian, Gallienus' sixth and seventh victories, celebrated by honouring the loyalty of the legions. Each type, which bears the appropriate legionary badge, associates the name and number of the legion with the honorific Pia Fidelis and the number of the appropriate victory, including that over the Alemanni in 259. (The legends are here abbreviated to name and number alone, so that the first, for example, would read LEG I ADI V P V F or LEG I ADI VI P VI F or LEG I ADI VII P VII F.)

28*a* LEG I ADI V (VI, VII), Capricorn r. Ant: 314−16/*C*443−50; 318/ *C*452−3

28*b* — — Pegasus r. Ant: 317/*C*451

28*c* LEG I ITAL VI, Boar r. Ant: 320/*C*455−7

28*d* — — Wolf suckling Romulus and Remus. Ant: 330/*C*475−6

28*e* LEG I ITAL VII, Hippocamp r. Ant: 321/*C*458

28*f* LEG I MIN VI (VII), Minerva stg. l. Ant; 322−3/*C*459−64

28*g* LEG II ADI VI (VII), PEGASVS r. Ant: 324−6/*C* 465−9

28*h* LEG II CL ADI VI, Capricorn r. Ant: 327/*C*470

28*i* LEG II ITAL VI, Capricorn r. Ant: 328/*C*471

28*j* — —Wolf suckling Romulus and Remus. Ant: 329/*C*472−4

28*k* — — VII, Ibis r. Ant: 321/*C*477

28*l* LEG II PART V (VI), Centaur l. Ant: 332−8/*C*478−86

28*m* LEG III ITAL VI (VII), Stork r. Ant: 339−41/*C* 487−98

28*n* LEG IIII FL VI (VII), Lion walking r. Ant: 342−4/*C*499−503

28*o* LEG V MAC VI (VII), Victory stg. l or r. Ant: 345/*C*504−7; 347/ *C*509

28*p* LEG VII CL/A VI (VII), Bull r. Ant: 346/*C*508; 348−50/*C*510−18

28*q* — — VII, Lion l. or r. A: 351/*C*519−20

28*r*   LEG VIII AVG V (VI, VII), Bull r. Ant: 352−4/C521−6
28*s*   LEG X GEM VI (VII), Bull r. Ant: 357−8/C529−32
28*t*   LEG XI CL VI, Neptune stg. r. Ant: 359/C533−6
28*u*   LEG XIII GEM VI, Victory walking r. Ant: 360/C537−9
28*v*   LEG VIII GEM VI, Capricorn r. Ant 361/C540−1
28*w*   LEG XXII VI (VII), Same type. Ant: 362−3/C542−7 (IIXX); 366/ C550−1
28*x*   LEG XXX VLP VI (VII), Neptune stg. r. Ant: 368−9/C553−7
28*y*   − − VI, Capricorn. Ant: 367/C552
29   COHH PRAET VI (VII), Lion r. Ant: 370−2/C104−14

Sole reign, 260−268

− − Arrival in Rome.
30   ADVENTVS AVG, Gallienus on horseback r. Ant: 22/C12−13
− − Celebration of victory over Regalian.
31*a*   VICTORIA AVG VII, Victory stg. or walking, usually with captive at feet. Aur: 85−6/C1128, 1130. Ant: 526/C1129, 1131. Dup: 410
31*b*   VICTORIA AVG III, Victory walking l. or r. Aur: 84/C1116. Avq: 130. Ant: 304−6/C1118−22; 524−5/C1115. Ses: 397−8/C1123−5. As: 434/C1126
31*c*   VICT GAL AVG III, Same type. Aur: 75/C1039
32   VICT GAL AVG (III), Three Victories stg. l. Ant: 294−5/C1032−7; 519
33*a*   VIC GAL/L AVG, Victory inscribing III on shield attached to palm tree. Ant: 292−3/C1031
33*b*   VICTORIA AVG, Same type. Ant: 521−2/C1087−8. Ses: 396/ C1089
261 Fourth consulate of Gallienus.
34   (P M TR P X) COS IIII P P, Gallienus in triumphal quadriga. Aur: 20/C836. Ant: 150/C146; 154/C837
35   − − P M TR P VIIII COS IIII P P, Gallienus sacrificing. Ant: 153, 462/C835
− − Celebration of a new beginning, with reference to Gallienus' ancestral home.
36   IANO PATRI, Janus stg. l. Aur: 45/C320
37   VIRTVS FALERI, Accoutrements of Hercules. Ant: 596/C1325−6

37   46

—— Arrival in Milan.

    38   ADVENTVS AVG, Gallienus riding l. Ant: 463/*C*14−16

262 Decennalia, with vows on completion of a decade, and in hopes of a second, donative, dedication of an oak-wreath by the Senate, and commemoration of the armies.

    39*a* VOTA DECENNALIA, Victory writing on shield attached to palm tree. Ant: 333, 540/*C*1332−4

    39*b* VOTA VICENNALIA, same type Ant: 541

    40*a* VOT/IS X (ET XX) in laurel wreath. Aur: 93−6/*C*1353−4, 1356. Ant: 598−9/*C*1350−2, 1355

    40*b* VOTIS DECENNALIB/VS in wreath. Aur: 92/*C*1337. Ant: 597/*C*1340. Ses: 406/*C*1345. Dup: 411. As: 440−2/*C*1346−9

    41   LIB/ERAL/IT AVG, Liberalitas stg. l. Aur: 55/*C*559−61. Avq. 111. Ant: 227−8/*C*556, 558, 562−3

    42   SPQR OPTIMO PRINCIPI in laurel wreath. Ant: 659/*C*998. Ses: 393/*C*999

    43*a* FID/EI PRAET, Genius stg. l., standard behind. Aur: 36−7/*C*214−15. Ant: 476/*C*210; 569 (FIDEI PRAET VOTA X)

    43*b* FIDEI PRAET, eagle between standards. Ant: 568/*C*216−17

    44   FIDEI LEG, Three trophies. Ant: 567/*C*213

    45   FIDEI EQVITVM in laurel wreath. Aur: 33−5/*C*211−12

—— Celebration of victory over the Macriani, Gallienus' eighth.

    46   VICTORIA AVG VIII, Victory walking l. Ant: 527/*C*1134−5

    47   FIDES EXERC VIII, Fides stg. l. Ant: 478/*C*220−3

263 Establishment of Siscia as base of operations, and reference to special military tactics called Cantabrian, associated with the new cavalry army (alternatively, honours to a local god of the region of Siscia).

    48   SISCIA AVG, Siscia std. on river bank, nymph swimming below. Ant: 582/*C*976−7

    49   IO CANTAB, Jupiter stg. l. Ant: 573/*C*339−40

264 Anticipated victory over Postumus, claiming restoration of liberty to the occupied provinces.

    50*a* OB LIBERTAT/EM REC/EPTAM, Libertas stg. l. Aur: 60−1/*C*676−7. As: 424/*C*679

    50*b* OB REDDIT LIBERTATEM, same type. Ant: 247/*C*681. As: 425/*C*682

—— Rescue of Gallienus from danger when wounded in campaign against Postumus.

    51   OB CONSERVAT SALVT, Salus stg. r. Aur: 59/*C*671

—— Peace settlement in the East, circumstances unknown.

    52   PAX FVNDATA, Trophy between two captives. Ant: 652/*C*769−71

266 Seventh consulate of Gallienus.

    53   PM TR P XV/I COS VII P P, Gallienus stg. l. Ant: 155/*C*850; 550/*C*851−2

—— Celebration of victory over the Heruli, with extravagant hopes of

universal peace, apparently the occasion for a remarkable series
whose meaning has been much debated. Its obverse legend is not,
as previously thought, to be taken as a feminine, but as an over-
correct form of the vocative (case of address), normally written
'Galliene'.

54   *Obv.* GALLIENAE AVGVSTAE, bust r. *Rev.* VBIQVE PAX, Victory in
biga r. Aur: 72–4/C1015, 1017–18. Avq: 121. Den: 359–60/
C1016, 1019.

54   ·   58*a*

267   Arrival of Gallienus in Siscia, to fight Aureolus.
55   ADVENTVS AVG, Gallienus riding r. Ant: 551–2/C14–16

267/8 Invocation of the gods as protectors of Gallienus against the
revolts of Aureolus and Postumus.

56*a*   APOLLINI CONS AVG, Centaur r. or l. Ant: 163–4/C72–4; 558/
C73–4

56*b*   — — Gryphon walking or stg. Ant: 165–6/C75–9

56*c*   — — Pegasus stg. r. Ant. 167/C80

57*a*   DIANAE CONS AVG, Doe or antelope l. or r. Ant: 176–7/
C153–6; 180–1/C163–7

57*b*   — — Stag stg. r. Ant: 178–9/C157–60

57*c*   — — Goat stg. r. Ant: 182/C161

57*d*   — — Boar walking r. Ant: 183

58*a*   HERCVLI CONS AVG, Lion walking r. Ant: 201/C316

58*b*   — — Boar running r. Ant: 202/C317–18

59   IOVI CONS AVG, Goat walking l. or r. Ant: 207/C341–8

60   LIBERO P CONS AVG, Panther walking l. or r. Ant: 229–30,
574/C586–92

61   MERCVRIO CONS AVG, Hippocamp r. Ant: 242/C631

61   NEPTVNO CONS AVG, Hippocamp or capricorn r. Ant: 244–6/
C667–70

63*a*   SOLI CONS AVG, Pegasus r. or l. Ant: 282–4/C978–81; 357/
C982

63*b*   — — Bull stg. r. Ant: 285/C983–5

SALONINA

Augusta, 254–268

Virtually nothing is known of Cornelia Salonina, made Augusta by
her husband Gallienus in 254. She was a patron of philosophy, and
was probably killed at Milan in 268. Her antoniniani of the type

AVGVSTA IN PACE (*RIC* 57−60), which have sometimes been taken as referring to Christianity, and thus reflecting Salonina's religion, have in fact, no such meaning.

264 Creation as Augusta.
   1   CONCORDIA AVGG, Gallienus and Salonina clasping hands. Ant: 63/C31.
268 Invocation of goddesses in time of crisis (*cf.* Gallienus *56−63*).
   2   DIANAE CONS AVG, Doe walking r. or l. Ant: 4/C37
   3   IVNONI CONS AVG, Same type. Ant: 14−16/C69−71

VALERIAN II

Caesar, 256−258

P. Licinius Cornelius Valerianus, the eldest son of Gallienus and Salonina, was made Caesar early in 256. He joined in the celebration of his father's and grandfather's victories and was sent to supervise the Danube frontier, where he died or was killed in 258. The coins which identify him with the infant Jupiter are an optimistic reflection of the golden age which the young Caesar was hoped to bring. Many obverses (struck in association with all reverse types) which portray him with close-cropped hair and one long lock extending below the right ear, show that he was identified with the Egyptian god Horus. They not only attest the great popularity of Egyptian cults at this time but are a further reflection of the idea of the golden age, since Horus, son of Serapis and Isis, was also a god of time and could symbolise its renewal. Valerian was consecrated after his death (Gallienus *23−26*).

256 Appointment as Caesar.
   1*a*   PRINC/IPI IVVENT/VTIS, Valerian stg. l. (several varieties). Aur: 11/C79; 23/C70, 74, 81; 44/C65. Ant: 5/C66; 49/C67; 51/C84. Den: 29. Qui: 30/C80. Ses: 34/C75. As: 37−40/C68, 71−2, 76, 83
   1*b*   PRINCIPI IVVENTVTIS, Valerian crowning trophy. Aur: 45/C77. Ant: 50/C78
   2   PIETAS AVGG (or AVGVSTORVM), priestly implements. Ant: 4/C52; 19−21/C45−7, 50−1, 56; 48. Ses: 33/C58. As: 36/C53−5

2

   3   IOVI CRESCENTI, Infant Jupiter on goat Amalthea. Aur: 1/C25. Ant: 3/C20; 13−17/C28−32. Ses: 32/C33

257 Victories of Valerian and Gallienus.

4 VICTORIA GERMAN, Victory presenting wreath to prince. Ant: 53/ *C*96

5 VICTORIA PART, same type. Ant: 54/*C*97

SALONINUS

Caesar 258, Augustus June−July (?) 260

P. Licinius Cornelius Saloninus Valerianus, younger son of Gallienus and Salonina, was made Caesar on the death of his brother Valerian late in 258. As in the case of his brother, his elevation to imperial rank was to herald the beginning of a golden age. He was sent to the Rhine frontier and had his headquarters at Cologne where he was besieged by Postumus during his revolt in 260. Although proclaimed Augustus in an effort to boost his prestige, he was captured and put to death by the usurper.

258 Accession as Caesar. Type *3*, showing Jupiter and Gallienus as the joint nurturers of the prince, is another reflection of hopes of a golden age.

1 PRINC/IPI IVVENT/VTIS, Saloninus stg. l. (several varieties). Aur: 3/ *C*86; 18−20/*C*82. Avq: 5. Ant: 10−12. *C*61−2, 64, 87; 27−8/ *C*60, 63, 73, Qui: 30; 31/*C*85. Ses: 32/*C*89. As: 33−4/*C*69, 90

2 PIETAS AVG/G, priestly implements. Aur 17/*C*48. Avq: 4/*C*42; 21/ *C*44. Ant: 9/*C*41; 26/*C*49. As: 37/*C*57

3 DII NVTRITORES, Jupiter presenting Victory to Gallienus. Ant: 35/ 21

Q. GALLIENUS (?)

A unique coin celebrates the memory of a prince who has been variously identified with Valerian II and Saloninus (in which case the Q has been taken to stand for 'quondam', meaning 'formerly'), or as an otherwise unknown son of Gallienus.

?? Consecration.

1 *Obv.* DIVO CAES Q GALLIENO, Radiate head r. *Rev.* CONSECRATIO, Altar Ant: 1

1

AUREOLUS

Late 267 (?)−Autumn 268

Aureolus, whose full name is unknown, rose through the ranks of the army to become commander of the new cavalry force instituted by Gallienus, and in 260 led it to crush the revolt of Ingenuus. In 268, he accompanied the emperor against Postumus in Gaul, but failed to follow up the successes gained there. Instead, he revolted against Gallienus himself and made an alliance with Postumus. He entered Italy, and gained control of Milan, which became the base of his revolt. Gallienus soon arrived there and besieged him, but in the course of the operations was himself murdered. Aureolus then surrendered to Claudius Gothicus, but was in his turn killed by the troops soon after.

The coinage struck in the name of Aureolus is of dubious authenticity; but the issues of Postumus at Milan, a city he never controlled, were in fact struck by Aureolus during the period of his alliance with Postumus.

267/8 Celebration of the cavalry army which Aureolus commanded.
Coinage in the name of Aureolus.
   1 CONCORDIA EQVITVM, Concord stg. l. Aur: 1
Coinage in name of Postumus, with his obverse types
   2 CONCORD(A) EQVIT(VM), Fortuna stg. l. Aur: 366/C16; Ant: 370−74/C17−21
   3 FIDES (A)EQVIT, Fides stg. l. Aur: 367−8/C56, 58
   4 VIRTVS EQVIT, Soldier walking r. Aur: 369/C440

MACRIANUS

September 260−end 261

C. Fulvius Macrianus was the son of Macrianus, an influential general of Valerian who commanded in the disastrous expedition against Persia in 260. When Valerian was captured, Macrianus the elder was offered the imperial power, but declined in favour of his two sons, Macrianus and Quietus. After establishing their power in the East, the two Macriani marched westward in hopes of taking control of Rome, but were met and defeated in Illyricum by Aureolus, after which both were murdered by the troops.

260 Prayers for a safe arrival in Rome.
   1 FORT REDVX, Fortuna std. l. Ant: 7/C5

QUIETUS

September 260–end 261

C. Fulvius Quietus was proclaimed emperor together with his elder brother Macrianus. He remained to manage the East, while his father and brother marched in the direction of Rome. When they were killed, he was attacked by Odenathus of Palmyra, and took refuge in Emesa, whose citizens put him to death.

260 Prayers for the successful arrival of the Macriani in Rome.
   1 FORT REDVX, Fortuna std. L. Ant: 4/C5

REGALIANUS

260

P. Caius Regalianus, who commanded the troops in Illyricum, revolted after suppressing the rebel Ingenuus. His base was at Carnuntum, where most of his exceptionally rare coins have been found. He was defeated and killed by the end of 260.

260 Donative, on announcement of the revolt.
   1 LIBERALITAS AVGG (The plural seems uncharacteristically to refer to Regalianus and his wife Dryantilla), Liberalitas stg. Ant: 5–6 (garbled description)

POSTUMUS

June/July 260–July/August 269

M. Cassianius Latinius Postumus, placed in charge of the Rhine frontier by Gallienus, was proclaimed emperor by his troops on news of the defeat and capture of Valerian. This apparently took place at Deuso (*3–4*) in lower Germany (though that has alternatively been considered as Postumus' birthplace). The usurper had first to deal with the legitimate Caesar Saloninus, whom he besieged in Cologne and eventually captured and executed. After this success, Postumus made a triumphal entry into the city where an arch (*1–2*) was erected in his honour. His defeat of the Germans who had broken through the frontier brought security (*5*) to the whole region. While still in the first year of his reign, however, Postumus was obliged to set out (*6*) against the Germans, whom he defeated at Magosa (*8*) in 281, the year of his second consulate (*7*).

During his third consulate (*9–10*) in 262, Postumus returned from an overseas expedition (*11*), evidently to Britain, and in 263 gained such a victory over the Germans (*12–13*) that he could claim to be 'Restorer of Gaul' (*14*). The celebration of his fifth anniversary (*15–20*) in 264, was marked by an abundant coinage, but the next year brought a serious attempt by Gallienus to recover control of Gaul. The emperor advanced far, but withdrew on being wounded, leaving operations to Aureolus; Postumus was thus saved from a major threat. During his fourth consulate (*21−22*) in 267, the mint of Cologne (*23*) and the monetary system were reorganised. The last year of the reign was marked by elaborate celebrations in honour of the decennalia (*24*), during which Postumus paid special devotion to his patron god, Hercules (*25−26*), and by the revolt of Laelianus which he successfully suppressed. When, however, Postumus refused to allow the troops to plunder Laelian's base of Mainz, they revolted and murdered him in the summer of 269.

Sources for the reign of Postumus are extremely sketchy and much of the history has to be reconstructed from the coins, whose dating and interpretation are subject to much debate. The coinage contains two remarkable series featuring gods who were Postumus' 'conservatores', and the Labours of Hercules. Although these are associated with the decennalia, they consist largely of extremely rare gold and billon pieces intended for distribution at the festival, rather than forming part of the regular coinage; they are therefore omitted here. In the following catalogue, the identification of the large radiate bronzes as double sestertii has been accepted.

260 Triumphal entry into Cologne, with erection of a commemorative arch.
1   ADVENTVS AVG, Postumus on horseback r. 2Ses: 115/*C*2. Ses: 115/*C*2. Dup: 191/*C*3
2   Elaborate triumphal arch inscribed FELICITAS AVG. 2Ses; 118−19/*C*47, 49. Ses: 119a/*C*79 (FILICITA)
— — Honours to the patron god of Deuso where Postumus was proclaimed emperor (or perhaps was born).
3*a*   HERC/VLI DEVSONIENS/I, Hercules stg. r. Aur: 20−1/*C*90. Ant: 64−5/*C*91−3. Den: 98/*C*93. 2Ses: 130−1/*C*89 94. Ses: 132−3/*C*96−7. Dup: 200−1/*C*88, 95
3*b*   — — Statue of Hercules in temple. Ant: 66/*C*98. 2Ses: 134/*C*99. Dup: 202/*C*100

3

4   Bust of Postumus as Hercules r. Aur: 22/*C*115. Den: 99. Ses: 137/*C*117. As: 247/*C*118
— — Defeat of the Germans, assuring safety for the province.
5   SALVS PROVINCIARVM, Rhine recumbent l. Ant: 38/*C*354; 87/*C*352−3, 355−6

5   7

—— Departure of Postumus on campaign against the Germans.
> 6   PROFECTIO AVGVSTI, Postumus riding r., preceded by Victory.
>   Ses: 155/*C*292

261 Second consulate.
> 7   P M TR P COS II P P, Postumus stg. l. Aur: 2/*C*240. Ant: 54/*C*243–
>   4. Qui: 104/*C*241–2. 2Ses: 106/*C*246,248; 110–11/*C*259. Ses:
>   167/*C*249, 252, 253, 255; 109/*C*256. Dup: 187–8/*C*247, 252. As:
>   242/*C*264

—— Honour to the patron god of Magosa where Postumus defeated the
   Germans (alternatively, honours to the Batavian troops who
   supported Postumus' uprising).
> 8   HERCVLI MAGVSANO, Hercules stg. r. Ant: 68/*C*129. 2Ses: 139/
>   *C*130

262 Third consulate.
> 9   P M TR P COS III P P, Postumus sacrificing. Aur: 4/*C*270
> 10 Type as *7*. Ant: 55/*C*261. 2Ses: 13/*C*262–3. As: 243/*C*250

—— Return from expedition to Britain.
> 11 NEPTVNO REDVCI, Neptune stg. l. Ant: 76/*C*205–6. Dup: 214–
>   17/*C*207–10

263 Victories over the Germans, with consequent restoration of
   Gaul. Type *14* revives a type of Hadrian.
> 12 P M G M TR P COS III P P, Trophy between captives. Aur: 3/*C*232
> 13 VICTORIA GERMANICA, Victory running r. Ant: 91/*C*405. Den:
>   102/*C*371. 2Ses: 177/*C*406
> 14 REST/IT/VTOR GALLIAR/VM, Postumus raising kneeling Gallia.
>   Ant: 82/*C*311–13, 319. 2Ses: 157–8/*C*320–1. Ses: 159/*C*322.
>   Dup: 223–5/*C*314–15, 317–18

264 Fifth anniversary of reign, with sacrifices, donative and celebration
   of German victories, events seen as marking the beginning of a new
   golden age.
> 15 QVINQVENNALES POSTVMI AVG, Victory writing Q or X or VOT X on
>   shield. Aur: 34–5/*C*308–10. Avq: 50–1/*C*306–7
> 16 VICTORIA AVG, Victory, std. on spoils before trophy, inscribing
>   VOT X on shield. Aur: 41/*C*395
> 17 VICT GERM TR P V COS III P P, Postumus crowned by Victory. Den:
>   97/*C*368
> 18 P M TR P IMP V COS III P P, Postumus, with citizen and child,
>   sacrificing at altar before two Vestal virgins. Aur: 9/*C*236

19   LIBERALITAS AVG, Donation scene, with Postumus and lictor, Liberalitas and citizen. Aur: 27−8/*C*188−9

20   I O M SPONSORI SAECVLI AVG, Jupiter and Postumus sacrificing over tripod. As: 248/*C*150

267   Fourth consulate.

21   P M TR P COS IIII P P, Postumus in triumphal quadriga l. Aur: 256−7/*C*234−5

22   −− Type as 7. Ant: 290/*C*266. 2Ses: 364/*C*267

−− Monetary reform; celebration of the capital.

23*a*   COL CL AGRIP COS IIII, Aequitas stg. l. Ant: 286/*C*14

23*b*   C C A A COS IIII, Same type. Ant: 285/*C*11

23

268   Decennalia, with celebration of Hercules. Most of the types featuring the Labours of Hercules appear on medallions rather than coins (*see above*).

24   P M TR P X COX V P P, Victory r., inscribing VOT XX on shield. Aur: 258/*C*284. Ant: 295/*C*285; 296/*C*364 (no P M)

25   HERCVLI ERYMANTHIO, Hercules carrying Erymanthian boar. Ant: *Bastien (1958)* 76, no. 22

26   HERCVLI INVICTO, Hercules stg. l., with foot on fallen Queen of the Amazons, whose belt he removes. Ant: 305/*C*124

LAELIANUS

June−July 269

Ulpius Cornelius Laelianus, who was apparently governor of Lower Germany under Postumus, revolted against him in June 269, with the support of the legion stationed at Castra Vetera (Xanten), and of Mainz, where he established his headquarters. His rebellion may have been coordinated with the actions of Claudius Gothicus who had just regained Spain and attacked Strasbourg. The revolt was suppressed in a short time, and Laelian put to death.

269   Celebration of legion XXX of Xanten, which supported the revolt

1   VIRTVS MILITVM, Virtus holding standard inscribed XXX. Aur: 3/*C*9. Den: 10/*C*10

MARIUS

July/August—October/November 269

Nothing is known of M. Aurelius Marius, who assumed power on the murder of Postumus and was killed later in the same year. A misinterpreted text had formerly seemed to suggest that he reigned only two or three days.

269   Reconciliation of the armies of Postumus and Laelianus under united rule.
>   1   CONCORDIA MILIT/VM, Two clasped hands. Aur: 1/C3. Ant: 5—6/C7—8

1

VICTORINUS

October/November 269—November(?) 271

M. Piavonius Victorinus, descendant of an aristocratic family, had served as consul with Postumus in 267. During the revolt of Marius he took control of Cologne, and gained supreme power when Marius was killed. In 269, when he held the consulate (*1—2*), he was occupied with the long siege of Autun, which had revolted and taken the side of Claudius Gothicus. When the city was captured and destroyed, Victorinus returned to Cologne (*3*), and celebrated his victory with vows (*4*), regarding it as equivalent to the restoration of Gaul (*5*). The large but extremely rare series commemorating the vexillations of the legions who fought with Victorinus, seems to consist of medallions rather than coins, and is thus not included here. Victorinus was murdered by an official whose wife he had seduced. Alone among the Gallic emperors, he was consecrated (Tetricus *2*).

269   Second consulate.
>   1   COS II, Victorinus presenting globe to std. Roma; soldier stg. behind. Aur: 1/C28
>   2   P M TR P (II) COS II P P, Victory walking l. Ant: 36—7/C94—5
> — —   Return to Cologne after victory at Autun, with vows and celebration of the restoration of Gaul.
>   3   ADVENTVS AVG, Victorinus riding l. Aur: 5/C7
>   4a   VOTA AVGVSTI, Jugate busts of Roma and Diana. Aur: 31—2/C138—9

4b — — Busts of Sol and Diana vis-à-vis. Aur: 33/*C*137
5 INDVLGENTIA AVG, Victorinus raising kneeling Gaul. Aur: 8/ *C*43

TETRICUS I

Autumn 271–Spring 274

C. Pius Esuvius Tetricus was governor of Aquitania when he succeeded to the Gallic throne on the death of his relative Victorinus. He made a formal entry into Cologne (*1*), consecrated Victorinus (*2*) and campaigned successfully against the Germans (*3*). Tetricus assumed the consulate (*4–8*) in 272 and in 273, when he raised his son, also called Tetricus, to be Caesar (*9*). The two emperors shared the consulate in 274 and celebrated decennial vows (*10–13*), but by this time the German threat, combined with constant military mutinies, had made the state ungovernable. Tetricus therefore surrendered to Aurelian, who displayed him in his triumph, but treated him with generosity, restoring his senatorial rank and making him governor of Lucania.

271 Entry into Cologne.
1 ADVENTVS AVG, Tetricus on horseback r. Aur: 8/*C*6
— — Consecration of Victorinus.
2 *Obv.* DIVO VICTORINO PIO, radiate head r. *Rev.* CONSECRATIO, Eagle on globe. Ant: 83–5/*C*23–6
— — Victory over the Germans
3 VICTORIA GERM, Tetricus crowned by Victory, captive at feet. Aur: 38/*C*195
272 First consulate.
4 P M TR P (II) COS P P, Tetricus std. l. Aur: 1/*C*125
5 — — Tetricus stg. l. or r. Aur: 2/*C*126; 4–5/*C*127–8
6 — — Tetricus in quadriga l. Aur: *Elmer* 807
7 — — Tetricus mounting horse, soldier behind. Aur: *Elmer* 808
273 Second consulate.
8 P M TR P III COS II P P, Tetricus stg. l. Aur: 7/*C*130
— — Elevation of Tetricus Jr. as Caesar.
9 P E TETRICVS C, Bust r. ½ Aur: *Elmer* 867
274 Joint consulate of the Tetrici, with celebration of their quinquennalia.
10 COS III, Tetricus stg. l. Ant: 45/*C*32
11 *Obv.* IMPP TETRICI AVGG, Busts vis-à-vis. *Rev.* P M TR P COS III P P VOTA (or VOT X), Tetricus I presenting globe to Tetricus II; altar between. Aur: 204–5/*C*10
12 — — Tetricus I holding globe and crowned by Victory facing Tetricus II who stands by altar. Den: 214–15/*C*11–12
13 *Obv.* IMP TETRICI PII AVGG, Type as previous. *Rev.* VICTORIA AVGG, Victory inscribing VOT X on shield. Aur: 210/*C*9

TETRICUS II

Caesar, early 273—Spring 274

C. Pius Esuvius Tetricus, son of Tetricus I, was made Caesar by his father in 273 and abdicated with him a year later.

273   Elevation to the rank of Caesar (*see also* Tetricus I *11—13*).
   1   PRINC/IPI IVVENT/VT/IS, Tetricus stg. (many varieties). Aur: *Elmer* 881—2. Ant: 260/C62—6. Den: 281

CLAUDIUS GOTHICUS

September 268—September 270

M. Aurelius Claudius, born in 214 in Illyricum, rose to high military command under Gallienus, serving against the rebels Ingenuus and Postumus. He became head of the new cavalry army (*2*) which Gallienus had created, and was sent to suppress the revolt of Aureolus. At Milan, however, he joined the conspiracy which murdered Gallienus and was proclaimed emperor, the occasion for the usual vows (*1*). He executed Aureolus, then had immediately to face the Alemanni, who had broken through the frontier which the rebel had stripped of troops. Claudius defeated the Germans (*3—4*) in northern Italy late in 268, then entered Rome (*5*) where he established a cordial relationship with the Senate and gave a donative (*6*) to the people.

   In 269, when he held the consulate (*7*), he sent a force against the breakaway state in the West, where Spain was restored to allegiance. Gaul, however, resisted, and no further attempt could be made because of a major threat from the Goths in Illyricum. They had attacked by land and sea, penetrating as far as northern Greece. In the process, they attacked Thessalonica, which was saved, it was believed, by the intervention of its local gods, the Cabiri, the sons of Vulcan (*8—9*). Claudius gained a decisive victory over the Goths (*10*) at Naissus and began to restore the devastated provinces, work which gained him the extravagant title of 'restorer of the world' (*11*). In the process, the army was struck by the plague, which carried off the emperor late in 270. His popularity and success earned Claudius a consecration which was long celebrated (see Quintillus *2—4* and Constantine *53—4*).

268   Vows on accession.
   1   VOTA ORBIS, Two Victories attaching shield inscribed SC to palm tree. Ant: 196, 226/C326—7
— —   Celebration of Claudius as head of the cavalry army.
   2   *Obv.* VIRTVS CLAVDI AVG, Radiate bust of Claudius l., holding horse's head by bridle. *Rev.* VIRTVTI AVGVSTI, Hercules stg. l. Ant: *Bastien (1983)* 4

— — Defeat of the Alemanni in northern Italy.

    3   VICTOR/IA GERMAN/IC, Trophy between two seated captives. Ant: 247−50/*C*289, 305−7

    4   VICTORIA Germanica MAXIMA, Victory stg. l., one or two captives at feet. Ant: 108/*C*304

— — Arrival in Rome, with donative.

    5   ADVENTVS AVG, Claudius on horseback l. Ant: 13/*C*3, 4

    6   LIBERA/LITAS AVG, Liberalitas stg. l. Ant: 57−9/*C*144−5, 183/*C*143

269 Assumption of the consulate.

    7   P M TR P II COS P P, Claudius stg. l. or walking r. Ant: 10−12/*C*214−16

— — Honours to the Cabiri and their father, Vulcan, who saved Thessalonica from Gothic attack.

    8   DEO CABIRO, Cabirus stg. r., holding hammer and nails. Ant: 204/*C*65

    9   REGI ARTIS, Vulcan stg. r., holding hammer and nails. Ant: 215/*C*239

— — Great victory over the Goths at Naissus.

    10   VICTORIAE GOTHIC SPQR, Two captives std. below trophy. Ant: 251−2/*C*308−10

10

— — Restoration of Balkan provinces after the Gothic invasions.

    11   RESTITVTOR ORBIS, Claudius sacrificing at altar. Ant: 189/*C*247

QUINTILLUS

September−November 270

M. Aurelius Quintillus, born in 229, was the younger brother of Claudius Gothicus. During the Gothic war, Quintillus was left in Aquileia to assure defence of the West, and was there proclaimed emperor on the news of his brother's death. He gave a donative (*1*), celebrated the consecration of Claudius (*2−4*) and assumed his name to gain support. As an Illyrian, he counted on the allegiance of the Pannonian troops, whose country he honoured (*5*), but the army rapidly took the side of the rebel Aurelian. Although well regarded by the Senate, Quintillus was deserted by his troops and committed suicide after a reign of about two months, during which he apparently remained in Aquilea.

270 Donative, probably on accession.
    1   LIBERALITAS AVG, Liberalitas stg. l. Ant: 23/*C*70
—— Deification of Claudius Gothicus: an abundant series of coins continued by Aurelian and frequently imitated in the irregular 'barbarous radiate' coinage of the West (*see also* Constantine 53−4).
    2 *Obv.* DIVO CLAVDIO (GOTHICO), radiate head or bust r. *Rev.* CONSECRATIO, Altar. Ant: 257/*C*39; 259; 261−4/*C*48−54
    3 Same *obv.* − Eagle r. or l. Ant: 265−6/*C*41−6. As: 267a/*C*47
    4 Same *obv.* − Funeral pyre. Ant: 256/*C*38; 267/*C*55−7

4

—— Celebration of the emperor's country of origin.
    5 PANNONIAE, Pannonia stg. l., holding laurel branch and standard. Ant: 60−61/*C*51

AURELIAN

November 270−Autumn 275

L. Domitius Aurelianus, born in Illyricum in 214, rose through the ranks of the army to become commander of the cavalry by 268, when he participated in the conspiracy which killed Gallienus. After the death of Claudius Gothicus, he was proclaimed emperor by the troops and achieved sole power on the suicide of Quintillus. His early coinage reflects the importance of the legions of the Danube, his main support (*1−3*). From his base in Sirmium, Aurelian marched against the Juthungi who had invaded Italy, then drove the Sarmatians from Rhaetia and Pannonia, and visited Rome (*4*). During his first consulate (*5*) in 271, he had to face attacking German tribes, who broke into Italy and badly defeated the imperial forces before they were finally overcome. Aurelian then returned to Rome to suppress the great revolt led by the mint workers, a campaign which involved thousands of troops and bitter fighting. Because of the constant threats which Rome now faced, he began construction of a defensive wall, the first built around the city in over five hundred years.
    In mid-271, Aurelian marched east against the Goths, defeating them (*6*) in Thrace. By this time, it had become impossible to guarantee the security of the exposed province of Dacia, which was therefore abandoned, and its population resettled in a new Dacia (*7*) south of the Danube. Aurelian was finally free to move against his major enemies in the Roman

East and West. Zenobia of Palmyra, whose kingdom now included most of the eastern provinces of the Empire, was attacked and, after a long campaign in which Aurelian defeated her Persian allies (*8*), her capital was taken in 272. Aurelian had now restored the East (*9–12*) to Roman rule, and could now direct his attention westward. After defeating the Carpi and suppressing a revolt in Palmyra, he moved in the summer of 273 against Gaul, where he received the surrender of the Tetrici. Aurelian was now master of the Roman world, reunited for the first time since 260, and could claim to be 'restorer of the world' (*13–15*), a title not original with him but now fully justified, and an action which could be seen in the classical terms of a restoration of a golden age (*18*). At the same time, he also restored the unity of the army (*19*).

The coins which celebrate the conquest of the East and portray Aurelian as pacifier of the world (*16–17*) show emperor and Sun-god in the same role (*9–11, 15–16*). This identification, which appears specifically on rare bronzes of Serdica where Aurelian is entitled 'God and lord' (*13b*), was part of the religious policy by which Aurelian fostered the cult of the Sun, favourite god of the armies, as a focus for loyalty and unity. Sol thus became chief god and received a splendid temple in the capital.

In 274, Aurelian celebrated a magnificent triumph in which Zenobia and the Tetrici were paraded; it was probably the occasion for a donative (*20*). It was about this time that the emperor promoted his wife Severina to be Augusta (*21–22*). In the same year, Aurelian carried out a reform of the coinage, whose details are much discussed, but which transformed the quality and appearance of the coins. After suppressing troubles in the West, Aurelian planned a great campaign against Persia, but only advanced as far as the region of Byzantium when he was murdered in a plot late in 275.

270 Celebration of the Danube provinces whose troops brought Aurelian to power.
    1 VIRTVS ILLVRICI, Mars walking r., captive at foot. Aur: 378–80/ C280–2. Ant: 388/C283
    2 GENIVS ILLVR, Genius stg. l. Ant: 110–11/C103–4; 172–3/ C101–2; 204–5; 222–4/C103–4
    3 PANNONIAE, Pannonia stg. Ant: 113/C165
—— Arrival of Aurelian in Rome
    4 ADVENTVS AVG, Aurelian riding r., captive(s) below. Ant: 42–3/ C3–4
271 First consulate.
    5 CONS PRINC AVG, Aurelian crowning trophy between two captives. Ant: 23/C72
—— Defeat of the Goths in Thrace.
    6 VICTORIA/E GOTHIC, Trophy between captives. Ant: 339–40/C260
—— Resettlement of Dacians and creation of a new province south of the Danube.
    7 DACIA FELIX, Dacia stg. l. Ant: 108/C73

271/2 Campaign against Zenobia, with defeat of her Persian allies; restoration and pacification of the East, with honours to Sol, identified with the emperor.

    8   VICTORIA PARTICA, Victory crowning Aurelian. Ant: 240

    9   RESTITVTOR/I ORIENTIS, Sol stg. l. Aur: 374−5/*C*213−14. Ant: 404

    10   RESTITV/TOR ORIENT/IS, Aurelian raising kneeling Orient. Ant: 141; 233; 350−1/*C*204−5

    11   (Same legend), Orient presenting wreath to Aurelian. Ant: 140/*C*192; 234/*C*201−2

    12   PACATOR ORIENTIS, Aurelian stg. r., captive at foot. Ant: 231/*C*164

273/4 Conquest of Gaul and reunification of the empire and army, victories which heralded a new golden age; exaltation of the emperor.

    13*a* RESTITVT/OR ORBIS, Orbis Terrarum presenting wreath to Aurelian. Ant: 53, 139/*C*192; 287−306/*C*192−200; 347−349/*C*209−11; 386/*C*193−4; 399/*C*192; 403/*C*215 (RESTITVTORI)

    13*b* *Obv.* (IMP) DEO ET DOMINO (NATO) AVRELIANO AVG. *Rev.* As previous. Ant: 305−6

    14   RESTITVTOR ORBIS, Victory presenting wreath to Aurelian; sometimes, captive at feet. Ant: 368−9/*C*208−12

    15   (Same legend), Sol and Aurelian together holding globe; two captives at feet. Ant: 367/*C*207

    16   PACATOR ORBIS, Sol walking l. Ant: 6−7/*C*161−2

    17   (Same legend), Aurelian stg. l. by altar. Ant: 4/*C*163

    18   RESTIT/VT SAECVLI, Woman presenting wreath to Aurelian. Ant: 52/*C*191; 235

    19   RESTITVTOR EXERCITI, Mars and Aurelian together holding globe. Ant: 366/*C*206

274 Triumph for victories in East and West, with donative.

    20   LIBERALIT AVG, Liberalitas stg. l. Ant: 229

— — Promotion of Severina to Augusta.

    21   CONCOR/DIA AVG/VSTOR, Aurelian|and|Severina|clasping|hands; (on bronzes) radiate head of Sol| in |field |above, Ant: 382/*C*39. Ses: 76/*C*34. Ant: 79−81/*C*20, 35−6

    22   SEVERINA AVG, Bust r. on crescent. Ses: 1/*C*1. Dup: 2−3/*C*2−3. As: 4

SEVERINA

Augusta 274−275

Ulpia Severina, wife of Aurelian, was made Augusta in 274; her subsequent fate is unknown.

274 Promotion to Augusta.
    1 CONCORDIA AVGG, Aurelian and Severina clasping hands
       (Aurelian *21*). Ant: 3, 16−7/C2, 3; 19/C1

VABALATHUS

Dux Romanorum 266/7−Augustus 271−272

L. Julius Aurelius Septimius Vabalathus Athenodorus, son of Odenaethus
and Zenobia, succeeded to the kingdom of Palmyra on the murder of his
father in 276 or 267, but remained under the tutelage of his famous
mother, who effectively ran affairs. By this time, Roman power had
virtually collapsed in the East and the Palmyrenes had extended their rule
over all the provinces from Asia Minor to Egypt. When Aurelian came to
the throne, he directed his efforts to the recovery of the East, taking
Egypt in 271 and defeating and capturing Zenobia and Vabalathus in 272,
when their kingdom came to an end. The initial coinage of Vabalathus
recognises the nominal supremacy of Aurelian, as part of a claim to
legitimacy. His later coins, as Augustus, bear no historical types.

270/1 Claim of legitimacy by sharing power with Aurelian.
    1 Obv. VABALATHVS vir CLArissimus REX IMperator DUX Roman-
       orum, laureate bust r. *Rev.* IMP C AVRELIANVS AVG, Radiate bust
       r. Ant: 381/C1

1

'THE INTERREGNUM'

It was formerly believed that there was an interval between the murder of
Aurelian and the proclamation of Tacitus during which the Senate exercised
authority. A series of coins bearing the Genius of the Roman People on
the obverse and the enigmatic reverse inscription INT VRB S C was attributed
to this period. More recently, these coins have been identified as commemorating an entry into Rome by Gallienus. They may in fact be
medallions; in any case, their significance is far from being satisfactorily
determined.

TACITUS

Autumn 275−June 276

M. Claudius Tacitus, born about 200 of an ancient family which claimed
connection with the famous historian, was a distinguished senator who

had become consul in 273 and was leader of the Senate when Aurelian was assassinated. The army left the choice of a successor to the Senate and the aged Tacitus reluctantly accepted the throne and undertook vows in the hope of a long reign (*1–2*). He appointed his brother Florian as praetorian prefect, and together they set out for the East to meet the threat of the Goths who had penetrated into Asia Minor. Although he soon won a victory (*3*) in Cilicia, Tacitus was murdered by the troops in a mutiny originally raised against one of his relatives whom he had appointed governor of Syria.

275 Accession, with decennial and vicennial vows.
  1   P M TR P CONSVL, Tacitus std. l. Aur: 70/*C*84
  2   VOTIS X ET XX, Tacitus, crowned by Mars, facing seated Victory holding shield inscribed VOTIS X XX. As: 109/*C*174
276 Victory over the Goths.
  3   VICTORIA GOTTHI/CA (COS II). Victory l. or r. Aur: 110/*C*164. Ant: 171–3/*C*157–60; 199–200/*C*161–2

FLORIAN

June–August 276

M. Aurelius Florianus was made praetorian prefect by his brother Tacitus and fought successfully with him against the Goths. When Tacitus was murdered, the troops proclaimed Florian emperor, and he celebrated the usual optimistic vows (*1–2*), along with the Gothic victory. Although Florian had much support, the armies of Syria and Egypt favoured Probus. After three months of undistinguished rule, Florian was murdered by his own troops at Tarsus, and a civil war was avoided. His coinage optimistically anticipated his return to Rome (*3*).

276 Decennial vows on accession, and celebration of Gothic victory.
  1   VICTORIA PERPET, Victory stg. r., inscribing X XX on shield attached to palm tree. Aur: 23/*C*92

1

  2   VICTORIAE AVGVSTI, Two Victories holding shield inscribed VOT XX. Ant: 43/*C*94

— — Anticipated return of Florian to Rome.
   3   REDITVS AVG, Florian stg., receiving globe from std. Roma. Ant:
       90−1/C79−80

PROBUS

Summer 276−September 282

M. Aurelius Probus, son of a soldier, was born in 232, supposedly at Sirmium, though the coins (*2−3*) appear rather to indicate Siscia. He followed a career in the army which led him to be commander on the eastern frontier when Tacitus was killed. The troops then proclaimed Probus emperor; the murder of Florian assured him the supreme power without a civil war. Probus advanced westward from his Syrian base, stopping in Cyzicus and Serdica, where his arrival (*1a−c*) was celebrated, before reaching Siscia, (*1d−f, 2−3*), where he spent the winter and restored order to the whole region (*4*). In this reign, when the mints are reasonably well identified, and the coinage arranged in a plausible sequence, it is possible to associate the unvarying ADVENTUS types with mint cities and thus to follow the imperial progress.

After assuming his first consulate (*5−6*) in 277, Probus briefly visited Rome (*7*) before proceeding to Ticinum where he rejoined the army and celebrated vows (*8−10*) for a successful reign, an occasion marked as the beginning of a new golden age, with titles borrowed from Aurelian. Emperor and army continued to Lugdunum (*11*) and then to the Rhine, where they inflicted severe defeats upon the Alemanni, Burgundians and Vandals, celebrated as victories over Goths (*13*) and Germans (*14−15*). During the campaigns Probus assumed his second consulate (*12*). He then returned to Ticinum (*16*) and Siscia where he entered his third consulate (*17*) and spent the year in 279. Probus could now claim, with some credibility, to be 'restorer of the world and the army' (*18−20*), again appropriating titles of Aurelian. Wars were not finished, however, for in 280 the emperor had to campaign against the Isaurians in Asia Minor, then suppress the revolt of Saturninus in Antioch where he spent the winter and entered his fourth consulate (*21*). News from Gaul, where Proculus and Bonosus had revolted, obliged Probus to hasten across the empire. After putting down these revolts, Probus finally returned to Rome for a great triumph late in 281, marked by a special issue of coins (*22−26*). While still in Rome, he entered his fifth consulate (*27*), then set out for a great expedition against the Persians. At Sirmium, however, the troops, dissatisfied with the strict discipline which Probus imposed and stirred by the revolt of Carus, murdered him in September 282.

276 Imperial progress westward from Syria: arrival in Cyzicus.
   1a   ADVENTVS AVG, Probus riding l., preceded by Victory. Aur: 890

1*b* ADVENTVS PROBI AVLG, Probus riding l., captive at foot. Ant: 903−4/C56, 69

—— Arrival in Serdica.

1*c* Type as *1b*. Ant: 836−7/C56−7, 69

—— Arrival in Siscia.

1*d* ADVENTVS AVG, Probus riding l., followed by soldier; two standards in background. Aur: 584/C30

1*e* —— As *1a*. Aur: 582−3/C29

1*f* ADVENTVS (PROBI) AVG/VSTI, Probus riding l., one or two captives under horse. Ant: 624−36/C46−51, 53, 56−7, 69, 71−2

276−7 Stay in Siscia; celebration of the city as Probus' birthplace and of restoration of order to the province.

2 SISCIA PROBI AVG, Siscia std. l. between two river gods. Ant: 764−6/C635, 637−8

2   7

3 ORIGINI AVG, Wolf and twins. Ant: 701−3/C393−4

4 RESTIT ILLVRICI, Two women stg. back to back between two standards. Ant: 730/C505

277 First consulate.

5 TRI POT COS P P, Probus in quadriga l. Aur: 1/C731

6 P M TR P COS P P, Probus stg. l. between standards. Ant: 606−9/C440−3. Den: 244/C439.

—— Arrival in Rome; decennial vows, with usual reference to return of a golden age.

7 ADVENTVS (PROBI) AVG, Type as *b*. Ant: 154−167/C36−43, 45, 55, 57−67, 69−70

8*a* VOTIS X ET XX FEL in laurel wreath. Ant: 457−461/C945−9

8*b* VOTIS X PROBI AVG ET XX in laurel wreath. Ant: 462−3/C950−1

9*a* RESTITVT SAECVLI, Probus, crowned by Victory, receiving globe from soldier who stands by palm tree bearing shield inscribed VOTIS. Aur: 310

9*b* —— Probus crowned by Victory; to l., soldier holding shield on cippus. Den: 253/C513

9*c* —— (Legend abbreviated), Probus, sometimes treading down enemy, crowned by Victory. Ant: 400−03/C511−12

9*d* —— As previous, but crowned by Sol. Ant: 404−6/C521−4

10*a* *Obv.* VIRTVS PROBI AVG, Bust of Probus r., holding shield inscribed VOTIS X ET XX. *Rev.* CONCORDIA MILIT, Probus and Concordia clasping hands Ant: 328/C118

10*b* — — *Rev.* FELICITAS SEC, Felicitas stg. l. Ant: 362/*C*232

10*c* — — *Rev.* HERCVLI PACIFERO, Hercules stg. l. Ant: 383/*C*296

10*d* — — *Rev.* VIRTVS INVICTI AVG, Probus galloping r., spearing fallen enemy. Ant: 454

— — Arrival in Lugdunum.

11 ADVENTVS PROBI AVG, Type as *1b*. Aur: 2/*C*54. Ant: 19−20/*C*68; 63−4/*C*68−70

278 Second consulate; victories over Goths and Germans.

12 P M TRI P COS II P P, Probus stg. l., captive at foot. Den: 245−6/*C*445−6

13 VICTORIA GOTHIC, Victory walking l., captive at foot. Aur: 10/*C*777

14 VICTORIA GERM, trophy between two captives. Aur: 141−2/*C*762−3. Avq: 149/*C*755. Ant: 220−3/*C*766, 768, 773, 775; 425. Den: 257−9/*C*765, 767. Qui: 273−8/*C*756−7, 769−72, 774, 776. As: 300/*C*764

15 — — Victory walking r. between two captives. Ant: 217−19/*C*759−60. Den: 254−6/*C*761. As: 299/*C*758

— — March eastward; arrival in Ticinum.

16 ADVENTVS (PROBI) AVG, Type as *1a*. Aur: (*Pink 1949*. 50). Ant: (*Pink 1949*. 51)

279 Probus in Siscia: third consulate and claims to have restored the Roman world.

17 P M TR/I P (V) COS III, Probus in triumphal quadriga r. Aur: 914. Ant: 614−16/*C*454−8; 835. Den: 247/*C*454

18 RESTITVT/OR ORBIS, Jupiter presenting globe to Probus. Ant: 856−9/*C*515−18.

19*a* — — Victory presenting wreath to Probus. Ant: 851−5/*C*506−7; 910/*C*519

19*b* — — Female presenting wreath to Probus. Ant: 731−6/*C*506−10, 519; 925/*C*509

20 RESTITVTOR EXERCITI, Soldier presenting globe to Probus. Ant: 909/*C*514

281 Fourth consulate; arrival in Rome, with triumph for victories in East and West; address to the troops; restoration of universal peace.

21 P M TR P V COS IIII P P, Probus stg. between standards. Den: 248

22*a* ADVENTVS AVG, Type as *1b*. Aur: 133/*C*35

22*b* — — Type as *1a*. Qui: 261/*C*31

23 VICTORIOSO SEMPER, Probus stg. l. between four suppliants. Aur: 143−4/*C*794−5. Ant: 224/*C*796

24 A(D) LOCVTIO AVG, Probus and praetorian prefect stg. on platform addressing soldiers and captives. Aur: 580−1/*C*18−19. Ant: 320−2/*C*24−7. Dup: 289/*C*23. As: 292/*C*22

25 PACATOR ORBIS, Probus stg. l., addressing four suppliants. Aur: 136/*C*395; 591

26 VBIQVE PAX, Victory in biga r. Aur: 139. As: 296/*C*732

282 Fifth consulate.
> 27 P M TR P VI COS V P P, Probus stg. between standards. Den: 249–
> 51/*C*460. Qui: 260/*C*461

BONOSUS

Rebel in Gaul *c*. 280: no historical types.

SATURNINUS

280

C. Julius Saturninus, the general of Probus in Syria, was proclaimed emperor by his troops. During his brief usurpation, he attempted to gain recognition from Probus, whom he claimed as a colleague, but instead was defeated and killed.

280 Claim to be colleague of Probus by striking coins in his name with an inscription ending in the plural 'Augustorum'. (The issues in Saturninus' own name do not have historical types.)
> 1 *Obv.* IMP C M AVR PROBVS AVG, Bust r. *Rev.* VICTORIAE AVGG,
> Victory driving biga r. Aur: 919

CARUS

September 282–July 283

M. Aurelius Carus, born in Illyricum *c*. 230, rose through civil and military office to become praetorian prefect under Probus, against whom he revolted in the Alpine region in the summer of 282. When the troops murdered Probus, Carus succeeded to the empire without further difficulty. Unlike his recent predecessors, he had two grown sons and thus could reasonably hope to establish a dynasty. He had the elder, Carinus, proclaimed Caesar (*1*) in October 282, and the younger, Numerian (*q.v.*) in December. By that time, Carus and Numerian, who were to share rule of the eastern provinces, had arrived in Siscia (*2*) where they fought a brief but successful campaign against the Sarmatians. At the end of the year, the two emperors set out for the East for a major effort against Persia; they arrived in February at Antioch, where the two Caesars were proclaimed Augusti (*3–5*). The Persian war was a great success: the Roman forces advanced deep into enemy territory, and took the capital, Ctesiphon. The victory earned Carus the title 'Parthicus', but this appears only on memorial issues (Carinus *8–9*) because, at the height of his success, Carus was struck down, supposedly by lightning, near the Persian capital in July 283.

282 Proclamation of Carinus as Caesar.

    1*a* KARINVS NOBIL CAES, Bust r. Aur 133−4/*C*3−4. Den: 144/*C*1

    1*b* M AVR CARINVS C, Bust l. Aqui: 145

— — Arrival in Siscia.

    2 ADVENTVS CARI AVG, Carus riding r. Aur: *C*6

283 Proclamation of Carinus and Numerian as Augusti.

    3 IMP (C M AVR) CARINVS (P F) AVG, Radiate bust r. Ant: 136−7/*C*2

    4 *Obv.* KARVS ET KARINVS AVGG, Jugate busts r. *Rev.* SPES PVBLICA, Carus and Carinus riding r. Aur: 135

    5*a* *Obv.* CARVS ET CARINVS AVGG, Jugate busts r. *Rev.* PAX AVG/G, Pax running l. Ant: 138−40/*C*5−7

    5*b* — — SAECVLI FELICITAS, Carus stg. r., holding globe. Ant: 141/*C*9

    5*c* — — VICTORIA AVGG, Victory stg. l., sometimes between captives. Ant: 142−3/*C*10

CARINUS

Caesar October 282/Augustus March 283−April 285

M. Aurelius Carinus, elder son of Carus, born *c.* 250, was made Caesar (*1*) in 282 and given charge of the West, where he protected Gaul by successful campaigns against the Germans (*2*). In 283, when he held his first consulate (*3*), Carinus visited Ticinum (*4*), then arrived in Rome, where he celebrated his father's and brother's Persian victories and his own marriage with Magnia Urbica (*5*); he was now proclaimed Augustus (Carus *3*−*5*). He next proceeded to the Danube to defeat the Quadi (*6*) and to Siscia where he entered his second consulate, held jointly with Numerian and the occasion for a donative (*7*). It was probably at this time that Carus was consecrated (*8*−*9*). He planned to celebrate their joint victories in East and West when they met in Cyzicus (*10*) but the murder of Numerian and the revolt of Diocletian changed the entire situation. Carinus then withdrew to Rome, where he celebrated the consecration of Numerian and of his own son Nigrinian, who had died in infancy (*11*−*16*); then, in a hasty campaign at the end of 284, he suppressed the revolt of Julianus at Verona. Early in the next year, Diocletian advanced into Moesia and engaged in a battle, in which the forces of Carinus had come close to victory when the emperor was murdered on the battlefield, probably in April 285.

282 Proclamation as Caesar (*see also* Carus *1*), with reference to Carinus' campaigns in Germany.

    1 PRINCIPI IVVENT/VI, Carinus stg. l. (many varieties). Aur: 147/*C*90; 199/*C*109. Ant: 150/*C*92−4; 151/*C*96; 158−60/*C*83−4, 102−4; 177−82/*C*84, 87−8, 97−8; 183−6/106−8; 197−8/*C*87, 89. As: 174/*C*81. Sem: 176/*C*82.

    2 VICTORIA CAESARIS, Victory in biga l. Aur: 201/*C*157

283 First consulate.
   3   P M TRI P COS P P, Carinus in triumphal quadriga r. Aur: 226/*C*79
— — Arrival in Ticinum.
   4   ADVENTVS AVG, Carinus stg. r. Aur: 294/*C*2
— — Marriage with Magnia Urbica.
   5   MAGNIA VRBICA AVG, Diademed bust r. Qui: 335/*C*1
— — Victory over the Quadi.
   6   VICTORIA GERMANICA, Victory in biga l., trampling enemy. Aur:
      319/*C*158
284 Donative for second consulate.
   7   LIBERALITAS AVGG, Liberalitas stg. r. Aur: 309/*C*48
— — Consecration of Carus.
   8   *Obv.* DIVO CARO PIO (OR PARTHICO), Ḧead r. *Rev.* CONSECRATIO,
      Eagle stg. r., sometimes on globe. Aur: 4/*C*14. Ant: 28–30, 47/
      *C*15, 18–19; 48/*C*17 (DIVO CARO PERS); 108–9/*C*19, 22; 112–13
      (CONSECRATIO AVG/VSTI); 126, 129/*C*16

8   16

   9   — — CONSECRATIO, Altar. Ant: 49/*C*20; 50 (DIVO CARO PERS),
      110/*C*23–4; 111 (CONSECRATIO AVG); 127/*C*21
— — Planned meeting at Cyzicus.
   10 ADVENTVS AVGG NN, Carinus and Numerian holding Victory on
      globe who crowns them both. Aur: 317
— — Consecration of Numerian and Nigrinian.
   11 *Obv.* DIVO NVMERIANO AVG, radiate head r. *Rev.* CONSECRATIO,
      Eagle stg. facing. Ant: 424–5/*C*10
   12 — — — — Altar. Ant: 426/*C*12
   13 *Obv.* DIVO NIGRINIANO, Radiate or bare head r. *Rev.* CON-
      SECRATIO, Image of Nigrinian in biga on pyre. Aur: 471/*C*1
   14 — — — — Eagle on altar. Ant: 473/*C*4
   15 — — — — Eagle stg. facing. Ant: 472/*C*2,3
   16 — — — — Altar. Ant: 474/*C*5

MAGNIA URBICA

Wife of Carinus, unknown to history, died in 283; for her coins, see
Carinus 5.

NIGRINIAN

Son of Carinus, died in 284; for his coins, *see* Carinus *13—16*.

NUMERIAN

Caesar December 282/ Augustus March 283—November 284

M. Aurelius Numerianus, younger son of Carus, was born *c*. 254 and was made Caesar (*1*) by his father at Siscia in 282, after their joint victory (*2*) over the Sarmatians. He was intended to share power in the East, and consequently accompanied Carus on his successful Persian expedition, prior to which he was made Augustus at Antioch in March 283. In spite of the death of Carus, the war continued and Numerian remained in the vicinity of Ctesiphon through the winter, during which he assumed the consulate (*3*). The great Roman victories were celebrated in the West with games and vows (*4—5*) in the name of the two emperors, and their joint arrival in Cyzicus was anticipated (*6*). Numerian, however, never lived to see the meeting, for he was murdered by his praetorian prefect Aper on the return from Persia, probably at Nicaea, in November 284.

282 Proclamation as Caesar, with celebration of the Sarmatian victory.

    1 PRINCIPI IVVENT/VT, Numerian stg. l. (several varieties). Aur: 352: 369/*C*65. Ant: 356—7/*C*72—3; 360—8/*C*66, 68—9, 72—4, 76—7, 80—1

1

    2 VICTORIA CAESARIS, Victory in biga l. Aur: 371/*C*98

283 First consulate.

    3 P M TR P COS P P, Numerian in triumphal quadriga r. Den: 427/ *C*64

—— Celebration of Persian victories, with vows.

    4 VNDIQVE VICTORES, Numerian stg. l., sometimes between captives. Ant: 422—3/*C*118—21

    5 VOTA PVBLICA, Numerian and Carinus sacrificing; standards behind. Ant: 461/*C*122

—— Anticipated meeting of Numerian and Carinus at Cyzicus.

    6 ADVENTVS AVGG NN, Numerian and Carinus holding Victory on globe, who crowns them both (Carinus *10*). Aur: 462/*C*5

JULIAN

October−December 284

M. Aurelius Julianus, governor of Venetia in northern Italy, briefly seized power on the Danube when Carinus left Siscia for Rome in October 284. This disturbance, which took place after Diocletian had also revolted, temporarily weakened Carinus' resistance, but the usurper was defeated and killed at Verona by the end of the year.

284   Celebration of Pannonia, the base of Julian's revolt.
   1   PANNONIAE, Two Pannoniae stg., r. hands outstretched.
       Ant: 4/C5−6

DIOCLETIAN

November 284−May 305

C. Valerius Diocletianus, originally named Diocles, was born in Dalmatia *c*. 236 and rose through the ranks to become commander of the imperial bodyguard under Carus. After the death of Numerian, Diocletian was proclaimed emperor by the army at Nicomedia on 20 November 284 and immediately dispatched Aper, the murderer of Numerian. He then marched westward against Carinus, and became sole ruler after defeating him in the spring of 285. Faced by troubles in East and West, Diocletian realised that he could not handle the whole situation alone, and appointed as co-emperor his old friend Maximian (*1−2*) at Milan in July 285. After their joint formal entry into Ticinum (*3*), Maximian was sent west to restore order to Gaul while Diocletian returned to his capital Nicomedia preparatory to moving against the Persians, over whom he gained a diplomatic triumph in 287, the year of his third consulate (*4*). The following years saw continuing troubles in East and West, and the fourth consulate (*5*) of Diocletian in 290, when he met Maximian at Lugdunum (*6*).

While residing at Sirmium in 291−293, Diocletian completed his plans for reorganising the state on a stable basis to prevent recurrence of the anarchy of the previous half century. A major element was the establishment of a college of emperors, the tetrarchy, with two Augusti and two Caesars, each responsible for the defence and administration of one part of the empire. On 1 March 293, therefore, during his fifth consulate (*7*), Diocletian appointed Constantius and Galerius as Caesars (*8−12*); later in the same year, he celebrated the tenth anniversary (*13−19*) of his own accession to power with a donative and games called secular. The Caesars were part of a far-reaching reform which created a new provincial structure, a vastly expanded bureaucracy and army, and a new financial system to meet the increased expenses. An important part of the reform concerned the coinage. In 294, coins were issued on a new standard, with pieces of fine silver, and bronzes of three denominations. Since their weight and quality were unfamiliar, the silver coins eventually had to be marked with a number indicating their value (*21*); small bronzes for the convenience of the public, who needed small change, were also issued (*22*). A major victory over the Sarmatians (*20*) in 294 enabled Diocletian to strengthen the Danube frontier. He spent much of the next two years in Sirmium, while Maximian was called to Africa (*24*) to suppress the tribes who were harrying that province. Diocletian, meanwhile, during his sixth consulate (*23*) in 296, proceeded to Egypt (*25*) where he put down the revolts of Achilleus and Domitianus. He stayed in the East, where Galerius won great victories over the Persians, through his seventh consulate (*26*) which he entered in Antioch in 299. These years saw simultaneous campaigns in East and West by all the emperors; consequently, vows were made to Fortune for their safe return, the last time the goddess appears on the coinage.

During his eighth consulate (*27*) in 303, Diocletian entered Rome for a magnificent festival in honour of his completion of twenty years (*28–34*) on the throne, together with celebration of the tenth anniversary of the Caesars, and the victories of Galerius. The occasion had special significance since Diocletian was the first emperor since Marcus Aurelius to stay in power long enough to celebrate his vicennalia. The following year, his ninth consulate (*35*), Diocletian returned to Nicomedia where he became extremely ill, incapacitated through the following spring. As a result, he put into effect the momentous decision he had made at the time of his vicennalia, and on 1 May 305, abdicated the imperial power (*36–37*), the only emperor ever to do so willingly. He obliged Maximian to follow his example, installed Constantius and Galerius as Augusti and Severus and Maximinus as the new Caesars. After thus, as he hoped, settling the affairs of the empire, Diocletian retired to his Dalmatian villa, where he died in 316.

The coinage of this momentous reign gives little hint of the great events and reforms which make Diocletian one of the most important of Roman emperors. Instead, most of it presents generalities, with special attention to the unity of the empire, as attested by the constant presence of the Genius of the Roman People (on the bronze) and the religious policy in which Jupiter was the special protector of the Jovian house of Diocletian and Hercules of the Herculian house of Maximian.

285 Appointment of Maximian as co-emperor; their arrival in Ticinum.
1   (IMP C) MAXIMIANVS AVG, laur, bust 1. or r. Aur: 334/C5. Den: 335/C12.
     Qui: 336–7/C9–10. Sem (?): 338
2   FIDES MILITVM, Diocletian presenting globe to Maximian. Ant: 266/C73
3   ADVENTVS AVG, Diocletian on horseback r. Ant: 203
287 Third consulate.
4*a*   COS III, Type as previous. Aur: 287, 310/C54
4*b*   — — Diocletian stg. r., holding globe. Aur: 129

290 Fourth consulate; entry into Lugdunum with Maximian.

5a   COS IIII, Type as *2*. Aur: 288, 311/C55

5b   CONSVL IIII P P PROCOS, Type as *4b*, sometimes with Victory on globe. Aur: 285–6, 307–8/C46–7

6   ADVENTVS AVGG, Diocletian and Maximian riding r. Ant: 11/C8

293 Fifth consulate.

7   CONSVL V P P PROCOS, Type as *4b*. Aur: Ant 5–6/C49

— — Appointment of Constantius and Galerius as Caesars; the coinage celebrates the whole imperial college, the foresight which created it, and the Illyrian origin of its members (the latter in a type which advertises the power of the emperor on land and sea).

8   MAXIMIANVS P F AVG, head r. Aur: Tic 6

9   CONSTANTIVS NOB CAES, head r. Aur: Tic 2

10   COMITATVS AVGG, Two Augusti riding r. Aur: Rom 1/C23; Tre 6, 7

11   PROVIDENTIAE AVGG, Four emperors sacrificing in turreted enclosure. Arg: Ale 7; Ant 31; Rom 10, 30, 34; Sis 33

11

12   VIRTVS ILLVRICI, Diocletian galloping r.; galley with rowers above. Aur: Tre 87/C515

— — Tenth anniversary of reign, celebrated with a donative and games called secular, probably because the occasion was taken as the beginning of a new age.

13   VOTIS X, Two Augusti sacrificing. Ant: 109–11/C532–3

14   VOT X M XX in laurel wreath. Ant: 108/C535

15   — — Victory stg. l. Ant: 125–6/C536–7

16   PRIMIS X MVLTIS XX, Jupiter stg. l. or facing. Ant: 175–6/C384–7

17   — — Victory inscribing VOT X (FEL) on shield on palm tree. Ant: 177–9/C388–9, 391.

18   AVSPIC FEL, Liberalitas stg. l., with altar or child at foot. Ant: 115/C15

19   SAECVLARES AVGG, Cippus inscribed COS X; MXX in ex. (these legends are apparently to be expanded as COS VOT X MVLT XX). Ant: *Bastien 1960.* 215; 78/*Bastien 1960.* 218 (no inscription on cippus)

— — Victory over the Sarmatians, with coinage celebrating the whole tetrarchy.

20a VICTORIA/E SARM/AT/IC/A/E, Four emperors sacrificing in turreted enclosure. Arg: Ale 8; Ant 32; Cyz 5; Her 2, 6, 10; Nic 19; Rom 14, 16, 19, 23, 31, 37; Sis 34, 36–7, 39–41; Tic 12, 16; Tre 100, 104, 108, 114, 119

20*b* — — Camp gate. Arg: Nic 22, 25

20   21

— — Reform of coinage, with eventual (*c.* 300) issue of silver with marks of value, indicating that 96 were struck to the pound; and bronzes issued to a fixed standard, with the smallest, the denarius, designated for the 'utility of the public'.

21   XCVI in wreath. Arg: Aqu 16; Car 15; Tic 20
22   VTILITAS PVBLICA, Utilitas stg. facing. Den: Rom 48; Tic 27

296 Sixth consulate.
23   CONSVL VI P P PROCOS, Type as *3b*. Aur: Ant 13

297 Triumphal entry of Maximian into Carthage.
24   FELIX ADVENT AVGG NN, Africa stg. Aur: Car 1. Arg: Car 10, 11, 13. Fol: Car 17, 19, 21, 23, 25

298 Vows for a safe return of the emperors from campaign; Diocletian was in Egypt (the last appearance of Fortuna Redux on the coinage).
25*a*   FORTVNAE REDVCI AVGG NN, Fortuna std. l. Fol: Tre 228−232
25*b*   — — but legend ends AVGG ET CAESS NN. Fol: Tre 240
25*c*   — — — — Fortuna stg. l. Fol: Tre 243
25*d*   FORTVNAE REDVCI CAESS NN Type as previous. Fol: Tre 247, 249, 251−2, 254−5

299 Seventh consulate.
26   CONSVL VII P P PROCOS, Type as *4b*. Aur: Ant 20−22

303 Eighth consulate.
27   CONSVL VIII P P PROCOS, type as *4b*. Aur: Sis 22

— — Vicennalia of Augusti (*28−33*) and decennalia of Caesars (*34*).
28   XX DIOCLETIANI AVG in wreath. Aur: Aqu 10, 12; Nic 13, 15; Tic 11
29   PRIMI XX IOVI AVG COS VIII in wreath. Aur: Tre 75
30   PRIMI XX IOVI AVGVSTI, Jupiter std. l. Aur: Tre 76
31   GAVDETE ROMANI, Two Victories holding tablet inscribed SIC XX SIC XXX. $\frac{1}{2}$ Aur: Aqu 14
32   VOTIS ROMANORVM, Type as previous. $\frac{1}{2}$ Aur: Aqu 15
33*a*   VOT/IS XX SIC XXX in wreath. Aur: Tre 96; 98. Arg: Tre 135−6. Den: Tre 612−3
33*b*   VOT XX AVGG (NN) in wreath. Aur: Aqu 7: Tre 93. Den: Tre 609−10
33*c*   VOT XX in wreath. Den: Car 37−8; Rom 76−7, 79−81, 83−6; Tic 36−8

34*a* VOT/IS X SIC XX in wreath. Den: Tre 568; 570
34*b* SIC X SIC XX in wreath. Den: Tre 565
34*c* MVLTIS XX in wreath. Den: Tre 563

304 Ninth consulate.

35 CONSVL VIIII P P PROCOS, Type as *4b*. Aur: Sis 24

305 Abdication of Diocletian and Maximian.

36 PROVIDENT/IA DEOR/VM QVIES AVGG, Providentia extending hand
to Quies. Aur: Ant 69; Ser 10. Fol: Ale 57−8; Ant 72−3,
76−7, 83, 96−7, 113−4, 136−7; Aqu 63−4; Car 41−2; Cyz
22−3, 28−9, 32−3; Her 27−9; Lon 76−7; Lug 200; Rom
116−9, 130−1; Ser 14−15; Sis 159, 161; Tic 56−7, 61−2,
65−8; Tre 671, 673−4, 676−7

37 QVIES AVGG (or AVGVSTORVM), Quies stg. l. Fol: Lon 81, 98;
Lug 216, 225; Tre 699, 712−3, 736. Den: Tre 681

36

DOMITIUS DOMITIANUS 296−297

Usurper in Egypt: no historical types.

MAXIMIANUS HERCULIUS

Caesar July 285/Augustus April 286−March 305;
February 307−late 308; 310

M. Aurelius Valerius Maximianus, born near Sirmium about 250, rose
through the ranks of the army and became a friend of Diocletian, with
whom he fought against Carinus. When Diocletian recognised the need
for a colleague, he appointed Maximian as Caesar (*1*) at Milan in 285,
and gave him charge of the West. Although the sources mention the rank
of Caesar, it does not appear on the coins. After suppressing the rebellion
of the Bagaudae in Gaul led by Amandus and defeating German invasions,
Maximian entrusted the campaign against the pirates of the Black Sea to
Carausius, who revolted, detaching Britain and parts of Gaul from the
Empire. Maximian meanwhile was promoted to Augustus in 286, and
assumed the consulate (*2*) in the following year, when he had constantly
to fight the Germans. A second consulate (*3*) followed in 288 and a third

(*4–5*) in 290, the year he devoted to problems in Gaul, where he and Diocletian apparently met (*6*).

During the fourth consulate of Maximinus in 293 (*7*), the tetrarchy was created (*8–10*) and Constantius became Caesar in the West. This coincided with the tenth anniversary of the joint reign, celebrated with 'secular' games and a donative (*11–18*). During the following years, when Diocletian's major reforms, including that of the coinage (*20–22*), were developed, and his Sarmatian victories (*19*) celebrated, Maximian stayed in Italy, which he made his base for the rest of his reign. From there he could direct the ultimately successful campaigns of Constantius against Carausius, and conduct campaigns in Africa, where the local tribes had been causing widespread devastation. After considerable success, Maximian entered Carthage (*24*) in triumph in 297, the year of his fifth consulate (*23*). Vows were made for his successful return to Italy (*25*), which he accomplished in 299, during his sixth consulate (*26*); there, he celebrated a formal triumph. His next consulate (*27*), in 303, was marked by a glorious event, the twentieth anniversary of the joint reign (*28–31*), celebrated by the Augusti together in Rome in November. Maximian assumed the consulate (*32*) once again in 394 before reluctantly joining Diocletian in retirement (*33–34*) on 1 May 305.

Maximian's retirement in Italy was short, for his son Maxentius revolted and called on him to resume the purple in February 307 in an effort to strengthen and legitimise his position (*35–37*). Maximian, now coruler with his son (*38–42*), justified his office by receiving the surrender of Severus, and then by making an alliance with Constantine, to whom he gave his daughter Fausta in marriage. After his defeat of Galerius at Rome, however, Maximian decided to aim for supreme power in Italy. When the troops remained loyal to Maxentius, he fled to Constantine in Gaul, where he again abdicated at the end of 308. Yet once again, this abdication was not final, for Maximian broke with Constantine in 310 and assumed the highest rank for the third time. This reign was ephemeral; he was soon forced to surrender, and committed suicide, probably early in 311. His memory was honoured by Maxentius (*15*).

285 Appointment as coemperor.
  1 FIDES MILITVM, Maximian receiving globe from Diocletian (Diocletian 2). Ant: 583
287 First consulate of Maximian.
  2 CONSVL P P PROCONSVL, Maximian stg. l., holding globe. Aur: 608/*C*77
288 Second consulate.
  3 COS II, Maximian riding r. Aur: 488, 598, 612/*C*86–7
290 Third consulate.
  4 CONSVL III P P PROCOS, Type as *2*. Aur: 596–7, 609–10/*C*78–9
  5 COS III, Type as *3*. Aur: 599, 613/*C*88
— — Arrival of the emperors in Lugdunum.
  6 ADVENTVS AVGG, Diocletian and Maximian riding r. (Diocletian 6). Ant: 347/*C*5, 6

293   Fourth consulate.
7   CONSVL IIII P P PROCOS, Type as 2. Aur: Ant 3−4/*C*80
— —   Creation of the tetrarchy.
8   COMITATVS AVGG, Diocletian and Maximian riding r. (Diocletian *10*). Aur: Rom 2, 3/*C*39; Tre 7
9   PROVIDENTIA/E AVGG, Four emperors sacrificing in turreted enclosure (Diocletian *11*). Arg: Ale 7; Rom 10, 12, 30, 34; Sis 33

9   24

10   VIRTVS ILLVRICI, Maximian galloping r.; galley with rowers above (Diocletian *12*). Aur: Tre 87/*C*621
— —   Tenth anniversary of reign of Diocletian and Maximian, with a donative and games, called secular celebrated by Maximian probably at Treveri.
11*a* VOTIS X, Diocletian and Maximian sacrificing (Diocletian *13*). Ant: 466−7/*C*669−71; 486 (one emperor)
11*b* VOTIS AVGG, Same type. Ant: 485
12   VOT X M XX in wreath (Diocletian *14*). Ant: 468/*C*678
13   — — Victory on globe l. (Diocletian *15*). Ant: 487/*C*677
14   PRIMIS X MVLTIS XX, Hercules stg. r. (*cf.* Diocletian *16*). Ant: 511−12/*C*472−3
15   — — Victory inscribing VOT X on shield on palm tree (Diocletian *17*). Ant: 513/*C*474−5; 514/*C*477 (two victories)
16   AVSPIC FEL, Liberalitas stg. l., altar or child at feet (Diocletian *18*). Ant: 469−71/*C*23−6
17   SAECVLARES AVGG, Cippus inscribed COS X (Diocletian *19*). Ant: *Bastien 1960.* 216/*C*507; 415/*Bastien 1960.* 219 (no inscription on cippus)
18   — — Elephant l. Den: *Bastien 1960.* 228/*C*506
294   Sarmatian victories of Diocletian.
19*a* VICTORIA/E SARM/AT/ICA/E, Four emperors sacrificing in turreted enclosure (Diocletian *20*). Arg: Cyz 5; Her 3, 7, 10; Nic 19; Rom 14, 17, 19, 20, 31, 37; Sis 34, 37; Tic 12, 16; Tre 104, 114, 119
19*b* — — Camp gate. Arg: Nic 22, 25.
— —   Reform of the coinage, with eventual use of marks of value, and issue of bronze for 'public utility'.
20*a* XCVI in wreath (Diocletian *21*). Arg: Aqu 16/*C*697; Car 15; Tic 20
21   VTILITAS PVBLICA, Utilitas stg. (Diocletian *22*). Den: Rom 62; Tic 27

22 — — Aequitas stg. l. Den: Sis 94
297 Fifth consulate.
23 CONSVL V P P PROCOS, Type as 2. Aur: Ant 11−12/*C*82
— — Victories in Africa and entry into Carthage.
24 FEL/IX ADVENT AVGG NN, Africa stg. (Diocletian *24*). Arg: Car 11/*C*91; 13/*C*92. Fol: Car 17, 19, 21, 23, 25.
298 Vows for safe return from Africa, and for the safe return of the other emperors from their campaigns.
25*a* FORTVNAE REDVCI AVGG NN, Fortuna std. l. (Diocletian *25a*). Fol: Tre 230, 232
25*b* FORTVNAE REDVCI AVGG ET CAESS NN, Fortuna stg. l. (Diocletian *25c*). Fol: Tre 243
25*c* — — but without AVGG ET (Diocletian *25d*). Fol: Tre 246, 248, 250, 253
299 Sixth consulate.
26 CONSVL VI P P PROCONSVL, Type as *2*. Aur: Ant 17−19/*C*83
303 Seventh consulate
27 CONSVL VII P P PROCONSVL, Type as *2*. Aur: Ant 27; Sis 21. ½ Aur: Sis 29.
— — Twentieth anniversary of Augusti; tenth of Caesars
28 XX MAXIMIANI AVG in wreath (*cf.* Diocletian *28*). Aur: Aqu 11, 13/*C*702−3; Nic 14, 16/*C*704; Tic 11/*C*705
29 GAVDETE ROMANI, Two Victories holding tablet inscribed SIC XX SIC XXX (Diocletian *31*). ½ Aur: Aqu 14/*C*130
30*a* VOT XX SIC XXX in wreath (Diocletian *33a*). Aur: Tre 97/*C*689. Den: Tre 613
30*b* VOT XX AVGG (NN) in wreath (Diocletian *33b*) Aur: Aqu 7/ *C*688; Tre 93. Den: Tre 610/*C*687
30*c* VOT XX in wreath (Diocletian *33c*). Den: Car 37; Rom 74−8, 82, 85; Tic 36−8
30*d* MVLTIS XXX in wreath. Den: Tre 608
31*a* SIC X SIC XX in wreath (Diocletian *34b*). Den: Tre 566
31*b* MVLTIS XX in wreath (Diocletian *34c*). Den: Tre 564
304 Eighth consulate.
32 CONSVL VIII P P PROCOS, Type as *2*. Aur: Ant: 30; Sis 23/*C*85
305 Abdication of Diocletian and Maximian.
33 PROVIDENT/IA DEORVM QVIES AVGG, Providentia extending hand to Quies (Diocletian *36*). Aur: Ser 10/*C*478. Fol: Ale 57−8; Ant 72−3, 76−7; Aqu 63−4; Car 41−2; Cyz 22−3, 28−9, 32−3; Her 27−8; Lon 76−7; Lug 200−1; Rom 116−9, 130− 1; Ser 14−15; Sis 158, 160; Tic 56−7, 61−2, 65−69; Tre 672−3, 675−8
34 QVIES AVGG, Quies stg. l. (Diocletian *37*). Den: Tre 681
307 Return to Rome as restored Augustus, with vows.
35 FELIX INGRESSVS SEN AVG, Rome std. l., holding shield inscribed VOT XXX. Aur: Rom 136, 145−6/*C*109
36*a* VOTIS XXX AVG/G (N/N) in wreath. Den: Tre 751−3, 793

36b   VOTIS XX in wreath. Den: Tre 754
37   PLVR NATAL FEL in wreath. Den: Tre 747

307−8   Joint reign with Maxentius: celebration of Rome and Carthage, their bases of power.

38a   CONSERV/ATORES VRB SVAE, Std. image of Roma in temple (Maxentius *4*). Fol: Aqu 121; Rom 165, 194, 198; Tic 84−5
38b   ROMAE AETER, Same type Fol: Lon 100
39   (Legend as *38a*) Victory presenting wreath to Roma in temple (Maxentius *5*). Fol: Aqu 118
40   CONSERVATOR AFRICAE SVAE, Africa stg. (Maxentius *2*). Fol: Car 52, 56
41   CONSERVATORES KART SVAE, Stg. image of Cathage in temple (Maxentius *7*). Fol: Car 59
42   FELIX KARTHAGO, Carthage std. l. (Maxentius *7A*). Aur: Car 46

AMANDUS

Rebel in Gaul 295−296; no historical types.

CARAUSIUS

286−293

M. Aurelius Mausaeus Carausius, a Menapian (from the Low Countries) of humble origin, was a sailor who entered the Roman army where he distinguished himself in the campaigns of Maximian against the Bagaudae in Gaul. As a result, Maximian entrusted him with the task of organising a fleet to defend the coasts against Frankish and British pirates (*6*). When, after some success, he was accused of embezzlement and threatened with death, he rebelled. Carausius was proclaimed emperor in 286 with the support of the detachments from the various legions (*8*) who manned the fleet, and crossed to Britain where he was received and recognised (*1−5*). Maximian, at first distracted by campaigns against the Germans, organised a great fleet to send against the breakaway state, but it met with disaster at sea in 288. Thereafter, the emperors tacitly recognised Carausius, and entrusted him with defence of the seas against pirates. Although Carausius claimed to be their imperial colleague (*7, 14*), the legitimate emperors never granted him official recognition. Carausius held four consulates, none of which was recognised elsewhere in the empire. For the fourth, which coincided with the fifth anniversary of his accession, he held games which he called secular, and gave a donative (*9−13*). Little is known of his reign in Britain, which ended when he was murdered by his praetorian prefect Allectus in 293. The coinage of Carausius contains many irregular issues and poses numerous problems of interpretation.

286 Arrival in Britain, with thanks to Neptune, who brought Carausius safely across the sea, and honours to Britain which received him.

1*a* ADVENTVS AVG/G, Carausius riding l., captive before. Den: 7, 190, 535−41, 706−8, 1067−8/*C*3−4, 7−11. Ant: 10−11, 598, 732, 1075−6/*C*5−6, 12

1*b* ADVENTVS CARAVSI, Same type. Ant: 734−5/*C*13−14

2 EXPECTATE VENI, Britannia greeting Carausius. Den: 554−8/ *C*56−58. Ant: 216−9, 605/*C*54−5, 59−61

2

10*a*

3 NEPTVNO REDVCI, Neptune stg. l. Ant: 472

4 GENIO BRITANNI, Genius stg. l. before altar. Ant: 240

− − Quinquennial vows, probably taken at accession.

5*a* PAX AVG VOT V, Pax stg. l. Aur: 3

5*b* PAX AVG MVLT X, Same type. Aur: 4/*C*189

− − Celebration of German victories, perhaps those over the Frankish and Saxon pirates, gained before Carausius' revolt.

6 VICTORIA GERMA, Trophy between captives. Ant: 432, 531−2, 1030−1/*C*385−6

− − Assumption of the title *princeps iuventutis*, indicating Carausius' claim of a subordinate position to the legitimate emperors.

7 PRINCIPI IVVENT, Carausius stg. l. Den: 721/*C*249. Ant: 947−8/ *C*250

− − Recognition of the legions whose detachments supported Carausius' revolt.

8*a* LEG I MINervia, Ram stg. r. Ant: 55−6, 268/*C*131

8*b* LEG II AVGusta, Capricorn l. Ant: 57−9/*C*132−3

8*c* LEG II PARTHica, Centaur l. or r. Ant: 60−4, 269−71/*C*134−6

8*d* LEG IIII FLavia, Lion walking l. or r. Ant: 69−70/*C*139−41; 568

8*e* LEG IIII FLAVIA, Two lions facing each other; youthful diademed head r. above. Ant: 71−2/*C*142

8*f* LEG VII CL/Avdia, Bull r. Ant: 74−6, 274/*C*144

8*g* LEG VIII AVGusta, Bull r. Ant: 77/*C*145

8*h* LEG XX valeria victrix, Boar r. Ant: 82−3/*C*148

8*i* LEG IIXX PRIMIGenia (XXII legion), Capricorn. Ant: 80−1/*C*147

8*j* LEG XXX VLPIA (victrix), Neptune stg. or std. Ant: 84−6/*C*146, 149

8*k* COH/RT PRAET, Four standards. Ant: 741−2/*C*21

290 Fourth consulate, apparently the occasion for vows, Secular Games and a donative.

9   VOTA QVI CAE, Carausius receiving Victory from std. Roma.
Ant: 1095/*C*405

10*a*   VOTVM PVBLIC/VM, Altar inscribed MVLTIS XX IMP. Den: 597/
*C*409−10. Ant: 620

10*b*   VOTO PVBLICO MVLTIS XX IMP in wreath. Den: 596/*C*407

11   SAECVLARES AVG, Cippus inscribed COS IIII. Ant: 393

12   − − Lion walking r. Ant; 391−2/*C*305−6

13   LIBERALIT, Donation scene with Carausius, prefect, Liberalitas
and citizen. Ant: 833/*C*151

290   and later. Claim to membership in the imperial college.

14*a*   *Obv.* CARAVSIVS ET FRATRES SVI, Jugate busts of Carausius,
Diocletian and Maximian 1. *Rev.* PAX AVGGG, Pax stg. 1. Ant:
1/*C*1

14*b*   Same type, but *obv.* legend C VAL DIO...AVGG. Ant: 2/*C*2

See also the types struck in the names of Diocletian and Maximian
from the London and the 'C' mints, *RIC* 3−49, and the coinage of
Carausius with reverse legends ending in AVGGG.

ALLECTUS

293−296

Allectus, the praetorian prefect, seized control of Britain when he murdered
Carausius in 293. He failed to extend his power to the continent, and
soon had to face the attacks of Constantius, who had been created Caesar
to bring Britain back under the control of the central government. Allectus
met the invading forces of Constantius in Hampshire, where he was
defeated and killed in 296.

293   Arrival in supreme power.

1   ADVENTVS AVG, Allectus riding 1., captive before. Ant: 62/*C*1

GALERIUS

Caesar March 293/Augustus May 305−May 311

Galerius Valerius Maximianus, born in 260 in the vicinity of Serdica, had
served in the army under Aurelian and Probus, and become a high
officer, probably praetorian prefect, when Diocletian named him Caesar
(*1−8*) in 293. He married Diocletian's daughter, and was adopted into
the Jovian family (*5*) as his son. He was given charge of the eastern
frontier where he had to deal with the attacks of the Persians, and
although his first efforts produced mixed results, he won a resounding
victory in 298 which resulted in the annexation of new lands in northern
Mesopotamia. His coinage, however, commemorates not this famous
triumph, but repeats the standard types of the Tetrarchy: the decennalia

of the Augusti (*9*), the Sarmatian victories of Diocletian (*10*), the coinage reform (*11−12*), the triumphs of Maximian in Africa (*13*), and the general prayers for a safe return of the Caesars and Augusti from campaign (*14−15*).

Galerius was the leader of the major persecution of the Christians launched by Diocletian at Nicomedia in 303. He participated in the great celebrations for the vicennalia (*17−21*), and on 1 May 305 received the purple mantle of Diocletian and the succession as Augustus (*22−24*) in the East; his colleague as Augustus was Constantius; his Caesar Maximinus. Much of Galerius' reign was occupied with civil war, first against Maxentius, then Constantine, and with his war against the Christian church. He ultimately failed in both. Shortly after agreeing to grant toleration to the Christians, he died at Serdica in May 311, on his way to his native village, Romuliana, where he was buried. He was consecrated, and his memory commemorated by Maxentius (*16−17*), Maximinus (*9*) and Licinius (*4−5*). His coinage is singularly uninformative, being confined almost entirely to stock types.

293 Proclamation as Caesar, with decennial vows; adoption of Galerius into the Jovian family; establishment of the Tetrarchy, with celebration of their Illyrian origin; donative on the tenth anniversary of the Augusti.

1 PRINCIPI IVVENTVTIS, Galerius stg. between standards. Aur: Sis 8−9. Ant: 704−7/C168, 172. Den: 708. Qui: 709−12/C166, 170−1, 173

2 PRAESIDIA REIPVB, Caesars holding globe between them; captive at feet. Ant: 716

3 VOTIS X, Galerius sacrificing at altar. Ant: 702/C235

4 VOT X M XX, Victory on globe. Ant: 703/C242

5 VIRTVS IOVI CAESARIS, Galerius riding r. Aur: Tre 90

6 COMITATVS AVGG, The two Caesars riding 1. (Diocletian *10*). Aur: Rom 4

7 PROVIDENTIA/E AVGG, Four emperors sacrificing in turreted enclosure (Diocletian *11*). Arg. Rom 11, 35; Sis 54

7

8 VIRTVS ILLVRICI, Galerius galloping r., galley above. (Diocletian *12*). Aur: Tre 88

9 AVSPIC FEL, Liberalitas stg. 1., altar or child at feet (Diocletian *18*). Ant: 693

294 Sarmatian victories of Diocletian.

    10   VICTORIAE SARM/AT/ICAE, Four emperors sacrificing in turreted enclosure (Diocletian *20*). Arg: Ant 33; Rom 22, 26, 36, 38–9; Sis 35, 38, 42; Tes 10; Tic 13, 17; Tre 105–6, 115, 220

— — Reform of coinage, with eventual need for marks of denomination.

    11   XCVI IN WREATH (Diocletian *21*). Arg: Aqu 17: Car 16; Tic 21–2

    12   VTILITAS PVBLICA, Utilitas stg. (Diocletian *22*). Den: Rom 49; Tic 28

297 Victories of Maximian in Africa.

    13   F/EL/IX ADVENT AVGG NN, Africa stg. (Diocletian *24*). Aur: Car 2. Arg: Car 12, 14. Fol: Car 18, 20, 22, 24, 26

298 Prayers for Galerius' safe return from the Persian wars, and for that of the other emperors from their campaigns.

    14   FORTVNAE REDVCI, Veiled and turreted head r. Aur: Ant 23

    15*a*   FORTVNAE REDVCI AVGG NN, Fortuna std. l. (Diocletian *25a*). Fol: Tre 237–9

    15*b*   — — legend adds ET CAESS (Diocletian *25b*). Fol: Tre 242

    15*c*   — — — — Fortuna stg. l. Diocletian 25*c* Fol: Tre 244–5

    15*d*   — — — — but CAESS NN only (Diocletian *25d*). Fol: Tre 258–60; 262–3

300 or 302 Joint consulate with Constantius (they shared office in both years).

    16   CONSVL CAESS, Galerius stg. l. Aur: Tes 1

303 Decennalia of Caesars (*17–20*) and vicennalia of Augusti (*21*).

    17*a*   VOT X CAESS in wreath; eagle at base. Aur: Aqu 5–6

    17*b*   VOT/IS X SIC XX in wreath (Diocletian *34a*). Aur: Tre 99; Den: Tre 569

    17*c*   VOT X in wreath. Den: Car 35–6; Tic 39–40, 42

    18   SIC X SIC XX (COS IIII) in wreath (Diocletian *34b*). Aur: Tre 82. Den: Tre 567

    19*a*   MVLTIS X in wreath. Den: Tre 562

    19*b*   MVLTIS XX in wreath (Diocletian *34c*). Den: Tre 607

    20   VOT XX CAESS in wreath. Den: Tre 611

    21*a*   VOT XX SIC XXX in wreath (Diocletian *33a*). Den: Tre 614

    21*b*   VOT XX in wreath (Diocletian *33c*). Den: Rom 87–89

305 Fifth consulate and elevation of Galerius to Augustus, with vows.

    22*a*   CONSVL V P P PROCOS, Galerius stg. r. Aur: Sis 149

    22*b*   CONSVL AVGG NN, Same type. Aur: Ser 5

    23   X MAXIMIANI AVG in wreath. Aur: Nic 38

    24   VOT XX AVGG (NN) in wreath. Den: Tre 94, 682

306 Sixth consulate.

    25   CONSVL VI P P PROCOS, Type as *22*. Aur. Ant 26

308 Seventh consulate.

    26   CONSVL VII P P PROCOS, Type as *22*. Aur: Ant 79

311 Eighth consulate.

    27   CONSVL VIII P P PROCOS, Type as *22*. Aur: Ant 128

CONSTANTIUS

Caesar March 293/Augustus May 305—July 306

Flavius Valerius Constantius, born of humble origins, rose through the ranks to become praetorian prefect of Maximian, under whom he led the struggle against Carausius and conducted successful campaigns in Germany. On 1 May 293 at Milan, he was made Caesar (*1—6*) and became a member of the imperial Herculian family by marrying the daughter of Maximian. On that occasion, he celebrated the 'secular' games and gave a donative with his colleagues (*7—8*). He conducted the fight against the breakaway state, and finally defeated Allectus, taking control of Britain in 296. From his residence at Treveri, he fought successfully against Franks and Germans until 305, when he succeeded as Augustus (*20*) on the abdication of Maximian. His coinage of these years is not distinctive, but like that of Galerius, repeats the standard types of the Augusti. As Augustus, Constantius continued to fight in the West, and crossed into Britain, where he penetrated far into the north, defeating the Picts before he died at York in July 306.

293 Proclamation as Caesar, with adoption into the Herculian family of Maximian; establishment of the Tetrarchy, with celebration of their Illyrian origin; donative and games for the decennalia of the Augusti.

1 PRINCIPI IVVENTVT/IS, Constantius stg. l. (several varieties = Galerius *1*). Aur: Sis 10. Ant: 658—62/C221, 223, 225. Den: 663—4. Qui: 665—8/C219—20, 222, 224

2 PRAESIDIA REIPVB, Caesars holding globe between them; captive at feet (Galerius *2*). Ant: 671/C218

3 VIRTVS HERCVLI CAESARIS, Constantius riding r. (*cf.* Galerius *5*). Aur: Tre 86

4 COMITATVS AVGG, The two Caesars riding l. (Diocletian *10*). Aur: Tre 7

5 PROVIDENTIA/E AVGG, Four emperors sacrificing in turreted enclosure (Diocletian *11*). Arg: Cyz 4; Her 1, 5, 9; Rom 11, 13, 35; Nic 18; Sis 54

5

10

6 VIRTVS ILLVRICI, Constantius galloping r., galley above. (Diocletian *12*). Aur: Tre 88

7 AVSPIC FEL, Libertas stg. l., altar or child at feet (Diocletian *18*). Ant: 649/C11

8   SAECVLARES AVGG, Cippus inscribed COS X (Diocletian *19*).
       Ant: *Bastien 1960.* 217

294 Sarmatian victories of Diocletian.

9*a*   VICTORIA/E SARM/A/T/I/CAE, Four emperors sacrificing in turreted
        enclosure (Diocletian *20a*). Arg: Ant 33; Rom 15, 18, 21−2,
        24−5, 36, 38, 43; Sis 35, 38, 58; Tic 13, 17; Tre 101, 105−7,
        115, 120, 127

9*b*   − − Camp gate (Diocletian *20b*). Arg: Rom 43

− − Reform of coinage, with eventual need for marks of denomination,
    and for small bronzes for public utility.

10   XCVI in wreath (Diocletian *21*). Arg: Aqu 17; Car 16; Tic 21.

11   VTILITAS PVBLICA, Utilitas stg. (Diocletian *22*). Den: Rom 49;
        Tic 28

297 Victories of Maximian in Africa.

12   F/EL ADVENT AVGG NN, Africa stg. (Diocletian *24*). Aur: Car 2.
        Arg: Car 12, 14. Fol: Car 18, 20, 22, 24, 26

298 Vows for a safe return from the Rhine, and for the other emperors
        from their campaigns.

13   FORTVNAE REDVCI, Veiled and turreted head r. (Galerius *14*).
        Aur: Ant 23

14*a*   FORTVNAE REDVCI AVGG NN, Fortuna std. l. (Diocletian *25a*).
        Fol. Tre 233−7

14*b*   − − legend adds ET CAESS (Diocletian *25b*). Fol: Tre 241

14*c*   FORTVNAE REDVCI CAESS NN, Fortuna stg. l. (Diocletian *25d*).
        Fol: Tre 256−9, 261, 263

300 or **302**   Joint consulate with Constantius.

15   CONSVL CAESS, Constantius stg. l. (Galerius *16*). Aur: Tes 1

303 Decennalia of Caesars (*16−17*) and vicennalia of Augusti (*18−19*).

16*a*   VOT X CAESS in wreath (Galerius *17a*). Aur: Aqu 5

16*b*   VOT/IS X SIC XX in wreath (Galerius *17b*). Aur: Tre 134. Den:
        Tre 571

17*c*   VOT X in wreath (Galerius *17c*). Den; Car 35; Tic 39−42

18   VOT XX CAESS in wreath (Galerius *20*). Aur: Tre 95. Den: Tre
        611

19*a*   VOT XX SIC XXX in wreath (Diocletian *33a*). Den: Tre 614

19*b*   VOT XX AVGG NN in wreath (Diocletian *33b*). Aur: Tre 94

19*c*   VOT XX in wreath (Diocletian *33c*). Den: Rom 87−89

305 Fifth consulate, held jointly with Galerius, and elevation of
        Constantius to Augustus, with vows.

20*a*   CONSVL V P P PROCOS, Constantius stg. r. (Galerius *22a*). Aur:
        Ant 65; Sis 20

20*b*   CONSVL AVGG NN, Same type (Galerius *22b*). Aur: Ser 5

21   X CONSTANTI AVG in wreath (*cf.* Galerius *23*). Aur: Nic 37

22   VOT XX AVGG (N) in wreath (Galerius *24*). Den: Tre 682, 684

MAXIMINUS DAIA

Caesar May 305/Filius Augustorum 309/
Augustus May 310—April 313

Maximinus Daia, the nephew of Galerius, was born in Illyricum on the very day that Diocletian became emperor. He rose through the ranks of the army to become an imperial bodyguard, and was adopted by Galerius who made him Caesar (*1—3*) in 305. He then changed his name to Galerius Valerius Maximinus. As Caesar, he had his headquarters at Antioch and ruled over the East and Egypt. When Licinius was made Augustus in 308, Maximinus demanded the title also, especially since it had been usurped by Constantine in the West. Instead, both he and Constantine received the novel rank of Filius Augustorum (*4*) in late 308 or early 309. This title appears on the coins struck for Maximinus in the West, but the issues of his capital, Antioch, stress his position as Caesar and member of the imperial Jovian family (*5—6*).

Maximinus was finally promoted to Augustus in May 310. In the same year, which marked his quinquennalia (*7*), he won a major victory over the Persians. In 311, when he held the consulate for the second time (*8*), Maximinus moved to Nicomedia on the death of Galerius (*9*), but in the next year, which saw Constantine's victory (*10*) in the West, he campaigned on the eastern frontier. These activities distracted Maximinus from the threat posed by Licinius, who attacked and defeated him in April 313; he committed suicide three months later.

Caesar, 305—309

305 Proclamation as Caesar, and vows on accession.

  1*a* PRINCIPI IVVENTVTIS, Maximian stg. r. Aur: Rom 149; Ser 8b, 9b, 19; Sis 151. Fol: Lug 275; Tre 733

  1*b* PRINCIPI IVVENT BONO REI PVBLICAE NATO, Same type. Fol: Lug 271

1

  2 P M TR P P P PROCOS, Same type. Aur: Sis 150
  3 VOT X CAESS in wreath. Æ3: Tre 685, 686, 688

Filius Augustorum, 309−310

309−10 Award of title Filius Augustorum; stress on position as Caesar in the East.

4   *Obv.* MAXIMINVS FIL AVGG, Bust r. *Rev.* GENIO AVGVSTI, Genius stg. l. Fol: Sis 200

4*b*   −− *Rev.* GENIO CAESARIS, Same type. Fol: Tes 32

4*c*   −− *Rev.* VIRTVTI EXERCITVS, Virtus adv. r. Fol: Tes 39

5   MAXIMINVS NOBILISSIMVS CAESAR, Maximinus stg. Fol: Ant 120, 135

6   IOVIO PROPAGAT ORBIS TERRARVM, Fol: Ant 134

Augustus 310−313

310 Accession as Augustus, with quinquennial vows.

7*a*   X MAXIMINI AVG in wreath. Aur: Ant 131

7*b*   VOTIS X ET XX in wreath. Aur: Ant 130

7*c*   VOT X MVL XX in wreath. Æ3: Tre 909

311 Second consulate.

8   CONSVL P P PROCONSVL, Maximin stg. r. Aur: Ant 127; Nic 62

−− Death and consecration of Galerius.

9   *Obv.* DIVO MAXIMIANO MAXIMINVS AVG FIL, Bust r. *Rev.* AETERNAE MEMORIAE GAL/ERI MAXIMIANI, lighted altar; eagle above or beside. Fol: Ale 133, 143, 148, 151, 154, 159; Cyz 75

312 Victory of Constantine over Maxentius.

10   VICTORIA CONSTANTINI AVG, Victory adv. r. Sol: Rom 285−6

SEVERUS

Caesar May 305/Augustus Summer 306−Spring 307

Flavius Valerius Severus was a native of Illyricum and friend of Galerius, who had him promoted to Caesar in 305, in charge of Italy and Africa. Severus was made Augustus on the death of Constantius and given the duty of suppressing the revolt of Maxentius. He set out from his head-quarters in Milan for Rome with a large army, but most of it was suborned by Maxentius and deserted, leaving Severus to flee for safety to Ravenna, where he surrendered on promise of his life. Nevertheless, he was executed at Rome a few months later.

305 Appointment as Caesar, with vows for the new Caesars and Augusti.

1   PRINCIPI IVVENTVTIS, Severus stg. r. Aur: Ser 8−9/C143. Æ3: Rom 125, 127

2   VOT X CAESS (NN) in wreath (Maximinus *3*). Den: Tre 685, 687

3   VOT XX AVGG in wreath (Galerius *24*). Den: Tre 683

307 Consulate of Severus.
    4a CONSVL P P PROCOS, Severus stg. r. Aur: Ant 78
    4b CONSVL AVGG NN, Same type. Aur: Ser 16

MAXENTIUS

Princeps October 306/Augustus April 307—October 312

M. Aurelius Valerius Maxentius, the son of Maximian Herculius, was born about 279. When the Tetrarchy was established, he was married to the daughter of Galerius and generally expected to become a member of the imperial college. On the abdication of the senior emperors, however, he was passed over and retired to Rome. When the new Augustus, Galerius, raised taxes and imposed them for the first time on Rome, the people and praetorians rose in revolt and proclaimed Maxentius emperor in October 306. At first, in deference to the tetrarchic principle, he took only the title *princeps* (*1—2*). His effort to secure legitimacy, however, was unsuccessful, and Galerius sent the new western Augustus, Severus, to suppress the revolt. Maxentius, now feeling the need of additional support, called his father from retirement and invested him with the title Augustus early in 307. Together, the two emperors defeated Severus, who surrendered at Ravenna. Maxentius now assumed the title of Augustus, and established his control over Italy, Africa and the islands, to which Spain was added later in 307. Rome was the base of his power and object of his special attentions, including an ambitious building programme in which a great basilica was erected in the Forum and the temple of Rome and Venus (*4—6*) rebuilt after its partial destruction by fire in 307. Consequently, the city is constantly featured in the coinage (*1, 3—6*); corresponding types celebrating Africa (*7*) were struck in Carthage.

Galerius, in his turn, attacked Italy in September 307, but was also obliged to withdraw. Maxentius' position now seemed secure, but in April 308 he broke with his father who had attempted to gain supreme power and fled to Gaul on his failure. Maxentius now assumed the consulate (*9*) in a definite break with the other emperors. In 309, he suffered a setback when Africa revolted under Domitius Alexander and when his son and intended successor Romulus died and was consecrated (*10*). Nevertheless, he was able to strengthen the defences of Italy against the attacks of Licinius. Maxentius celebrated his third consulate (*12*) in 310, the year when he honoured the memory of Maximian (*15*) who had committed suicide after revolting against his ally Constantine. In 311, Maxentius similarly honoured Galerius and Constantius (*16—18*), the latter as part of his collegiality with Constantine. In these years, Maxentius lost Spain but suppressed the revolt of Alexander in Africa (*11*). This important victory justified a triumph, which coincided with the celebration of the emperor's quinquennalia (*13—14*). Wars and the temporary loss of the African grain supply, however, diminished Maxentius' support in Rome. When Constantine attacked in 312, therefore, he met

little resistance. In spite of prayers for victory (*19*), Maxentius was defeated and killed at the battle of the Milvian bridge on 28 October 312.

Princeps, 306—307

(Coins of Carthage also use the title Caesar.)
306 Benefactions to Rome and Carthage, principal bases of Maxentius.
    Obv. MAXENTIVS PRINC INVICT, Bust r.
     1   CONSERVAT/OR VRBIS SVAE, Roma std. l. Aur: Rom 135/*C*48;
        143—4
     2   CONSERVATOR AFRICAE SVAE, Africa stg. Fol: Car 53—4, 57

Augustus, 307—312

307 Continuing honours to Rome and Carthage, with celebration of the
    rebuilding of the temple of Rome, the main coin type of the reign.
    3a CONSERVATOR VRBIS SVAE, Type as *1*. Aur: Rom 177—8; Ost 2
    3b ROMA AETERNA, Same type. Aur: Car 48
     4   CONSERV/ATOR/ES VRB/IS SVAE (The plural 'Conservatores' refers
        to Maxentius and Maximian), Statue of Rome in temple of
        Rome and Venus. Arg: Rom 187/. Fol: Aqu 119, 116, 118A,
        121—6; Rom 162—3, 194—5, 198—9, 202, 204—5, 208—12,
        258—63, 278—80; Tic 84—5, 91, 94—5, 100—5, 108—9

          4   10

     5   CONSERV VRB SVAE, Victory presenting wreath to Roma in temple.
        Fol: Aqu: 115; Tic 106—7
     6   — — Rome in temple giving globe to Maxentius. Fol: Aqu
        113—4; Rom 213; Tic 110
     7   CONSERVATORES KART SVAE, Carthage stg. in temple. Fol. Car 60
     7A FELIX KARTHAGO, Carthage stg. facing. Aur: Car 47
— — Consecration of Constantius.
     8   *Obv.* DIVO CONSTANTIO PIO (or AVG), Veiled head r. *Rev.* MEM/
        ORIA DIVI CONSTANTI, Eagle stg. on shrine or altar. Fol: Aqu
        127; Tic 96—7
308 First consulate.
     9   FELIX PROCESS CONSVLAT AVG N, Maxentius stg. r. Aur: Rom
        179/*C*64. Arg: Rom 188/*C*65

309 Death and consecration of Romulus.

    10*a*   *Obv.* DIVO ROMVLO N V BIS COS, Head r. *Rev.* AETERNAE MEMORIAE, Domed shrine surmounted by eagle. Fol: Ost 34; Rom 207, 257. ½ Fol: Ost 58–9. Den: Rom 226, 239–40

    10*b*   *Obv.* DIVO ROMVLO N V FILIO MAXENTIVS, Head r. *Rev.* as previous. Fol: Ost 32; Rom 249, 256

    10*c*   *Obv.* IMP MAXENTIVS DIVO ROMVLO N V FILIO, Head r. *Rev.* as previous. Fol: Ost 33

— — Address to troops, on expedition to reconquer Africa.

    11   ADLOCVTIO AVG N, Maxentius addressing troops. Fol: Ost 23; Rom 206, 242

310 Third consulate.

    12*a*   FEL PROCESS CONS III AVG N, Maxentius in facing quadriga or six-horse chariot. Fol: Rom 216, 264.

    12*b*   — — Maxentius in quadriga of elephants. Fol: Rom 215

311 Fifth anniversary of the reign, with celebration of African victories.

    13   VICTORIA AETERNA AVG N, Victory inscribing VOT V (or VOT/IS X or VOT XX FEL) on shield. Aur: Ost 8, 9/. ½ Fol: Ost 60–64

    14*a*   VOT QQ MVL X (FEL) in wreath. ½ Fol: Rom 237. ⅓ Fol: Rom 281

    14*b*   VOT QQ MVL XX in wreath. ½ Fol: Rom 238. ⅓ Fol: Rom 281

    14*c*   VOT X FEL in wreath. Den: Aqu 128; Rom 241

310–311 Death and consecration of Maximian and Galerius; celebration of them, together with Constantius, as relatives of Maxentius. Types 15, 16 and 18 all have *rev.* AETERNA/E MEMORIA/E, Eagle on domed shrine.

    15*a*   *Obv.* DIVO MAXIMIANO SEN AVG, Veiled head r. Fol: Ost 24; Rom 250

    15*b*   *Obv.* DIVO MAXIMIANO PATRI MAXENTIVS AVG, Same type. Fol: Ost 25; Rom 243

    15*c*   *Obv.* IMP MAXENTIVS DIVO MAXIMIANO PATRI, Same type. Fol: Ost 26; Rom 244, 251

    16*a*   *Obv.* DIVO MAXIMIANO IVN AVG, Veiled head r. Fol: Rom 246, 253

    16*b*   *Obv.* DIVO MAXIMIANO SOCERO MAXENTIVS AVG (socer = 'father-in-law'), Veiled head r. Fol: Ost 30; Rom 247, 254

    16*c*   *Obv.* IMP MAXENTIVS DIVO MAXIMIANO SOCERO, Same type. Fol: Ost 31; Rom 248, 255

16c

17   *Obv.* DIVO MAXIMIANO AVG, Veiled head r. *Rev.* MEMORIA FELIX, Lighted altar flanked by eagles. Fol: Rom 271

18*a*   *Obv.* DIVO CONSTANTIO COGN MAXENTIVS AVG (cognatus = 'relative'; Constantius was Maxentius' uncle-in-law), Same type. *Rev.* As 15. Fol: Ost 27

18*b*   *Obv.* IMP MAXENTIVS DIVO CONSTANTIO COGN, Same type. Fol: Ost 28; Rom 245, 252

18*c*   *Obv.* DIVO CONSTANTIO ADFINI MAXENTIVS AVG (adfinis = 'relative by marriage'), Veiled head r. Fol: Ost 28A

18*d*   *Obv.* IMP MAXENTIVS DIVO CONSTANTIO ADFINI, Same type. Fol: Ost 29

311   Prayers for success against Constantine.

19   VOT OPTATA ROMAE FEL, Victory writing on shield. Fol: Ost 57

ROMULUS

Valerius Romulus, son of Maxentius and Maximilla the daughter of Galerius, was born about 294 and named for his maternal grandmother Romula. Although he held the consulate in 308 and 309, he was never made Caesar. He died in 309 and was consecrated; for his coins, *see* Maxentius *10.*

DOMITIUS ALEXANDER

Usurper in Africa 308−310

L. Domitius Alexander, of Pannonian origin, became vicar of Africa at an advanced age. When Maxentius took control of the West, he became suspicious of Alexander, who was persuaded to revolt in 308. His control of Africa enabled him to cut off the grain supply of Rome, a serious danger which led Maxentius to send an expedition against him in 310. A brief campaign sufficed to defeat the usurper, who was put to death. His coinage celebrates his province, Africa, and expresses hopes of recognition by Rome.

308−310   Celebration of Africa and Carthage and its army; hopes of equality with Rome, and official recognition.

1   INVICTA ROMA FEL KARTHAGO, Carthage stg. Aur: Car 62/*C*3

2   − −Roma std. Aur: Car 63/*C*5

3   GLORIA EXERCIT/VS KART, Alexander riding r. Fol: Car 65−6/*C*2

4   AFRICA AVG N, Africa stg. Fol: Car 64/*C*1

LICINIUS

Augustus, November 308−September 324

Valerius Licinianus Licinius, born of humble origins in Dacia *c.* 265, was a friend of Galerius, with whom he fought against the Persians in 297 and by whom he was sent against Maxentius in 307. In 308, Galerius appointed him Augustus to replace Severus and to lead the fight to regain control of Italy. At the same time, Constantine was recognised as emperor in the East; he and Licinius shared the consulate in 309 and 312 (*1–2, 6*), and Licinius celebrated Constantine's anniversaries (*3*) and victories (*7*) on his coins. After the death and consecration of Galerius (*4–5*), Licinius shared the East with Maximinus, who moved rapidly to occupy Asia Minor and in 313 attacked the European provinces (*8*), but was defeated and killed, leaving Licinius supreme in the East. He then took up the consulate which Maximinus had vacated (*8A*).

Although the rest of his reign was eventful, the coinage of Licinius presents only his anniversaries and consulates. In 316, Constantine attacked and won some victories, but Licinius resisted vigorously, appointing Valens as co-emperor and securing a settlement. In this, Licinius' young son Licinius was made Caesar along with Constanine's sons, and Valens was deposed. Later, during the final struggle with Constantine in 324, Licinius appointed Martinian as co-emperor, but both were swiftly driven from Europe and decisively defeated at Chrysopolis opposite Byzantium. Licinius surrendered to Constantine and was exiled to Thessalonica, where he was executed the next year, ostensibly for involvement in a plot against the emperor.

309 Joint consulate with Constantine
  1 CONSVL DD NN, Licinius stg. r. (Constantine *18*). Aur: Tes 27/C8
  2 CONSVL/I P P PROCO(N)S/VL, Type as previous. Aur: Ant 101–2/ C10
310 Quinquennalia of Constantine.
  3 VOT X MVL XX in wreath (Constantine *21a*). Den: Tre 908
311 Death and consecration of Galerius.
  4 *Obv*. DIVO MAXIMIANO, Veiled bust r. *Rev*. MEM DIVI MAXIMIANI, Eagle on domed shrine. Fol: Tes 48
  5 *Obv*. DIVO GAL VAL MAXIMIANO (AVG), Veiled bust r. *Rev*. FORTI FORTVNAE, Fortuna stg. r. Fol: Sis 205–6, 220–1, 223–4, 226
312 Second consulate, with Constantine.
  6 CONSVL P P PROCONSVL, Type as *2*. (Constantine *31*). Aur: Ant 156
— — Constantine's defeat of Maxentius.
  7 VICTORIA CONSTANTINI AVG, Victory advancing l. (Constantine *32*). Sol: Rom 285/C169
313 Departure to meet the attack of Maximinus.
  8 PROFECTIO AVGG, Licinius riding r.
     Aur: Sis 218/C243
— — Third consulate, replacing Maximinus.
  8A CONSVL P P PROCONSVL, Type as *2*. Aur: Ant 6
— — Fifth anniversary of reign.
  9a VOTIS V MVLTIS X, Victory stg. r., holding shield inscribed VICTORIA AVG. Aur: Ant 2–4; Her 4; Nic 2, 6

9*b* VICTORIA AVGG NN, Victory stg. r., holding shield inscribed VOT V MVL X. Aur: Nic 3

315 Fourth consulate.

10 CONSVL P P PROCONSVL, Type as 2. Aur: Ant 9

317 Decennalia of Licinius.

11 IOVI CONS LICINI AVG, Jupiter std. l. on platform inscribed SIC X SIC XX. Aur: Ant 20; Nic 18–20

12 VICTORIA AVGG NN, Victory stg. r., inscribing VOT X MVL XX on shield. Aur: Nic 10

13 SIC X SIX XX in wreath. Aur: Her 7, 9–10

13

318 Fifth consulate.

14 CONSVL P P PROCONSVL, Type as 2. Aur: Ant 19, 23

320 Fifteenth anniversary of the reign of Constantine, celebrated in the west as also the fifteenth anniversary of Licinius.

15 VIRTVS EXERCIT, Standard inscribed VOT X or XX, captive below (Constanine *68*). Fol: Aqu 39–40 (x), 50–1, 59, 63; Sis 110, 119 (x), 121, 128–9, 135; Tes 76, 82; Tic 115–6, 123, 128; Tre 267, 294–5

16 ROMAE AETERNAE, Roma std. l, with shield inscribed XV (Constantine *69*). Fol: Rom 151, 196

17*a* VOT X ET XV F in wreath (Constantine *70a*). Fol: Rom 202–3

17*b* VOT XV FEL XX in wreath (Constantine *70b*). Fol: Rom 215, 221

17*c* VOT XX MVLT XXX in wreath (Constantine *70c*). Fol: Tes 33–5

18*a* D/OMINI N (LIC) LICINI AVG/VSTI around VOT XX in wreath. Fol: Aqu 67, 86; Are 224, 229, 234, 240; Rom 225, 233; Sis 150, 160; Tes 89, 97, 102–4, 110–2

18*b* LICINI AVG/VSTI around VOT XX. Fol: Are 209, 214, 218–9; Sis 141

18*c* D N LICINI INVICT AVG around VOT XX (Constantine *71c*). Fol: Tic 132–3, 146–7

18*d* D N LICINI MAX AVG around VOT XX in wreath. Fol: Sis 149

18*e* D N CONSTANTINI MAX AVG around VOT XX in wreath (Constantine *71a*). Fol: Aqu 66; Tic 144

321 Quinquennalia of Licinius II.

18 *Obv.* LICINIVS AVG OB DIEM V (annorum) FILII SVI, Bare head r. *Rev.* IOVI CONS LICINI AVG, Type as 11. Aur: Ant 31–2; Nic 41

LICINIUS II

Caesar March 317–September 324

Fl. Valerius Constantinus Licinianus Licinius, born about 313, was made Caesar as a child and deposed with his father in 324. He was exiled with Licinius, and condemned to slavery in 335.

317   Proclamation as Caesar.
1   PRINCIPI/A IVVENTVTIS, Licinius II stg. l. Avfrac: Tic 113. Fol: Sis 40. $\frac{1}{2}$ Fol: Rom 139
320   Fifteenth anniversary of Constantine.
2   BEATA TRANQVILLITAS, Altar inscribed VOTIS XX (Constantine *67*). Fol: Tre 310–1
3*a*   VIRTVS EXERCIT, Standard inscribed VOT XX, captive below (Constantine *68*). Fol: Aqu 54–5; Are 203, 206; Sis 139; Tes 79; Tic 118–20, 125; Tre 256, 271–2, 298–9
3*b*   — — Standard inscribed VOT X. Aqu 44; Sis 114–5, 125, 132
4   ROMAE AETERNAE, Roma std. l. with shield inscribed XV (Constantine *69*). Fol: Rom 153–4, 198–9
5*a*   VOT X ET XV F in wreath (Constantine *70a*). Fol: Rom 205, 208
5*b*   VOT XV FEL XX in wreath (Constantine *70b*). Fol: Rom 217, 223
5*c*   VOT XX in wreath (Constantine *70d*). Fol: Rom 212
321   Quinquennalia of the Caesars, celebrated in the West with the fifteenth anniversary of Constantine (also types of his sons).
6*a*   CAESARVM NOSTRORVM around VOT/IS V, sometimes in wreath. Fol: Aqu 71–3, 91–2; Are 211, 215, 221, 227, 231, 236, 238 (VOT X), 242; Rom 230, 235; Sis 143, 154–5, 162; Tes 86, 92–3, 99, 107, 114, 119
6*b*   DOMINOR/VM NOSTROR/VM CAESS around VOT V in wreath. Fol: Tic 136–7, 151
6*c*   VOT V MVLT X CAESS in wreath. Fol: Tes 41–2
— —   Quinquennalia of Licinius II.
7   IOVI CONSERVATORI CAES, Jupiter std. on platform inscribed SIC V SIC X, eagle at feet (Licinius *18*). Aur: Ant 33; Nic 42

7

VALENS

Augustus October 316—January 317; no historical types.

MARTINIAN

Augustus July—September 324; no historical types, but *see* Constantine *99b*.

CONSTANTINE

Caesar July 306 / Augustus Autumn 307 (in the West); Filius
Augustorum 309 / Augustus 310 (in the East) — May 337

Flavius Valerius Constantinus, known to posterity as Constantine the
Great for his accomplishments in transforming the history of Rome and
the entire western world, was born in Naissus (now Nish, in Yugoslavia)
c. 272, the illegitimate son of Constantius, then an army officer, and
Helena, who entertained guests in an inn. After his father became Caesar
in 293, Constantine moved to the court of Diocletian in Nicomedia
and there received his education. When Diocletian abdicated in 305,
Constantine joined his father, and together they crossed to Britain. He
was proclaimed emperor (*1—4*) at York when Constantius died in 306. He
had his father consecrated (*5—8*; *cf. 55—56*), but nevertheless showed a
clear partiality for Christianity.

Constantine's proclamation had been made by the troops, without the
approval of the senior Augustus Galerius who, however, granted him the
title of Caesar. The elevation of Constantine stirred Maxentius, son of
Maximian, who revolted in Italy. He was soon joined by his father,
restored as Augustus (*9—10*), and faced with the open hostility of Galerius.
In order to find a counterweight, the two Italian emperors appealed to
Constantine, who made an alliance with them (*12—15*) and married
Maximian's daughter Fausta. As a result, Maximian granted him the title
Augustus (*16—17*). In 308, however, Maximian rebelled against his son
and took refuge with Constantine in Gaul. The situation was becoming
so anarchic that Galerius summoned a meeting with Maximian and
Diocletian, now in retirement, at Carnuntum, where Maximian was
obliged to abdicate once again and Constantine's position in the West was
officially recognised, but not as Augustus. Instead, he and Maximinus,
the eastern Caesar, received the novel title *Filius Augustorum*, 'sons of
the Augusti' (*18—19*). This appears on coins struck in the territories of
Licinius and Galerius; in his own domains, Constantine never abandoned
the title Augustus. In May 309, however, Maximinus, discontent with the
subordinate title, claimed that of Augustus and was so recognised by
Galerius. Consequently, Constantine also became Augustus, once again,
in the year which marked the fifth anniversary of his reign (*20—21*).

During this period, Constantine was constantly occupied on the frontier with the attacks of the Franks and Alamanni. Thanks to the effectiveness of his Gallic troops he was successful (*22–27*), even though his efforts were interrupted by the revolt and third proclamation of Maximian (who was soon suppressed and executed). Constantine's campaigns took him to Britain twice in these years (*9, 28*) to consolidate his position in the West. He also made successful use of propaganda in his advance to supremacy, by revealing the surprising discovery that he was descended from Claudius Gothicus, whose victories had led Rome toward stability; although announced in 310, this relationship was not advertised on the coinage until 316 (*53–54*). As part of the same effort, Constantine reestablished good relations with Galerius, recognising his consuls in the West (*29–30*) and, when he died, made an alliance with Licinius (*31*) who had taken control of the Balkans. He was now free to move against Maxentius.

The campaign in Italy was brief, decided by one battle at the Milvian Bridge outside Rome, where Constantine became master of the entire West (*32–38*). The war was attended by an event of momentous significance when Constantine saw a vision of a cross in the sky before the battle, and ordered the labarum, the Christian sign, placed on the standards of his troops. From this time, he was a defender of the Church and functionally a Christian, whatever the exact nature of his beliefs. The central event, the vision, appears not on Constantine's coins, but on those of Vetranio issued in 350. The coinage of Constantine, however, does show a clear, if gradual, transition in which the pagan types die out to be replaced by images which are neutral (most of them related to the emperor), but rarely specifically Christian. The last openly pagan types were struck in the West in 321 and in the East (which Constantine did not control) in 324 (for Christianity on the coins, see the appendix, with types *93–110*).

Constantine, now master of the West, still had to face Licinius, who was equally supreme in the East. At first, relations were friendly (*39, 42*), for Constantine was busy in Gaul where he won further victories against the German tribes (*43*), and in Britain, which he again visited (*44*). In 315, he entered his fifth consulate in Treveri where, in antique style, he was proclaimed imperator and gave a donative (*45–47*), the last appearance of Liberalitas on the coinage; this year was also the tenth anniversary of his reign (*48–50*). Constantine now turned to the East and in the Spring of 316 invaded Licinius' territory, after addressing the troops and claiming universal supremacy (*51–52*). Although the advantage was initially with Constantine, he won no decisive victory, but settled on terms instead. By the agreement reached in March 317, Constantine's sons, Crispus and Constantine, were promoted Caesars, together with Licinius's son Licinius. Constantine used this occasion of founding an imperial dynasty to celebrate his imperial ancestors Claudius Gothicus, Constantius and Maximian (*53–59*).

After the war, Constantine spent much time in his newly conquered Balkan territories and in northern Italy (*60, 62–3*), and twice held the consulate (*61,63*). The West was entrusted to Crispus, now an adult, who justified his position by defeating the Franks (*64*). In 320, Constantine celebrated his fifteenth anniversary with an extensive coinage (*65—71*) and the next year the quinquennalia of the Caesars (*72—73*). In 322, Constantine crushed a Sarmatian invasion of the Balkans, which led his army into Licinius' territory. Because of this transgression, the coins which Constantine issued to celebrate the victory (*74*) infuriated Licinius who refused to allow them to circulate in the East. War between the two was in any case imminent and soon broke out: Constantine attacked Thrace with a huge army and drove Licinius first to take refuge in Byzantium, then to cross into Asia where he was decisively defeated in September 324. Constantine was now sole ruler of the empire.

In supreme power, Constantine actively patronised Christianity and closed many pagan shrines. He visited his new domains, reaching Antioch (*75—76*) in 324, then returning to Nicomedia for the celebration of his vicennalia (*77—82*) in 325. The anniversary was a suitable occasion for raising his third son, Constantius, to Caesar (*83*); it also coincided with a meeting of universal importance (not celebrated on the coinage), the first ecumenical council of the Church held in Nicaea. In the next year, the Caesars celebrated their decennalia (*84*).

Wars continued along the northern frontier, where Constantine was generally successful. Control was secured by construction of the fortress of Daphne (*85*) on the north bank of the Danube. Since the main threats to the empire came from the Balkan region and the East, Constantine undertook another work of universal significance by establishing a base convenient to both when he refounded Byzantium as Constantinople (*86—90*), the new capital of the empire, in 330. That year was his twenty-fifth anniversary (*91a*); the thirtieth (*91b—92*) was celebrated in 335. This was a remarkable occasion, for no emperor since Augustus had reigned so long. By now, Constantine was planning a great expedition against Persia, and gave his nephew Hanniballianus the title King of Kings as a sign that he would replace the Sassanian monarch. In 337, however, before the war could begin, Constantine fell ill and died near Nicomedia. Much of the activity of his enormously significant and eventful reign is reflected in the coinage, which contains the last instances of many classical types. His is the last reign to produce a coinage of real interest; as Christianity and despotism took firm root, the message of the coins became limited and unvarying, focusing ever more on the emperor himself.

Caesar 306—307 (310)

306   Proclamation as Caesar, with vows.
  1   PRINCIPI IVVENTVT/IS Constantine stg. between standards (several varieties). Aur: Rom 141, 150; 151; Ser 20; Sis 152; Tre 627. Fol: Tre 733—5; 743. Den: Tre 679—80
  2   VOT X FELICITER in wreath. ½ Arg: Tre 641

3   HAEC VOTA MVLT ANN in wreath. ½ Arg: Tre 639

4   PLVR NATAL FEL in wreath. ½ Arg: Tre 640/*C*394. Fol: Tre 745−6

— — Consecration of Constantius. Many of these were struck by Constantine as Augustus.

5   *Obv.* DIVVS CONSTANTIVS, Bare head r. *Rev.* CONSECRATIO, Pyre surmounted by image of Constantius in quadriga. Sol: Tre 809/*C*28

6   *Obv.* DIVO CONSTANTIO PIO, Laureate or veiled head r. *Rev.* CONSECRATIO, eagle. Fol: Lug 202, 251

7   — — MEMORIA FELIX, Eagle stg. in temple. Fol: Lug 269

8   — — — — Altar with eagle above or beside. Fol: Lon 110; Lug 264−8, 297; Tre 789. ½ Fol: Tre 790

307 Restoration of Maximian, with joint vows.

9*a*   VOTIS X in wreath. Den: Tre 750

9*b*   VOT X CAESS (NN) in wreath. Den: Tre 748−9

10   MVLT NATAL FEL in wreath. Den: Tre 744

— — Visit to Britain.

11   ADVENTVS AVGG, Constantine riding l., captive below. Fol: Lon 82

307−311 Alliance with Maxentius, reflected in common types, most of which continued to be struck by Constantine as Augustus.

12   CONSERV/ATORES VRB SVAE, Image of Rome std. in temple (Maxentius *4*). Fol: Aqu 117, 120, 121; Rom 164, 196−7, 200−1, 203; Tic 93

13*a*   ROMAE AETER, Same type. Fol: Lon 99

13*b*   ROMA AETERNA, Roma std. l. (Maxentius *3b*) Aur: Car 48

14   CONSERVATOR/ES KART SVAE, Carthage stg. in temple (Maxentius *7*). Arg: Car 49/*C*72 (XCVI in ex). Fol: Car 61

14   23

15   CONSERVATOR AFRICAE SVAE, Africa stg. (Maxentius *2*). Fol: Car 55, 58

Augustus 307−337

307 Proclamation as Augustus, with vows.

16   CONSTANTINO P AVG BONO REI PVBLICAE NATO, Constantine stg. r. Fol: Lug 252, 286

17   VOT X AVG N in wreath. Den: Tre 791–2

Filius Augustorum (in East) 309–310

309–10   Recognition as Filius Augustorum by Galerius, and joint consulate with Licinius. *Obv.* (FL VAL) CONSTANTINVS FIL AVG/G, Laureate bust r.

18   CONSVL DD NN, Constantine stg. r. Aur: Tes 28/*C*115

19*a*   GENIO AVGVSTI, Genius stg. l. Fol: Sis 200

19*b*   GENIO CAESARIS, Genius stg. l. Fol: Ale 99–100; Ant 104; Nic 56; Sis 203; Tes 32

19*c*   GENIO FIL AVGG, Same type. Fol: Ant 105, 111

19*d*   VIRTVS EXERCITVS, Virtus adv. r. Fol: Ale 113, 117, Tes 39 (VIRTVTI)

Augustus 310–337

310   Celebration of fifth anniversary of reign.

20   VOTIS V MVLTIS X, Victory inscribing VICTORIA AVG on shield. Aur: Ant 129. Sol: Tre 821

21*a*   VOT X MVL XX in wreath. Den: Tre 901–2, 907–13

21*b*   VOTIS X in wreath. Den: Tre 903–6

310   Victories over Franks and Alemanni, won with Constantine's Gallic troops.

22   GAVDIVM ROMANORVM, ALAMANNIA in ex., Alamannia std. l. on ground, trophy above. Sol: Tre 823

23   – – FRANCIA, Francia std. l. on ground, trophy above. Sol: Tre 824/*C*168

24   GAVDIVM REI PVBLICAE, Trophy between std. captives Alamannia and Francia. Sol: Tre 811/*C*163

25   FELICITAS REI PVBLICAE, Constantine std. on platform with two officers; three kneeling figures below. Sol: Tre 810

26   GLORIA EXERCITVS GALL, Constantine riding r. Sol: Tre 812

27   VIRTVS EXERCITVS GALL, Mars advancing r. (This type was repeated in 317 at Ale, Sis, Tes and Tre.) Sol: Tre 820

– –   Visit to Britain.

28   ADVENTVS AVG/G (N), Constantine riding r., captive below. Fol: Lon 133–45

311   Reconciliation with Galerius; recognition of Galerius and Maximinus as consuls; quinquennium of Maximinus.

29   CONSVL P P PROCONSVL, Galerius stg. Aur: Ant 127

30   AVGG above crossed hands within wreath. Aur: Ant 126

30*a*   VOTIS V MVLTIS X, Victory stg. r., placing shield inscribed VICTORIA AVGVSTORVM. Aur: Ant 129

312 Joint consulate with Licinius.

    31   CONSVL P P PROCONSVL, Constantine stg. l. Aur: Ant 156−7

—— Defeat of Maxentius at the battle of the Milvian Bridge and conversion of Constantine (for Christianity on his coins, *see* Appendix, types *93−110*); 'liberation' of Rome, with types reflecting those of Maxentius; praise of Constantine's Gallic troops.

    32   VICTORIA CONSTANTINI AVG, Victory advancing l. Sol: Ost 70; Rom 285; Tre 819/C600

    33   RESTITVTORI LIBERTATIS, Roma presenting globe to Constantine. Sol: Tic 31−2; Tre 22−6

    34   LIBERATORI VRBIS SVAE, Image of Rome in temple. Fol: Rom 303−4

    35   RESTITVTOR VRBIS SVAE, Type as previous. Fol: Rom 312

    36*a*   ROMAE RESTITVTAE, Roma std. l. Fol: Lon 272−4

    36*b*   ROMAE AETER AVGG, Same type. Fol: Lon 269−71

    37   RECVPERATORI VRB SVAE, Soldier presenting Victory to std. Constantine. Fol: Are 13, 33−4

    38   VIRTVS EXERCIT GALL, Virtus leaning on spear. ½ Fol: Rom 359−60

313 Joint consulate with Licinius.

    39   CONSVL P P PROCONSVL, Type as 31. Aur: Ant 5

—— Transfer of the mint from Ostia to Arelate.

    40   PROVIDENTIAE AVGG, Arelate receiving female who holds cornucopia and stands on ship. Fol: Are 30−1

    41   VTILITAS PVBLICA, Soldier receiving Utlitas who stands on ship holding cornucopia and scales. Fol: Are 49−51

—— Quinquennalia of Licinius.

    42   VOTIS V MVLTIS X, Victory stg. r., holding shield inscribed VICTORIA AVG (Licinius *9a*). Aur: Ant 1; Her 3; Nic 1, 5

—— Successes in war against the Germans.

    43   GAVDIVM ROMANORVM, FRAN ET ALAM in ex., Trophy between captives. Sol: Tic 28, 37

313 or 314 Visit to Britain.

    44   ADVENTVS AVG N, Constantine riding l. Fol: Lon 1, 21

315 Entry into fourth consulate at Treveri, with proclamation as imperator and distribution of money to the army.

    45   FELIX PROCESS COS IIII (AVG N), Constantine stg. l. Sol: Aqu 28; Tic 26; Tre 12

    46   (P M) TR(I)B P CO(N)S IIII P P PROCO(N)S(VL), Constantine std. l. on curule chair. Fol: Are 48, 69; Tic 30, 38; Tre 18−21

    47   LIBERALITAS XI IMP IIII COS P P, Liberalitas stg. l. (The numerals are to be associated with the word following them. This is the last appearance of Liberalitas on the Roman coinage.) Sol: Tic 53

—— Decennalia of Constantine.

    48   VOTA PVBLICA, Constantine stg. between Respublica (l.) who offers Victory on globe and Pax (r.) who offers wreath. Sol: Tre 89−91

49*a*   VICTORE N AVG N VOTIS (X), Victory std. r. with shield inscribed (X) MVL XX. Sol: Tic 40, 50, 58

49*b*   VICTORE AVG N (VOTIS), Victory inscribing X (MVL) XX on shield. Sol: Tre 86–8

49*c*   VICTORIA/E AVGG NN, Victory stg. r., inscribing VOT X (MVL XX) on shield. Aur: Nic 9; Fol: Lug 28

49*d*   VICTORIA AETERNA AVG N, Victory std. r., inscribing VOTIS XX on shield. Fol: Are 70

49*e*   VICTORIBVS AVGG NN VOTIS, Victory facing, holding shield inscribed X. Den: Tre 38

50   SIC X SIC XX in wreath. Aur: Her 8

316 Campaign against Licinius: address to troops, and propaganda claiming supremacy as a ruler subject not to the stars, but only to God.

51   ADLOCVTIO AVG, Constantine on platform addressing soldiers and captives. Sol: Tic 48

52   RECTOR TOTIVS ORBIS, Constantine, crowned by Victory, std. l., holding zodiac. Sol: Tic 54

— —   Creation of Crispus and Constantine Jr. as Caesars, the occasion for celebrating the memory of Constantine's real or imaginary ancestors; Claudius Gothicus, from whom he claimed to be descended; Constantius, his father; and Maximinus, his father-in-law.

53

53   *Obv.* DIVO CLAVDIO (OPT/IMO IMP), Veiled head r. *Rev.* REQVIES OPT/IMOR/VM MER/ITOR/VM, Claudius std. l. Fol: Rom 106. ½ Fol: Aqu 23, 26; Are 173, 176; Rom 109; Sis 43, 45; Tes 26; Tre 203, 207

54*a*   — —*Rev.* MEMORIA AETERNAE, Eagle l. or r. Fol: Rom 112. ½ Fol: Rom 115–6, 119

54*b*   — — — — Lion adv. l. or r. ½ Fol: Rom 122, 125, 128

55*a*   *Obv.* DIVO CONSTANTIO (PIO PRINC/IPI), Veiled head r. *Rev.* REQVIES OPT/IMOR/VM MER/ITOR, Constantius std. l. Fol: Rom 105. ½ Fol: Aqu 22, 25; Are 175,178; Rom 108; Sis 42,26; Tes 25

55*b*   — — but *obv.* DIVO CONSTANTIO OPT/IMO IMP. ½ Fol: Tre 201–2, 206

56*a*   *Obv.* as 55a. *Rev.* as 54a. Fol: Rom 111. ½ Fol: Rom 114, 118

56*b*   — — *Rev.* as 54b. ½ Fol: Rom 121, 127

57a   *Obv.* DIVO MAXIMIANO SEN (FORT IMP), Veiled head r. *Rev.* REQVIES OPT/IMOR/VM MER/IT/OR, Maximian std. l. Fol: Rom 104. ½ Fol: Aqu 21,24; Are 174,177; Rom 107; Sis 41,44

57b   — — but *obv.* DIVO MAXIMIANO OPT/IMO IMP. ½ Fol: Tes 24; Tre 200, 204−5

58a   *Obv.* as 57a. *Rev.* as 54a. Fol: Rom 110. ½ Fol: Rom 113,117

58b   — — *Rev.* as 54b. ½ Fol: Rom 120,123,126

59   GAVDIVM REIPVBLICAE, Constantine stg. between sons, to one of whom he presents globe. Sol: Tre 185

318   Arrival in Aquilea, Constantine's base for the year.

60   ADVENTVS AVGVSTI N, Constantine riding l. Sol: Aqu 27

319   Fifth consulate.

61   CONSVL P P PROCONSVL, Type as 31. Aur: Ant 22

320   Sixth consulate, entered in Sirmium.

62   FELIX PROCESS COS VI (AVG N), Constantine stg. l. Sol: Ant 41; Aqu 34; Sir 1, 4; Tic 104

63   P M TRIB P COS VI P P PROCOS, Type as 46. Sol: Tre 244−5

— —   Victories of Crispus in Germany.

64   GAVDIVM, ROMANORVM, FRANCIA in ex., Francia stg. l. Sol: Sis 23; Den: Tre 365

— —   Fifteenth anniversary of reign.

65   VICTORIA AVGG ET CAESS NN, Victory std. r., holding shield inscribed VOT XX; in front, trophy with captive below. Sol: Sir 10; Tic 110

66   VICTORIAE PERPETVAE, Victory stg. r., inscribing VOT XX on shield. Sol: Aqu 37; Tic 109. Den: Sir 12−3

67   BEAT/A TRANQVILLITAS (often TRANQLITAS), Altar inscribed VO/TIS XX. Fol: Lon 199−207, 217, 220−7, 238−46, 261−72; Lug 125−31, 153−61, 197−201; Tre 303−6, 316−9, 341−5, 368−71, 389−92, 416, 423−4

68   VIRTVS EXERCIT, Standard inscribed VOT XX, captives below. Fol: Aqu 47−9, 57−8; Are 202, 205; Lon 185−6, 191−3; Lug 106−7, 113−5, Sis 109, 120, 127, 134; Tes 72, 75; Tic 114, 122, 127; Tre 254, 266, 291−3

69   ROMAE AETERNAE, Roma std. r. with shield inscribed XV. Fol: Rom 146−50, 194−5

70a   VOT X ET XV F in wreath. Fol: Rom 201, 207

70b   VOT XV FEL XX in wreath. Fol: Rom 213−4, 219−20

70c   VOT XX MVLT XXX in wreath. Fol: Tes 27−32, 52−6

70d   VOT XX in wreath. Fol: Rom 211

71a   D N CONSTANTINI (MAX) AVG around VOT XX in wreath. Fol: Aqu 64−5, 85, 104; Are 223, 228, 233, 239, 246, 252−3; Her 56, 60, 64, 66; Rom 225−7, 232, 237, 245; Sis 148, 159, 168, 171, 174, 177, 180; Tes 84 (no DN), 88, 96, 101, 109, 117, 123−4; Tic 130−1, 140−3, 163, 167; Tre 439

71b   CONSTANTINI AVG/VSTI around VOTIS XX. Fol: Are 208, 213, 216−7; Lug 91−2, 96−7; Sis 140

71a   71b

71c   D N LICINI INVICT AVG around VOT XX in wreath. Fol: Tic 145

71d   LICINI AVG around VOTIS XX. Fol: Lug 94

321   Quinquennalia of the Caesars.

72   CRISPVS ET CONSTANTINVS CC, Busts vis-à-vis. Arg: Sir 14

73   CAESARVM NOSTRORVM around VOT X in wreath (type issued 323−4, perhaps in anticipation of decennalia of Caesars). Fol: Tre 430

322   Victories over the Sarmatians.

74   SARMATIA DEVICTA, Victory advancing r., captive on ground. Are 257−8; Lon 289−90; Lug 209, 212, 214, 219, 222; Sir 48; Tre 429, 435

324   Visit to Antioch, with series struck to commemorate the imperial family; type 76 was struck also for Crispus, Constantine II, Helena and Fausta.

75   ADVENTVS AVG N, Constantine riding l. Sol: Ant 48

76   CONSTANTINVS AVG, Wreath above. Fol: Ant 52, 57

325   Twentieth anniversary of the reign of Constantine; arrival in Nicomedia for the celebration.

77   ADVENTVS AVGVSTI N, Type as 60. Sol: Nic 58

78   VICTORIA CONSTANTINI AVG, Victory std. r. with shield inscribed VOT XX. Sol: Nic 103; Rom 273; Sir 9. Avfrac: Rom 274; Sir 11,66; Tes 140; Tic 197

79   VICTORIA AVGG ET CAESS NN, As previous, with trophy and captives in front.
Sol: Cyz 22−3; Nic 63−5

80   VOTA PVBLICA, Type as 48. Sol: Nic 66−7

81   D N CONSTANTINI MAX AVG around VOT XXX in wreath. Fol: Her 69−73, 82, 87, 90−4, 106; Rom 318−20, 322; Tic 174, 186

82   PLVRA NATAL FEL in wreath. Fol: Rom 321

− −   Promotion of Constantius to Caesar.

83a   FELICITAS ROMANORVM, Constantine stg. in arch with Crispus, Constantine II and Constantius II. Arg: Nic 88−9

83b   − −   but two sons only (struck after the execution of Crispus). Arg: Her 105; Sir 15; Tes 140A

326   Decennalia of the Caesars.

84   NOBB CAESS, Busts of Crispus and Constantine II vis-a-vis. Arg: Con 6

328   Construction of the fortress of Daphne on the Danube.

85   CONSTANTINIANA DAFNE, Victory std l., kneeling captive at feet. Sol: Con 36; Arg: Con 37; Fol: Con 29−35, 38

85   88a

330   Restoration of Byzantium, and its refoundation as Constantinople.

     86   PIETAS AVGVSTI NOSTRI, Constantine, crowned by Victory, raising kneeling turreted female. Sol: Nic 165–8

     87   *Obv.* CONSTANTINOPOLIS, Helmeted bust r. *Rev.* (No legend), Victory stg. r. on prow. Fol: Ale, Ant, Aqu, Are, Con, Cyz, Her, Lug, Nic, Rom, Sis, Tes, Tre *passim.*

     88a   *Obv.* VRBS ROMA, Helmeted bust l. *Rev.* (No legend), She-wolf l., suckling twins. Fol: Ale, Ant, Aqu, Are, Con, Cyz, Her, Lug, Nic, Rom, Sis, Tes, Tre *passim.*

     88b   As previous, but VRBS ROMA BEATA. Fol: Rom 408

     89   *Obv.* POP ROMANVS, Draped bust l. *Rev.* (No legend), Milvian bridge. Æ4: Con 21

     90   – – *Rev.* (No legend), Star in wreath. Æ4: Con 22

330   Twenty-fifth anniversary of the reign.

     91a   VICTORIA CONSTANTINI AVG, Victory std. r., holding shield inscribed VOT XXX. Sol: Con 51; Nic 171. Avfrac: Con 52; Nic 172

335   Thirtieth anniversary of the reign.

     91b   Type and legend as *91a.* Sol: Aqu 130; Con 107; Nic 175–80, 185; Sis 242–3, 257. Avfrac: Con 117; Nic 185; Tes 179; Sis 258

     91c   As previous, but VOT XXXX. Sol: Con 108. Avfrac: Con 118

     91d   – – Victory advancing r., holding shield inscribed VOT XXX; foot on captive. Sol: Sis 244

     91e   – – Victory advancing l.; VOT XXX in field r. Sol: Ant 96

     92   VOTIS XXX in wreath. Aur: Tes 206–7

92

Appendix: Constantine and Christianity

In terms of world history, the central event of the reign of Constantine was his conversion to Christianity in 312, on the eve of the battle of the

Milvian bridge. According to the story, he saw a cross in the sky with the inscription IN HOC SIGNO VINCES, thereupon ordered his troops to paint the *labarum*, the monogram of Christ, on their shields, and proceeded to win the decisive victory which gave him control of the West. Although the miracle does not appear on the coins of Constantine (though it does form a type of Vetranio: *1*), the labarum is occasionally present, first as a mark of issue in the reverse field, then as part of the decoration of Constantine's helmet, and finally as a major type. In some cases, the Christian significance of the symbol may be ambiguous, but the presence of the labarum, which Constantine adopted as his personal emblem after the battle, may generally be taken as numismatic evidence for his conversion. A mark which resembles the sign of the Cross appears on a few types; its interpretation as a Christian symbol, rather than a simple design, has also been disputed.

Other evidence for the triumph of Christianity relates to the pagan gods. Between 317 and 312, they disappear from the coinage of the West, never to return; a tradition as old as the Roman coinage itself was at an end. The change came later in the East, controlled by Licinius, but here too, the pagan gods vanish after the triumph of Constantine. They never appear on the coins struck in his new capital, Constantinople. The last pagan types, therefore may also be taken as historical, representing the end of the ancient state religion. Since these coins were issued under the authority of Constantine and Licinius for themselves and their Caesars, they will be listed here by type, followed by indication of the ruler and the date of their last issue. Coins which show the labarum and the sign of the cross will follow.

The following abbreviations are used:
Cr=Crispus; Con II=Constantine II; Lic=Licinius.

316–321 Last pagan types in the West; coins struck in the name of Constantine unless otherwise specified.

93 SOLI COMITI AVG N, Sol presenting Victory to Constantine. Sol: Aqu 35 (320); Sir 8 (321); Tic 108 (320)

94 SOLI INVICTO COMITI, Sol crowning Constantine. Sol: Sir 21–2 (321)

95 − −Sol stg. 1. Fol: Aqu 3–5 (317); Are 180, 184 (319); Lon 137–41, 149–51; 142–4, 152 (Cri); 145–7, 153 (Con II) (all 318); Lug 51–62 (316); Rom 136 (318); Sis 31–4 (317), 36 (Con II); Tic 67–8 (318), 69 (Lic); Tre 157–62, 164–7 (318), 163, 168 (Con II)

96 CLARITAS REIPVBLICAE, Sol stg. l., the normal type for the Caesars. Sol: Tes 8 (317), 9 (Con II). Fol: Aqu 14 (317), 15–20 (Con II); Are 181–2 (Con II 319); Lon 124–6, 148 (318), 127–30 (Cr), 131 (Con II); Rom 129–30 (Cr 318); Sis 35 (317), 37 (Cri), 38 (Lic II); Tes 23 (Con II 318); Tic 79 (Cr 318), 80–1 (Con II); Tre 175–8 (Cr), 182 (Cr), 179–81 (Con II), 183 (Con II)

97   VIRTVS EXERCIT, Sol stg. above plan of Roman camp. Fol: Tes 66−7 (320), 68 (Lic), 69 (Cr), 71 (Con II), 70 (Lic II)

98   IOVI CONSERVATORI AVG, Eagle carrying Jupiter; types of Licinius. Fol: Are 196−7 (319); Tre 210−2 (319)

99*a*   IOVI CONSERVATORI, Jupiter stg. l. Types of Licinius unless specified. Fol: Aqu 6−8 (317); Rom 131−2 (318), 133 (Lic II); Tes 19 (Con 317); Tic 70 (318), 71−2 (Lic II)

321−4   Last pagan types in the East.

99*b*   As previous. Fol: Ale 28, 32 (Lic), 27 (Con), 29 (Cr), 31 (Con II), 30,33 (Lic II); Ant 35 (Lic), 34 (Con), 36 (Lic II); Cyz 15 (Lic), 14 (Con), 16 (Martinian), 17 (Cr), 19 (Con II), 18 (Lic II); Her 52 (Lic), 51 (Con), 53 (Cr), 55 (Con II), 54 (Lic II); Nic 44 (Lic), 43 (Con), 45−7 (Martinian), 48 (Cr), 50 (Con II), 49 (Lic II)

316−335 The cross as a field mark on the reverse. The Christian significance of these types is questionable.

100   SOLI INVICTO COMITI, Type *94*, cross in field (316). Fol: Tic 43−5, 46 (Lic)

101   MARTI CONSERVATORI, Mars stg. r., cross in field (316). Fol: Tic 47

104

102   GLORIA EXERCITVS, Two soldiers stg. with two standards between them; cross in field (334−5). Fol: Aqu 124 (Con), 125 (Con II), 126 (Constantius II), 127 (Constans)

320−337 The labarum as a field mark on the reverse.

103   VIRTVS EXERCIT, Type *68* (320). Aqu 58 [Con], 59 (Lic), 60−1 (Cr), 62 (Con II); Sis 138 [Lic], 139 (Lic II); Tes 82 (Lic), 83 (Con II); Tic 118−120, 125 (Lic II), 121, 126, 129 (Con II)

104   GLORIA EXERCITVS, As *102*, but one standard with labarum (324). Fol: Are 381 (Con), 382 (Con II), 383 (Constantius II), 384 (Constans)

105   CONSTANTINOPOLIS, Type *80* (330). Fol: Are 386

109   110

106   VRBS ROMA, Type *86a* (330). Fol: Are 385
107   VICTORIA CONSTANTINI AVG, Victory advancing l. (337). Sol:
Ant 98−100 (Con), 101 (Con II)
319−320   The sign of the Cross as a design.
108   VICTORIAE LAETAE PRINC PERP, Two Victories stg. facing each
other, holding shield inscribed VOT P R on altar decorated
with cross in wreath (319−20). Fol: Lon 166−73 (Con),
174−9 (Cr), 180−2 (Con II): Note that only some of these
actually bear the cross: see the note in *RIC*; Tic 86 (Con; plain
cross)
319   Labarum on Constantine's helmet.
109   *Obv.* IMP CONSTANTINVS AVG, Bust l., with shield, spear and
helmet decorated with labarum. *Rev.* As *108*, but no cross on
altar. Fol: Sis 61
327   The labarum as a main type.
110   SPES PVBLIC, Labarum with three medallions piercing serpent.
Fol: Con 19, 26

HELENA

Flavia Julia Helena was born about 250 in a town of Bithynia which was
later named Helenopolis for her. She had a son, Constantine, by
Constantius who was an army officer at the time. Constantine made her
Augusta in 324, by which time she had been converted to Christianity.
The enormous wealth derived from her position enabled her to devote
much attention to the church, including a pilgrimage to the Holy Land
during which she is reputed to have discovered the true cross. She died at
an advanced age around 330.

324   Promotion to Augusta, as part of the celebrations for the victory
over Licinius.
1   SECVRITAS REIPVBLICAE, Helena stg. l. Sol: Nic 79−80; Sir 60;
Tes 134, 149; Tic 183. Fol: Ale 38−39, 44,48,53,57; Ant
67,75,80; Are 278,299,307,317,324; Con 11; Cyz 28,39,49,54;
Her 79,85,89, 95; Lon 29; Lug 234; Nic 95; Sis 187,196,204,218;
Tic 190,202, 209; Tre 458,465,481,515

1

−− Imperial visit to Antioch.
2   FL HELENA AVGVSTA, Star with crescent above. Fol: Ant 61

FAUSTA

Flavia Maxima Fausta, the daughter of the emperor Maximian, married Constantine in 307; she bore him three sons, Constantine, Constantius and Constans. Fausta revealed the intrigues of her father to Constantine and was an active supporter of the church. In 326, however, she was involved in the death of Crispus (with whom she was rumoured to have committed adultery) and executed soon after. She apparently became Augusta in 324, at the same time as Helena.

324   Promotion of Fausta to be Augusta.
    1   SALVS REIPVBLICAE, Fausta stg. facing, holding children Constantine and Constantius. Sol: Nic 77−8; Tic 182. Fol: Ale 39−40; Ant 68, 76; Are 277,298; Con 12; Lon 300; Lug 235; Nic 96; Sir 55; Tes 160; Tre 459,483

1

    2   SPES REIPVBLICAE, Same type. Sol: Sir 61; Tes 137. Fol: Ale 40; Ant 69,77; Are 279, 285,300,308; Cyz 29,40,50; Her 80,86; Nic 97; Rom 271, 292−4; Sis 187.197,205; Tes 161−2; Tic 191,203−4
− −   Imperial visit to Antioch.
    3   FLAV MAX FAVSTA AVG, Star with crescent above. Fol: Ant 56,62

CONSTANTIA

The daughter of Constantius and sister of Constantine, Constantia married Licinius in 313 as part of his alliance with Constantine. After the deposition of Licinius, she successfully pleaded for his life. She retained the favour of Constantine, and lived at his court though no longer with the title Augusta, but merely *nobilissima femina*.

324   Celebration of Constantia's relation to the imperial family at the same time as Helena and Fausta became Augustae.
    1   SOROR CONSTANTINI AVG in wreath. Fol: Con 15

CRISPUS

Caesar October 316−Autumn 326

Flavius Julius Crispus, the eldest son of Constantine, was born *c.* 303 to his concubine Minervina, and made Caesar (*1*) in 316.

He was sent to govern Gaul, where he successfully defeated the Germans (*2–3*) in 320, the year which marked the fifteenth anniversary (*4–10*) of Constantine's accession. In 321, Crispus entered his second consulate (*11*) at Serdica, the headquarters of his father, and celebrated his quinquennalia (*12–15*) in Sirmium. As the result of further victories over the Germans (*17*) in 323, he was awarded the consulate (*18*) for the next year. He commanded the fleet in the war against Licinius, after which he visited Antioch (*19*) with Constantine. He celebrated his decennalia (*21*) in 325, the year of the council of Nicaea. He left for the West after it, but was executed on the way at Pola in northern Italy for reasons which are now mysterious. Contemporary gossip accused him of indulging or refusing an affair with his stepmother Fausta who seems in any case to have been implicated in his death.

316   Appointment as Caesar.
   1a   PRINCIPI IVVENTVT/IS, Crispus stg. r. or l. Sol: Aqu 29, 36; Sir 5–6; Tic 106; Tre 186–7. Fol: Rom 137–8; Tre 138–42, 169–71. Æ3: Tic 111–12
   1b   PRINCIPIA IVVENTVTIS, Crispus stg. r. or l. Fol: Aqu 9–10; Are 106–7, 113; Lon 133; Rom 60–2, 87–90, 93, 95–6, 102–3, 135, Sis 39; Tes 20–1; Tic 65, 73–8
   1c   — — Mars stg. r. or l. Fol: Are 129–35, 143, 161–3, 168, 172, 179, 183
320   Victories in Germany.
   2   GAVDIVM ROMANORVM, ALAMANNIA in ex., Alamannia std. l. on ground before trophy. Sol: Tre 243, 362
   3   — — but FRANCIA, Francia std. Sol: Tre 363. AV FRAC: Tre 366
— — Fifteenth anniversary of Constantine.
   4   VICTORIAE PERPETVAE, Victory stg. l., holding shield inscribed VOT XX (Constantine *66*). Sol: Aqu 38
   5   BEATA TRANQVILLITAS, Altar inscribed VOT/IS XX (Constantine *67*). Fol: Lon 208–15, 218, 228–35, 247–52, 273–81; Lug 132–9, 162–75, 202–4; Tre 307–9, 320–5, 329–33, 346–51, 372–79, 393–407, 417–8, 425–6

6a   14

   6a   VIRTVS EXERCIT, Standard inscribed VOT X; captives below Fol: Aqu 41–3; Sis 112–3, 123–4, 130–1
   6b   — — Standard inscribed VOT XX (Constantine *68*). Fol: Aqu 52–3, 57A, 60–1; Lon 187–9, 194–6; Lug 108–10, 116–21; Sis 111, 122, 136–7; Tes 73, 77–8; Tic 117, 124; Tre 255, 268–70, 296–7

7   ROMAE AETERNAE, Roma std, l., holding shield inscribed XV (Constantine *69*). Fol: Rom 152, 197

8   VOT X ET XV F in wreath (Constantine *70a*). Fol: Rom 204

9   VOT XV FEL XX in wreath (Constantine *70b*). Fol: Rom 216, 222

10   CONSTANTINI AVG around VOTIS XX (Constantine *71b*). Fol: Lug 93

321 Second consulate of Crispus.

11   FELIX PROCESSVS COS II, Crispus stg. l. Sol: Sir 20A

— — Quinquennalia of the Caesars. The numerals V and X refer to the Caesars, XX to the fifteenth anniversary of Constantine.

12   VICTORIA CRISPI CAES, Victory stg. r., with shield inscribed VOT X. Sol: Sir 23–4, 26, 32–3

13*a*   DOMINOR/VM NOSTROR/VM CAESS around VOT V in wreath. Fol: Tic 134–5, 148–50, 153

13*b*   — — VOT X Fol: Her 57–8, 61; Tic 155–60, 164, 168–71

14*a*   CAESARVM NOSTRORVM around VOST/IS V in wreath (*cf.* Constantine *73*). Fol: Aqu 68–70, 87–90; Are 210, 220, 225, 230, 235, 241, 244; Lug 95, 98–100; Rom 229, 234; Sis 142, 145, 147, 151–3, 161; Tes 85, 90–1, 105–6, 113, 118

14*b*   — — VOT X. Fol: Aqu 78, 97–100, 106–10; Are 247–8, 254, 259–60; Lon 291; Lug 210, 213, 215–16, 220, 223; Rom 238–40, 246; Sis 165, 169, 172, 175, 178, 181; Tes 121, 125–7; Tre 431–2, 440

15*a*   VOT V MVLT X (CAESS) in wreath. Fol: Tes 36–40, 57–8

15*b*   VOT V CAESS NN in wreath. Æ3: Tre 339

322 Victories of Constantine over the Sarmatians (Constantine *74*).

16   SARMATIA DEVICTA, Victory adv. r., with captive. Fol: Tre 436–7

— — Victories of Crispus in Germany.

17   ALAMANNIA DEVICTA, Type as *16*. Fol: Sir 49

324 Third consulate of Crispus.

18   FELIX PROCESSVS COS III, Crispus stg. l. Sol: Sir 43, 57

— — Visit to Antioch, with celebration of the imperial family.

19   CRISPVS CAESAR in wreath (*cf.* Constantine *76*). Fol: Ant 53, 58

325 Promotion of Constantius II to be Caesar.

20   FELICITAS ROMANORVM, Constantine stg. l. with three sons (Constantine *83a*). Arg: Nic 89

— — Decennalia of Crispus.

21   DOMINOR NOSTROR CAESS around VOT XX in wreath. Fol: Tic 175, 187

DELMATIUS

Caesar September 335–Summer 337

Fl. Julius Delmatius, born *c.* 313, was the son of Julius Constantius and grandson of Constantius I. He was made Caesar by Constantine in 335 and given charge of Thrace, Macedonia and Greece. Delmatius was murdered together with the other members of his family two years later.

335 Creation as Caesar.
   1 PRINCIPI IVVENTVTIS, Delmatius stg. r. Sol: Con 113; Sis 247; Tes 213

HANNIBALLIANUS

Rex Regum, 335–337

Fl. Hanniballianus, the youngest brother of Delmatius, born *c*. 315, was appointed by Constantine as King of Kings of Armenia to secure Roman influence in the East, preparatory to the planned campaign against Persia. At the same time, he married Constantine's daughter Constantina. He made his headquarters at Caesarea in Cappadocia, where he perished in the general massacre of his family.

335 Advertisement of the eastern realm of Hanniballianus, with its frontier at the Euphrates.
   1 FELICITAS PVBLICA, Euphrates reclining l. Arg: Con 100

1

   2 SECVRITAS PVBLICA, Euphrates stg. r. on ground. Fol: Con 145–8

CONSTANTINE II

Caesar October 316/Augustus September 337–April 340

Fl. Claudius Constantinus, eldest son of Constantine and Fausta, was born in Arelate in 316 and made Caesar (*1*) in the same year, together with his half-brother Crispus. He held the consulate in 320, 321, 324 and 329 (*20*), and celebrated his quinquennalia (*8–11*) in 321 and decennalia (*19*) in 325. He participated in the German campaigns of Crispus (*15–16*) in 323. After the murder of Crispus, Constantine replaced him in Gaul and led successful campaigns against the Alamanni. In 332, he won major victories over the Goths and Sarmatians (*21*). Constantine took control of the western provinces in May 337 on the death of his father whom he and his brothers consecrated (*33–34*), and assumed the title Augustus (*24–32*) together with his brothers after the massacre of his other relatives that Summer. At first he exercised a tutelary supremacy over his youngest brother Constans, then decided to annex his territory, but met defeat and death when he invaded Italy in 340.

316 Appointment as Caesar, and subsequent advertisement as imperial heir (types struck until 337).

1   PRINCIPI IVVENTVTIS, Constantine stg. r. or l. Sol: Ant 47, 94; Con 109–11; Nic 71–5; Sir 7, 40–1; Sis 209, 226; Tes 209; Tic 107; Tre 188, 447, 472, 560, 572–4. Avfrac: Nic 114–5, 183; Sis 251. Fol: Rom 91–2, 94 (PRINCIPIA); Tre 143–5, 172–4. Æ3: Tre 199

320 Fifteenth anniversary of Constantine.

2   BEATA TRANQVILLITAS, Altar inscribed VOT/IS XX (Constantine *67*). Fol: Lon 216, 219, 236–7, 253–60, 282–8; Lug 140–52, 176–96, 205–8; Tre 312–5, 326–8, 334, 352–5, 380–8, 408–15, 419–22, 427–8

2

3*a*   VIRTVS EXERCIT, Standard inscribed VOT X; captives below Fol: Aqu 45–6; Sis 116–8, 126, 133

3*b*   — — standard inscribed VOT XX (Constantine *68*). Fol: Aqu 56, 62; Are 204, 207; Lon 190, 197–8; Lug 111–2, 122–4; Tes 74, 80–1, 83; Tic 121, 126, 129; Tre 257, 273–8, 300–2

4   ROMAE AETERNAE, Roma std. l. with shield inscribed XV (Constantine *69*). Fol: Rom 155–7, 200

5   VOT X ET XV F in wreath (Constantine *70a*). Fol: Rom 206, 209

6   VOT XV FEL XX in wreath (Constantine *70b*). Fol: Rom 218, 224

7   VOT XV in wreath. Fol: Rom 210

321 Quinquennalia of the Caesars (Vota v and x).

8   VICTORIA CONSTANTINI CAES, Victory std. r., with shield inscribed VOT X (Crispus *12*). Sol: Sir 25, 27, 34

9*a*   DOMINOR/VM NOSTROR/VM CAESS around VOT V in wreath (Crispus *13a*). Fol: Her 59, 63; Tic 138–9, 152, 154

9*b*   — — VOT X (Crispus *13b*). Fol: Her 62; Tic 161–2, 165–6, 172–3

10*a* CAESARVM NOSTRORVM around VOT/IS V in wreath (Crispus *14a*). Fol: Aqu 74–7, 93–6; Are 212, 222, 227, 232, 237, 243, 245; Rom 231, 236; Sis 144, 146, 156–8, 163–4; Tes 87, 94–5, 100, 108, 115–6

10*b* — — VOT X (Crispus *14b*). Fol: Aqu 79, 101–3, 111–5; Are 249–51, 255–6, 261–3; Lon 292; Lug 211, 217–8, 221, 224; Rom 241–4, 247; Sis 166–7, 179, 173, 176, 170, 182; Tes 122, 128; Tre 433–4, 441

11*a* VOT V MVLT X CAESS in wreath (Crispus *15a*). Fol: Tes 43−7
11*b* VOT V CAESS NN in wreath (Crispus *15b*). Æ3: Tre 340

322 Sarmatian victories of Constantine.

12 PRINCIPIA IVVENTVTIS, SARMATIA in ex., Constantine stg. Sol: Tre 364A, 536

13 GAVDIVM ROMANORVM, SARMATIA in ex., Sarmatia std. on ground; trophy behind. Sol: Tre 364. Æ3: Tre 367

14 SARMATIA DEVICTA, Victory adv. r., with captive (Constantine *74*). Fol: Tre 438

— — German victories of Crispus.

15 GAVDIVM ROMANORVM, ALAMANNIA in ex., Alamannia std. l. on ground by trophy. Sol: Tre 516, 535

16 ALAMANNIA DEVICTA, Type as 14 (Crispus *17*). Fol: Sir 50−2

324 Visit of Constantine to Antioch, with celebration of the imperial family.

17 CONSTANTINVS CAESAR in wreath (*cf.* Constantine *76*). Fol: Ant 54−5, 59−60

325 Promotion of Constantius II to Caesar.

18*a* FELICITAS ROMANORVM, Constantine stg. l. in archway, with three sons (Constantine *83a*). Arg: Cyz 42; Rom 275

18*b* — — but two sons (struck after the execution of Crispus) (Constantine *83b*). Arg: Nic 142; Tes 140C; Tre 474B

— — Decennalia of the Caesars.

19 DOMINOR/VM NOSTROR/VM CAESS around VOT XX in wreath (Crispus *21*). Fol: Tic 176, 188

329 Fourth consulate.

20 PRINCIPIA IVVENTVTIS COSS IIII, Constantine std. l. Avfrac: Tre 517

332 Victories of Constantine over the Goths and Sarmatians.

21 GAVDIVM ROMANORVM, ALAMANNIA in ex., Type as 15. Sol: Tre 535

336 Vicennalia of Constantine.

22 VICTORIA CONSTANTINI CAES/AR, Victory stg. r., inscribing VOT XX on shield held by Genius. Sol: Con 116, 119−20

23 XX in wreath. Arg: Nic 198; Sis 260

337 Accession to imperial power, combined with continued celebration of the vicennalia. Types *30−31* celebrate the entire imperial college, with their respective anniversaries.

24 GAVDIVM POPVLI ROMANI around SIC XX SIC XXX in wreath. Sol: Sis 19, 20. Mil: Sis 47. Sil: Sis 70

25 — — Victory std. r., inscribing VOT XX MVLT XXX on shield supported by Genius. Sol: Aqu 4

26*a* VICTORIA AVGVSTORVM, Same type. Sol: Ant 23

26*b* VICTORIA DD NN AVG, Same type. Sol: Sis 28

27 VICTORIA/E DDD NNN AVGGG, Two Victories holding wreath inscribed VOT/IS XX MVLTIS XXX. Sol; Sis 26−7

28*a* VICTORIA AVGVSTORVM, Type as *25*, but shield inscribed VOT XXX. S: Ant 13—16, 20

28*b* VICTORIA AVGVSTI, Same type. Sol; Ant 10

29 VICTORIA CONSTANTINI AVG, Victory adv. r., holding shield inscribed VOT XXX and kicking std. bound captive. Sol: Sis 3—4

30 — — Type as *28a*. Sol: Sis 1,2

31 VICTORIA CONSTANTI AVG, Same type, but shield inscribed VOT XX. Sol: Con 3

32 VICTORIA CONSTANTIS AVG, Same type, but VOT V MVLT X. Sol: Sis 33

— — Consecration of Constantine.

33*a* *Obv.* D(I)V(VS) CONSTANTINVS AVG P(A)T(ER) AVGG, Veiled head r. *Rev.* (No legend), Hand of God above Constantine in quadriga. Sol: Con 1. Æ4: Ale 4, 12, 22; Ant 37, 39; Con 37, 39, 52; Cyz 4, 19, 25, 30; Tre 44, 68

33*b* As previous, but *obv.* DIVO CONSTANTINO AVG (or P). Æ4: Are 42; Lug 12, 17

34 AETERNA PIETAS, Constantine stg. l. or r. Æ3: Are 17, 40—1; Lug 1—3; Tre 37

CONSTANS

Caesar December 333/Augustus September 337—January 350

Flavius Julius Constans, born to Constantine and Fausta in 323, was made Caesar (*1*) on Christmas 333 and entrusted with the rule of Italy in 335. As Augustus (*2—10*), after the murder of his relatives in 337, he ruled the central part of the empire, from the Alps to Africa. Constans held his first consulate in 339; others, held jointly with Constantius, followed in 342 and 346. When his eldest brother Constantine tried to take over his territories, Constans gained the support of Constantius, and defeated and killed Constantine, assuming control of the entire West in 340.

During these troubles, Franks attacked in 341. Constans defeated them so thoroughly in the following year that they were forced into alliance with the Romans, and the Rhine frontier was pacified. He celebrated these victories together with his own decennalia (*11—18*). Constans travelled frequently throughout his realm, from Britain to the Danube, but the coinage makes no mention of events beyond the usual *vota* (*19—28*), occasions for donatives to the troops. The only exception is the vast issue to celebrate the 1100th anniversary of Rome (*29—35*) in 248. In 350, when Magnentius revolted, Constans fled, but was captured and killed in southern Gaul.

333 Elevation of Constans to Caesar.

1 PRINCIPI IVVENTVTIS, Constans stg. l. Sol: Sis 228, 245—6; Tes 212; Tre 575—6. Avfrac: Nic 184

337 Accession to imperial power, considered as celebration of the quinquennalia of Constans and vicennalia of Constantine II (*10*).

2   GAVDIVM POPVLI ROMANI, Two Victories holding wreath inscribed SIC V SIC X. Sol: Sis 22

3*a*   — — around SIC V SIC X in wreath. Sol: Tes 8−9. Mil: Sis 49,
51−2; Tes 42. Sil: Sis 72−3; Tes 43

3*b*   — — VOT V MVLT X. Sol: Her 1; Tes 10

3*a*   13

4   VICTORIA AVGVSTORVM, Victory std. r., inscribing VOT V MVLT X
on shield supported by Genius. Sol: Ant 29

5   VICTORIAE D/D/D N/N/N AVG/G/G, Two Victories holding wreath
inscribed VOT V MVLT X. Sol: Aqu 6−7; Sis 112; Tes 14, 31. Sil:
Aqu 52A; Tre 164−5

6   — — Victory adv. l., holding shield inscribed VOT V MVLT X,
and kicking std. bound captive. Sol: Her 2

7   VICTORIA CONSTANTIS AVG, Same type. Sol: Her 3; Sis 37−8

8*a*   — — Type as *4*. Sol: Her 5; Sis 34−5, 36 (VICTORIA D N
CONSTANTIS AVG)

8*b*   — — Shield inscribed VOT V. Sol: Nic 2

8*c*   — — Shield inscribed VOT X. Sol: Con 7−8

9   FELICITAS PERPETVA VOT V, Three emperors enthroned. Mil:
Tes 52

10   VICTORIA AVGVSTI (or AVGVSTORVM), Victory std. l., with shield
inscribed VOT XXX. Sol: Ant 12, 19

342 Decennalia of Constans, combined with celebration of his victories
over the Franks.

11   GAVDIVM POPVLI ROMANI, Two Victories holding wreath inscribed
SIC X SIC XX. Sol: Tre 169

12   — — around SIC X SIC XX in wreath. Mil: Sis 149, 151, 153−4

13   GAVDIVM ROMANORVM, Standard inscribed VOT X MVLT XV (or
XX) flanked by two captives. Mil: Tre 152, 158−9

14   OB VICTORIAM TRIVMPHALEM, Two Victories holding wreath inscribed VOT X MVL/T XV. Sol: Aqu 38−9; Sis 113, 114A, 115,
116 (VOT X MVL XX); Tre 124

15   VICTORIA AVGVSTORVM, Type as *4*, but VOT VX MVLT XV. Sol: Ant
28

16   — — Victory std. l., inscribing VOT X MVLT XX on shield. Sem:
Tes 65−6. Mil: Aqu 50 (VOT X MVLT XV), 51−2, 57, 57A, 61−3

17   VICTORIAE D/D N/N AVG/G, Two Victories holding wreath inscribed
VOT X MVLT XV. Sil: Aqu 53−5; Tre 166−7

18 — — VOT X MVL/T XX. Sol: Aqu 45; Sis 120, 124−5, 130, 132, 134, 136, 138−9; Tes 72−4, Tre 129, 138. Sem: Sis 142−3. Sil: Tre 167A, 168

— — Vicennalia of Constantius II.

19 GLORIA REIPVBLICAE, Rome and Constantinople enthroned holding wreath inscribed VOT XX MVLT XXX. Sol: Nic 34

20 VICTORIAE DD NN AVGG, Type as *17*, but VOT XX MVLT XXX. Sol: Sis 140

21 VOT XX MVLT XXX in wreath. Æ3: Ale 34, 37, 40, 43; Ant 115; Con 70, 73, 77; Cyz 50−52, 57, 61, 64; Her 47, 48, 52, 55, 60; Nic 51−2, 56, 59

346 Joint consulate of Constans and Constantius, celebrated as their respective fifteenth and twenty-fifth anniversaries.

22 FELICITAS REI PVBLICAE around VOT XV MVLT XX in wreath. Sol: Con 56

23 VICTORIA AVGVSTORVM, Victory std. l., with shield inscribed VOT XV MVLT XX. Sol: Ant 26

24 VICTORIAE DD NN AVGG, Two Victories holding wreath inscribed VOT XV MVLT XX. Sol: Aqu 46

25 VICTORIA CONSTANTIS AVG, Type as *23*, but shield inscribed VOT XV. Avsem: Aqu 41

26 VOT XV MVLT XX in wreath. Æ4: Ant 116, 120

27 VICTORIA AVGVSTORVM. Victory adv. l., holding wreath inscribed XXV; trophy and palm branch over shoulder; captive before. Sol: Nic 27−8

28 VOTIS XXV MVLTIS XXX in wreath. Sil: Nic 42−4

30   31

348 Celebration of the 1100th anniversary of Rome. Types 29−31 are those of Constans: 29 continues the celebration of his vicennalia, 30 represents his crossing to Britain, and 31 his defeat and settlement of the Franks. The phoenix of 32 is the general symbol of renewal and rebirth; 32−34 celebrate the Persian wars and victories of Constantius. All have the inscription FEL TEMP REPARATIO.

29 Victory stg. r., inscribing VOT XX on shield supported by kneeling figure Sil: Rom 61−3

30 Constans, holding phoenix on globe and labarum, stg. on galley steered by Victory. Æ2: Ant; Ale; Aqu; Are; Con; Cyz; Her; Lug; Nic; Rom; Sis; Tes; Tre *passsim*. Æ3: Aqu 108−9; Are 117; Lug 96, 98−9; Rom 146−7; Tes 120−2; Tre 238

32

31 Soldier leading captive from hut beneath tree. Æ2: Ale; Ant; Aqu; Are; Con; Her; Lug; Nic; Rom; Sis; Tes; Tre *passim*. Æ3: Aqu 101, 103, 106, 121

32 Radiate phoenix stg. on rocky mound or globe. Æ3: Ant 131; Aqu 111−2; Are 109, 113, 115; Cyz 88, 90−1; Lug 90−1; Rom 142−3, 145; Sis 228, 232, 236, 241, 247, 249; Tre 226, 228−30, 232, 234, 236. Æ4: Ale 70−1

33 Soldier spearing fallen Persian horseman (many varieties). Æ2: Ale 48−9; Ant 136; Aqu 116; Are 103, 123; Cyz 68; Lug 80, 82; Rom 136; Sis 211, 254, 258; Tes 116

34 Constantius stg., holding labarum; two captives before. Æ2: Ale 56−7, 64−5; Cyz 76; Sis 224, 226

35 Nimbate Constantius galloping r., thrusting at two barbarians with pointed caps. Æ2: Rom 155

CONSTANTIUS II

Caesar November 324/Augustus September 337−November 361

Flavius Julius Constantius, the third son of Constantine and Fausta, was born in 317 and made Caesar (*1−2*) in 324. He held his first consulate in 326; nine others followed. Constantius participated in the campaigns of his brother Constantine II against the Germans in Gaul (*4*) in 332, and in 336 went to Constantinople for the thirtieth anniversary of Constantine's reign; there he married his cousin, the daughter of Constantine's brother Julius Constantius. In the same year, he was sent east against the Persians. He succeeded to the rule of the eastern half of the empire (*6−13*) on the death of Constantine (*14−15*) in 337. War with the Persians broke out in 338, and continued for many years, with several Roman victories, none of them decisive. It kept Constantius from dealing with problems in the West, where Constans took full control in 340. Constantius celebrated the twentieth anniversary of his reign (*16−29*) in 342, the year he and Constans were joint consuls, and the twenty-fifth (*32−34*) in 346. Peace was finally made with Persia in 350, just in time for Constantius to march west against Magnentius who had gained control of the western provinces (*43*). In the final stages of his revolt, the city of Treveri defected from Magnentius and struck distinctive coins in the name of Constantius (*45−47*). Constantius defeated Magnentius in 351, and gained full control of the West, and thus of the whole empire, by 353.

To leave himself free to deal with the West, Constantius had appointed his cousin Gallus Caesar (*44*) in 351. He ruled with such violence and cruelty, however, that he had to be recalled and executed three years later. In 355, when the Frank Silvanus revolted in Gaul, Constantius appointed his cousin Julian Caesar (*53*) and sent him west, where he gained such success that his troops proclaimed him emperor in 360. Constantius moved against him, but died at Tarsus in 361 before a new civil war could begin. His coinage reflects few events besides the 1100th anniversary of Rome – a vast issue (*35–42*) – and the promotion of the Caesars. Instead, it is dominated by the frequent imperial anniversaries of this long reign, the occasions for donatives to the troops. Since many of these *vota* types continued to be struck long after the appropriate anniversaries, assignment to a specific occasion is often problematic.

324 Accession as Caesar (type struck until 335).
    1   PRINCIPI/A IVVENTVTIS, Constantius stg. l. or r. Sol: Ant 95; Aqu 117; Con 112; Nic 78; Sir 59; Sis 227; Tes 133, 176, 191, 193, 210–1; Tic 181; Tre 448, 473–4; 501. Avfrac: Nic 116; Arg: Sir 16
    2*a*   FELICITAS ROMANORVM, Constantine stg. in arch with three sons (Constantine *83a*). Arg: Cyz 43
    2*b*   – – two sons (struck after the execution of Crispus). (Constantine *83b*). Nic 143
– – Twentieth anniversary of Constantine, celebrated with vows for the Caesars.
    3   D N CONSTANTINI MAX AVG around VOT V in wreath (cf. Constantine *81*). Fol: Tes 129–30
332 Victories of Constantine II in Gaul.
    4   DEBELLATORI GENTIVM BARBARARVM, GOTHIA in exergue, Emperor and soldier; captive below. Sol: Tre 534
333 Decennalia of Constantius.
    5   VICTORIA CONSTANTI CAES, Victory std. r., inscribing VOT XV on shield. Sol: Con 72, 115
337 Accession to imperial power, considered as the fifteenth anniversary of Constantius' reign, celebrated with the vicennalia of Constantine II (*10d, 10e, 10f, 13*) and the quinquennalia of Constans (*9b*).
    6   FELICITAS PERPETVA, Victory std. r., inscribing VOT X MVLT XX on shield supported by Genius. Sol: Aqu 5
    7   FELICITAS REIPVBLICAE around VOT XV MVLT XX in wreath. Sol: Con 11–12. Sil: Con 58; Nic 37
    8   FELICITAS ROMANORVM, Same type. Sol: Ant 30–1
    9*a*   GAVDIVM POPVLI ROMANI around SIC X SIC XX in wreath. Sol: Sis 20A, 21. Mil: Sis 48. Sil: Sis 71
    9*b*   – – SIC V SIC X (Constans). Sol: Are 59
    10*a* VICTORIA/E DD/D NN/N AVG/G, Victory std. as type *6*, SIC X SIC XX on shield. Sol: Sis 23–5
    10*b* – – VOT X MVLT XX. Sol; Sis 29–31; Tre 15

10*c*   VICTORIA AVGVSTORVM, Same type, VOT XV MVLT XX. Sol: Ant 22, 25

10*d*   — — VOT XX MVLT XXX. Sol: Ant 24

10*e*   — — VOT XXX. Sol: Ant 17–18

10*f*   VICTORIA AVGVSTI, Same type, VOT XX MVLT XXX. Sol: Ant 9, 11

11*a*   VICTORIAE D N AVG, Two Victories holding wreath inscribed VOTIS XV MVLTIS XX. Sol: Sis 117–8; Tes 15, 30

11*b*   — — VOT X MVLT XV Sil: Aqu 56

12*a*   VICTORIA CONSTANTI AVG, Type as 6, VOT X. Sol: Nic 1

12*b*   — — VOT X MVLT XV. Sol: Her 4

12*c*   — — VOT XV. Sol: Con 4–6, 9; Her 6–10

13   VICTORIA CONSTANTINI AVG, Constantine II stg., holding standard inscribed VOT XX; captive to r. Sol: Sis 5–7

— — Consecration of Constantine.

14   *Obv.* DV CONSTANTINVS PT AVGG, Veiled bust r. *Rev.*: VENERATA MEMORIA, Constantine stg. r. Æ4: Ale 32, 35, 38, 41; Ant 112, 117; Con 68, 71, 75; Cyz 46, 54, 59, 62; Her 44, 51, 53, 58; Nic 48, 54, 57

15   — — *Rev.*: IVST VEN/ER MEM/OR, Aequitas stg. l. Æ4: Ale 28; Ant 64; Con 62; Cyz 35; Her 41; Nic 45

342 Vicennalia of Constantius, celebrated with the decennalia of Constans (*24–29*), during their joint consulate.

16   GLORIA REI PVBLICAE, Rome and Constantinople holding wreath inscribed VOT XX MVLT XXX (This became a stock type, struck as late as 352). Sol: Ant 81–6; Con 57; Cyz 38; Nic 29–33; Rom 225–7; Sir 1; Sis 297–8

17   VICTORIAE DD NN AVGG, Victory as type 6, VOT XX MVLT XXX. Sol: Aqu 44; Sis 119, 121–3; Tes 63, 69–71; Tre 128, 133, 137. Sem: Sis 141, 141A; Tes 64

18   — — Two Victories holding wreath inscribed VOT XX MVLT XXX. Sol: Sis 119, 121–3, 129, 131, 133, 135, 137, 141

19   VICTORIA CONSTANTI AVG, Victory as type 6, VOT XX MVLT XXX. Sol: Con 10

20   FELICITAS PERPETVA around VOT XX MVLT XXX in wreath. Mil: Aqu 59–60

21   FELICITAS REI PVBLICE around VOT XX MVLT XX in wreath. Sil: Con 59; Cyz 3, 3A; Her 40

22   GAVDIVM POPVLI ROMANI around SIC XX SIC XXX in wreath. Mil: Sis 150, 152

23   VOT/IS XX MVLT/IS XXX in wreath. (Type struck for several years). Sil: Ant 36, 105, Æ4: Ale 33, 36, 39, 42; Ant 113, 114A, 118; Con 67, 69, 72, 76; Cyz 47–49, 55–6, 60, 63; Her 45–6, 54, 59; Nic 49–50, 55, 58, 58A

24   VICTORIA AVGVSTORVM, Victory as type 6, VOT VX MVLT XV. Sol: Ant 27

25*a*   OB VICTORIAM TRIVMPHALEM, Two Victories holding wreath inscribed VOT X MVL XV. Sol: Sis 114

25*b*   — — VOT XV Sem: Sis 126

26*a*   VICTORIAE DD NN AVGG, Two Victories holding wreath inscribed
      VOT X MVLT XX (Type *18*). Sol: Tre 134−6

26*b*   VICTORIAE D N AVG, Two Victories holding wreath inscribed
      VOT X MVLT XV. Sil: Aqu 56

27   VICTORIA AVGVSTORVM. Victory std. r., inscribing VOT X on
      wreath supported by Genius. Sem: Lug 32

28   FELICITAS PERPETVA around VOT X MVLT XX in wreath. Mil: Aqu
      58

29   GAVDIVM ROMANORVM, Standard with banner inscribed VOT X
      MVLT XV flanked by two captives. Mi1: Tre 151, 156−7

346 Twenty-fifth anniversary of Constantius and fifteenth of Constans,
      celebrated during their joint consulate.

30   VICTORIAE D N AVG, As type 27 but VOT XXV MVL XXX. Sol: Tes
      75

31   VICTORIA AVGVSTORVM, Victory adv. r., holding wreath inscribed
      XXV; trophy and palm branch over shoulder; captive before.
      Sol: Ant 79; Con 55; Nic 26

32   VOTIS XXV MVLTIS XXX in wreath. Sil: Ant 106−7; Con 60−1;
      Cyz 43−4; Nic 40−1

33   FELICITAS REI PVBLICE around VOTIS XV MVLTIS XX in wreath. Sil:
      Nic 37

34   VOT/IS XV MVLT/IS XX in wreath. Sil: Ant 35. Æ4: Ant 114, 119

348 Celebration of the 1100th anniversary of Rome. Type *35* continues
      the vows for the vicennalia; *36−38* celebrate the Persian victories of
      Constantius; the phoenix of *39* is the general symbol of renewal; *40*
      and *41* are types of Constans; and *42* is a type of Gallus, struck after
      354. This is a vast coinage which continued to be struck until the
      end of the reign. All have legend FEL TEMP REPARATIO.

35   Victory inscribing VOT XX on shield supported by kneeling
      figure. Sil: Rom 59−60

36   Soldier spearing fallen Persian horseman; many varieties. Æ2:
      Ale, Amb, Ant, Aqu, Are, Con, Cyz, Her, Lug, Nic, Rom,
      Sir, Sis, Tes, Tre *passim*. Æ3: Ale, Ant, Aqu, Are, Con, Cyz,
      Her, Lug, Nic, Rom, Sir, Sis, Tes *passim* (though less frequent
      than Æ2).

37   Constantius holding standard with labarum; two bound captives
      before. Æ2: Ale 54−5, 62−3; Ant 125, 127; Aqu 107, 119−
      20, 149; Con 84, 87, 89−90; Cyz 70−1, 75, 80, 83−4; Her 63,
      69, 72, 75; Nic 67−8, 71; Rom 186−190; Sis 224−5

  36   52

38   Nimbate Constantius galloping r., thrusting at two barbarians with pointed caps. Æ2: Rom 153−4, 184−5

39   Radiate Phoenix stg. r. on rocky mound or globe. Æ3: Ant 129−30; Aqu 110; Are 110−2, 114; Con 93−4; Cyz 89; Lug 92−4; Nic 73; Rom 141, 142A, 144; Sir 26; Sis 227, 231, 235, 240; Tre 227, 231, 233, 235, 237. Æ4: Ale 69

40   Constans on galley (Constans *30*). Æ2: Ale, Aqu, Are, Lug, Rom, Sis, Tes, Tre *passim*. Æ3: Are 116; Lug 95−7; Sis 229, 233, 237, 243; Tes 119

41   Soldier leading barbarian from hut (Constans *31*). Æ2: Ale, Aqu, Are, Con, Cyz, Her, Nic, Rom, Sis, Tes, Tre *passim*.

42   Emperor, holding victory and labarum, kicking captive. Æ2: Tes 172, 178

350−1 Civil war with Magnentius. Emphasis on the legitimacy of an emperor descended from Constantine. Type created by Vetranio, *q.v.*

43   HOC SIGNO VICTOR ERIS, Constantine, holding labarum, crowned by Victory (Miraculous vision and victory at the Milvian Bridge in 312). Æ2: Sir 23, 30; Sis 272, 278, 282, 286, 291, 304−5, 309, 311

351 Creation of Gallus as Caesar.

44   FELICITAS ROMANORVM, Constantius and Gallus stg. under arch. (Type derived from Constantine *83*.) Mil: Aqu 182; Sir 11, 13

353 Revolt of Treveri against Magnentius in favour of Constantius, with advance celebration of his tricennalia.

45   VICTORIAE DD NN AVGG, Two Victories holding wreath inscribed VOT XXX. Sol: Tre 328

46   VICTORIA AVG NOSTRI, Victory adv. l., leading Constantius. Sol: Tre 329−31

47   SALVS AVG NOSTRI, Labarum between alpha and omega (an answer to the propaganda of Magnentius *9*). Æ1: Tre 332−7

−− Thirtieth anniversary of the reign.

48   GLORIA REI PVBLICAE, Rome and Constantinople std., holding wreath inscribed VOT XXX MVLT XXXX. Sol: Ant 87−8, 162, 165, 168, 170; Aqu 179−81; Are 233−4, 236, 238, 280; Con 95−6, 98; Cyz 39; Her 81; Lug 178; Med 2; Nic 74; Rom 228−30, 289−91, 293; Sir 2−9; Sis 297−8, 320, 322; Tes 147−8, 150, 152−4, 193, 195−6; Tre 338−46

49*a*   VICTORIAE D/D N/N AVG/G, Victory std. r., holding shield inscribed VOT XXX MVLT XXXX Sem: Tes 155, 199

49*b*   VICTORIA AVGVSTORVM, Same type but VOT XXX Sem: Ant 92

50   VICT DD NN AVG ET CAES, Two Victories holding wreath inscribed VOT XXX. Æ2: Rom 251−2

51   GAVDIVM POPVLI ROMANI around VOTIS XXX MVLTIS XXXX in wreath. Mil: Sir 10

52   VOT/IS XXX MVLT/IS XXXX in wreath. Sil: Ant 108, 183−4, 186; Aqu 183−4; Are 203, 207−8, 253−4, 258−9, 261, 291; Con

101−4, 133; Cyz 44A, 45; Lug 180, 216−7; Nic 80−1, 103; Rom 234−5, 302−3; Sir 15, 17, 19−20, 66, 68; Sis 324−5, 360; Tes 163, 205

355 Appointment of Julian as Caesar.

53 GLORIA REI PVBLICAE, Rome and Constantinople holding shield inscribed FELICITER V. Sol: Rom 294

357 Thirty-fifth anniversary of reign.

54 FELICITAS ROMANORVM, Rome and Constantinople holding shield inscribed VOT XXXV MVLT XXXX. Sol: Rom 296−8

55a GLORIA REI PVBLICAE, Same type. Sol: Aqu 210; Sir 55−64; Sis 357−9

55b − − VOT XXXX. Sol: Ant 172−3; Con 129; Nic 100; Sir 65; Tes 198

56a VICTORIA AVGVSTORVM, Victory std. r., holding shield inscribed VOT XXXX. Sem: Ant 93; Nic 101

56b VICTORIA CONSTANTI AVG, Same type. Sem: Rom 299

56c VICTORIA AVGVSTI, Same type. Mil: Con 132

57a VOTIS XXXV MVLTIS XXXX in wreath. Sil: Aqu 211

57b VOTIS XXXX in wreath. Sil: Con 134

360 Quinquennium of Julian.

58 VOTIS V MVLTIS X in wreath. Sil: Are 262, 294; Sol: Rom 296−8

MAGNENTIUS

January 350−August 353

Flavius Magnus Magnentius, born in 303 at Ambianum of a British father and Frankish mother, rose through the army to become commander of legions. He assumed the purple (*1*) at Augustodunum in Gaul, and soon defeated and killed Constans, who had fled to the south. Magnentius gained the allegiance of the entire West, but his progress eastward was halted by the promotion of Vetranio to emperor in Illyricum. He then tried to gain recognition from Constantius who, however, refused, and stirred up the German tribes against him. Magnentius suppressed the revolt of Nepotian in Rome (*2−3*) then, to strengthen his position, proclaimed his brother Decentius as Caesar. Decentius took charge of the defence against the Germans, while Magnentius looked to the East. Magnentius hoped to gain control of the Balkans by making an alliance with Vetranio, but here too he failed. In September 351, the year he held the consulate (*4*), Magnentius was badly defeated in Pannonia and withdrew to Italy. Further defeats caused him to flee to Gaul, where he committed suicide in 353. Magnentius was a pagan, but strove to gain the allegiance of the Catholics (*9*) whom he hoped to rouse against the Arian heretic Constantius.

350 Accession, considered as marking the beginning of a new age, with a type adapted from Constantius.

    1 FEL TEMP REPARATIO, Magnentius stg. l., holding labarum. Æ2: Lug 108

— — Recovery of Rome from Nepotian; liberty was 'twice restored' because Magnentius had first freed Rome from Constans.

    2 BIS RESTITVTA LIBERTAS, Victory and Libertas supporting trophy. Sol: Rom 168

    3 RENOBATIO VRBIS ROME, Roma std. l. Æ2: Rom 207

3

351 Consulate of Magnentius, with celebration of vows.

    4 BEATITVDO PVBLICA, Magnentius in consular robes std. on curule chair. Æ3: Aqu 164–6

    5 VICTORIAE DD NN AVGG, Victory std. r., inscribing VOT V MVLT X on shield (the plural AVGG refers to Constantius, whose recognition Magnentius hoped to gain). Mil: Aqu 143–5; Are 160; Lug 107

    6 FELICITAS PERPETVA around laurel wreath containing VOT V MVLT X. Mil: Aqu 142

    7 GLORIA ROMANORVM, Two Victories holding wreath inscribed VOT X. Æ4: Rom 194

9

    8 VICT/ORIAE DD NN AVG ET CAES, Two Victories holding wreath inscribed VOT V MVLT X. Æ2: Amb, Aqu, Are, Lug, Rom, Tre *passim*. Æ3: Tre 310, Æ4: Lug 125, 144A-B

351–353 Propaganda to rouse the Catholics against the Arian Constantius.

    9 SALVS DD NN AVG ET CAES, Christogram flanked by alpha and omega. Æ1–2: Amb, Are, Lug, Tre *passim*.

DECENTIUS

Caesar Summer 350–August 353

Magnus Decentius, the brother of Magnentius was chosen as Caesar after the revolt of Nepotian was suppressed, to meet the threat from the Germans who had been stirred up by Constantius. Since many troops had been withdrawn by Magnentius, Decentius' forces were too weak to meet the attacks, and Gaul was severely ravaged. After a defeat on his way to help Magnentius during his final struggle with Constantius, Decentius committed suicide soon after his brother's death.

350 Recovery of Rome from Nepotian.
   1   RENOBATIO VRBIS ROME, Roma std. l. (Magnentius *3*). Æ2: Rome 208
351 Joint vows with Magnentius, on his consulate.
   2   VICT/ORIAE DD NN AVG ET CAE/S, Two Victories holding wreath inscribed VOT V MVLT X (Magnentius *8*). Mil: Are 162. Æ2: Aqu, Are, Lug, Rom, Tre *passim*. Æ4: Lug 143–4; Tre 311

VETRANIO

March–December 350

Vetranio, born in Moesia, was a distinguished officer who had served under Constantine when Constans made him commander of the infantry. The revolt of Magnentius found Vetranio in Illyricum and raised the real danger that his army might go over to the usurper. The sister of Constantius, therefore, persuaded Vetranio to assume the purple, an act which Constantius willingly recognised. The strategic region which Vetranio's army occupied made him a desirable ally, but after negotiations with both Magnentius and Constantius, Vetranio declared for Constantius. The two emperors met at Naissus on Christmas day, and there Vetranio formally abdicated. Constantius allowed him to retire with wealth and honour to Prusa in Bithynia where he died in 356.

350 Allegiance of Vetranio to Constantius, proclaimed by striking a type which featured Constantine, the founder of the dynasty. Vetranio also struck this type in the name of Constantius (Constantius II *43*).
   1   HOC SIGNO VICTOR ERIS, Constantine, crowned by Victory, stg., holding labarum (portrayal of the miracle at the battle of the Milvian Bridge). Æ2: Sis 275, 279, 283, 287–8, 292

1

NEPOTIAN

June 350

Fl. Popilius Nepotianus (whose name first appears as Julius Nepotianus and finally as Fl. Nepotianus Constantinus), was a nephew of Constantine who revolted against Magnentius and took control of Rome. During his month-long reign, he violently persecuted the followers of Magnentius, but was captured and executed by forces loyal to the usurper.

350 Celebration of Rome, base of Nepotian's power.
  1   VRBS ROMA, Roma std. l. Sol: Rom 16−7. Æ2: Rom 201−3

CONSTANTIUS GALLUS

Caesar March 351−Winter 354

Flavius Claudius Gallus, the son of Julius Constantius and nephew of Constantine, was born in Etruria in 325 or 326. When his father was killed after the death of Constantine in 337, Gallus and his brother Julian were exiled to the family estates in Asia Minor and educated in relative isolation. During the revolt of Magnentius in 351, Constantius II, then sole emperor, called Gallus to his court at Sirmium and appointed him Caesar (*1−2*) to rule the East, while he went in person to deal with the revolt. Gallus thereupon took the name Constantius and married the emperor's sister Constantia. He made Antioch his headquarters, and ruled from there with such cruelty and ferocity that Constantius, fearing that a revolt might break out, recalled him to the court and had him executed. His coinage is typically dominated by the 1100th anniversary of Rome (*3−6*) and the quinquennial (*7−10*) vows which were celebrated together with the thirtieth anniversary of the reign of Constantius.

351 Appointment as Caesar.
  1   FELICITAS ROMANORVM, Constantius II and Gallus stg. under an arch (*cf.* Constantine *83*). Mil: Sir 12, 14

1

−− Proclamation of the legitimacy of the new Caesar as part of the family of Constantine, propaganda against Magnentius.
  2   HOC SIGNO VICTOR ERIS, Victory crowning Constantine who holds labarum (reference to the victory of the Milvian Bridge: Constantius II *43*) S: Tes 146. Æ2: Sir 24, 31; Sis 306, 312

351–355 Continuing celebration of the 1100th anniversary of Rome. Type *3* was struck primarily for Gallus, *4* for Constantius, and *5* and *6* originally for Constans (now deceased); the phoenix of *6* is the general symbol of renewal. All have the inscription FEL TEMP REPARATIO.

3   Gallus, adv. l., holding labarum and kicking std. captive. Æ2: Tes 173, 179

4   Soldier spearing fallen Persian horseman. Æ2: Amb 47; Are 213; Lug 185; Ale, Ant, Aqu, Con, Cyz, Her, Nic, Sir, Sis, Tes, Tre *passim*. Æ3: Ale 81; Ant 154, 156; Aqu 200, 203–204A, 206, 209; Are 217–18, 221, 223; Cyz 106–7, 109; Her 91; Lug 188, 191–2; Nic 97; Rom *passim*; Sir 49, 51, 53; Sis 351, 354; Tes 190–1

5   Emperor stg. on galley, holding labarum. Æ2: Rom 250; Sis 329–31; Tes 169–70, 175

6   Radiate phoenix stg. on rocky mound. Æ3: Ant 137A; Sir 27

353 Quinquennalia of Gallus, celebrated with the thirtieth anniversary of Constantius.

7   GLORIA REIPVBLICAE, Rome and Constantinople holding wreath inscribed VOT V MVLT X. Sol: Con 97; Lug 179; Sis 321; Tes 149, 151; Tre 347

7b   ——VOTIS V Sol: Ant 89–90; Nic 75

8a   VICTORIAE DD NN AVGG, Two Victories holding wreath inscribed VOT V MVLT X. Sem: Tes 156

8b   VICT DD NN AVG ET CAES, Same type. Æ2; Rom 253

9   VICTORIA AVGVSTORVM, Victory std. r., holding shield inscribed VOTIS V. Sem: Ant 94–5

10a   VOT/IS V MVLT/IS X in wreath. Sil: Aqu 185; Con 105; Nic 82–3; Sir 16, 18; Sis 300, 326; Tes 164

10b   VOTIS V in wreath. Sil: Ant 109

JULIAN

Caesar November 355/Augustus February 360–June 363

Flavius Claudius Julianus was born in Constantinople in 332, the son of Julius Constantius, and thus nephew of Constantine and younger brother of Gallus. Spared from the massacre of his family because of his age, Julian pursued his studies with increasing enthusiasm, especially at Pergamum and Ephesus where he became converted to the worship of the old pagan gods by local philosophers. For the time being, however, he kept his religious beliefs secret. In 355, Julian was summoned to court from Athens where he was studying and was made Caesar (*1–3*) to deal with the German invasions of Gaul. At that time, he married the sister of the Augustus Constantius.

Julian achieved great success during his five years in Gaul, constantly defeating the Germans and carrying out extensive administrative reforms. His success roused the suspicions of Constantius, which proved justified when the troops proclaimed the reluctant Caesar as emperor in 360 at Paris (*6–8*). After defeating further German attacks, Julian marched east but avoided having to fight a civil war because Constantius died at Tarsus in 361, naming Julian as his successor.

As sole Augustus, Julian distinguished himself for contemporaries and posterity by openly abjuring Christianity and making a determined effort to restore paganism. For this, he has been called 'the Apostate'. His policy roused little enthusiasm in the Christian East, least of all at Antioch, which he made his base in July 362 for a great expedition against Persia. Preparatory to this he celebrated his decennalia early (*11–12*), to have an occasion for giving a large donative to the troops. In March 363, the army departed for the East, and advanced successfully as far as Ctesiphon, but Julian was killed in a skirmish near the Tigris in July. His restoration of paganism perished with him. His coinage is far less interesting than might be expected: most of it celebrates the usual anniversaries; only one type (*10*) may reflect the pagan revival.

Caesar, 355–360

355 Appointment as Caesar.
    1   GLORIA REI PVBLICAE, Rome and Constantinople std., holding shield inscribed VOTIS V. Sol: Are 233A, 235, 237, 239
    2   VICTORIA AVGVSTORVM, Victory std. r., inscribing VOT V on shield. Sem: Are 240
    3   VOTIS V in wreath. Sil: Nic 102A
360 Quinquennalia.
    4   GLORIA REIPVBLICAE, As 1 but VOT V MVLT X. Sol: Tes 194, 197
    5   VOT V MVLT X in wreath. Sil: Are 260, 263–5; Sir 67; Tes 206

Augustus, 360–363

360 Continuing celebration of quinquennalia, coincident with proclamation as Augustus.
    6   GLORIA REI PVBLICAE, Type as *4*. Sol: Are 281–7; Lug 205–6; Tre 362
    7   VICTORIAE DD NN AVGG, Victory inscribing VOT X on wreath. Sem: Lug 207
    8   VOT/IS V MVLT/IS X in wreath. Sil: Are 292–3, 295–7; Lug 218–19, 227–30; Sir 102–3; Tes 221; Tre 363–5.
361 Praise of the troops of Gaul, leaders of the revolt and its success.
    9   VIRTVS EXERC GALL, soldier holding trophy, with hand on head of kneeling captive. Sol: Are 303–4; Lug 226

10

362 Discovery of a bull representing the god Apis in Egypt (or perhaps symbolic representation of pagan sacrifice; in any case, the closest to a pagan type on this coinage).

    10   SECVRITAS REIPVB, Bull stg. r. Æ1: Aqu 242–3; Are 313–23; Con 161–4; Cyz 125–8; Her 101–4; Lug 236–8; Nic 118–22; Sir 105–7; Sis 411–3, 417–9; Tes 222–6

— — Early celebration of decennalia at Antioch.

    11   GLORIA REIPVBLICAE, As type *1* but VOTIS X MVLTIS XX. Sol: Lug 225A

    12   VOT/IS X MVLT/IS XX in wreath. Sil: Ant 211–4; Are 309–12; Con 159; Lug 231–5. Æ3: Ale 90–91; Ant 219–21; Aqu 244–5; Are 324–6; Con 165–7; Cyz 129–31; Her 105–6; Lug 239; Nic 122A–25; Rom 328–30; Sir 108; Sis 414–6, 420–2, Tes 227–8

JOVIAN

June 363–February 364

Flavius Jovianus, born at Singidunum (Belgrade) in 331, rose to become commander of the imperial bodyguard under Julian, on whose death he was proclaimed emperor. He brought the Roman army back from Persia, though at the great price of surrendering the provinces east of the Tigris. He restored the supremacy of the Christian church, but died suddenly in Asia Minor soon after assuming the consulate at Ancyra in 364.

363 Vows on accession.

    1   GLORIA REI PVBLICAE, Rome and Constantinople std., holding wreath inscribed VOT V (MVLT X). Sol: Tes 230–1

2

2   SECVRITAS REIPVBLICAE, Same type. Sol: Ant 222−4; Aqu 246;
     Are 327; Con 169−70; Lug 240; Nic 126; Rom 331; Sir 113−6
3a   VOT/IS V MVL/T/IS X in wreath. Mil: Ant 225. Sil: Ant 227; Are
     329, 331−2; Con 172−4; Nic 127; Sir 117. Æ2: Ant 232−3;
     Aqu 247; Are 333−4; Con 179; Cyz 132; Her 110−1; Lug 241;
     Nic 128−9; Rom 333−4; Sir 118−20; Sis 425−6; Tes 239
3b   VOT V in wreath. Æ2: Ale 92; Ant 230−1; Con 178; Cyz 133;
     Her 108−9; Sis 423−4

VALENTINIAN I

February 364−November 375

Flavius Valentinianus, born in 321 in Pannonia, entered the army and had
become commander of the guards when Jovian suddenly died. The high
officials of the empire debated on a successor, and finally chose Valentinian,
who was proclaimed at Nicaea. Valentinian chose his brother Valens as
co-emperor to rule the East, while he departed for his headquarters,
Milan. As emperor, he was a rather puritanical Christian who legislated
in favour of the poor, promoted German generals in the army, and spent
most of his reign repelling German attacks and reorganising the defences
of the frontier. In 367, after an illness, he appointed his eight-year-old son
Gratian as Augustus, an occasion for additional vows. He transferred his
attention in 375 to Pannonia, where he suddenly collapsed and died
during negotiations with the Quadi. His uninteresting coinage, typical of
the period, reflects nothing of the reign but its consulates, anniversaries
and vows.

364 Accession, with customary vows.
    1   VICTORIA AVGVSTORVM, Victory std. r., inscribing VOT V on shield
         supported by winged Genius. Tre: Ant 3
    2   VICTORIAS AVGVSTORVM, Two Victories holding shield inscribed
         VOT V. Mil: Con 10
    3   VOT V in wreath. Arg: Con 11. Sil: Con 13
365 Joint consulate with Valens, entered by Valentinian at Milan.
    4   VOTA PVBLICA, Valentinian and Valens enthroned, each holding
         mappa. Sol: Med 3
368 Joint consulate with Valens, entered at Treveri.
    5   VOTA PVBLICA, Type as previous. Sol: Ant 23; Con 29; Nic 16;
         Tre 18
− − Vows for fifth anniversary of reign, with celebration of accession of
     Gratian (8).
    6a   VICTORIA AVGVSTORVM, Victory std. r., inscribing VOT V MVL X
         on shield. Sol: Con 26.
    6b   VICTORIA AVG, As 1, but VOT V MVLT X. Tre: Con 30
    7   GLORIA REIPVBLICAE, Rome and Constantinople enthroned,
         holding shield inscribed VOT V MVLT X. Sol: Nic 13

5   20

8   SPES R P, Valentinian and Gratian std.; between them, small
      togate figure bearing shield inscribed VOT V MVLT X. Sol: Ant
      20
9   VICTORIAE D N AVG, Type as *1*, but VOT V MVLT X. Sem: Tes 23
10   PAX PERPETVA, Same type, VOT V MVL X. Tre: Tes 5
11   VICTORIA AVGVSTORVM, Victory stg. r., inscribing VOT V MVLT X
      on shield. Mil: Rom 8
12   VOT/IS V MVLT/IS X in wreath. Mil: Aqu 3; Lug 4; Tes 9. Sil:
      Aqu 5; Con 36; Rom 10; Tre 3
373 Vows for tenth anniversary of reign, with delayed celebration of
      quinquennalia of Gratian (*20−21*).
   13*a*   VICTORIA AVGVSTORVM, Type as *6a*, but VOT X MVL XX. Sem: Ant
         22.
   13*b*   — — Type as *1*, but VOT X MVL XX. Sol: Ant 24
   14   GLORIA ROMANORVM, Type as *7*, but VOT X MVL XX. Sol: Ant
         15−16
   15   VICTORIA D N AVG, Victory stg., holding wreath surmounted by
         shield inscribed VOT X MVLT XX. Mil: Con 31
   16   VOT X MVLT XX in wreath. Arg: Con 34. Sil: Ant 33−4; Con 37:
         Nic 22; Sis 12
   17   GLORIA REIPVBLICAE, Type as *7* but VOT X MVLT XV. Sol: Tre 12
   18   VICTORIA AVGVSTORVM, As *11*, but VOT X MVLT XV. Mil: Are 13
   19   VOTIS X MVLTIS XV in wreath. Mil: Are 12; Lug 17
   20   VICTORIA AVGVSTORVM, As *11*, but VOT V MVLT X Mil: Tre 24
   21   VOT/IS V MVLT/IS X in wreath. Mil: Are 11; Lug 16; Tre 23. Arg:
         Nic 19. Sil: Nic 20−21
(373) Vows for the fifteenth anniversary of the reign (which would have
      taken place in 378 after the death of Valentinian), apparently
      celebrated at Constantinople and Siscia together with the decennial
      vows, in anticipation.
   22   VOT/IS XV (or VX) MVLT/IS XX in wreath. Mil: Sis 9. Arg: Con
         35. Sil: Con 38

VALENS

March 364−August 378

Flavius Valens, born in Pannonia in 328, was an imperial bodyguard
when his brother Valentinian chose him as co-emperor and gave him

charge of the eastern provinces. His first problem was to establish himself at Constantinople where Procopius had seized power. After defeating the usurper, he fought the Goths in Thrace, then turned his attention to the East where war had broken out with Persia over the control of Armenia. During his stay at Antioch, Valens gained a reputation for extreme cruelty during his persecution of pagans and philosophers. In 376, he was called back to the West, where the Visigoths had launched a major attack. Valens met them at Adrianople and fought one of the decisive battles of world history. He was killed − the first emperor since Decius to fall in battle against a foreign foe − and his army crushed. His coinage closely follows that of his brother.

364   Accession, with customary vows.

   1   VICTORIA AVGVSTORVM, Victory std. r., inscribing VOT V on shield supported by winged Genius (Valentinian *1*). Tre: Ant 3

   2   VICT DD NN AVGG, Two Victories holding shield inscribed VOT V (*cf.* Valentinian *2*). Arg: Rom 9

   3   VOT/IS V in wreath (Valentinian *3*). Arg: Con 11. Sil: Ant 8; Con 13

365   Joint consulate with Valentinian.

   4   VOTA PVBLICA, Valentinian and Valens enthroned, each holding mappa (Valentinian *4*). Sol: Med 3.

368   Joint consulate with Valentinian, with celebration of quinquennalia and the accession of Gratian (*8, 11*).

   5   VOTA PVBLICA, As previous (Valentinian *5*). Sol: Ant 23; Con 29; Nic 16−7; Tre 18

   6*a*   VICTORIA AVG/VSTORVM, Victory std. r., inscribing VOT V MVLT X on shield (Valentinian *6a*). Sol: Con 26

   6*b*   VICTORIA AVG, Type as 1, but VOT V MVL X (Valentinian *6b*). Tre: Con 30

   7   GLORIA REIPVBLICAE, Rome and Constantinople enthroned, holding shield inscribed VOT V MVLT X (Valentinian *7*). Sol: Con 23; Nic 13

   8   SPES R P, Valentinian and Gratian std.; between them, small togate figure bearing shield inscribed VOT V MVLT X (Valentinian *8*). Sol: Ant 20

8

   9   VICTORIA AVGVSTORVM, Victory stg. r., inscribing VOT V MVL X on shield (Valentinian *11*). Mil: Rom 8

10   VOT V MVLT X in wreath (Valentinian *12*). Mil: Aqu 3. Sil: Con
     36; Lug 8; Rom 10; Tes 14; Tre 4

11   VOTIS V in wreath. Sil: Con 39

373 Vows for tenth anniversary, and for the quinquennium of Gratian
(*18–19*)

12*a* VICTORIA AVGVSTORVM, As *6a*, but VOT X MVL/T XX (Valentinian
       13a). Sol: Ant 22; Con 38

12*b* — — Type as *1*, but VOT X MVL/T XX (Valentinian *13b*). Sem:
       Ant 24, 26; Tre 20

13   GLORIA ROMANORVM, Type as *7*, but VOT X MVL XX (Valentinian
     14). Sol: Ant 16

14   VOT X MVL/T XX in wreath (Valentinian *16*). Mil: Arg 28. Arg:
     Con 34. Sil: Ant 33–4; Con 37; Lug 19; Nic 22; Sis 12; Tes
     25.

15   GLORIA REIPVBLICAE, Type as *7* but VOT X MVLT XV (Valentinian
     17). Sol: Tre 12

16   VICTORIA AVGVSTORVM, As *9*, but VOT X MVLT XV (Valentinian
     18). Mil: Are 13

17   VOTIS X MVLTIS XV in wreath (Valentinian *19*). Mil: Lug 17.

18   VICTORIA AVGVSTORVM, As *9*, but VOT V MVLT X (Valentinian *20*).
     Mil: Lug 18; Tre 24–5

19   VOT/IS V MVLT/IS X in wreath (Valentinian *21*). Mil: Ant 27;
     Are 27; Lug 16; Tre 23. Arg: Nic 19. Sil: Nic 20–1

(**373**) Vows for fifteenth anniversary, celebrated in anticipation, on the
decennalia at Constantinople and Siscia.

20   VOT/IS XV (or VX) MVLT/IS XX in wreath (Valentinian *22*). Mil: Sis
     9. Sil: Con 38; Sis 13

376 Decennalia of Gratian.

21   VOTIS X MVLTIS XX in wreath. Mil: Tre 41. Sil: Aqu 14

22   VOT X MVLT XV in wreath. Sil: Tre 44

378 Third quinquennium of Valens.

23   VOT/IS XV (or VX) MVLT/IS XX in wreath. Mil: Sis 16. Sil: Sis 19,
     Tes 30

(**378**) Anticipation of vicennalia (would have been 383), at Constantinople.

24   VOT XX MVLT XXX in wreath. Sil: Con 42

PROCOPIUS

September 365–May 366

Procopius, a native of Asia Minor and relative of the emperor Julian, was
born about 326 and had a distinguished military career which brought him
to command the eastern frontier under Julian who, according to rumour,
chose him as his successor. When Julian was killed, however, Procopius
withdrew to private life in favour of Jovian, but on the accession of

Valentinian became an object of suspicion and disappeared from view. He soon arrived in Constantinople where the troops proclaimed him emperor. After a series of battles in Asia Minor, however, he was defeated by Valens and executed.

365 Vows on accession.

    1 VOT V in wreath. Sil: Con 13; Cyz 3; Nic 6

1

GRATIAN

August 367−383

Flavius Gratianus, the son of Valentinian I, was born at Sirmium in 359. He became Augustus at the age of eight, but only ruled after the death of his father in 375. He controlled the entire West, having effective charge of the regions nominally ruled by his younger brother Valentinian II. After fighting the Alemanni from his base at Treveri, he moved to Sirmium, where he appointed the general Theodosius to replace Valens after the catastrophe of Adrianople (*15*). He returned to the West, where he received news of the revolt of Magnus Maximus in 383. Gratian hastened to Paris to meet the threat, but his soldiers deserted him and he fled to Lugdunum where he was killed.

367 Accession, with customary vows.

    1 PRINCIPIVM IVVENTVTIS, Gratian stg. r. Sol: Ant 19; Con 24; Nic 14; Tre 13

    2 GLORIA NOVI SAECVLI, Gratian stg. facing, crowned by two small images of Victory. Sol: Are 10, Lug 15. Æ: Are 15 (no Victories)

    3 VOTIS V in wreath. Sil: Con 39

368 Quinquennium of Valentinian and Valens, with further celebration of Gratian's accession.

    4 SPES R P, Valentinian and Valens std.; between them, small togate figure bearing shield inscribed VOT V MVL X (Valentinian *8*). Sol: Ant 20

373 Joint consulate of Valentinian and Valens (*5*), with celebration of their decennalia (*6−7*) and of the quinquennalia (*8−10*) of Gratian, which actually fell in 371.

    5 VOTA PVBLICA, Valentinian and Valens enthroned, each holding mappa. Sol: Tre 18

6   VICTORIA AVGVSTORVM, Victory std. r., inscribing VOT X MVLT XX on shield (Valentinian *13a*). Sol: Con 28

7   VOT X MVLT XX in wreath. Sil: Ant 34

8*a*   VICTORIA AVGVSTORVM, Type as *6* but VOT V MVL/T X. Sol: Ant 21; Con 27

8*b*   — — As previous, but shield supported by Genius. Sem: Tre 19.

8*c*   — — Type as 8b, but VOT X only. Tre: Ant 25

9   — — Victory stg. r., inscribing VOT V MVLT X on shield (Valentinian *20*). Mil: Lug 18; Tre 24

10   VOT/IS V MVLT/IS X in wreath (Valentinian *21*). Mil: Are 11, 14; Lug 16; Tre 23. Sil: Ant 32; Con 36; Nic 20; Sis 11.

(**373**) Anticipated vows for the fifteenth anniversary of Valentinian and Valens, celebrated at their decennalia.

11   VOT XV MVLT XX in wreath (Valentinian *22*). Sil: Sis 13

376 Decennalia of Gratian.

12   VOTIS X MVLTIS XX in wreath. Mil: Tre 41. Sil: Aqu 14

13   VOT X MVLT XV in wreath. Sil: Tre 44

378 Fifteenth anniversary of Valens.

14   VOT/IS XV (or VX) MVLT/IS XX in wreath (Valens *23*). Mil: Sis 16. Sil: Sis 19; Tes 30, 36 (VOT XV MVLT XXX)

379 Recovery of the Empire with the appointment of Theodosius.

15   REPARATIO REIPVB, Emperor stg l., raising kneeling turreted female. Æ2: Ale 8; Ant 42; Aqu 30; Are 20; Con 54; Lug 28; Nic 27; Rom 43; Sis 26; Tes 37; Tre 65

380 Joint consulate of Gratian and Theodosius (*16*), which Gratian entered at Treveri; vows for third quinquennium (*17*) of Gratian (actually 381) and first (*18*) of Valentinian II (379).

16   VOTA PVBLICA, Gratian and Theodosius enthroned, each holding mappa. Sil: Tre 51

17   VOT/IS XV MVLT/IS XX in wreath. Mil: Tre 52. Sil: Sis 25; Tre 63. Æ4: Ale 12; Ant 53; Are 24; Lug 30; Nic 35; Sis 31; Tes 43; Tre 74

18   VOT V MVLT X in wreath. Sil: Sis 24. Æ4: Ant 52; Aqu 36; Sis 29; Tre 73

383 Accession of Arcadius (*22*), celebrated with anticipatory vows for the vicennalia (*19*) of Gratian (which would have fallen in 386) and the decennalia (*20–21*) of Valentinian II (384).

19   VOT XX MVLT XXX in wreath. Æ4: Ant 58; Con 64; Cyz 22; Her 20; Nic 39

20   VOT X MVLT XV in wreath. Sil: Tre 61

21   VOT X MVLT XX in wreath. Æ4: Ale 13; Ant 56; Cyz 21; Her 19

22   VOT V in wreath. Æ4: Cyz 20; Her 18; Nic 37

VALENTINIAN II

November 375–May 392

Flavius Valentinianus, the son of Valentinian I, was born at Treveri in 371 and made Augustus on the death of his father in 375, with nominal jurisdiction over Italy, Illyricum and Africa; actual power was exercised by Gratian until his death in 383. Thereafter, Valentinian ruled the entire West, much troubled by ecclesiastical disturbances. Valentinian was forced to flee from Magnus Maximus but was re-established in power by Theodosius whose triumph he shared. He subsequently fell under the influence of the German army commander, Arbogast, who had him killed when he attempted to restrict the general's power in 392.

378 Quinquennium, celebrated in anticipation, with the fifteenth anniversary of Valens.
  1 VOT V MVLT X in wreath. Sil: Tes 29
  2 VOT XV MVLT XX in wreath (Valens *23*). Sil: Sis 19.
  — — Recovery of the empire, and appointment of Theodosius.
  3 REPARATIO REIPVB, Emperor raising turreted female (Gratian *15*). Æ2: Ale 8; Ant 42; Aqu 30; Are 20; Con 54; Lug 28; Nic 27; Rom 43; Sis 26; Tes 37; Tre 65
380 Quinquennium, celebrated with the fifteenth anniversary of Gratian.
  4 VOT V MVLT X in wreath (Gratian *18*). Sil: Sis 24. Æ4: Aqu 36; Con 59; Sis 29; Tre 73
  5 VOT XV MVLT XX in wreath (Gratian *17*). Æ4: Ale 12; Aqu 38; Rom 51; Tre 74
383 Decennalia of Valentinian (*6–7*), celebrated early, like the vicennalia (*8*) of Gratian (which would have fallen in 386), to coincide with the quinquennalia (*9–10*) of Theodosius and the accession of Arcadius (*11–12*).
  6 VOT X MVLT XV in wreath (Gratian *20*). Æ4: Aqu 50
  7 VOT X MVLT XX in wreath (Gratian *21*). Æ4: Ale 13; Ant 56, 65; Aqu 37, 51; Con 63; Cyz 21; Her 19; Nic 38; Sis 30, 37; Tes 49
  8 VOT XX MVLT XXX in wreath (Gratian *19*). Æ4: Ale 14; Ant 58; Cyz 22; Her 20; Nic 39
  9 VICTORIA AVGVSTORVM, Victory std. r., inscribing VOT V MVL X on shield. Sem: Con 73. Tre: Con 50
  10 VOT V MVLT/IS X in wreath. Sil: Con 51; Tre 59–60. Æ4: Aqu 49.
  11 VICTORIA AVGVSTORVM, As *9*, but VOT V on shield. Sol: Ant 39
  12 VOT V in wreath (Gratian *22*). Æ4: Con 62: Cyz 20: Nic 37
387 Joint consulate of Valentinian and Theodosius (*13*), which Valentinian entered at Milan. Celebration of the fifteenth anniversary (*14–16*) of Valentinian (389), and decennalia (*17–19*) of Theodosius (388).
  13 VOTA PVBLICA, Valentinian and Theodosius enthroned, each holding mappa. Sol: Med 9, 21.
  14 CONCORDIA AVGGG, Constantinople enthroned, holding shield inscribed VOT XV MVLT XX. Sol: Tes 54

15 GLORIA ROMANORVM, Rome and Constantinople std., holding shield inscribed VOT XV MVLT XX. Sol: Rom 61

15

16 VOT XV MVLT XX in wreath. Arg: Lug 42
17 CONCORDIA AVGGG, As 14, but VOT X MVLT XX on shield. Sol: Med 7
18 — — VOT X MVLT XV on shield. Sol: Aqu 39, Med 7
19 VOT X MVLT XX in wreath. Sil: Med 14; Rom 62; Tes 58. Æ4: Ale 19
390 Consulate of Valentinian, entered at Trier.
20 VOTA PVBLICA, Two emperors std., holding mappa. Sol: Tre 91

THEODOSIUS

January 379–January 395

Flavius Theodosius, born in 346, was the son of Theodosius, a distinguished Spanish general who had risen to command the imperial cavalry. The son served in his father's staff, and was promoted to become *magister militum* in 378 by Gratian who made him co-emperor in the following year after the death of Valens at Adrianople. Theodosius dealt successfully with the Goths by allowing them to settle on Roman territory, but repelled all further threats from them. In 383, problems in Armenia obliged him to recognise Magnus Maximus in the West, but a long-lasting treaty with Persia in 387 left him free to move against the usurper whom he defeated the next year. Theodosius was a devout and intolerant Christian who persecuted heretics and pagans. Moves to forbid the pagan cult provoked the revolt of Eugenius, which Theodosius suppressed in 394. On this death in 395, he divided the empire (which was never again reunited) between his sons Arcadius and Honorius. Although Theodosius was one of the more important Roman emperors, his coinage merely features the stock abstractions and vows, with a posssible reference to the battle of Adrianople (*1*).

379 Recovery of the empire, with appointment of Theodosius.
1 REPARATIO REIPVB, Emperor raising turreted female (Gratian *15*). Æ2: Ale 8; Ant 42; Aqu 30; Are 20; Con 54; Lug 28; Rom 43; Sis 26; Tes 37; Tre 65
380 Vows for the fifteenth anniversary of Gratian and fifth of Valentinian II.

2   VOT XV MVLT XX in wreath (Gratian *17*). Æ4: Aqu 38; Con 60;
     Cyz 19; Rom 51; Sis 31; Tre 74

3   VOT V MVLT X in wreath (Gratian *18*). Sil: Sis 24. Æ4: Aqu 36;
     Con 59; Sis 29; Tre 73

383 Quinquennium (*4–6*), celebrated with the accession of Arcadius
      (*7*), the anticipated vicennalia (*8*) of Gratian (which would have
      been in 386) and the decennalia (*9–11*) of Valentinian II (384). The
      AVGGGG of *4a* refers to the short period, January–August 383, when
      there were four emperors: Gratian, Valentinian, Theodosius and
      Arcadius; type *4b*, with AVGGG, was struck after the death of Gratian.

4a   CONCORDIA AVGGGG, Constantinople enthroned, holding shield
      inscribed VOT V MVLT X. Sol: Con 47

4b   CONCORDIA AVGGG, As previous. Sol: Con 68

5   VICTORIA AVGVSTORVM, Victory std. r., inscribing VOT V MVLT X
      on shield (Valentinian II *9*). Sem: Con 73. Tre: Con 50

6   VOT V MVLT X in wreath (Valentinian II *10*). Sil: Con 51; Tre
      59.

7   VOT V in wreath (Gratian *22*). Æ4: Aqu 48; Cyz 20; Tes 48

8   VOT XX MVLT XXX in wreath (Gratian *19*). Æ4: Ant 66; Con 64;
      Cyz 22; Her 20; Nic 39;

9   VICTORIA AVGVSTORVM, Type as *5*, but VOT X MVLT XV. Tre: Con
      74

10   VOT X MVLTIS XV in wreath (Gratian *20*). Sil: Tre 61

11   VOT X MVLT XX in wreath (Gratian *21*). Æ4: Ale 13; Ant 56;
      Aqu 37, 51; Con 63; Cyz 21; Her 19; Nic 38; Rom 50; Sis 30,
      37, 65; Tes 49

387 Joint consulate with Valentinian II; vows for decennalia (388) and
      quinquennalia (*15*) of Arcadius (387).

12   VOTA PVBLICA, Valentinian and Theodosius enthroned, each
      holding mappa (Valentinian II *13*). Sol: Med 21

13a CONCORDIA AVGGG, Type as *4*, but VOT X MVLT XX (Valentinian
      II *17*). Sol: Med 7

13b — — VOT X MVLT XV (Valentinian II *18*). Sol: Aqu 39; Con 71;
      Med 7

14   VOT X MVLT XX in wreath (Valentinian II *19*). Sil: Con 77; Med
      14; Rom 62; Tes 58. Æ4: Ale 19

15   CONCORDIA AVGGG, Type as *4* (VOT V MVLT X). Sol: Med 7

393 Decennalia of Arcadius, celebrated with the accession of Honorius.

16   VOT X MVLT XX in wreath. Sil: Con 87

MAGNUS MAXIMUS

Spring 383–August 388

Fl. Magnus Maximus, a Spaniard and distant relative of Theodosius,
served with distinction in Britain and Africa, and rose to command the

army in Britain under Gratian, against whom he rebelled in 383. When Gratian, deserted by his troops, was defeated and killed, Maximus gained supreme power in Gaul, Britain and Spain and associated his son Victor with him. He entered into negotiations with Theodosius who, being fully occupied in the East, recognised Maximus as Augustus, as did Valentinian II in Italy. In 387, however, Maximus invaded Italy and put Valentinian to flight, though still recognising him as co-emperor. In the following year, Theodosius attacked and defeated Maximus who was killed by his troops.

383 Vows on accession.
  1 votis v in wreath. Æ4: Are 28
388 Celebration of quinquennium.
  2 victoria avgvstorvm, Victory std. r., writing vot v mvlt x on shield. Sem: Tre 78
  3 vot/is v mvlt/is x in wreath. Mil: Tre 80−1. Sil: Log 4. Æ4: Lug 35; Tre 86

FLAVIUS VICTOR

383−August 388

The infant son of Magnus Maximus, made Augustus soon after his father assumed power, was killed together with him after the victory of Theodosius.

383 Vows for the quinquennium of Magnus Maximus.
  1 victoria avgvstorvm, Victory std. r., writing vot v mvlt x on shield. Sem: Med 17

EUGENIUS

Augustus 392−September 394

Fl. Eugenius, a rhetorician and teacher of Latin, rose to high civil office in Rome, where he was proclaimed Augustus by the German general Arbogast who controlled the West after his murder of Valentinian II. When he failed to gain recognition from Theodosius, he allied himself with the pagan aristocracy of Rome (though he was himself a Christian) but was soon defeated and killed. His brief reign represented the last hope for paganism in the empire.

392 Vows on accession (with numbers usually employed for a quinquennium).
  1 vot v mvlt x in wreath. Mil: Med 30
393 Joint consulate with Theodosius, proclaimed by Eugenius, but not recognised by Theodosius in the East.

2 VOTA PVBLICA, Eugenius and Theodosius enthroned, holding mappa. Sol: Tre 102

ARCADIUS

January 383–May 408

Fl. Arcadius, the elder son of Theodosius, was born in Spain in 377 and proclaimed Augustus at the age of six. He was entrusted with the East when Theodosius marched against Eugenius and acceded to full power on the death of his father in 395. Arcadius was virtually a cipher during his reign, with power being exercised by his wife Eudoxia and by the high ministers of the court. His territories were generally at peace, while serious troubles were beginning in the West. He died peacefully in 408.

383 Accession to imperial power (*1*), celebrated with the quinquennalia of Theodosius (*2–4*), the decennalia (*5*) of Valentinian II and the anticipated vicennalia (*6*) of Gratian.

1 VOT V in wreath (Gratian *22*). Æ4: Con 62; Cyz 20; Her 18; Nic 37; Sis 36; Tes 48

2 CONCORDIA AVGGGG, Constantinople enthroned, holding shield inscribed VOT V MVL X (Theodosius *4a*). Sol: Con 47

3 VICTORIA AVGVSTORVM, Victory std. r., writing VOT V MVL X on shield (Valentinian II *9*). Tre: Con 50

4 VOT V MVLT X in wreath (Valentinian II *10*). Æ4: Aqu 49; Rom 58

5 VOT X MVLT XX in wreath (Gratian *21*). Æ4: Ale 13; Ant 56, 65; Aqu: *LRBC* 1099; Cyz 21

6 VOT XX MVLT XXX in wreath (Gratian *19*). Æ4: Ant 58

388 Quinquennium (*7*), celebrated with the decennalia (*8–11*) of Theodosius.

7 CONCORDIA AVGGG, Type as 2 (VOT V MVLT X) (Theodosius *15*). Sol: Med 7; Tes 51

8 — — but VOT X MVLT XV (Valentinian II *18*). Sol: Con 17; Tes 52

9 GLORIA ROMANORVM, Rome and Constantinople std., holding shield inscribed VOT X MVLT XX. Sol: Rom 60

8

10 VICTORIA AVGVSTORVM, Victory std. r., writing VOT X MVLT XX on shield supported by winged Genius. Sem: Med 22

11   VOT X MVLT XX in wreath (Valentinian II *19*). Sil: Con 77; Rom 62; Tes 58. Æ4: Ale 19

393 Decennalia, celebrated with the accession of Honorius.

12   VOT X MVLT XX in wreath (Theodosius *16*). Mil: Med 24. Sil: Con 87

13   VOT X MVLT XV in wreath. Sil: Med 27

402 Nomination of Theodosius II as Augustus, and vicennalia of Arcadius.

14   NOVA SPES REIPVBLICAE, Type as *3*, but XX XXX. Sol: *Tolstoy* 28

403 Decennalia of Honorius.

15*a*   VICTORIA AVGVSTORVM, Type as *3*, but VOT X MVLT XX. Sem: *Tolstoy* 40: Rom

15*b*   — — Type as *10*. Sem: *MonMed* 81: Med; *Tolstoy* 39: Rom

16   VOT X MVLT XX in wreath. Mil: *RSC* v. 28: Med; Rav; Rom. Sil: *RSC* v. 28A: Con

HONORIUS

January 393—August 423

Fl. Honorius, the younger son of Theodosius, born in 384, was made Augustus in association with his father and elder brother in 393. He assumed power in the West on the death of his father in 395, and ruled it from Ravenna after 402 because of the danger from the Goths. His reign, which was dominated by his generals, ministers and his sister Galla Placidia, saw the Germans overwhelm Gaul and the Goths capture Rome in 410 — the first time the city had fallen to a foreign enemy in 800 years. To defend the empire against these constant menaces, Honorius elevated Constantius to be co-emperor in 421, but he died the same year. Honorius himself succumbed to disease in 423.

394 Accession to imperial power, and decennalia of Arcadius; celebration delayed because of the usurpation of Eugenius.

1   VOT X MVLT XV in wreath (Arcadius *13*). Sil: Med 27

396 Joint consulate with Arcadius, entered by Honorius at Milan.

2   VOTA PVBLICA, Arcadius and Honorius std. facing, each holding mappa. Sol: *C*60—61: Med

397 Quinquennium of Honorius.

3   VICTORIA AVGVSTORVM, Victory std. r., inscribing VOT V MVLT X on shield. Sem: *MonMed* 77: Med

4   VOT V MVLT X in wreath. Mil: *MonMed* 78: Med. Sil: Med 26

403 Decennalia of Honorius.

5   VICTORIA AVGG, Honorius stg., foot on captive, holding standard inscribed VT X and shield inscribed MVLT XX. Sol: *C*37: Med

6   VICTORIA AVGVSTORVM, Type as *3*, but VOT X MVLT XX (Arcadius *15*). Sem: *C*51: Med; Rav

7   VOT X MVLT XX in wreath (Arcadius *16*). Mil: RSC v. 64: Med; Rav; Rom. Sil: RSC v. 65: Con.

408   Fifteenth anniversary of Honorius.

8   VOT XV MVLT XX in wreath. Mil: RSC v. 66: Con; Rom. Sil: RSC v.67: Con

411   Vicennalia, celebrated with decennalia of Theodosius II.

9   CONCORDIA AVGG, Constantinople enthroned, holding shield inscribed XX VOT XXX (*cf.* Theodosius II *1*). Sol: *Hahn (1979)* 4: Con

10   VICTORIA AVGVSTORVM, Type as *3*, but VOT XX MVLT XXX Sem: *C*52: Rav

11   VOT X MVLT XV Sil: *C*50: Rav

421   Vicennalia of Theodosius II.

12   VOT XX MVLT XXX, Victory stg l., holding long cross (Theodosius II *5*). Sol: C68: Con

422   Thirtieth anniversary of Honorius. Type *13* was struck for the actual festival, *14* for circulation during the following years.

13   VOT XXX MVLT XXXX, Honorius std. facing on curule chair, holding mappa and sceptre. Sol: *C*69: Rav

14   (No legend), Rome and Constantinople std., holding shield inscribed VOT XXX MVLT XXXX. Sol: *C*73: Rav

CONSTANTINE III 407–411 and CONSTANS 408–411

Usurpers in Gaul; no historical types.

MAXIMUS 409–411

Usurper in Spain: no historical types.

ATTALUS

November 409–June 410; 414–early 415

Priscus Attalus, a pagan of an Antiochene family, lived in Rome, where he became prefect of the city in 409 after its first siege by Alaric. When the Gothic king's attempts to come to terms with Honorius failed, he blockaded Rome and had Attalus installed as emperor; Attalus in his turn granted Alaric the high military command he requested. Attalus had ambitions of defeating Honorius and of gaining control of Africa, but when both attempts failed and the governor of Africa stopped the grain supply of Rome, Alaric deposed Attalus in order to reach an accommodation with Honorius. When this proved abortive, Alaric marched on Rome, which he captured and plundered in August 410, a momentous event in history. Attalus then accompanied Alaric northward, retaining considerable influence. In 414, he was again proclaimed emperor, this time in Gaul, but was soon defeated and captured by Constantius. After being paraded in the triumph of Honorius, he was exiled to the isle of Lipara.

409 Celebration of the city of Rome, where Attalus ruled, the last time it could be described as 'unconquered'. The gold coins, along with the medallions of the same type, were struck for payment to the Goths.

    1   INVICTA ROMA AETERNA, Rome std. l. Sol: *C*3: Rom. Tre: *C*4: Rom. Sil: *C*7: Rom

1

JOVINUS

411−Autumn 413

Ruler in Gaul; no historical types.

SEBASTIANUS 412−413

Brother of Jovinus, and co-ruler with him: no historical types.

CONSTANTIUS III

February−September 421

No historical types.

GALLA PLACIDIA

Aelia Galla Placidia, the daughter of Theodosius, born in 388, lived in Rome until its sack by the Goths, when she was captured and eventually married to their king, Ataulf in 414. Two years later, she was returned to Rome by treaty and married the general Constantius. When he was made co-ruler, she became Augusta. After his death, she took refuge in Constantinople where she used her influence to have her son Valentinian

III installed as western emperor in 425. She then became Augusta again, and virtual ruler of the West. Although she withdrew from public life after the marriage of Valentinian in 437, she retained considerable influence until her death in 450.

421 Vicennalia of Theodosius II.

   1   VOT XX MVLT XXX, Victory stg. l., holding long cross (Theodosius II 5). Sol: *C*13–14: Rom

1

JOHANNES 423–425

Ruler in the West: no historical types.

THEODOSIUS II

January 402–July 450

Fl. Theodosius, the only son of Arcadius and Eudoxia, was born in 401 and made Augustus when less than a year old. He succeeded Arcadius in 408, but hardly ruled, being dominated by his ministers and his sister Pulcheria. He married Eudocia in 421; among their children was Eudoxia who married Valentinian III. Theodosius died from a hunting accident, after a reign of forty-nine years, the longest in Roman history. His coinage, unusually for this period, includes a type with an apparent specific historical reference. According to a contemporary source, Quotvultdeus of Carthage, writing about 450, Type 5 was issued to celebrate a miracle which took place during the Persian war of 421–22. The date of its first issue, however, is disputed; it was, in any case, struck over a long period. Characteristically, the rest of the coinage is concerned with the anniversaries of the emperor, which were celebrated at somewhat irregular intervals.

411 Decennalia.

   1   CONCORDIA AVGG, Constantinople enthroned, holding shield inscribed X VOT XX. Sol: *Hahn (1979)* 3: Con

   2   VOT X MVLT XX in wreath. Sil: *RSC* v. 20*b*: Con. Æ4: *LRBC* 2242: Con

415 Fifteenth anniversary.

   3   GLORIA REIPVBLICAE, Rome and Constantinople std., holding shield inscribed VOT XV MVLT XX. Sol: *Hahn (1979)* 5: Con

   4   VOT XV MVLT XX in wreath. Sil: RSC v. 20C: Con

            8   11

422 Vicennalia: type 5*a* was struck for the festival; 5*b* for general circulation, probably over the next ten years. Both may refer to the Roman victory over Persia, in a war begun to save the Christian Armenians from persecution.

   5*a*   VOT XX MVLT XXX, Victory stg. l., holding long cross. Consular obverse. Sol: *Hahn (1979)* 6: Con

   5*b*   — —As previous, but helmeted bust on *obv*. Sol: *Hahn (1979)* 15, 18: Con

   6   VICTORIA AVGG, Victory std. r., inscribing XX XXX on shield. Sem: *Hahn (1979)* 39−41: Con

   7   VOT XX MVLT XXX in wreath. Sil: *RSC* v. 20D: Con

425 Joint consulate of Theodosius and Valentinian III.

   8   SALVS REIPVBLICAE, Theodosius enthroned, with child Valentinian stg., each holding mappa. Sol: *Hahn (1979)* 22: Aqu; Con

426 Joint consulate of Theodosius and Valentinian III.

   9   SALVS REIPVBLICAE, Theodosius and Valentinian std. facing, each holding mappa. Sol: *Hahn (1979)* 23: Con

430 Joint consulate of Theodosius and Valentinian, with celebration of the thirtieth anniversary of Theodosius. Type *10* was struck for the occasion; *11* for circulation after.

   10   VOT XXX MVLT XXXX, Theodosius and Valentinian enthroned, each holding mappa. Consular obverse. Sol: *Hahn (1979)* 7: Con

   11   — — Constantinople std. l., holding cross on globe. Sol: *Hahn (1979)* 25, 56: Con; Tes

   12   VICTORIA AVGG, As type 6, but XXX XXXX on shield. Sem: *Boyce (1965)* no. 129

   13*a*   VOT XXX MVLT XXXX in wreath. Sil: *RSC* v. 20E: Con

   13*b*   VOT XXX in wreath. Æ4: *LRBC* 2243: Con

435 Thirty-fifth anniversary of reign.

   14   VOT XXXV MVLT XXXX, Theodosius enthroned, wearing consular robes Consular obverse. Sol: *Hahn (1979)* p. 129: Con

> 15   VICTORIA AVGG, As *6*, but XXXV on shield. Sem: *Boyce (1965)*
>   no. 128
> 16   VT XXXV in wreath. Æ4: *LRVC* 2244: Con

437   Marriage of Valentinian II and Eudoxia.
>   17   FELICITER NVBTIIS, Theodosius stg. between Valentinian and
>   Eudoxia, who clasp hands. Sol: *Hahn (1979)* 9: Con

17

439   Seventeenth consulate of Theodosius and fortieth anniversary of
reign. Type *18* was struck for the occasion; *19* in 443, apparently
for use as tribute to the Huns of Attila.
>   18   SECVRITAS REIPVBLICAE, Type as *14*. Consular obverse. Sol: *Hahn*
>   *(1979)* 10: Con
>   19   IMP XXXXII COS XVII P P. Roma std. l. *Hahn (1979)* 33: Con
>   20   VICTORIA AVGG, As *6*, but XXXX on shield.
>   Sol: *Tolstoy 63*: Con
>   21   VOT MVLT XXXX in wreath. Sol: *RSC* v. 21: Con

444   Eighteenth consulate of Theodosius. This is the last time that an
imperatorial acclamation appears on the coinage, but here it is
merely used as a date.
>   22   IMP XXXXIIII COS XVIII, Type as *14*. Consular obverse. Sol: *Hahn*
>   *(1979)* 11: Con

— —   Forty-fifth anniversary of reign.
>   23   VICTORIA AVGG, As *6*, but XXVXX on shield. Sem: *Tolstoy 61–2*:
>   Con

EUDOCIA

Athenais was the beautiful and accomplished daughter of a famous soph-
ist of Athens. She came to Constantinople when her brothers deprived
her of her inheritance, and attracted the attention of Pulcheria, the sister
of Arcadius. As a result, she was married to Theodosius II in 421 after
becoming a Christian and taking the name Aelia Eudocia. She was made
Augusta in 423, but exiled to the Holy Land in 443 because of a suspicion
of adultery and her involvement in the ecclesiastical disputes of the day.
There, she performed works of piety until her death in 460.

422   Celebration of the vicennalia of Theodosius II.
>   1   VOT XX MVLT XXX, Victory holding long cross (Theodosius II 5).
>   Sol: *Hahn (1979)* 20: Con

430 Thirtieth anniversary of Theodosius II.
  2 VOT XXX MVLT XXXX, Constantinople std. 1. (Theodosius II *11*).
     Sol: *Hahn (1979)* 28: Con

PULCHERIA

Aelia Pulcheria, the oldest child of Arcadius and Eudoxia, born in
399, played a dominant role in the empire during the reign of her
brother Theodosius II. She was proclaimed Augusta in 414, and led
a life of piety and virginity, never losing her influence. In order to
secure a peaceful succession, she entered into a kind of marriage
with Marcian in 450, and died three years later.

421 Vicennalia of Theodosius II.
  1 VOT XX MVLT XXX, Victory holding long cross (Theodosius II 5).
     Sol: *Hahn (1979)* 17, 19: Con
430 Thirtieth anniversary of Theodosius II.
  2 VOT XXX MVLT XXXX, Constantinople std. 1. (Theodosius II *11*).
     Sol: *Hahn (1979)* 27: Con

VALENTINIAN III

Caesar October 424/Augustus October 425−March 455

Flavius Placidus Valentinianus, the son of Constantius III and Galla
Placidia, was born in 419 and proclaimed Caesar, then Augustus by
Theodosius II while still a child. At first under the influence of his mother
and her advisers, Valentinian established a certain independence after his
marriage to Eudoxia in 437. His reign saw the loss of Africa, Britain and
the Balkan provinces, though imperial authority was maintained in Spain
and Gaul. Although the empire survived the attacks of Attila the Hun
during his reign, Valentinian could not survive his own treacherous murder of his best general, Aetius, and was himself killed soon after, having
ruled for thirty years.

425 Joint consulate with Theodosius II and celebration of accession.
  1 SALVS REIPVBLICAE, Theodosius enthroned and Valentinian stg.,
     each holding mappa. (Theodosius II 8). Sol: *C*9: Con
430 Thirtieth anniversary of Theodosius II.
  2 VOT XXX MVLT XXXX, Constantinople std. 1. (Theodosius II 11).
     Sol: *C*42: Con
435 Joint consulate with Theodosius, and decennial vows.
  3 VOT X MVLT XX, Valentinian enthroned facing, holding mappa
     and cross. Sol: *C*41: Rav
  4 VICTORIA AVGVSTORVM, Victory std. r., holding shield inscribed
     VOT X MVLT XX. Sem: *Boyce (1965)* no.122: Rom

445 Twentieth anniversary of reign.

    5*a* VOT XX MVLT XXX in wreath. Sil: *RSC v.* 41A: Con

    5*b* VOT XX in wreath. Æ4: *LRBC* 847: Rom

455 Consulate, with celebration of thirtieth anniversary. Type *6* was issued for the festivities; *7* for circulation thereafter. Type *6* is the last example of the 'restitutor' type in the Roman coinage; it may have been issued to portray Valentinian as restoring the Roman world after the defeat of Attila.

    6   VOT XXX MVLT XXXX, Valentinian in consular robes stg. facing, raising kneeling female figure. Consular obverse. Sol: *Boyce (1965)* no. 124: Rom

    7   — — Valentinian stg. facing, holding Victory and long cross, foot on human-headed serpent. Sol: *Boyce (1965)* no. 123: Rom

LICINIA EUDOXIA

Licinia Eudoxia, the daughter of Theodosius II and Aelia Eudocia, born in 422, married Valentinian II in 437 (Theodosius II *17*) and was proclaimed Augusta in 439. After her husband was murdered in 455, she was forcibly married to the usurper Petronius Maximus against whom, according to rumour, she summoned the Vandal king Gaiseric who swiftly arrived, captured and plundered Rome, and led the empress captive to Carthage. She was released in 462 and retired to Constantinople.

455 Thirtieth anniversary of the reign of Valentinian III.

    1   VOT XXX MVLT XXXX, Valentinian and Eudoxia stg. facing. Sol: *C2*: Rom

MARCIAN

August 450–January 457

Fl. Valerius Marcianus, an Illyrian soldier who was promoted through the influence of his commander, the German general Aspar, attracted the favour of Pulcheria who arranged for him to succeed her brother Theodosius II and married him in 450. He died after a competent reign whose main feature was the ecumenical council of Chalcedon in 451. Marcian had a daughter who married Anthemius, later emperor of the West.

450 Marriage with Pulcheria.

    1   FELICITER NVBTIIS, Christ stg. between Marcian and Pulcheria. Sol: *Tolstoy* p. 99: Con

PETRONIUS MAXIMUS 455

Usurper in Rome: no historical types.

AVITUS 455–456

Emperor in the West: no historical types.

LEO I

February 457–January 474

Fl. Leo, a Thracian born *c.* 400, was made emperor by the general Aspar who hoped to rule through him. Leo, however, found a counterweight in the Isaurian chief Tarasios who married his daughter Ariadne and took the name Zeno. Leo's reign saw the collapse of Roman authority in the West, in spite of his efforts in installing Anthemius (467) and Julius Nepos (474) on the throne. His problems were compounded by the failure of his great expedition against the Vandals of Africa in 468, but the East remained peaceful and prosperous. In 473, he chose his young grandson Leo as his successor, and proclaimed him Augustus in the following year; he died soon after.

458 or **462** Consulate, occasion not specified.
    1 VICTORIA AVGGG, Leo enthroned, holding mappa. Consular obverse. Sol: *Tolstoy* 15–6: Tes

476 Appointment of Leo II as Augustus.
    2 SALVS REIPVBLICAE, Two Augusti enthroned facing. Sol: *Tolstoy* 21: Con

LEO II

Caesar October 473/Augustus January–November 474

Son of Zeno and Ariadne, and grandson of Leo I, Leo was raised to imperial office by his grandfather whom he succeeded in 474 at the age of seven. He died later in the same year after naming his father as co-emperor.

474 Creation of Zeno as co-emperor.
    1 *Obv.* D N LEO ET ZENO P P AVG, Facing bust. *Rev.* SALVS REIPVBLICAE, Leo II and Zeno enthroned facing. Sol: *Tolstoy* 1–3: Con

MAJORIAN

April 457–August 461

Fl. Julius Valerius Maiorianus, a successful army commander, had retired from active service when Valentinian III called on him to conciliate the troops after the murder of Aetius. When Valentinian was also killed,

Majorian was favoured by Eudoxia as his successor. In 456, in alliance with the German general Ricimer, he rebelled against Avitus, and was proclaimed emperor. He had the support of the eastern emperor Leo. Majorian entered Ravenna in December 457 and gained some success against the German invaders until failure of an expedition to Africa provoked Ricimer into deposing and executing him.

458 Joint consulate of Majorian and Leo I.
    1 VOTIS MVLTIS, Majorian and Leo, holding mappa and cross, stg. facing each other. Sol: *C*12: Rav

LIVIUS SEVERUS 461–465

Emperor in the West; no historical types.

ANTHEMIUS

April 467–July 472

Procopius Anthemius, a Constantinopolitan of an aristocratic Anatolian family, was a descendant of the usurper Procopius. He married the daughter of the eastern emperor, Marcian, became his chief general, and won considerable victories over the Goths and Huns. Since the situation in Italy had degenerated into virtual anarchy, with Ricimer alone exercising power, Leo I appointed Anthemius ruler of the West, and gave him military support. Ricimer was conciliated by marriage with Anthemius' daughter, and Anthemius was installed as emperor in Rome. As a Greek, Anthemius was never popular in Italy; he eventually broke with Ricimer whose revolt in 472 provoked the murder of Anthemius.

467 Accession, with the support of Leo.
    1*a* SALVS REIPVBLICAE, Leo handing globe to Anthemius. Sol: *C*6–12: Med; Rav; Rom
    1*b* — — Leo and Anthemius stg. Facing, holding a cross. Sol: *C*2–5, 16–17: Rav

1b

OLYBRIUS 472

Emperor in the West; no historical types.

GLYCERIUS 473–474

Emperor in the East; no historical types.

ZENO 474–491

Emperor in the West; no historical types.

BASILISCUS

January 475–August 476

Brother of Verina, the wife of Leo I, Basiliscus had a military career marked with success in the Balkans but a catastrophic defeat when commanding the great fleet sent against the Vandals in 468. With the encouragement of Verina, he rebelled against Zeno, whose Isaurian origin made him unpopular, and seized control of Constantinople. Since, however, he was not orthodox, and lacked the military strength of his rival, he could not maintain his position, and was soon ousted and executed by Zeno, along with his son Marcus whom he had elevated to Caesar in 475 and Augustus in 476.

476 Promotion of Marcus to Augustus.
   1 *Obv.* D N BASILISCI ET MARC P AVG, Facing bust. *Rev.* SALVS REIPVBLICAE, Two Augusti enthroned facing. Sol: *Tolstoy* 88: Con

JULIUS NEPOS 474–475

Emperor in the West; no historical types.

ROMULUS AUGUSTUS 475–476

Last Roman emperor in the West; no historical types.

Index

NOTE: This index concentrates on significant types, with a few noteworthy legends; it does not include emperors or their relatives; provinces and their inhabitants are listed by their Latin name (e.g. for Germany, Germans, or types relating to Germany, see Germania; for Egypt, Aegyptus). *Passim* is used to indicate that the type appears on almost all of a range of pages.